DEVELOPMENT AID

CHARLES BEVAN

First published 2021 by Compass-Publishing UK

ISBN 978-1-913713-72-0

Edited and typeset by The Book Refinery Ltd
www.thebookrefinery.com

Cover photos (top to bottom)
Jamuna Bridge in Bangladesh © baborbd
Kainji Dam © Africa-bi.com
A rock carving in the Laongo Park in Burkina Faso © Charles Bevan

Printed and bound by CMP, Poole, Dorset, UK.

A note on the cover photo: The bottom picture on the front cover is of a rock
carving in the Laongo Park in Burkina Faso. It demonstrates the artistic creativity
of West African craftsmen and the tortured symbolism of a continent crying out
for change but held back by stultifying traditions.

Foreword

This is an extraordinary time of change throughout the world. Covid-19 has resulted in a huge increase in human misery and slowed down large sectors of the economy; climate change and the consequent increase in extreme weather events are already having a significant impact; and the increasing polarisation of society and political views is threatening governance systems that have fostered stability in much of the world for several decades in the recent past. To exacerbate things, the United Nations (UN) has estimated that the world's population will grow by almost 1.9 billion people between 2021 and 2050. Against this backdrop, this timely and fascinating book explores some of the reasons for and consequences of the Western world's declining confidence in some of its long-held beliefs and practices. It focuses especially on those institutions and programmes that were designed to help the poorest countries of the world to develop socially and economically.

Charles Bevan highlights the hypocrisy, self-interest and failure associated with much of the official development assistance, or foreign aid, provided to low- and middle-income countries. The book recognises that the provision of such assistance is far from being purely altruistic, and it is one of the key 'soft power' policies of the United States and its allies. Of course, not all aid funding was or is wasted; indeed, one of the key attributes of this book is its identification of what aid works and what doesn't. Nevertheless, the failure of many of the West's aid programmes has helped to discredit the soft-power aspirations of Western governments. It has also handed to other powers, notably China, a golden opportunity to elicit support from developing-country leaders by implying – and in some cases, demonstrating – that they do things differently and better.

The book begins with a history and analysis of the economic policies supporting aid, and it provides thumbnail sketches of the main institutions involved. The core of the book is an in-depth review of 20 selected investment projects that clearly demonstrate the political motives behind much Western aid – investments that were often made based on cursory feasibility studies and being in a hurry to get the money out of the door.

The author makes no apology for his focus on agriculture, as for many years, much aid funding was aimed at improving agricultural production, both to help fight hunger and malnutrition and to improve the livelihoods of the world's poorest people. It is also a subject he obviously knows well, having studied agricultural science at Cambridge University before embarking on a career in international agricultural development – a career that occasioned his involvement in more than

100 projects and programmes in some 40 developing countries in Africa, Asia and the Caribbean. He has also gained wide-ranging experience of different aid agencies through projects supported by the World Bank, the United Kingdom bilateral aid agency, the private sector, the Bill & Melinda Gates Foundation and the Food and Agriculture Organization of the UN. His observations, analyses and views are thus those of an international development expert, an insider of a somewhat shady world that is frequently reluctant to give up its secrets.

In addition to the core case studies, this book provides a broader analysis of the policies and processes of aid agencies. Among other things, this analysis shows that both providers and recipients of aid have been learning by doing, and that many of the lessons learned have played a role in the changing nature of aid over at least the past 10 years. Based on this, the author suggests some of the changes needed or anticipated in the aid sector of the future, and also provides some useful guidelines for policymakers, whether they be in the West, China or elsewhere. The author believes that, while humanitarian aid will continue to be a factor in global politics, overall aid budgets are likely to shrink and continue to become more focused on the direct interests of the funding countries. Indeed, this trend is already apparent.

This book should be prescribed reading for everyone in the aid business, whether a foot soldier at the front or a policymaker back in a capital city. Charles Bevan is to be congratulated on having written a book in which everyone will find something of interest and value. Having been written with a minimum of jargon and technical terms, I believe it will also appeal to all who are interested in international and current affairs. After all, providing foreign development assistance impacts us all – funders and recipients alike.

Geoff Hawtin, *well-respected plant scientist and administrator, and former director of both the International Plant Genetic Resources Institute (now Bioversity International) and the International Center for Tropical Agriculture (CIAT)*

Contents

Epilogue....315

Acknowledgements....357

Introduction

Aims of the Book

This book has been many years in the making. It began with the family Christmas letter. Forty years ago, I started including a few thoughts on development aid in our annual letter to friends and relatives. One very dear old friend, David Fabian, who had just taken a holiday in The Gambia in the early 1990s, wrote and asked me why it was that countries such as The Gambia seemed to be stuck in a time warp of underdevelopment. I started thinking about how to reply to David and jotted down a few ideas. The more I thought and wrote, the longer my intended reply became, and that forms the structure of this book.

The material about aid in this book largely refers to what happened in the period from 1970 to 2010. Since then, there have undoubtedly been some significant policy changes, but many of the criticisms of the way aid funds are used or wasted are still relevant to aid in the 10 years between 2010 and 2020. Whether they will still be relevant to the world post Covid-19 is impossible to tell.

The book is an attempt to shed some light on official development assistance (ODA), often just called 'aid', based on my personal experience. The term 'ODA' is used to describe the transfer of resources from richer countries to poorer ones for three basic reasons:

1. National/global security
2. Commercial interest
3. Humanitarian concerns

Underlying all three reasons are the objectives of helping poorer countries grow their economies, reduce poverty and become stable, responsible members of the global community of nations.

The book has been written mainly for people with an interest in politics and current affairs, and more generally for rich countries' taxpayers who are interested in knowing whether the portion of their taxes used for aid has been – and is being – used wisely. It aims to explain to the uninitiated the politics behind much aid, plus what works and what does not work. It is not intended to be another textbook on the economics of aid and development. I am no academic, and there are far too many such books out there already. Most academic texts, in my opinion, are of limited value and are generally written to support a pet theory or two, rather than provide a cogent analysis of reality. The paradox of academic texts is that some experts say the important thing is to simply get the money out and into the hands of the poor, while on the same shelf are books that say the important thing is to help the economy of a poor country to grow and that aid solely directed to the poorest does not work.

So why have I now chosen to write this book? At the present time, with many countries still struggling to develop economically, I sense that an increasing number of people do now want to know whether their aid dollars – be it from taxation or donation – have been used wisely, and I feel the time is right to put them on record for a wider audience. It is also the case that, while I never seemed to find enough time to do the necessary research and background reading while I was working, in retirement, I have had fewer excuses for not putting pen to paper.

An Outline of the Content

The core of this book is based largely on a critical review and analysis of a carefully selected number of aid projects, programmes and technical ideas that I have been associated with over a lifetime of working in development. I have read quite widely about aid (some of the books I have read were clearly written to meet some political agenda; others were more critical) and I have tried to indicate herein those authors whom I think have written the most useful books.

The projects described in *Chapters 3* and *4* have been selected to illustrate project design, implementation and evaluation. They also attempt to show the importance of global politics with respect to much of what was done, and to show that – even if not always successful – the overall support provided to many countries was good value for money, as far as the promotion of important Western values and global peace are concerned.

In the last chapters of the book, I attempt to predict the future paths of aid, based on some of the lessons learnt in its first 75 years of existence, and the changes in global power interplays since the end of the Cold War and the rise of China. I do not see an end to aid or indeed a fundamental change in its rationale or objectives. I do, however, see some clear changes of scale and scope within the overall objectives. Of these, the most obvious are the increasing importance of China, international security and climate change.

As the famous United States (US) politician Tip O'Neill is reported to have once said, 'All politics is local', and if rich-world[1] taxes are used to finance aid in poor countries, it is a local issue in so far as it means less money for public services inside donor countries. The United Kingdom (UK), one of the few Western economies that meets the UN target for aid, has retained a legal obligation since 2015 to spend 0.7% of its annual gross national income (GNI)[2] on aid. This is a commitment that translates into some £14 billion[3,4] a year, and it is money that could otherwise be spent on the National Health Service or our schools.

I have included a chapter on the background and history of aid, and a chapter on the main aid agencies. The latter is by no means comprehensive. There are thousands of organisations involved in aid, and I have focused on what I believe are the more important ones. If the reader wants to know more about a specific agency, I recommend a visit to its website, even if this only provides the 'good news'.

I have written quite extensively about the World Bank because of its pivotal role in aid throughout the years since the Second World War. The World Bank was the main global agency for intellectual and political development for much of the second half of the 20th century. It is also the basic model for the regional development banks, such as the African Development Bank (AfDB), Asian Development Bank (ADB) and Inter-American Development Bank (IADB). I have also shared some observations about a number of United Nations (UN) agencies, especially those involved in agriculture and rural development, which I hope will help the reader appreciate some of the structural constraints faced by aid agencies.

Throughout the book, I have included some of my personal travel experiences associated with the aid projects I have been involved with. This not only lightens up the text but also underlines the fact that, at the end of the day, aid is about people: their strengths and weaknesses.

Putting Aid into Perspective

It is important to put aid into a historical and political perspective. In many ways, aid as we know it today is a follow-on or development of the Marshall Plan, which was designed to rebuild Europe after the Second World War. Furthermore, just as the Marshall Plan was an American initiative, so the US has been the major

---

1. 'Rich world' is a loose term for the 36 countries in the Organisation of Economic Co-Operation and Development (OECD) plus the oil-rich countries of the Middle East.
2. GNI is the total sum of a country's national income, usually described as the market value of all goods and services plus earnings from foreign sources. Gross domestic product (GDP) is similar, but it excludes interest and dividends from foreign sources.
3. In 2018/19, the UK aid budget was £14 billion.
4. In this book, a billion is taken to mean a thousand million (1,000,000,000).

player on the aid stage. Most Western nations have their own bilateral aid agency or agencies and a degree of independence in where and for what they provide aid, but it has been and still is almost always under the umbrella of Uncle Sam. As Helen Thompson (2019) points out in a recent article, the Western countries have been allowed a degree of freedom in their international relations, but when push comes to shove (Vietnam or Iraq), it is difficult for nations to refuse to do the US's bidding. I say more about this (notably the origins of the UN and the World Bank) in *Chapter 2*, but a good place to start one's awareness of this is with the ownership of the World Bank, which is based in Washington, DC. The World Bank had 185 member nations in 2019; of these, the largest shareholder was the US, with just under 16%. And guess what? The president of the World Bank is always a US national.

The Cold War was the result of the West's commitment to the containment theory of the US diplomat George Kennan, who served in Moscow in the 1940s. He believed the only way the West was going to win the ideological race with the Union of Soviet Socialist Republics (USSR) and the other command economies was through a containment of Soviet expansionist tendencies. This is well documented in the book *The Cold War* (Gaddis, 2005). Kennan believed it would take time, but that in the end, internal tensions and failures in the international arena would result in the collapse of the Stalinist ideology. Kennan's message was lapped up in the West, and it formed the basis of many of the foreign policy strategies adopted there until the fall of the Berlin Wall in 1989 and the end of the Cold War. Something similar may happen in the future between the West and China, although there are few signs of the necessary tension with China at the time of writing (2020).

The World Bank and the UN agencies, together with other Western development agencies, provided much of the soft power[5] of the containment strategy. The basic idea was to show that the West was in the business of providing much more training, expertise and finance than the USSR could ever afford, and that alignment with the West and the encouragement of free – albeit regulated – markets was a win-win situation. If this meant a few billion dollars was wasted here and there, no one was really very worried. Jaw-jaw was far better than war-war. And by no means was all the money wasted. On the whole, big expenditure on infrastructure investments such as the Jamuna Multipurpose Bridge over the Brahmaputra River in Bangladesh have more than justified the investment and helped the country's economy grow.

During the Cold War, the West poured millions of dollars into aid projects and programmes in newly independent and developing nations in the hope that, if

---

5. 'Soft power' is the ability to attract and co-opt, rather than coerce (hard power). Soft power is the ability to shape the preference of others through appeal and attraction.

nothing else, this financial support would keep open the channels for dialogue, regardless of internal political direction. In many cases, the justification was undoubtedly political. For many years after the Second World War, the leaders of India had clear socialist leanings and, indeed, very good relations with Moscow. The Indian Air Force was still flying Russian jets (MIG 21) in 2019 when they had one shot down by a Pakistani F-16 (made in the US). In fact, the Communist Party of India had some 3 million members in 1965 and was seen as a big threat by the West. To counter this influence, the West's strategy was to keep as large a foot as possible in the door – mainly through aid flows – in the hope that, eventually, India would move towards free-market thinking, which it has, slowly but surely.

I have already referred to the Cold War as being a major driver of aid after the Second World War, but there was another very important political dimension, which – as far as much of Europe was concerned – was the exit from 'empire'. After the Second World War, it was apparent to the wiser politicians and their advisers that the days of colonial rule were over. The war had, after all, been fought in the name of freedom and open society. It hardly made sense for those colonies that had helped the Allies win the war to be back in chains as vassal states. And perhaps of even greater concern was the rising cost of colonisation. No longer was it possible for the coloniser to exploit a colony's resources with a minimum of infrastructure and administration. Expectations had been raised, and colonies needed massive investment in infrastructure, education and health if their economies were to flourish. This was investment the weakened colonial masters simply could not afford. The solution was to turn an economic scuttle into a handover of sovereignty by awarding independence.

After the Second World War, when the Europeans gave up their colonies, the hope was that the newly independent nations would sooner or later decide for themselves what their economic and development priorities should be. Not all observers fell for this aspiration. Some wiser men, such as Guy Hunter, with his experience of colonial Africa, challenged this line of thinking in his book *The Best of Both Worlds?* (Hunter, 1967). He asked whether it was realistic to telescope into a few decades the process of development that took centuries in Europe.

Another sceptic was Lord Peter Thomas Bauer. His studies of rural entrepreneurs in Malaysia and Nigeria convinced him that the priority was for a newly independent government to provide the right environment for individuals to improve their lives. He believed that government-to-government aid could actually hinder development as it could increase the power of government, leading to corruption, the misallocation of resources and the erosion of civil liberties. Bauer believed this:

If all conditions for development other than capital are present, capital will soon be generated locally, or will be available to the government or to private businesses on commercial terms from abroad, the capital to be serviced out of higher tax revenue or from the profits of enterprise. If, however, the conditions for development are not present, then aid – which in these circumstances will be the only source of external capital – will be necessarily unproductive and therefore ineffective. (Bauer, 1971).

In my files, I have a copy of an article he published in the *Daily Telegraph* (Bauer, 1965) in which he explains his concerns about conventional foreign aid at the time. His basic contention was that large-scale aid had not served to raise living standards appreciably. His ideas were dismissed by his economist colleagues then, but from the perspective of 2020, it is clear that Hunter and Bauer were remarkably prescient in much of what they questioned.

Some 75 years after the Second World War, it is notable that those countries that have made real progress are, in general, those that have recognised the importance of being self-reliant – most notably South Korea and China, but increasingly, many other Asian countries also. This factor is likely to become progressively more important over the coming years as the rivalry between the West and China takes shape. The West might be wise in future to focus the bulk of its aid in countries that show serious understanding and commitment to self-reliance, and let China provide charity to the others.

My Career in Development

I have spent almost all of my professional working life in agricultural development, first as a junior technical assistance (TA) adviser in Lesotho in the early 1970s, and subsequently, I've mainly been involved in rural and agricultural investment project design and evaluation for the World Bank. I have also worked for bilateral and multilateral aid agencies, and charities such as the Bill & Melinda Gates Foundation. For nearly 10 years, I worked for a commercial consultancy based in the UK, before joining the Food and Agriculture Organization (FAO) of the UN in Rome.[6]

My work has taken me to most of the countries of South Asia, 20 countries in sub-Saharan Africa, Brazil, parts of the Caribbean, North Africa, the Pacific Islands and Eastern Europe. I cannot claim to have seen it all by any means, but I have seen

---

6. I actually worked for the FAO / World Bank Cooperative Programme (FAO/CP), a division of FAO that has special responsibility for preparing investment projects on behalf of emerging nations. The thinking behind the FAO/CP was that the FAO would be a neutral partner between the World Bank and a borrowing country, and would only design and endorse technically and economically viable projects. Some two-thirds of the unit costs were met by the World Bank and the other third by the FAO.

and learnt a lot about the problems from and solutions to rural poverty in more than 40 countries on five continents. I would be the first to admit that farming is a somewhat traditional activity, with little glamour compared to many other sectors of an economy. However, it is important to remember that, in much of the world, agriculture still employs more people than all the other sectors put together, and without the farmers producing a surplus, many of the world's 7.7 billion people would not have enough food to survive. Any government – whether democratic or autocratic – ignores the needs of its agricultural sector at its peril.

During the various stages of my career, I have tried to understand the reasons behind and purposes of the aid work I was involved with, and I have also attempted to assess how effective it was. As might be expected, my beliefs regarding the value of aid have changed over the years, largely in response to first-hand experience but also from reading extensively about the subject. It is also the case that, during my working life (1972–2017), there has been a sea change in academic economic thinking and writing about aid. It was never explained to me in the early days that we coalface workers were each but a small cog in a series of global political wheels or games. I do not think we were deliberately kept in the dark by our employers. In fact, they too were probably just as ignorant of the policies and practices of aid and were simply doing what they thought was right.

Another huge change in aid thinking, which is closely related to these new ideas, is the growing realisation that the basic engine for economic growth is the private sector. In the early years after the Second World War, much aid was carried out by Western experts filling key posts in the civil service of a developing country, together with feasibility studies and some infrastructure investment (roads, dams, etc.). I think the idea was that if the donors held the hands of the politicians and civil servants in developing countries for long enough, they would learn how to manage an economy and its administration. It was also a time when state involvement in an economy was hardly questioned.

It is also the case that many in the aid business now realise that one size does *not* fit all; therefore, to be effective, aid has to be tailored to circumstances, and new approaches may be needed in some parts of the world. Some 50 years after I started working in development, many of us have – or are – losing our faith in simple solutions, at least where much of the continent of Africa is concerned. Martin Meredith, in his book *The State of Africa* (Meredith, 2005) points out that, of the 50-plus countries on the aforementioned continent, only two (South Africa and Botswana) had higher standards of living in the early years of the 21st century than they did some 40 years earlier.

In an article on Africa (*The Economist*, 2018A), the statistics provided are similarly depressing.[7] The article reports that some 42% of the African continent's population in 2013 were classified as living on under US$1.90/day (the World Bank's benchmark indicator of poverty). Furthermore, with projected economic growth rates for most African countries of under 4% over the next few years, coupled with growing populations, incomes are only expected to creep up by 1% a year. Clearly, the aid approaches and initiatives promoted by the rich world since independence have largely failed in much of Africa and it is time for a rethink.

One of the most poignant personal accounts of aid failure that I know of is a report of a return visit to Soche in Malawi at the turn of the century, given by the famous US writer Paul Theroux in his book *Dark Star Safari* (Theroux, 2003). He returned to the school where he had taught as a Peace Corps volunteer in 1964 and was dismayed to find the school effectively abandoned and in ruins. He also spoke with people he had known at the time and came to the conclusion that the country was actually less developed than it was when he lived there, soon after its independence. He comments that aid seems to have achieved little other than keeping the elite in power. Shortly after writing this travelogue, he wrote a convincing article (Theroux, 2005) in which he remonstrates with those who say all Africa needs is more charity in the form of volunteer labour and debt relief, and that Bono and Co. are completely wrong to persuade Westerners to simply give money to Africa.

When he was working in Malawi, it was believed that once the country was self-sufficient in terms of trained specialists such as teachers, there would be no need for any more aid workers and volunteers from overseas. In fact, what seems to have happened in Malawi and in many other countries is that trained nationals have simply emigrated to richer parts of the world and the services remain dreadful nationally. He also refers to the poor evaluation of aid initiatives that prevent any analysis of what aid works best and how to reduce corruption. The article is not, however, without hope. Theroux clearly has much sympathy for Africa and Africans, and he also believes they have the potential to help themselves. What they need is less poor aid and patrimony from the West but greater efforts to encourage skilled nationals to stay at home.

It is equally clear, however, that some countries have – and are – making enormous strides, with or without much aid. In 1953, South Korea was as poor as Ghana. However, it was 20 times richer by 2004, according to Robert Guest (2004) in *The Shackled Continent*. At independence in 1971, Zambia had a higher per capita GDP than South Korea. In 2006, South Korea's GDP was 32 times that of Zambia.

7. African statistics should always be read with a degree of caution as the methods of collection and collation are far from reliable, but in this case, I consider they are likely to be more rather than less optimistic.

Other countries in Asia – including countries such as Bangladesh, which was written off as a basket case by Henry Kissinger when he was US Secretary of State – are actually making substantial progress in the fight against poverty. In the early years of the 21st century, the annual economic growth rate in Bangladesh was over 5%. The garment industry in Bangladesh has raised millions out of poverty through its capture of global markets. In 2017, aid funding accounted for less than 5% of government spending in Bangladesh. Not so long ago (in 1971), it was the poorest country in Asia. The economies of India and China, which is home to some one-third of the world's population, have grown at breakneck speed (+/-6%) annually, with very little aid since 2000. This simple, little geographical analysis confirms that countries can improve the livelihoods of their populations and reduce poverty levels. I believe it also shows that economic development is essentially a home-grown product, and that it is delivered by the private sector more often than not, with the government providing the essential institutions (e.g. a civil service, education facilities and legal frameworks) to support the private sectors. Governments do, of course, have a responsibility to support and invest in essential infrastructure, regulations and services.

Nevertheless, it is not all doom and gloom in Africa. In the first 15 years of the 21st century, 10 countries in Africa had annual economic growth rates of some 7% per annum, which are among the fastest in the world. Much of this growth has come from China's surging demand for raw materials and rising commodity prices. These growth rates have slowed since 2015, reflecting the slowing economic growth in China. It is also the case that the exploitation of commodities does not provide many jobs. Given the population explosion in many African countries, if per capita incomes in Africa are to rise, many more jobs need to be created.

Aid Terminology

At this point, I think a few simple definitions might help the reader. ODA is defined by the Development Assistance Committee (DAC) of the Organisation of Economic Co-Operation and Development (OECD)[8] as 'government aid that promotes and specifically targets the economic development and welfare of developing countries' (OECD, n.d.A). ODA excludes funds used for military assistance.[9]

Public sector aid is provided by multilateral agencies such as the World Bank, regional development banks and the United Nations Development Programme (UNDP); and by bilateral agencies such as the UK's Department for International

---

8. The OECD is a group of 36 of the world richest countries. Headquartered in Paris, it provides a forum for discussion of economic development and related policy. China is not a member. .
9. US figures for aid, however, usually include military assistance, which can account for nearly 50% of US aid.

Development (DFID), the United States Agency for International Development (USAID) and the Millennium Challenge Corporation (MCC) of the US. Broadly speaking, these aid flows are in the form of grants or concessional loans at lower rates of interest than a country would have to pay for commercial loans.

Aid (mainly humanitarian aid) is also provided by numerous non-governmental organisations, (NGOs) such as Oxfam and Save the Children; and by a number of countries within the Organization of the Petroleum Exporting Countries (OPEC) and non-OECD countries. The annual total of ODA over the past 70 years is provided in Table 1. Although there has been a marked increase in aid flows since 1960, flows since 2000 have not really kept up with inflation, and in terms of spending power, aid flows have remained relatively constant. There are a number of reasons for this, but one of the most significant is the emergence of China as a donor, rather than as a recipient of aid. China is not a member of the OECD, so its aid flows are not shown in Table 1. Other reasons for the relative constancy of aid flows are the increase in private sector investment in developing countries and a more cautious approach to aid by many Western donors.

Table 1. Aid Flows (Current Dollars, 1960–2019) and Remittances (2005–19)

Year	1960	1970	1980	1990	2000	2005	2010	2011
Aid Flows*	4.6	6.7	26	54	54	108	128	135
Remittances*						284	469	528

Year	2012	2013	2014	2015	2016	2017	2018	2019
Aid Flows*	127	134	137	131	144	147	149	147
Remittances*	549	580	603	595	589	632	689**	715

* US$ billions

**India was the recipient of the largest flows (US$80 billion), followed by China and then the Philippines.

Sources: Organisation of Economic Co-Operation and Development (OECD)(n.d.A; n.d.B); World Bank (2019A); World Bank (2019B)

The other key feature demonstrated in Table 1. is that remittances have dwarfed ODA for many years. Of course, it is important to be aware that while ODA is given to governments, ostensibly for the benefit of the whole nation, remittances are to private bank accounts for individual benefit. However, it is the remittances that largely enable the import of goods and services, as well as paying for domestically produced goods and services; as such, they help a national economy to grow through the expansion of domestic businesses. Some countries, notably the oil-rich states of the Middle East, also give substantial amounts of aid, mainly to Islamic countries, but no data is available on the amounts provided or the names of the recipient countries. Saudi Arabia gave Egypt US$10 billion in the form of a soft loan soon after Abdel Fattah el-Sisi took over as president in 2014. There is a grey area associated with a substantial amount of Chinese aid flows, which some authorities consider to be commercial loans rather than aid. In addition to ODA and remittances, private sector financial investment flows are an important and growing source of funding for development, but no figures for these flows are readily available.

Aid, Agriculture and Population Growth

I make no apology for the focus of this book being on agriculture and the agencies involved in helping to improve agricultural productivity; given that some 75% of the world's poor still live in rural areas, agriculture remains at the root of all economic development. Farming, we are told, began in the fertile crescent of Asia Minor, where man first learnt how to farm – rather than hunt – to get his food. Wheat, as we know it today – upon which so much of mankind depends for food – was selected from the wild grasses growing in the area. The importance of this cannot be overestimated, as it was the surpluses provided by these new wheat plants that allowed men and women to spend time on things other than just looking for and growing food. In many ways, it was the seed that grew into what we today call 'civilisation', which was subsequently the basis for the 'enlightenment', and as such was the basis of our modern technologically advanced world.

Nor for that matter can we ignore the Malthusian predictions of population growth and resource shortages outlined by the Club of Rome in 1972, just when I started my career. A best-selling book *The Limits to Growth* (Meadows *et al.*, 1972) at the time predicted mass starvation. Right then, the Club of Rome had no idea that the green revolution was about to occur and that the world was going to be able to feed all the new mouths that the demographers had accurately predicted would be born.

At the start of the third decade of the 21st century, the demographic projections again look awesome, with a population of 9 billion expected by 2050. There is every reason to think that these projections are fairly accurate, as they are based on well-known population growth trends adjusted for known reductions in fertility as countries get richer. However, on the supply side, there is perhaps less room for optimism. In many of the poorest countries of the world, where population growth is the greatest, the scope for boosting food production is increasingly limited, with or without climate change. What is more, much – if not most – of this population growth is expected to be in Africa, so much of the future of aid will revolve around what happens there, which is why so much of this book focuses on Africa, the world's largest and poorest continent.

According to experts Clapp and Cohen (2009) in the book *The Global Food Crisis*, some 80 countries – one-third of the world's countries – are expected to remain in food deficit and will have to rely on imports to feed themselves. They will only be able to do this if they can develop their economies (so as to be able to export goods and services to cover the costs of their imports) or they will become increasingly dependent on food aid from the rich world. Either way, aid is likely to remain an important fact of life for all of us.

I am not sure I accept Clapp and Cohen's (2009) pessimism entirely. In theory, there is potential to increase food production in Africa and parts of Latin America if modern production techniques – notably the use of mineral fertiliser, irrigation and conservation farming practices – are more widely adopted. However, African soils in the tropical regions are generally very deficient in plant nutrients, and the annual use of mineral fertiliser in Africa is on average less than 10 kilogrammes/hectare compared to over 100 kilogrammes/hectare in India. These figures alone suggest that Africa has the potential to produce much more food, and Africa is big – very big. The Democratic Republic of Congo (DRC) is twice the size of France, and it is blessed with good rainfall and water supplies.

There is little doubt that Africa could feed itself if it got a few basic things sorted out. That said, there are major hurdles to overcome. Any increase in fertiliser usage would require the roads and credit systems to enable its timely delivery. Better marketing systems are also needed if surpluses are to be sold off-farm. What is more, a shifting culture and a lack of land tenure are major issues in Africa that inhibit investment in land used by all (see 6.1. and *Appendix E*). It is far easier for African governments to rely on food aid, which is shipped to the main ports for distribution to urban centres linked by paved roads, than to address the fundamental problems of African farming.

On a more optimistic note, new plant-breeding techniques, such as gene editing by clustered regularly interspaced palindromic repeats (CRISPR),[10] might herald a new green revolution. The development of new and intensive 'agri-tech'[11] production technologies also suggests the world may not run out of food anytime soon. However, it will not be equitably available and will require a massive redistribution effort that will almost certainly involve aid.

---

10. CRISPR is a complicated technique that allows scientists to edit the genes of organisms. It facilitates more rapid plant breeding and is expected to revolutionise the development of new varieties of crop plants.
11. 'Agri-tech' is the term given to precision farming (the accurate placement of inputs, according to soil type), aquaculture, hydroponics and vertical farming.

Finally, my interest in agriculture extends to a warning that is sadly related to the pressures on land and resources referred to previously. It is a warning to development workers and developing countries' governments to be wary of donors bringing false gifts. For some 30 or so years, at least since the early 1990s, donors have talked endlessly about 'the rural space' and how livelihoods can be improved in rural areas by carefully planned and executed projects. Such projects almost invariably have an agricultural focus, either through providing farmers with simple improved technology to grow crops, helping the landless raise more livestock, or adding value by processing primary agricultural products. Regrettably, the facts of the matter are that all land has a finite carrying capacity and only so many people can be supported by agriculture in any given location.

Just look at any so-called 'developed' country: most of the people are urban, being supported by a rural population that is very rarely more than 5% of the total. In the well-known article 'The Economic Stages of Growth' (Rostow, 1959), the first stage given is the exodus from the land. Why should the poor countries of the world be subject to different economic laws? Of course, they are not; it is just that the idea of finding real jobs for the multitudes from the rural areas of the developing world is simply too frightening to countenance. So, rather than face reality, the rich world has – as it has so often – turned to hypocrisy, having tried to convince the developing world that they can reverse the laws of economics and provide work for all in the countryside. It is rubbish, and the more-honest development economists know it, but they cannot challenge the shibboleths of the politicians who pay their salaries, so they too go along with the myths.

This book should not be seen as an apology for having had an interesting and well-rewarded career that achieved little of obvious substance. One of my colleagues in the UN – Roger, who had a wry sense of humour – once told me that he had started working in development to do good, but had ended up doing quite well, in fact – for himself and his family.

In early 2017, I had dinner with an old colleague from the agricultural consultancy company I worked for in the 1980s. He had retired as the managing director, having been responsible for spending millions of pounds of taxpayers' money on development projects. 'All wasted,' was David's trenchant assessment. And it is true that much money has been wasted, especially before the fall of the Berlin Wall in 1989.

A year later, I asked Edward, a development-expert friend, how many of the projects that he had been associated with in Bangladesh had been successful. He thought for a minute or two and said with considerable certainty, '50%'. He then offered to provide me with a list of the good, the bad and the ugly projects he had been associated with over nearly 40 years. I said that would be great, but that I was sure he had better things to do with his time.

To a considerable extent, the failure of much aid is because farming is essentially a private sector activity, whether done by a small peasant or a large company. Governments have support and regulatory roles (research, pricing, standards, provision/regulation of markets, safety, etc.) but have no comparative advantage in production. If you want proof of this, just look at food production in the USSR after the Second World War compared with post-communist-period Russia. In the 1970s, the USSR had to import grain from the West. By 2016, Russia it was exporting a surplus to many countries in Africa. What had changed was the collapse of 'collective' farming. Something very similar in terms of increased output can also be seen in China following Deng Xiaoping's reforms. Additional evidence comes for the change in the World Bank's involvement in lending for agriculture.

In the last decades of the 20th century, some 30% of World Bank lending was for agriculture and rural space. Agriculture became a popular destination for aid funds, in part because of the West's need for investment opportunities in developing countries during the Cold War. By 2015, agriculture accounted for less than 10% of the total World Bank lending. It should perhaps be noted that the World Bank's support for agricultural development in Africa post 2000 is linked to land reform and to individual tenure in particular, according to the book *The Politics of Land Reform in Africa* (Manji, 2006). I think this policy makes good sense from a technical perspective, but it is very difficult to achieve socially. The message is quite clear that there are far better sectors of the economy for the World Bank's money.

Aid and Corruption

I should perhaps say a word here about one of the less spoken about but common features of aid, namely corruption. There is no doubt that much aid funding has ended up in the pockets or accounts of civil servants, politicians and consultants. No one, as far as I know, has added up the numbers, but at a guess, I am sure that at least 25% (and probably more) of all aid money never reached the intended beneficiaries. I outline a couple of small cases of corruption I came across in Bangladesh, Lesotho and Zambia in *Chapters 3* and *4*.

Projects and programmes usually have mechanisms incorporated in them to minimise fraud, but it is almost impossible to prevent leakage entirely, as it is as much about cultural attitudes as accountancy or auditing. If the money is coming from the World Bank or the British government, stealing a bit on its way to its intended beneficiaries does no obvious harm to the intended beneficiaries. Sure, they might get less than originally intended, but without the aid, they would have got nothing. Concerns about aid fraud led to the establishment of Transparency International, a good institution, but one that works everywhere not just in aid-receiving countries.

No, the real thing about corruption and aid is that the West saw it as a price that had to be paid to get the money out of the aid agencies' doors. It is also the case that at least some aid was tied; that is to say, a developing country would get aid to buy goods from the donor country. I relate a possible case of tied aid in Egypt (see 3.5.). The UK abolished tied aid when Clare Short was the minister of overseas development in the 1970s, as she believed it discouraged recipients from buying the best-value-for-money products and services. To some extent, she had a point (see 3.2.). However, the pendulum had swung back the other way by the end of the second decade of the 21st century, when the then Tory government was in favour of using as much aid money as possible to buy goods and services from British companies and organisations.

As indicated earlier, it is also the case that corruption was, in many ways, encouraged by the very organisations giving aid, and their tears about losses were crocodile tears. An economist I know, who has spent much of his working life undertaking ex-post-project evaluations, says his main professional concern has been that few of the agencies he worked for wanted honest evaluations. I can endorse his views from personal experience. I was once about to embark on a series of evaluation consultancies for the World Bank. In fact, I started looking at half a dozen projects. But I soon realised my initial comments were too near the bone for the World Bank's management. Instead of watering down my comments, I decided to quit the job. This is one of the best professional decisions I have ever made.

Another important aspect of corruption was the competition with the Soviet Block during the Cold War. Many poor countries' governments, in their infancy after independence, were spoilt with cheap loans and grants from the West in the process of keeping them from the bear's claws. The problem was that some of the aid was little more than a Ponzi scheme. The mantra from the West was this: the more you borrow, the better the ultimate returns will be. You need capital for infrastructure, industry, education, health, governance and security. If you spend it well, your economic growth will be more than enough to repay all these loans.

The trouble was that it was only partly true. The economic theories of growth had not been fully tested in poor developing countries, and rich-country models proved misleading, to say the least. There is a splendid illustrative story about this Ponzi lending in the book *The World's Banker* (Mallaby, 2004). It describes the events of an evening during Jim Wolfensohn's visit to Côte d'Ivoire in 1995, soon after he became president of the World Bank. The visit was an opportunity for him to see the results of a World Bank-funded 'educational adjustment loan'. On the first day, his wife was taken to see a school, while he was introduced to Henri Konan Bédié, the then president of the country. In the evening, after an official dinner, he sat down with some World Bank staffers. He asked to be told the location of the schools that had been financed by the loan. According to Mallaby (2004), there was a brief silence, after which a staffer explained to him that it was an adjustment operation, not an investment operation. Basically, he was told the sad truth that the country was in such bad economic shape that, in order to repay previous World Bank loans, it had needed to borrow more money via an adjustment loan funded by the International Development Association (IDA).[12] Jim went ballistic and said he did not like what he had just heard. Kim Jaycox – whom I once met and consider a decent man, and who was the World Bank vice president for West Africa at the time – was present and agreed with him, but said there was no alternative.

The point is that the West was so hooked on buying the allegiance of poor countries that it had conveniently overlooked one of the basic rules of government borrowing: the rule that says governments can only afford to borrow today if future taxation revenue and inflation will cover the cost of the loan and its interest costs. In many African countries, there was insufficient tax revenue to cover the basic costs of government, let alone finance loans. This was conveniently overlooked for many years. To be fair to Jim, he did at least address the problem to some extent while he was president of the World Bank. He managed to get the World Bank's shareholders to agree to a programme of debt forgiveness for the most indebted countries.[13] However, in many ways, it was too late as it had encouraged many developing countries' governments to believe that there is a magic money tree and there is no need to balance income and expenditure. At the start of the third decade of the 21st century, this tree – if it does still exist – is growing roots in China. We do not yet know if China will follow the West and forgive debts. It probably will, but there will be a catch or two. Any country lucky enough to secure debt relief will have to support China in its global affairs, give China long-term leases for facilities created by the failing loans and/or support the establishment of Chinese businesses in the debt-stressed country. Already, there are some signs of this practice in Djibouti, Ethiopia and Sri Lanka (see 6.3.).

In some cases, notably during the Cold War, the West deliberately and knowingly turned a blind eye to rapacious autocratic leaders in developing countries. 'He may be a son of a bitch, but he is our son of a bitch,' was the kind of justification for dealing with guys like Mobutu Sese Seko of Zaire (now the DRC) during the Cold War. In fact, the Zaire situation was politically complicated. The country has some of the world's richest deposits of uranium and other vital minerals, and there was no way the West was going to let the USSR get its hands on these resources.

---

12. The IDA is a section of the bank that lends money at concessional rates to the poorest countries. IDA money was raised partly from the 'profits' on full bank loans and contributions from member countries. In the case of Cote d'Ivoire, the money came from France.
13. The Highly Indebted Poor Country (HIPC) Investment Programme.

What Went Wrong?

I think the main problem was the Western powers having far too much optimism and faith in representative democracy. There is little doubt that effective representative democracy can and does contribute to the raising of living standards overall. But it requires the elite to recognise that they have to share more – usually through progressive taxation, plus legal systems that work and are fair – and there have to be leaders of integrity. The optimists in the West failed to appreciate that these effective systems of governance do not come into force overnight, but over years – sometimes over centuries. Indeed, in the UK, the world's oldest democratic state, the devolution of power from the monarch to the people took the best part of 1,000 years. It began with the Magna Carta in 1215, continued through the Civil Wars of the 1640s, but was not really completed until the Atlee government in 1945, after the Second World War. It was only then that the UK really became a pluralist representative democracy with a greater emphasis on sharing the benefits of wealth creation.

If my travels have taught me anything it is that cultural traditions, especially systems of governance, change at glacial speed. There are cases of revolutionary and rapid change, but rarely do revolutions precede the adoption of effective democracy. In Rwanda, Paul Kagame was hailed as a democrat by the West when he took political control in 2000. He had previously led the militia that ended the civil war there in 1994. Things seemed to start on the right track, and the West poured in resources, but within a short period, he was ruling like any other autocrat. The same thing happened in Cambodia. Hun Sen pushed out the dreadful regime of Pol Pot and was festooned with cash and goodwill from the West. Today, Cambodia is yet again run by an autocrat named Hun Sen.

For nearly 20 years, it looked as though South Africa might prove the democratic pessimists wrong by showing that a young nation can be governed in an effective way by representative democracy. Sadly, all the evidence suggests the optimism might have been misplaced and that more traditional rule by powerful elites has returned. The country has also suffered from massive corruption, as revealed in recent book *Gangster State* (Myburgh, 2019). Not all has been lost in South Africa. Cyril Ramaphosa, President Zuma's more competent successor, seems to be moving the country in the right direction. If he and his successors succeed, it will largely be due to the institutional framework and related political culture established in earlier years.

A weakness of representative democracy is that, unless it is backed up by a culture that respects the 'rule of law', it is too easily abused by the wealthy and powerful, either by direct bribes or promises that can never be fulfilled. What is more, there is often no way to challenge such abuse legally (judges can be bribed), and the moment force is used, the whole concept of representation evaporates. As we enter the third decade of the 21st century, the problem for the West is that the democratic ideals we peddled so furiously during the Cold War have, with few exceptions, not delivered the results promised. Sadly, the fastest economic growth – again, with few exceptions – is now in autocratic regimes such as China and Vietnam. These are places where the concepts of human rights are more often ignored than followed. It is rather terrifying to think that the UN could soon be heavily influenced – if not dominated by – such autocratic regimes (see *Chapter 6*).

One of the key themes that comes across when reading some of the tales about aid and development outlined in the subsequent chapters of this book is how we were all really flying by the seat of our pants. We had terms of reference for our projects and missions, but there was no guidebook that told one what to do and how to do it. There was also a massive amount of politics. Those of us involved in aid were part of so-called 'soft power' or influence. If poor countries' governments could be persuaded to look towards London, Paris or Washington, rather than Moscow, it did not really matter if the aid money actually reached all the intended beneficiaries – if some leaked, that was a shame, but in the short run, it did not matter very much. A good example is the helicopter engine story in the piece about the Philippines in 1975 (see 4.4.).

It is also true that much aid was in the form of loans, the bulk of which have been or are still being serviced. To put it less poetically, development only really happens when the people concerned decide they want to make the necessary social and cultural changes – changes that require strong, motivated, competent and determined leadership (think China, Singapore or Uruguay). In much of the developing world, the default position seems to be to keep things as they have always been. Cultural change really only comes about following major events. In Europe, the First and Second World Wars brought about far more economic and social change than any amount of intellectual initiative, such as that promised by the Fabians in England in the early 20th century or Thomas Hobbes in the 17th century.

I had thought about giving this book the title *Beer & Boats* as a punchy shorthand way of drawing attention to and alluding to some of the follies of aid, but on further reflection, I decided that the current title more accurately describes its contents. The former idea followed a conversation I had with a colleague one lunchtime in the mid-1990s, sitting in the cafeteria of the FAO. David had just returned from a visit to Grenada on behalf of the International Fund for Agricultural Development

(IFAD), which is possibly the most political of all the UN agencies.[14] The task of his mission was to design a second phase of a fisheries project. They started their work by reviewing the achievements of the first phase. They found that the cold store, built under the first phase project, was full of beer, and the boats provided were being used for a series of races around the bay of the capital, St George's. To be fair, it was a holiday weekend, and we all need a bit of fun now and again. However, it soon became clear that the first project had not helped the fishing industry very much. Closer analysis showed that Grenadians like their fish fresh, not frozen.

In its own small way, this project was symptomatic of the worst kind of aid. The problem starts with the donor agency having to get its money out the door. A team is hired and sent out to the borrowing country, where – in a series of hurried interviews – they discuss possible projects with civil servants. The civil servants then talk to the politicians, and eventually, some ideas are thrown together and agreed. The team then submit a glowing report of their mission and a positive response from the government. This is reviewed by an in-house team of the funding agency that suggests a few minor changes, and sooner or later, the project gets the green light from its board of directors.

14. The IFAD was born soon after the oil crisis in 1973. The oil nations of the gulf ramped up the price of oil by several hundred per cent. Some smart guys in the West pointed out that the price rises were crippling many poor developing nations. They suggested that, in compensation, the oil producers should make some credit available to help these nations manage until their economies picked up. To encourage such largesse, the rich Western countries said they would also chip in to this new fund (40%), but as the biggest contributors (60%), the oil-rich countries would have the first choice of the head or president of the agency. The agency was based in Rome, alongside the FAO and the World Food Programme, as it was considered that the bulk of the funds' loans would be for agriculture and rural investments. See *Chapter 3*

1.
Historical Background

1.1. Pre-Independence Aid

Before the independence period, there is considerable evidence that the colonial powers of the 19th and early 20th centuries were mindful of the need to provide infrastructure and train their subjects in some of the skills needed in a growing economy. It was not seen as aid so much as a way of maximising the economic returns to colonialism, but it undoubtedly contributed to economic growth and laid some foundations for the future.

The main motive for any such interventions was not so much to help the individual country but to contribute to the overall economy of the imperial power and meet the costs of governing the colony. Let it not be forgotten that a key objective of the colonisers was for each colony to generate sufficient income to cover its administrative costs and be self-supporting financially, as reported in the book *The Best of Both Worlds?* (Hunter, 1967). To achieve this, some economic resources had to be generated to pay for the necessary services and a small cadre of nationals trained to fill basic service positions. Although not seen as development assistance at the time, the schools and training colleges, infrastructure, and institutions started in most colonies should be considered as important, even vital, first steps.

One of the best examples of early colonial investment is the establishment of the Gezira cotton scheme in Sudan in the early years of the 20th century. It is described in detail in the book *Gezira: A Story of Development in the Sudan* (Gaitskell, 1959). At the end of the 19th century, for strategic reasons (given its position on the Red Sea), the UK took over suzerainty of Sudan, but realised that the prospect of raising taxes to pay for administration was unrealistic from such a subsistence economy. To generate economic activity, it was decided to develop a massive irrigated-cotton scheme to produce valuable long-staple cotton. On completion, the Gezira scheme covered more than 1 million acres, and was the largest such scheme in the world. The initial capital cost was £13 million in 1924 (£700 million today), and it had to be guaranteed by the government in London, as investors considered the risks too high. However, in the event, the investment was recovered from an annual charge on the income from the scheme, and the massive investment paid off. It not only provided an income for thousands of tenant farmers but also finances for running the country. Nearly 100 years later, the scheme is still operational in parts.

Another better-known example is the railway network (all 68,000 kilometres of it) built by the British in India, much of which is still operating today, providing vital internal trade links throughout the country. The 14 steel spans of the massive Hardinge Bridge over the Ganges in Bangladesh gives one a sense of the enormous technical, economic and emotional investment the UK was prepared to put into its colonies in the 19th century. In real terms, far more money than we spend on development assistance today. Allied to these kinds of physical investments, of course, was the projection of power. Power to rule, which was bought fairly cheaply by simply having the best technology and most efficient administration available at the time. In particular, maritime power that enabled most of the world's seas to be controlled relatively cheaply by the Royal Navy, allowing trade to flourish. Control of the seas was perhaps the most significant benefit to the UK and, indeed, the free world of *Pax Britannica*, according to Mead (2007) in his book *God and Gold*.

1.2.   Post-Second World War History of Aid

It is important to recognise that aid is a relatively new addition to the skills of statecraft and realpolitik – one that really only took off after the Second World War and that is evolving as new methods are tried, tested and analysed, and new problems emerge. I think the evolution of development theory can best be viewed from two perspectives: the historical and the ideological.

If one is looking for a decisive starting point for development aid, I think it is difficult to find a better moment than the signing of the Atlantic Charter by Churchill and Roosevelt onboard various warships in the Atlantic Ocean in 1941. The charter was the price Churchill had to pay to gain US support for the UK in the Second World War, which was largely designed to blow away the mercantilism[15] that had protected the British Empire, and to open up its markets to new suppliers, especially those in the US. The US also insisted that the UK abrogated its related rules that gave British ships the sole right to transport cargoes to and from empire ports.[16] However, as is usual in the affairs of state, it was dressed up in such a way as to give it a broader rationale in terms of liberty and self-destiny. At the same time, although not publicly admitted, it was effectively the death warrant for the British Empire and other colonial empires. Thus, if the wealth of empire and its markets

---

15. One definition of 'mercantilism' is an economic policy that is designed to maximise the exports and minimise the imports for an economy ('Mercantilism', 2021).
16. Today, shipping is generally much more open, but it is interesting that only US-owned vessels can transport American grain on behalf of the World Food Programme.

could no longer be controlled, albeit for modest financial reward and largely to meet local running costs, what was the point of empire? And if the empires were to be dissolved, constituent countries would have to be given their independence. Some reports suggest that Churchill thought he could reverse the charter if the war was won. But as we know, Churchill did win the war, but he lost power in the 1945 general election.

Better known than the Atlantic Charter, but also of long-lived effect, was the momentous UN Monetary and Financial Conference, usually just called the 'Bretton Woods Conference', in New Hampshire in July 1944. The conference was attended by delegates from 44 nations, and it was aimed at rebuilding the international monetary system as the end of the war appeared to be in sight. Two famous institutions, the World Bank and the International Monetary Fund (IMF), were born at the conference and both have played enormously important financial roles in the world ever since. In the same year, at the instigation of US President Franklin D. Roosevelt, a smaller number of delegates from the UK, China, the USSR and the US met at Dumbarton Oaks (a private estate outside Washington, DC) and agreed to create the UN. Following the surrender of Germany in April 1945, the UN Charter was signed in San Francisco on 26 June 1945. The Bretton Woods Institutions, and the UN and its agencies were established to help all countries – big or small, rich or poor – and they have played a massively important role in development aid for more than 70 years (see *Chapter 2*).

1.3.   Independence

Having been bequeathed a constitution, a representative system of government, no debts, a little cash in the bank and a modestly sized and trained civil service, it was hoped to be only a matter of time before independence would lead to the all-important economic growth needed to improve the livelihoods of the people of the newly independent nations. Most had been bequeathed primary industries (mining, oil or plantations) to exploit and build on; however, few (with the possible exception of India) had anything in the way of significant manufacturing or service industries.

With the benefit of hindsight, it is now possible to identify three major flaws in the thinking that independence was the necessary and key solution to economic development. The first was the failure to take into account the rapid growth in the populations and expectations of the independent peoples. Where were the jobs to come from? In the heady days surrounding independence, only a handful of doomsayers asked such questions, such as Roy Welensky in what is now Zimbabwe (Welensky, 1964), and Guy Hunter and Thomas Bauer in Britain. For the most part, the colonialists wanted out as soon as possible at the lowest cost, and so did not raise these issues.

The second issue, related to the first in many ways, was the ownership structure of the newly independent economies. Typically, the public sector dominated, with commercial activities largely limited to trading rather than manufacturing. The all-important private sector engine for growth and its supporting institutional environment simply did not exist. Even today, many of the poorest countries have a limited private sector. In Ethiopia, one of the poorest countries in the world, the private sector only controlled some 14% of the economy in 2007. The rest was in the inefficient hands of the state or, more accurately, the elite that actually runs the country. The private sector has increased its share of the economy to some 35% since 2007, but the state still dominates.

The third flaw was the failure to address the cultural gap between the colonisers and the colonised. For example, if one looks at the history of Nigeria over the past 100 years or so and at how Western ideas of economics and governance have failed to take root, it is difficult to avoid the conclusion that much can be attributed to a massive cultural divide. During the colonial period, this was well recognised, if not widely shared. The colonists were motivated by commerce and were anxious to minimise the costs of administering the country. This was achieved through dependence on existing governance structures, which was often referred to as 'native administration'. These were financially supported to a degree, but were essentially there to maintain law and order, not to encourage economic development. A very small group of expatriate staff filled key government positions and kept the show on the road. To put things in perspective, it is reported that, during the heady days of the British Rule in India, the Indian Administrative Service had a total of only 1,000 senior officers.

The colonial powers knew how weak the foundations for independence were, but they were desperate to leave. They conveniently convinced themselves that – with a little preparation in the form of establishing the rudiments of democracy (parliaments and political parties), together with a small cadre of trained technicians and some money in the state coffers – all would be well.

In a few colonies, especially where there were white settlers, there were also liberation movements; therefore, rather than fighting them at great cost, it made much better sense to call their bluff and let them try to run the show. Kenya is a good case study. The British tried through surrogates to hang on after the war, but the nasty Mau Mau insurrection hinted that hanging on to power could be very expensive at a time when the UK was borrowing massively just to keep everyone fed and clothed back home. According to the book *Inside Africa* (Gunther, 1955), during the three years from 1952–55, the British spent some £26.5 million (equivalent to at least £250 million today) to contain the Mau Mau. On reflection, decolonisation was a no-brainer, and in Kenya, it was eventually done in such a way that reasonably good relations between the UK and Kenya were established at independence and remain some 50 years later.

Furthermore, 'independence' and tariff-free access to new markets was what the US wanted as part of its price for helping the Allies defeat Germany in the Second World War, and for which Uncle Sam had guaranteed to help the newly emerging nations. On paper, it all looked like a win-win situation. The US had deep pockets, and some might say a naïve confidence in how to run a country. They would show these emerging nations how to do things, and they had come up with a brilliant way of helping countries to help themselves in the form of concessional loans and technical expertise.

The ex-colonial powers and the US were all well aware that independence alone was insufficient to generate economic growth, and they searched for ways in which they could help the newly emerging nations in mutually beneficial ways. In developing these ideas, they were helped considerably by the theories of Carl Popper. In his seminal work, *The Open Society and Its Enemies* (Popper, 1945), he had convincingly shown that socialism and the autocratic government control of wealth-generating enterprises does not work, or at any rate, it does not work as well as had been predicted by Messrs Marx, Engels, Trotsky, Lenin and Co., and that totalitarian states would eventually fall behind their liberal democratic competitors because of their inability to adapt to change. Of course, what this boils down to is representative democracy with regular elections. This is nicely summarised by Bryan Magee (1985) in his little book, *Popper*. Proof of Popper's thinking, if it were still needed, comes from the collapse of the command economies of the USSR and Eastern Europe in 1989 – a watershed in human affairs if ever there was one.

The big problem associated with Popper's concept of liberal democracy and economic growth is not its theoretical basis, which is now well accepted by most political scientists, but how to nurture it. In most ex-colonies, there were noble attempts before independence to encourage the development of Western-type political parties, parliaments and electoral procedures. The problem was – and still is in many countries – that the Western ideas of left- and right-wing political beliefs were alien concepts in countries where the traditional systems of governance depended largely on allegiance to traditional chiefs or monarchs, compounded by caste politics, and ethnic or tribal rivalry, and not just in the least-developed countries of the African continent.

I well recall talking to a taxi driver in Johannesburg in 2008, just before Jacob Zuma became president of South Africa. The papers were full of stories about how fickle he was and concerns that he would be a lousy president – concerns that were borne out by the time he stood down in 2018. I asked the taxi driver why Zuma stood such a strong chance of being elected. The simple answer I got was that it was the turn of the Zulus to take power, and he was the choice of the Zulus. His predecessor, Thabo Mbeki, is a Xhosa, and South Africa's first black president, Nelson Mandela, was a Thembu.

In Kenya, one of the more developed East African countries, the largest ethnic group is the Kikuyu. Apart from a longish period in the 1980s, they have held the presidency since independence in 1963. In recognition of this, Raila Odinga, a Kalenjin who has failed to secure office more than five times, decided in 2019 to work with the current Kikuyu president, Uhuru Kenyatta, rather than challenging him. Leaving aside this power sharing, the presidency of Uhuru Kenyatta – who is the son of Jomo Kenyatta, the first president of Kenya – hints at the African tendency to retain power in the family.

These political stories are by no means unique to Africa, but they go some way to explaining why Western ideas of liberal democracy have not become widely adopted. Instead, in much of the continent, power still resides with traditional leaders. Their power base does not rely on electoral promises but on ethnic support, which has to be rewarded to the extent possible by preferential treatment for jobs, training opportunities and contracts for members of the tribe. This kind of governance fails a fundamental aspect of Popper's thinking, namely the ability of the governed to change their leaders. There is no easy solution to this problem, and I fear it will almost certainly continue to hold back economic growth in much of the continent of Africa for the foreseeable future. (I say a bit more about this in *Chapter 6*.)

Another big name in early development thinking was the Swedish social economist Gunnar Myrdal. He was a Nobel Prize winner who claimed that the economic theories of developed countries did not necessarily apply to developing countries. In particular, he believed that the dependence on markets and free enterprise as engines for growth was not relevant in a country with no infrastructure, a shortage of capital and a shortage of skills. Instead, he recommended central planning, much along the lines of the command economies. This would help prioritise the investment needed to build up the basic social and infrastructure capital needs of an economy.

This 'soft socialism' fitted in well with the early Western thinking and practices of the Cold War. In particular, it provided an intellectual policy basis for much of the World Bank lending for infrastructure. It also supported the idea of a broad-based plan for economic growth, with supporting capital and technical expertise for priorities within a 'country assistance programme'. To a considerable extent, this thinking picked up on the Keynesian idea of pump priming to kick-start economic growth. However, with hindsight, we now know that provision of capital alone is insufficient and, even worse, it has resulted in massive debt overhangs in many countries. To be fair to Keynes, he only recommended pump priming for restarting an economy, not for building it up from scratch. He argued that it was okay for a government to build up temporary debt as long as the long-term benefits would allow such a debt to be serviced and repaid.

1.4.   The Cold War

The second historical period, which overlaps the period of independence to a considerable extent, was the Cold War; that is, the period of rivalry between the Western capitalist economies and the Eastern command economies. This was hinted at by Churchill in his Iron Curtain speech – given at Fulton, Missouri, in 1946 – about Europe: 'An iron curtain has descended across the Continent.' The implications of this speech were not fully appreciated by the majority of world leaders at the time, and it took a while for his message to sink in. When battle did commence, the actual battlefields were in the developing world.

Indeed, the policy of 'containment' of the USSR, as dreamt up by the US diplomat George F. Kennan, was designed to strengthen European and American ties to developing nations. Its aims were to avoid direct conflict between the West and the East, and to play a game of cat and mouse on the global stage until the USSR and its acolyte command economies surrendered to Western capitalism. Both sides were determined to win by whatever means necessary, including the support of the newly independent countries through a combination of ideological and economic means. The Cold War continued until November 1989 when the Berlin Wall was breached, and the failures of the command economies could no longer be hidden. I saw the tail end of this policy in practice in 1986 when I was on a ridiculous mission to Pakistan, ostensibly to help endorse a technical project, but one that was really aimed simply at shovelling money into that country; the money being needed to help Pakistan in its efforts as a bulkhead against Soviet expansion in Afghanistan (see 3.9.).

The main weapon of both sides was, of course, money – either as grants or loans (usually with conditions), or sadly, often as military aid in support of terrorist groups. For years, the West supported the União Nacional para a Independência Total de Angola (the National Union for the Total Independence of Angola) (UNITA) in Angola, while the Eastern bloc supported the Movimento Popular de Libertação de Angola (People's Movement for the Liberation of Angola) (MPLA). This is well described in the book *Africa: Altered States, Ordinary Miracles* (Dowden, 2008). In addition to supporting nominally pro-Western decision makers in the newly emerging nations, much Western aid was linked to introducing policy and institutional changes that were favourable to the Western capitalist system (e.g. market liberalisation). The message from both sides was this: do it our way if you want more support. However, the leverage or conditions had to be fairly subtle as, being mindful of the vestigial feelings and sentiments associated with colonisation, most of the richer countries were very cautious about meddling too obviously in the internal affairs of developing nations.

The UN agencies, the World Bank and the other development banks provided good Trojan horses for the West. Supposedly, these were independent and objective development agencies, which were able and willing to support all ideologies, but in reality, they were promoting the Western capitalist way of doing things. The command economies were not members of the development banks, rarely paid their contributions to the UN and its agencies, and had few nationals serving in UN agencies. To some people, Western influence on newly independent governments was seen as little more than subliminal, as described in *Aid as Imperialism* (Hayter, 1970) and *Inside Foreign Aid* (Tendler, 1975). I can think of countless examples of scandalous loans to poor countries designed to keep their governments friendly to the West (see *Chapter 3*). But while there was much hypocrisy associated with aid during the Cold War, I am convinced that the aid policies of the West were justified. Indeed, I would go further and say the soft power of aid during the Cold War was infinitely better than the alternative of hot lead or, worse, nuclear hard power. All the more so, as recognising the disaster of many non-performing development loans, the rich world subsequently provided substantial debt relief.

1.5.   Monetarism

Following the end of the Cold War, there was a period from 1989, lasting about 10 years (and containing a number of sub-periods), which was characterised by tough economic thinking, conveniently described as 'monetarism'. At this point in time, with the end of the Cold War effectively stopping any belief in the command economy approach to governance and economics, the emphasis moved to finding better ways of making the free-market approach work. It was also a time when a debt crisis emerged in much of Latin America, following a binge of investment in infrastructure using borrowed funds that could not be serviced due to roaring inflation. At the time, the view of many in the US was that there was a need to secure as much in the way of repayments as possible before things got worse. John Williamson (*The Economist*, 2021B), a British economist, wrote a document to frame the proceedings of a conference held in Washington, DC, to discuss the problem that, *inter alia*, proposed a more gradual, measured approach; he is considered to have coined the term Washington Consensus (WC).

I call the first of the aforementioned sub-periods the 'WC period', which reigned supreme in the early 1990s. On becoming increasingly aware of the failure of many aid initiatives, a rethink was necessary. This was spearheaded by the ideas of the neoclassical Chicago School of Economics (Milton Friedman), and it led to the belief that the only things needed to secure economic stability were macroeconomic discipline, a market economy and free trade. It was an informal policy that evolved from the adoption of monetarism by many OECD countries. In its purest form, its adherents believe that economic growth – and hence poverty alleviation – will result from the adoption of appropriate fiscal and economic policies; in particular, market liberalisation, privatisation and free trade.

The approach was supported by the work of Hausmann *et al.* (2004). They looked at 83 countries with annual and sustained economic growth of more than 2%. A summary of their work was reviewed in an article in *The Economist* (2004). Their studies conclude that one of the key factors was an increase in private sector activity in response to the relaxing of specific constraints. Crucially, for this to work, it also demanded the rule of law, freedom of expression and a degree of political pluralism.

Another way of looking at it is to say that when countries adopt policies encouraging business and investment, everything else will follow suit. The big difference between this approach and earlier approaches to development is the restriction of government intervention, mainly through the establishment and regulation of policy, and large infrastructure investment, rather than large-scale public sector involvement in the economy. There is no room within the consensus for the state ownership of productive enterprises, which was so popular in socialist regimes.

Encouraged by the results achieved by such fiscal and monetary policies in the US and the UK, the aid bandwagon started promoting them globally in a big way. The World Bank went into overdrive to promote privatisation and slim down state-owned enterprises (SOEs); the International Finance Corporation (IFC) and bilateral aid agencies established dozens of pseudo-projects aimed at helping entrepreneurs improve their act. However, the results were frequently disappointing.

In 1994, I led a mission to China to prepare a 'seeds commercialisation' project for World Bank funding (see 3.11.). At the time, most states (and even provinces) in China had their own seed companies, which were dreadfully overstaffed and inefficient. The World Bank planned to solve this problem by privatising the industry. It was an uphill struggle to convince the Chinese that this was what they needed for many reasons, but the biggest challenge was the pensions – or rather the lack of pensions – for seed-company staff. Instead of receiving a pension, staff stayed on the payroll until they fell off their perch. I was never convinced we really got our message across, and the World Bank completion report for the project is fairly muted about its achievement. However, China has since introduced a national pension system to replace those of state companies.[17]

---

17. It requires employers to contribute 20% of employees' salaries, plus employees a further 8% of their salary into the national scheme. It is, however, predicted to run out of money by 2035, as the population is ageing and there are too few new employees to contribute financial support.

Another good example of the failure of this approach is that of cashew nut processing in Mozambique (once the world's largest producer of these nuts). The edible bit of the nut has to be recovered by cracking its curved protective shell and scooping out the nut. It is tedious work, but provides useful jobs in a country with very high unemployment. In the 1990s, in an attempt to liberalise the industry, the World Bank told the government to remove controls and taxes on the export of raw nuts. The result was catastrophic. Trading firms shipped out the nuts, as foreign buyers pounced on access to cheap supplies of unprocessed nuts, and some 8,000 jobs were lost as domestic processors closed down. Since 2001, the government has reversed the policy imposed by the World Bank, and the domestic processing industry is recovering slowly, with an estimated 17,000 jobs in processing factories at time of writing. Too much market liberalisation is not always a good thing, especially when and where it destroys jobs.

The pure WC period was quite short and was followed by a modified second sub-period, loosely referred to as the 'post-Washington Consensus (pWC) period', which overlapped with the millennium period to a considerable extent. The economic recession in 2008 led to a rethink about free markets; in particular, the unimpeded flow of capital (Birdsall and Fukuyama, 2011). The economics is quite complicated, but basically, the risks associated with the large-scale flow of capital require the sophisticated regulation of the financial sectors – regulations that are very difficult to effect, especially in developing countries.

Doubts emerged about the ability of the monetarist system to do the job in developing countries. It is all very well closing down state-owned industries or privatising them to make them efficient, but what happens to all those thrown out of work or who cannot find jobs in a competitive free-market economy? The pWC was really a hybrid between private and state involvement in the economy, with the caveat that governance has to be good governance.

It is interesting that a one-time chief economist at the World Bank – Nobel Prize winner Joe Stiglitz – is on record as saying that markets do not always work satisfactorily and state intervention is sometimes needed. Stiglitz is quite a character and was released by the president of the World Bank for going too public with his views at a time when World Bank policy was almost pure WC. Now, it seems, he was ahead of the curve in fact, and more and more people were beginning to challenge the purist WC.

The problem, as I see it, is really one of scale. No one really challenges the view that economic growth and wealth creation are best done by the private sector / free enterprise, but – and it is a huge but – the private sector cannot address the magnitude of the problem or, to put it in simple language, create sufficient jobs quickly enough. During a visit to Kenya in 2003, I was told by the owner of the ranch where Prince William spent some of his gap year that 14% of Kenyans had a paid job. The rest are subsistence farmers, but there is no more suitable land to farm. What happens to the next generation of people looking for a job or land to farm? The pWC recognises that market failures have to be addressed as appropriate by government intervention. The problem here is knowing what jobs to create. It may be okay for an oil-rich nation to create jobs for all the unemployed; however, it is not so easy for a country with a growing workforce but few valuable resources to exploit. Some interventions that largely depend on human skills, such as garment-making, have worked in a number of countries with a large number of unemployed workers.

The third sub-period can conveniently be called the 'millennium period'. It began around the turn of the 20th century, at the time of the eight Millennium Development Goals (MDGs),[18] and it can best be seen as a return to earlier policies of grants and loans, but also as a time of evaluation and reflection on the responsibilities of rich and poor countries. Folk in the West began to realise that the peace heralded by the end of the Cold War was not, as Fukuyama had said, 'The End of History' (i.e. the universalisation of Western liberal democracy). They also began to realise that, until and unless the issue of poverty was addressed, it was likely there would be more terrorist attacks and more illegal immigration.

In support of the recognition of this awareness of the linkages between poverty and terrorism – as reported by Beale (2001) in the *Financial Times* – Horst Kohler, the then managing director of the IMF, went on record to say that there was an urgent need to promote economic growth in Africa, and the IMF had a role to play in helping countries achieve the macroeconomic stability needed for growth.

A year later, in 2002, a huge gathering of heads of state, ministers and international agency staff[19] met in Monterrey, Mexico, and came up with the name Monterrey Consensus. This called for, *inter alia*, more funding for aid and for the better use of aid funds. At the conference, the rich world agreed to finance the eight MDGs in return for the recipient nations agreeing to political and economic reform. It was at this meeting that the idea of rich countries each contributing 0.7% of their GNI to aid[20] was born. At the time, the US contribution was 0.18% of GNI.

As far as the MDGs are concerned, a final monitoring of the results in 2011 found that only one target had been fully achieved, which was the coordination

---

18. In September 2000, at the annual UN conference in New York, the member nations agreed on an agenda for development. There were eight goals: (1) eradication of poverty and hunger; (2) universal primary education; (3) promotion of gender equality; (4) reduction in child mortality; (5) improved maternal health; (6) combating disease; (7) promotion of environmental stability; and (8) development of a global partnership for development. As with all political promises, there was much hypocrisy involved, as no reliable monitoring was established to record whether the objectives would be achieved. It was, however, seen as a seal whereby the poor countries would endeavor to reform in return for continued financial assistance.
19. In total, there were over 50 heads of state, 200 ministers, and representatives from the UN, the World Bank, the IMF and the WTO.
20. Some 20 years later, only a handful of European countries have met this target.

of technical cooperation. In the foreword to the MDG Report (2015), the then Secretary-General of the UN, Ban Ki-Moon, referred to the MDGs helping lift 1 billion people out of extreme poverty, making inroads against hunger and enabling more girls to go to school. All good things, but not necessarily due to the MDGs alone, and closer inspection of the numbers tells a rather different story as most of the improvement has come from China. It is also the case that there has been no formal evaluation of the MDGs. But if nothing else, the MDGs do show that economic growth can be achieved if a government gets its economic priorities and policies right. An important criticism of the MDGs is that they were focused on the issues of the development community (poverty, growth and social inclusion). They were only marginally focused on the issue of concern to the environmental community (the survival of the planet), which affects both poor and rich countries.

1.6.   Post-Millennium Development Approaches

Around the time of the MDGs, some well-known economists were arguing that the best way to solve the problems of poverty in poor countries was simple: just give the poor folk money. Loosely called the Make Poverty History (MPH) approach, it is closely associated with the US economist Jeffery Sachs, the UN, and celebrities such as Bono and Bob Geldof. Using a number of simple numerical examples, Sachs tried to show that, for a relatively small amount of money, poverty could be reduced substantially for most of the world's poor.

It is essentially a safety net approach, similar to but on a larger scale than what has been tried to date. Give the poor all the money they need now, and the problems of poverty will somehow evaporate. This says that the starting point is to provide resources (funds), and economic growth will then take place. It is a seductive approach that appeals to the uninformed in the donor world as it impacts heavily on the conscience of the rich, and when dressed up in seemingly rigorous economic argument by a reputedly brilliant economist like Jeffery Sachs, who would doubt its efficacy? It also appeals greatly to the would-be recipients, who simply have to wait for the low-hanging fruit to fall! The approach basically says that if folk are well fed, educated and fit, they will be able to work, and if they can work, they will generate an income that will enable them to improve their livelihoods.

However, there are two fundamental problems with this approach, which is why there is still a struggle for it to be widely accepted. The first is what might be termed a 'cart or horse issue'. Thus, will creating a workforce generate jobs or will creating jobs lead to a trained workforce? Evidence from economic history suggest that the jobs have to come first, and that simply producing a workforce is more likely to lead to further problems of frustration, and possibly insurrection and terrorism, as young, unemployed, fit, educated men and women fall prey to organisations such as Al-Qaeda, as there are no other jobs to go to.[21]

An article by Peter Neuman (2007), the then director of the Centre for Defence Studies at King's College, London, refers to a fair number of Islamic terrorists being highly trained chemists, engineers and even doctors who faced extreme tension in their personal lives in the West, which they resolved by embracing jihadism. One swallow does not a summer make, but the story hints that job creation precedes the establishment of a workforce. It is, of course, nice to think that everyone in a country should be able to read and write, but in fact, being able to read and write has little value if the only employment available is manual work.

It is interesting to me that the question of whether to educate people to produce a workforce or whether to provide employment was considered in the 1960s (Hunter, 1967), at the time of decolonisation, when the feeling was that the priority was to create jobs. So what went wrong? Why were the earlier experts' views ignored? I suspect that the real problem has been – and, indeed, always will be – that it is a lot easier for governments to educate people (at all levels) than it is for them to create real jobs.

The second fundamental trouble with the MPH approach is that – even if the economics made sense – all else being equal, all is not equal in the real world of the poor. In particular, the Sachs approach conveniently ignores the malign power and influence of corrupt elites who are – or would be – in control of the safety net funds. Again, evidence from (albeit recent) history confirms that aid funds are almost impossible to target accurately, and that much is always lost, stolen or squandered by those in positions of influence. Sachs makes no provision in his thinking for this reality, but Thomas Bauer did. He referred to such aid as 'taking money from the poor in rich countries and giving it to the rich in poor countries' (Bauer, 1971).

Another important development in US aid policy around this time was the MCC, which was established in 2004. The MCC forms partnerships with developing countries that are committed to good governance, economic freedom and investing in their citizens. The MCC uses a set of third-party metrics to assess annually the extent to which more than 100 developing countries are ruling justly, investing in their people and promoting economic freedom. Those that meet the necessary criteria are eligible for financial support from the MCC. It is still early days, but there is some empirical evidence that the MCC's eligibility standards are effective at incentivising reform (Parks, 2019)(see 2.19.).

---

21. The Egyptian government does its best to employ some of its citizens, 2 million of whom serve in the not-so-well-armed forces.

An interesting study of 72 rich and poor countries by William Easterly and Ross Irvine (*The Economist*, 2002B) suggests that institutions matter far more than policy or geography. Their study shows that countries with good institutions tend to do alright with good or bad policies, and countries with bad institutions tend to do badly regardless. However, the study does suggest that geography also matters. They posit that the countries settled by large numbers of people from Europe – such as Canada, North America, Australia and New Zealand – tend to have good institutions. Countries that were not settled by Europeans – such as most of Africa and much of Latin America – have poorer institutions. The reasons why some countries were settled can be attributed to them having fewer pests and diseases, and vice versa. So, geography did – and still does – play a role in development. I think one can add a footnote to this conclusion to say that the settled Europeans brought with them cultural values that have helped them to develop their new-found countries (see *Chapter 6*).

Following the MDGs, the Sustainable Development Goals (SDGs) aim to meld the issues and actions needed by both rich and poor countries. They are based on the work of an open working group set up at the UN Rio+20 conference held in Rio De Janeiro in 2012. There are 17 SDGs, which are listed in *Appendix C*. The biggest single difference from the MDGs is that the commitment for change is no longer focused on the poorer countries but on both poor and rich countries, although the SDGs still call on the rich countries to pick up the lion's share of the costs.

The SDGs are also focused on the well-being of Planet Earth, as well as the elimination of poverty and hunger. While it is hard to deny the logic and, indeed, the rationale behind the SDGs, it is difficult to see them taking precedence over the selfish interests of individual nations. Some, such as number 5 (gender equality), are simply wishful thinking as far as some cultures are concerned. Others, such as number 7 (affordable and clean energy) and number 12 (responsible production and consumption), are not really within the realistic remit of the UN, as they require individual countries to change the way things are done.

More specific criticism is that some of the SDGs challenge one of the key tenets of economics, namely that of comparative advantage. It is not realistic to expect poorer countries to introduce responsible production methods if that means raising the costs of production and losing any comparative advantages they might have. Given the general erosion of confidence in the UN and its organisations, I see the SDGs remaining largely as aspirations rather than achievable goals. In many ways, they resemble the manifesto of a global green political party, and they have about as much chance of electoral success as the UK's Green Party, which has one Member of Parliament for the slightly alternative constituency of Brighton Pavilion (at time of writing in 2020).

Yet again, it is all about politics, really. Most countries are basically in favour of the UN, if only as a talk shop, but the institution also needs to be able to show some concrete activity. The SDGs list a whole lot of aspirations that all can subscribe to, even if Nelson's eye will be turned to several of them by many countries. The arrival of the mass movement Extinction Rebellion might encourage more action on SDG number 7 (affordable and clean energy) than heretofore.

1.7.   Debt Relief

Recognising the failure of many development loans to realise their objectives of solving the problems of development, at the G8 Gleneagles summit of the rich countries' world leaders in 2005 it was agreed to write off the entire US$55 billion of debt owed at the time by the 18 poor countries most highly indebted to the World Bank, the IMF and the AfDB. This was known as the Multilateral Debt Relief Initiative (MDRI), which was similar to but not the same as the Heavily Indebted Poor Countries (HIPC) Initiative started by the World Bank and the IMF in 1996.

Although the HIPC initiative was dressed up as ensuring that no poor country would face a financial burden it could not manage, it was really an admission that, in fact, much World Bank lending had been very irresponsible and too few projects achieved their economic aspirations. Furthermore, it was recognition of the fact that many such loans were adding to the economic meltdown in many countries and contributing to political instability, which were therefore encouraging many developing-country nationals to emigrate illegally.

The MDRI meant that a further 20 countries could now also see their debt cancelled if they met targets on fighting corruption and removed impediments to private investment. This was a massive change in aid thinking and practice, for which the then UK Chancellor of the Exchequer, Gordon Brown, must be given much of the credit. By 2018, 36 countries (30 in Africa) had received debt relief totalling US$99 billion for both HIPC and MDRI, provided by the rich world. If nothing else, this debt forgiveness was an admission that much aid up to this point in time had not achieved its objectives, and a further rethink on aid policy and practices was called for. It was also an implicit recognition that some countries will need financial support in the future just to survive.

1.8.   Realism

Towards the end of the second decade of the 21st century, a fourth historical period was emerging, which was based around the most detailed evaluation of aid since the Second World War, and a simultaneous recognition of a new political challenge in the form of China. It can conveniently be called an 'age of realism'.

The Commission on State Fragility, Growth and Development, chaired by David Cameron (ex-prime minister of the UK), produced a report in 2018 that reinforced current thinking about the importance of realism, not idealism; the importance of national, not international, priorities; and the importance of institution building (Cameron, 2018). It also identifies the essential early steps that need to be taken to develop plurality in politics before elections, and it recognises that fragile states are likely to contain more than 2 billion people before long, providing perhaps the most difficult challenges facing development. A review of the report's main recommendations is provided in *Chapter 6*.

Along similar lines, in April 2019, the Congressional Research Service of the US government published a detailed policy paper on foreign aid (Lawson and Morgenstern, 2019). It is a short document of some 30 pages that reviews the rationale, types and mechanisms of US aid. Its key features are the emphasis on aid being associated with national (US) security policy, as well as more traditional humanitarian, economic and social reasons.

It should be recalled that, unlike most aid programmes, US aid includes that spent on military initiatives. The report (Lawson and Morgenstern, 2019) reveals that total US aid in 2017 was just under US$50 billion, of which 35% was for military expenditure. Consequently, the US is the largest single aid donor, accounting for some 25% of total donor assistance. Adjusted for inflation, US aid in 2017 was running at a level similar to that of the Marshall Plan after the Second World War. Over the past decade, the report notes that aid has been focused on global health programmes, increased security assistance directed against terrorism, and humanitarian assistance in response to crises. In other words, the trend is moving away from more traditional aid designed to assist economic development. Furthermore, given the failure of many earlier aid initiatives, most US aid is now given in the form of grants rather than loans.

These UK and US policy trends clearly recognise the failure of much early aid policy, notably that extant during and after the Cold War; there are signs that these concerns, backed up by academic studies, are becoming widely accepted. Paul Collier (professor of economics and director of the Centre for the Study of African Economies at Oxford University, and earlier in his career, a senior research economist at the World Bank) has developed a more pragmatic approach to economic growth. In his book *The Bottom Billion*, Collier (2008) has used powerful statistical methods to support his arguments, all of which led to the same basic conclusion, namely that it is not enough to rely on the 'goodwill' of developing countries' politicians to introduce and adopt the necessary changes needed to stimulate economic growth –

some kind of intervention from outside may be necessary. His work has identified four principal traps that prevent economic growth:

1. Conflict
2. Dependence on natural resources (e.g. hydrocarbons or minerals)
3. Being landlocked with bad neighbours
4. Bad governance

In the case of conflict, this might need some form of intervention, such as the UK's military intervention in Sierra Leone in 1999 to stop a civil war. To address problems associated with the natural-resource curse, he suggests better systems of taxation for exports and the establishment of sovereign wealth funds to accumulate reserves for all nationals, rather just the elite. Landlocked countries can overcome the trap if they can achieve regional economic integration. The improvement of governance is a tough one, but he suggests more transparency and accountability to taxpayers. Apart from military intervention, he suggests other initiatives from outside, such as helping to improve institutions, notably taxation and wealth management; shining a spotlight on poor governance; and in some cases, withholding aid until better practices are carried out. Overall, Collier is calling for more – not less – intervention from the richer world, and he has been accused by some of having a neocolonial mentality.

I think the important thing is not *what* Collier recommends but *how* his recommendations are undertaken. In many ways, his thinking can be seen as an update or reiteration of that of Guy Hunter in the 1960s (Hunter, 1967), who said economic growth in independent nations would be constrained by the lack of fundamental institutions on which a successful economy depends. In practical terms, this means that the priority help needed by such nations is how to establish and sustain the fundamental institutions of a successful economy. Although he does not spell it out, he clearly implies that such change will require the donors' benign and intelligent hand-holding of developing-country governments for many years to come.

In his book *The Great Escape* (2013), Deaton provides the most coruscating criticism of conventional aid I have read. His basic argument is that economic growth is the best way of reducing poverty. He discusses the fact that statistical analyses of economic growth in many countries shows a strong correlation between growth and the amount of national income and foreign capital invested. However, the problem with this thinking, as far as many poor countries are concerned, is that it assumes capital for investment is the single missing ingredient. It ignores the other key factors – such as financial institutions, legal systems and non-toxic politics – that enable capital to be used wisely. In fact, he reiterates what Peter Bauer

(1971) said: 'if all conditions for development are not present, then aid, as the source of capital, will be ineffective.' Deaton (2013) then goes on to ask the question as to whether countries that receive more aid per capita grow faster than other countries, and subsequently shows that both India and China – which have received less aid per head compared to much smaller countries – have grown substantially. In contrast, many much smaller countries in Africa that have received much more aid per capita have much less impressive records of economic growth.

Deaton (2013) also is very critical of how aid is evaluated, implying that donors shy away from rigorous evaluations, and he identifies much aid as having been provided for political rather than economic reasons. His overall conclusion is that giving money (aid) does not, in fact, reduce poverty, and that people in rich countries need to be aware of this. Furthermore, he believes that much aid has been provided largely in the interests of donors and those involved in giving aid, either because the population of the donor country calls for aid on humanitarian grounds or because of political interests. He is particularly critical of aid that has enabled politicians and civil servants in poor countries to rely on aid to solve a nation's problems rather than finding home-grown solutions.

A good example of such misuse of national funds is the collection of luxury cars owned by Teodorin Obiang, the son of the president of Guinea, which were sold at auction in Switzerland in late September 2019 for US$27 million. The cars were seized by the Swiss authorities in connection with a money laundering scandal associated with Obiang. The money from the auction will be used for social welfare programmes, which the despotic regime had failed to finance.

Deaton (2013) goes on to suggest that, by and large, poverty reduction will come about when poor countries copy what the rich countries (which had received no aid) did to get rich in the first place. He believes that this can best be achieved by letting poor countries help themselves by 'getting out of the way' and stopping doing things that are obstructive. He thinks this might be done by linking aid to good policies, as is the case for aid provided by the MCC (see 2.19.), although this is not a watertight way of containing or moderating repressive regimes.

Somewhat similar in thinking is the cash-on-delivery approach proposed by the Center for Global Development. Under such schemes, funds are linked to timed targets (e.g. vaccinating a given percentage of children by a given date). However, there is plenty of opportunity for slippage, and once again, one of the big ironies of development rears its head. Thus, good regimes do not require incentives to undertake good projects.

Deaton (2013) does not rule out the provision of some aid, but he thinks the future emphasis should be on reducing the amount of aid. He also suggests that aid funds need not be spent directly in recipient countries. He gives the example of medical research to eliminate malaria. The rich world could – and, indeed, should – finance this research, which would be of enormous benefit to Africa. Similarly, aid funds could be used to help develop drugs and other treatments for pests and diseases that affect Africa but are not of significant interest to Western pharmaceutical companies. This would not be easy, as a way would have to be found to share the aid funds among the participating companies, but it should be possible. Other ideas include increasing the use of aid funds to provide technical advice, and the realignment of agricultural prices for commodities, so that developing countries do not suffer from the effects of subsidies paid to farmers in rich countries. One might add to this list the creation of more favourable markets in rich countries for products made by infant industries in developing countries, along the lines of the US African Growth and Opportunities Act (AGOA), which allows preferential tariffs on garments from approved countries in Africa. The difference in approach between Collier and Deaton is considerable. Collier is an interventionist, whereas Deaton advocates minimal intervention and a return to basic, common-sense-based economics.

Abhijit Banerjee and Esther Duflo are two Nobel Prize-winning development economists who were often in the news in the second decade of the 21st century. Their work (Banerjee and Duflo, 2019) has contributed to a better understanding of what types of aid work and how donors need to do better evaluations of aid initiatives. Basically, they divide a homogenous rural population into two groups: one group gets special treatment and the other does not. They specialise in undertaking randomised controlled trials (RCTs)[22] to answer economic questions. In one interesting case study in Hyderabad, India, one group received microfinance loans, while the other did not. The results were positive in so far as the microcredit helped to address poverty in the selected districts, but not as much some of its promoters claim.

Banerjee and Duflo (2019) are perhaps less extreme in their thinking than Collier and Deaton, as they consider it inhumane in this day and age for nearly one-sixth of mankind to be living in abject poverty, and believe we must all do something about the situation. However, like Collier and Deaton, they suggest that economic growth is the starting point, not the end point, and that ways have to be found to facilitate growth in those countries that have not grown fast enough in recent years, and where the roughly 2 billion poor people still live. They also see conventional development assistance as often being part of the problem in these countries. In particular, they see aid funds as effectively being rents obtained from selling

---

22. An RCT is where a large population is split into two, with one half receiving a treatment, whereas the other half does not. Both populations are then surveyed by trained teams who ask a number of specialised questions. The results are then compared statistically, and a conclusion can be drawn as to whether the treatments had a measurable effect.

natural resources (oil, copper, etc.), which actually depresses economic growth as it leads to the 'Dutch disease' (where too much dependence on a single commodity or export, especially hydrocarbons, has a tendency to depress other sectors of an economy). If there is plenty of aid money around, why should developing countries' governments do anything to create jobs?

As these summaries indicate, aid thinking and policy were beginning to mature by the beginning of the third decade of the 21st century. Perhaps the most important lesson from nearly 70 years of aid, as supported by Deaton's work, is that aid works best when the developing country takes responsibility for its own development and prioritises the right investments and institutional policies. China is the clearest example of this, but there are others in Asia and Latin America, and a handful in Africa.

A second lesson is the growing evidence that, despite its failings, liberal democracy is a prerequisite for stable and prolonged economic growth. (China – a notable exception to this as far as politics is concerned – has encouraged free-market entrepreneurship, albeit with socialist or party strings attached.)

Thirdly, economic theories have become much more robust, with the views of Deaton (2013) widely accepted by Western politicians, if not all those in the aid game. The politics has become clearer too, with much aid continuing to be in the political interests of the donor as well as the receiver, and the admission of economists that they do not know how to transform poor countries into rich ones (*The Economist*, 2019D). This recognition is a welcome breath of fresh air and honesty. It is perhaps best summed up in the book *Good Economics for Hard Times* (Banerjee and Duflo, 2019), which broadly supports the views of Collier and Deaton. What it means in practical and policy terms is not yet clear, but it suggests that much future aid will be for reasons other than just supporting economic growth (see *Chapter 6*).

There is already some evidence that it is influencing policy. In early 2019, the UK's then Secretary of State for International Development, Penny Mordaunt, denounced the UK's commitment to spending 0.7% of GDP on aid. She also recommended spending the aid budget jointly with other departments, notably the armed forces (similar to how this is done in the US) and to review the funding of multilateral bodies such as the United Nations Education, Scientific and Cultural Organization (UNESCO). Boris Johnson, when he was Foreign Secretary, called for her department to be closed. The debate about aid seems likely to continue for some time to come.

2.

Aid Infrastructure

There are believed to be more than 150 multilateral bodies involved in aid, together with any number of specialist funds, NGOs, community-based organisations and bilateral agencies. There are probably more than 500 international organisations involved in aid in one way or another. It would be almost impossible to give details of all of these, as new ones keep popping up, and old ones keep folding or merging. What follows is a summary of the main features of the more important and well-established multilateral and bilateral agencies, and some of the newer ones (at time of writing) that seem to portend the future approach to aid, such as the MCC.

It is fairly clear from any review of aid architecture that it is a mess (*The Economist*, 2008). A major problem, according to this article, is not insufficient funding but too many cooks spoiling the broth. The article details that one of the main problems is there being too many aid operatives from international/bilateral aid agencies and NGOs seeking audiences with government officials in developing countries. There simply is not the time to consider the needs in sufficient detail to decide how aid agencies can best help. I read somewhere (unfortunately, I can no longer find the source) that donors conducted over 15,000 missions in 54 recipient countries in 2007.

According to some observers, another problem is the preference of international organisations for using their own staff, rather than nationals of the recipient countries, to prepare projects. This means a loss of practical learning experience for nationals and a much higher cost. I am not sure how serious this problem really is. I recall a big World Bank project in Zambia that was an abject failure (see 3.14.). The World Bank claimed it had been largely prepared by Zambian nationals and that this gave it a special seal of approval in Washington, DC. In fact, the local team did some careful research, during which they determined what the World Bank was looking for and served it up on a plate.

It is also the case that some of the best projects, especially those in disease control, have been designed by outsiders with help from nationals. I think a far bigger problem is the 'pressure to lend' that is faced, especially by organisations such as the World Bank and IFAD, which are often judged by how much money they have lent rather than on the quality of their projects. A good example is provided by the small fisheries project in Grenada (see 3.16.).

This chapter starts with the 'father' of the industry – the UN – along with its family of organisations and related organisations such as the IAEA. The latter has limited direct aid roles, but it plays a vital role in securing world peace and trade relations, without which no effective aid initiatives would be possible. I then provide summaries of some other important international and national aid agencies, together with information about several of the important private sector foundations involved with aid.

2.1.   United Nations (UN)

The UN is a direct, but more secure, sustainable and better-designed descendent of the League of Nations.

Like the League of Nations, the UN has very limited powers, other than those of persuasion. It has no armed forces of its own but relies on the mercenary forces of its members, which are rarely given the authority to fire, except in self-defence when on UN peacekeeping duties. I say 'mercenary forces' because, typically, the richer UN countries hire troops from poorer countries to do most of their front-line work. This weakness has been criticised by many, who blame it for the UN failing to resolve many crises in recent years. However, when you think about it, the idea of the UN having a strong fighting force is oxymoronic. How could a UN force ever take up arms against a fellow member country? Of the 195 recognised countries in the world (at time of writing in 2020), 193 are members of the UN. The two non-members are the Holy See (the Vatican) and Palestine, which have special status. There is also a small handful of states that are not recognised as countries by the UN, such as Taiwan, and are therefore not members, though they would dearly like to be. The big difference between the League of Nations (which was based in Switzerland) and the UN (which is headquartered in New York) is that the US was the driving force behind the UN and it still calls many, if not most, of the shots.

The UN Charter was signed in San Francisco on 26 June 1945, as part of the peace-building efforts after the Second World War. A summary of the UN, its functions and achievements is available in a short book entitled *The United Nations: A Very Short Introduction* (Hanhimäki, 2008), and is given in more detail in a longer book called *The Oxford Handbook on the United Nations* (Weiss and Daws, 2008). Neither book provides much information on the UN's specialist agencies that do much of the work.

The UN has four basic aims:

1. To safeguard peace and security
2. To reaffirm faith in fundamental human rights

3. To uphold international law
4. To promote social progress

With headquarters in New York, the UN consists of the following:

- The General Assembly
- The Security Council
- The International Court of Justice (ICJ) (based in The Hague)
- The Secretariat

The General Assembly is perhaps best seen as a global parliament or talking shop. All 193 member nations (as of 2020) have the right to a seat in the General Assembly and have a single vote.

The Security Council is like the executive committee or cabinet of the General Assembly. It consists of five permanent members (the US, the UK, France, Russia and China) – in essence, the victors of the Second World War, all of which have a veto on proposals put to the Security Council. That said, with the UK and France firmly in the Western camp, the US can usually be secure in having its interests looked after. In addition, the Security Council has a further 10 members, each elected for terms of two years.

The ICJ is headquartered in the Netherlands and has responsibility for judicial disputes that cannot be resolved bilaterally. For example, in 2019, the ICJ decided unanimously in favour of the claim that the UK had wrongly removed the Chagos Islands from the sovereignty of Mauritius some 50 years earlier.

The Secretariat is headed by the Secretary-General, who is elected from the member nations for a period of five years (which is renewable). Although a prestigious position, it was described by the second Secretary-General, Dag Hammarskjöld from Sweden, as 'the most difficult job on earth'. I think he meant that you have all the world's problems on your desk, but very few powers, other than persuasion and perhaps a bit of special funding. That said, the UN has been instrumental in resolving a number of regional conflicts since 1945; however, the crisis in Syria in the second decade of the 21st century has tested the UN almost to breaking point, with permanent members of the Security Council at loggerheads and literally sniping at each other, albeit mainly via surrogates.

The contrast between the aspirational and actionable powers of the UN has perhaps been the greatest paradox of international politics over the last 75 years. On the one hand, the UN is supposed to be the guardian of peace, and yet, ultimately, it does not have the power to enforce it. The only power the UN actually has is the power of agreement by consensus, and when there is no consensus, the UN fails. Take the case of the Falklands War in the 1980s. Both the UK and Argentina were members of the UN, but no amount of discussion by diplomats could prevent armed conflict. The UN was also powerless to stop the eight years of war between Iran and Iraq, and the three wars between India and Pakistan. Many interstate conflicts have also raged in Africa since the UN was founded.

Of perhaps even greater significance in terms of alleviating human suffering, the UN is – or has been – powerless to intervene in internal conflict or the suppression of subject peoples by autocratic dictators such as Saddam Hussain in Iraq, Hun Sen in Cambodia, the military in Burma (now Myanmar), Omar al-Bashir in Sudan, and Omar Bongo in Gabon, to name a few of the world's worst leaders. It was similarly powerless to do anything in the case of failed states such as Somalia, or to resolve civil wars (e.g. Sri Lanka, Sudan, and more recently, Libya and Yemen), because it has no mandate over and above that of a sovereign state. But it is worth recalling the words of Secretary-General Dag Hammarskjöld[23] who said, 'The UN was created not to lead mankind to heaven, but to save it from hell.'

In addition to the core institutions of the General Assembly and the Security Council, the UN's 2020 family of institutions is a multifaceted complex of specialist agencies, funds and programmes, and related organisations. Not all members of the family have a distinct aid function, but the four basic principles of the UN give most of the organisations an aid role. I summarise the more important funds, specialist agencies and related organisations in the following sections.

Economic and Social Council (ECOSOC)

Located at UN headquarters, the ECOSOC – in theory – coordinates the economic and social work of the UN and its family of organisations, and it has a key role in fostering international cooperation for development and economic security. It grew out of the recognition at the Dumbarton Oaks meeting of the important link between peace, security and economic well-being, and it was originally intended to play an important role in guiding the global economy.

The ECOSOC has 54 member nations, which are elected by the General Assembly for three-year terms. It oversees human rights, sustainable development and five regional commissions. It also oversees the work of the specialist agencies, UN funds and programmes, such as the United Nations International Children's

---

23. Hammarskjöld, a Swedish national, died in a plane crash in September 1961, en route to Ndola in what was then Northern Rhodesia (Zambia today), where he was due to meet some of the leaders of the rebellion in the Congo. To this day, the crash of the DC6 has never been satisfactorily explained. Conor Cruise O'Brien, in his book *To Katanga and Back* (1962), speculates that it was an assassination organised by the men of the Organisation of African Security, a right-wing group of French ex-colonialists. In 2019, evidence emerged that would seem to confirm that a Belgian pilot of a small war plane fired on Hammarskjold's plane as it came in to land, confirming the assassination theory. It is generally believed that the Congo was the first serious battleground between the West and the USSR in the Cold War. Recent research commissioned by the UN would seem to support this theory.

Fund (UNICEF). As with much UN activity, it has a largely passive role, based on monitoring and reporting. It has not much power, if any, and some observers consider it of little real value.

United Nations Development Programme (UNDP)

One of the more important organisations of the UN is the UNDP, which is also based in New York. It was founded in 1965 and is basically a source of funding for specific development purposes. Sadly, like much in the aid business, it too has a distinct political flavour. When I joined the UN's FAO in 1984, there were some 400 FAO staff employed through UNDP funds to administer and implement a huge programme of agricultural development projects (ADPs) all over the globe. Staff and funds were made available for research teams, analytical laboratories, and specific crop and livestock projects in dozens of countries. The ostensible reason was to provide hands-on training for nationals who would take over when the expatriates left.

Five years later, in 1989, when the Berlin Wall fell, UNDP support for the FAO collapsed almost overnight. Clearly, these vital training projects were no longer vital. UNDP funding is provided on a voluntary basis by richer member countries, with the US being the biggest contributor; with the demise of the command economies, the US reassessed its aid priorities, followed by many of the other richer countries.

United Nations International Children's Fund (UNICEF)

UNICEF is one of the best-known and most-respected UN bodies. It was founded in 1946 by Dr Ludwik Rajchman, a Polish doctor, to provide emergency relief to mothers and children in the countries devastated by the Second World War. In 1950, its mandate was expanded to include mothers and children in developing countries, and in 1953, it joined the UN system as a fund, not as a specialist agency. It has headquarters in New York and a supply division in Copenhagen. In 2019, the executive director (ED) was Henrietta Fore, a US national.

UNICEF is governed by a board of 36 members, who are elected by members of ECOSOC for a period of three years.

In 2018, UNICEF had one of the largest UN budgets of US$5.2 billion, most of which was comprised of contributions raised by the national UN committees that raise funds through selling things such as trick-or-treat campaigns, especially in the US; selling greetings cards, notably at Christmas and New Year; and by sponsorship. The famous Barcelona football club is a sponsor. UNICEF is operational in 192 countries and has field offices in 150 countries.

UNICEF is no longer an emergency-response organisation; its mandate calls for it to advocate for the protection of children's rights, to help meet their basic needs and to expend to develop their full potential. It achieves this in the field by helping governments to improve health and education policies and facilities. It is particularly associated with vaccination programmes in the developing world, and has worked closely with the Bill & Melinda Gates Foundation in its campaign to eliminate polio. In its first 25 years of operation, UNICEF secured the vaccination of 400 million children against tuberculosis. In 1965, it was awarded the Nobel Peace Prize for its global work in improving the lives of children. While it is not easy to evaluate the work of UNICEF quantitatively, there is no doubt that it has helped millions of children in poor countries to grow up healthier.

World Food Programme (WFP)

Although only a programme, not a specialist agency, the WFP has one of the largest budgets of any UN-specified organisation and is almost entirely involved in aid, both in emergencies and also at other times, as needed. It is the world's largest humanitarian organisation. In 2019, its budget was some US$6.2 billion, of which 33% is provided by the US. In recent years, it has provided 4 million tonnes of food annually for more than 90 million people in 83 countries.

Its mandate is to eradicate hunger and malnutrition, and it has an ambitious target to eliminate hunger globally by 2030. It is also unusual in that, apart from a couple of short periods with an acting ED, most of the 10 appointed EDs have been US nationals. The exceptions to this were the Australian James Ingram (1982–92), the Canadian G.N. Vogel (1977–81) and A.H. Boerma from the Netherlands (1962–67). The current (2020) ED, David Beasley, is a US national.

The WFP started life at the suggestion of US President Dwight D. Eisenhower in 1961. The idea was to see if the UN could help provide food aid to victims of an earthquake in Buin Zahra, Iran. Following further emergencies in Thailand, Algeria and Togo, it was established as a fully fledged UN programme in 1965, based alongside the FAO, which was already headquartered in Rome. When I joined the FAO in 1984, the WFP shared an office with the FAO, a few kilometres from the main FAO building. The WFP also had the FAO as one-half of its governing body, the other half being 36 representatives from member states appointed by the ECOSOC.

Things worked quite well for the first 15 years or so, but a serious problem arose when Edouard Saouma from Lebanon became the director general (DG) of the FAO and began to treat the WFP as one of his departments, rather than an independent institution. Saouma's luck ran out when he agreed to the appointment of James Ingram, who came to the WFP having been head of Australia's International Development Assistance Bureau. Ingram soon realised the extent to which his actions would be circumscribed by Saouma, and he began to keep close notes in a diary, which eventually he turned into a book called *Bread and Stones* (Ingram, 2006). This book details all the tricks that Saouma tried and succeeded in playing on the WFP, and Ingram's own efforts to gain real independence for WFP. In essence, Ingram clarified the legal position of the WFP within the UN, and in particular, clarified the powers and responsibilities of the ED. This led eventually to a separate headquarters agreement and a new constitution, which became operational in 1992, on Ingram's retirement.

Today, the WFP has its own headquarters building in Rome, where some 10% of its 17,000 staff are based. The others are in some 80 county offices. It has worked in 42 of the 54 countries in Africa. The WFP claims to be one of the most efficient UN organisations, as it only spends 6.5% of its budget on administration. In the early days, it sourced much of its food from North America, but today, it sources 85% of its food from other developing countries. It also has programmes to provide hungry people with cash to buy food in local markets, and it has farmer training programmes (Purchase for Progress [P4P]) to help raise food production. At the time of writing (early 2020), the WFP had emergency programmes operational in the DRC, North-Eastern Nigeria, the Sahel, Somalia, South Sudan and Yemen – all parts of the world with serious conflict that is preventing any food production.

Although there is no doubt that the work of the WFP has saved millions of lives, it does have its critics. In the early days, and even now (2020), the dominant role played by the US has led some observers to suggest that it is really little more than a way of getting rid of surplus US-produced grain. Although that in itself is no bad thing, it does take the pressure off receiving governments to increase their domestic output. This is probably why it has developed alternatives such as the 'money-for-food' and P4P initiatives. At the end of the day, it would be great if all countries could feed their own populations from their own resources, but until that is possible, and while there are major conflicts raging, the WFP would seem to be one of the more valuable UN organisations.

United Nations Environment Programme (UNEP)

The UNEP is one of the youngest and smallest UN agencies. It was established in 1972 and has its headquarters in Nairobi, Kenya. A relatively small organisation, it has an annual budget of around US$40 million and employs some 300 staff, mostly in Kenya. The governing body is the UN Environment Assembly in New York. This means all UN member countries are members of UNEP, although only 83 contribute funds. UNEP has a broad environmental responsibility, covering climate change, ecosystem management and environmental governance. It played an important role in developing the Montreal Protocol of 1987 that led to the phasing out of the use of chlorofluorocarbons (CFCs) in refrigeration and their replacement with fluorine hydrocarbons to protect the ozone layer in the atmosphere, and in the Minamata convention on the use of toxic mercury. Some observers think this success led to overconfidence, and the UNEP thought it would inherit a similar responsibility for addressing the problems of climate change. It failed to realise that, whereas the ozone problem had a single solution in the banning of the use of CFCs, which was relatively easy to persuade member nations to adopt, climate change is vastly more complex.

Additional Specialist Agencies

In addition to the funds and programmes, there are 17 autonomous or specialist agencies, including the World Bank Group (International Bank for Reconstruction and Development [IBRD], IDA and IFC) and the IMF. The aforementioned four are loosely linked to the UN; however, apart from using UN travel documents (*laissez-passer*) they do not follow UN terms of employment and have their own distinct organisational structures.

The specialist agencies are part of the UN family insofar as their staffing, salaries and conditions are very similar, and they have similar structures and administrative systems, largely based on the US civil service. However, a country is not automatically a member of all the UN agencies, only those it chooses to join. At the outset, the USSR wanted to have individual membership of FAO for each Soviet state, which would have effectively given them overall voting control; unsurprisingly, the rest of the world said no. Russia joined on its own in the 1990s on the break-up of the USSR.

The specialist agencies have a particular mandate or focus, which is by no means exclusively related to aid, but all the agencies have an aid profile of sorts – if only to provide training to staff from developing countries. They are funded partly by voluntary contributions, usually for special activities, and by regular assessments provided by member nations, usually biennially. They are relatively autonomous, headed by a DG or president who is elected by the member nations for a fixed-but-renewable four- or five-year term. He or she is subject to a programme of work and a budget approved by the member nations. Staff are retained to deliver the work programme and write reports.

Regional Offices

Most agencies also have country and/or regional offices, each headed by a senior member of staff, to deal with local and regional issues. When I joined the FAO in 1984, many if not most of its country offices were headed by Westerners. Today, the majority are headed by nationals from developing countries. I suspect the quality of the heads of these country offices has not really changed that much. I recall a number of US nationals in post who were fairly incompetent. Conversely, the developing-country nationals were often among the smartest. However, what cannot be denied is that, in the 1980s, the West was interested in and willing to pay to have its nationals in senior UN posts around the world, perhaps as useful eyes and ears. Nowadays, after the end of the Cold War, they no longer see any benefit in such posts.

Something similar has happened at headquarters. During the Cold War, the Western powers were ready to bolster most UN agencies. Towards the end of the second decade of the 21st century, the opposite is true, with UN-agency budgets constantly being trimmed and programmes reduced – yet more evidence, if it were needed, of the political nature of the UN. In some ways, China is taking over the West's interests in the UN specialist agencies. In 2020, three of the 14 key agencies (other than the World Bank Group and the IMF) are headed by Chinese nationals. Forty years ago, few agencies had any Chinese staff other than translators.

Most of the agencies have at least one claim to fame, whether it is the eradication of a disease or globally respected agreements, such as those on civil aviation, telecommunications or marine pollution. Most also have some history of scandal, be it regarding politics, nepotism or simple financial mismanagement. UNESCO very nearly lost the plot with its 'new information and order' in the 1980s (see 2.10.).

2.2.   The Food and Agriculture Organization (FAO)

The FAO (whose motto is *'fiat panis'* – or 'let there be bread') is the second-largest specialist agency of the UN. At its peak in the mid-1980s, it employed more than 4,500 staff. In 2020, it was still quite large, but the number of staff employed had dropped somewhat to 3,100 worldwide, many of whom are on short-term eleven-month contracts, as compared to earlier employees who had three-year contracts that often turned into full-time careers. It is also one of the oldest agencies, pre-dating the UN itself by some eight days.

The idea for a global agriculture agency can be traced back to an international conference called by President Roosevelt at Hot Springs, Virginia, US, in 1943. Many of the free world's leaders were acutely aware of the severe shortages of food as a result of the Second World War, which had led to food rationing and severe hunger all over the world, except in those few countries (mainly in the Americas) not directly affected by the war. Forty-four countries got together and agreed to set up an interim commission based in Washington, DC, to work out the details of the agency's structure and mandate. It formally started life in Washington, DC, in 1945, after a conference of members in Quebec on 16 October 1945. After five rounds of voting, and by a margin of two votes (30 votes to 28), it was agreed that the headquarters would be in Rome, Italy, not Copenhagen, Denmark, and it moved to Rome in 1951.

Given that Italy was not exactly one of the Allies, it might seem odd that Rome eventually won the ballot, but I think there are a number of good reasons why Rome was chosen. In the first place, there were concerns that if it were to have been based in the US, it might simply have become a department or section of the UN in New York. Secondly, Rome was the home of the International Institute of Agriculture, which had been founded in 1908 by David Lubin, with the support of King Victor Emmanuel III of Italy.

A third less-discussed reason is global politics, or more specifically, communism and the Cold War. As mentioned earlier, George Kennan's confidential telegram to US President Harry Truman in 1946, recommending the 'containment' of the USSR, led to the Cold War policy of the Western powers preventing the spread of communism wherever possible. Denmark was one of the candidate countries for the FAO's permanent location. However, Denmark was firmly and squarely in the Western camp. In contrast, by 1951, Italy had a very large communist party, which had close links to Russia, going back to 1921, as outlined in the book *Modern Italy* (Clark, 1984). In the June 1946 Italian election, the communists won 104 seats, some 20% of the total. Together with the 115 seats won by the socialists, the left parties held more seats than the 207 seats held by the Christian democrats.

Placing the FAO – a large, international agency – in Italy was potentially a convenient 'spy in the cab'. The biennial FAO conference would be a venue for senior politicians from all over the world to meet and rub shoulders. On a more routine basis, it meant the chance for individual countries to have a dedicated senior diplomat posted in Rome, ostensibly with responsibility for keeping an eye on the FAO's activities, but also keeping an eye on the involvement of the Italian communists in matters of Italy's agricultural policies and activities. The FAO also provided a convenient vehicle in its early days, as each emerging or developing country had a senior FAO staff member posted in the capital city. Almost all of these posts were filled by senior Western experts, quite a few of whom had backgrounds in espionage as well as agriculture. Although there is little hard evidence of this aspect of the FAO's activities, the posting to the FAO of John Cairncross – the fifth member of the Cambridge spy ring – after his confession in 1962, hints at its political use to the West.

The overarching *raison d'être* for the FAO was, and still is, to increase food production and alleviate hunger worldwide. This is clear from the agency's constitution, which begins as follows:

> *The nations accept this constitution being determined to promote the common welfare by furthering separate and collective action on their part for the purposes of: raising levels of nutrition and standards of living of the peoples*

under their respective jurisdiction, securing improvements in the efficiencies of production and distribution of all food and agriculture products.

(Food and Agriculture Organization [FAO], 1944).

The FAO has two basic mandates. The first, or normative, mandate is as a source of information and a forum for the dissemination of knowledge about agriculture and food. For example, the FAO is the only organisation in the world that collates statistics about crop production worldwide. Together with the World Health Organization (WHO), the organisation is also responsible for global standards for food additives, the Codex Alimentarius (CA) (or Food Code), and such things as acceptable levels of residues of antibiotics and hormones used in animal production (see 3.20. for an interesting case study). This mandate also relates to the control of transboundary animal diseases, including zoonoses,[24] such as highly pathogenic avian influenza, more commonly known as 'bird flu'.

The second mandate is as a development agency to pilot and demonstrate the use of better production technology, mainly but not exclusively in developing countries. During the immediately postcolonial period (1960–90), this was an important and relevant aspect of the organisation's work. As the colonial powers left, they took with them the agricultural technicians who had helped run the plantations, research stations and colleges. To fill the void, before the nationals could be trained to take over, the FAO provided much-needed short-term expertise in everything, ranging from apiculture to zoonotic disease control.

Today, the survival of this mandate is in jeopardy for two main reasons. The first is that most emerging nations now have their own cadre of agricultural scientists and technicians, so there is little need for the FAO to provide expertise. The second and perhaps more important reason is that, with few exceptions, the private sector now leads in the development of new agricultural technology. In fact, if anything, the FAO discourages new agricultural technology. It sat firmly on the fence when the genetic modification of crops became commercial; closed down its fertiliser service in response to pressure from the Greens in Germany; and promoted the use of integrated pest control (IPM), which does not really work.[25] In 2019, the FAO, together with the WHO, produced a fatuous report (World Health Organisation and Food and Agriculture Organisation of the United Nations, 2019) suggesting that the control of insect pests by modern agricultural sprays was leading to the loss of insect species that could result in a long-term deleterious effect on the environment. To be fair, it has had some success in promoting conservation

---

24. Zoonoses are animal diseases that can also infect humans.
25. This was in response to concerns raised nearly 50 years ago by Rachel Carson in her book *Silent Spring* (1962), a time when many pesticides in use were very toxic and persistent. Today (2020), things are very different, and modern pesticides are far more specific and short-lived.

agriculture – otherwise known as 'no-till farming' – in appropriate locations, which does away with the need for the expensive ploughing of fields before sowing crop seeds, and with the elimination of rinderpest, a serious disease of bovines.

The basic structure of the organisation – or 'secretariat', as it calls itself – is fairly simple and similar to that in most other UN agencies. The membership elects a DG every four years (well, that was the original idea, based on the US constitution). The DG appoints a series of assistant director generals (ADGs) to cover the different departmental subsectors (viz. crops, livestock, forestry, fisheries, development, communications and administration), as well as one for each of the four regional offices (Accra, Bangkok, Cairo and Santiago). There are also two or three deputy DGs, with the senior most traditionally being a US national. The ADG posts are nominally technical, but in practice, most are political appointees.

In addition to the staff at the headquarters in Rome and the regional offices, the FAO has some 130 country offices, each with five to ten staff members on average. Most but not all of these are in developing countries and are staffed by nationals. It is by no means clear why the FAO still has offices in countries such as Argentina, Brazil, China and India, which have their own highly competent agricultural scientists and administrators, by and large. The only realistic explanation I can see is the modest political advantage that being considered a developing country can have in some arenas.

Membership is open to any country that agrees to pay an annual assessment or membership fee. In 2019, there were 194 member countries. There is a complicated formula to determine each country's assessment, but basically, the richer the country, the more it pays. For example, the US currently pays 22% and Japan pays 20%, while the UK pays 5% and India 0.3%. Membership entitles nationals from member countries to employment as professionals with the organisation on a pro rata basis to the assessment paid. Thus, as the biggest payers, the US and Japan have the right to the most employees, although in fact, they never manage to fill their quota.

To guide and oversee the secretariat, the members nominate nationals to a council and various committees (e.g. finance, food and agriculture). The council is supposed to meet in Rome at least five times within a biennium, and it reviews the position and policy papers prepared by the secretariat before general acceptance by all members at the biennial full conference meeting. Ideally, that is attended by the ministers of agriculture from member countries. Soon after I joined in 1984, I remember a cocktail party during the conference where I shook hands with Chris Patten when he was the UK minister for overseas development. (I may be wrong, but I think he was the last full UK minister to attend the conference.)

The council has 49 members, who are appointed for two-year periods, renewable for a further two years. It was established in 1947, soon after the FAO was established, to provide the secretariat with executive guidance. It was seen as an important way of ensuring the secretariat followed practical and financial policies acceptable to the member nations. In those days, of course, most of the member nations were developed countries, and it was relatively easy for the council to be a rubber stamp for the wishes of the West.

Today, the boot is on the other foot. In 2019, more than half the member states were developing countries, according to the DAC classification, and would be net recipients of FAO resources rather than contributors. The council still acts as a rubber-stamp agency; however, these days it does so in the interests of the developing rather than the developed nations. Currently, it is also subject to more than a degree of influence, as well as outright politics. Thus, members can be persuaded to support policies in return for favours, such as jobs.

More seriously, the council has recently shown little interest in or regard for the proposed reform of the agency. Following the lengthy and expensive independent external evaluation (IEE) of the FAO, which reported in 2007 (discussed later on page 62), the then DG agreed to almost all the reform proposals. The council, however, was less concerned with the need for the reforms, and the reform proposals were quietly forgotten and never endorsed. In many ways, this confirmed the changing political power base of the organisation. No longer could the West secure the policies it favoured, as political power was largely in the hands of the developing world.

At the biennial conference, a programme of work and the related budget for the next two years is approved. The funding of the FAO is quite complicated as it consists of a regular programme budget plus extra-budgetary funds, which are mainly for emergencies and rehabilitation. In fact, in recent years, the shares of the regular programme and the emergency budgets have each been around 50% of the total. For 1994/95, the regular programme budget was US$480 million; for 2004/05, it was US$576 million; and for 2020/21, it was set to US$1,005 million. When inflation is taken into consideration, these budgets suggest substantial cuts in real terms. The total FAO budget of voluntary contributions, including regular member assessments for 2020/21, was set at US$2.9 billion.

Headquarters-based staff are primarily concerned with normative work, and they undertake such tasks as supervising the collation and publication of statistics, arranging meetings of experts to make decisions on things such as permitted food additives, and mounting campaigns to eradicate animal diseases (rinderpest, for example, has been eradicated largely through FAO expertise) or pests, such as locusts, when there are outbreaks.

The development mandate is generally undertaken in the field, although it requires a large back-up staff of technical experts in Rome. TA projects for developing new production technologies and transferring knowledge from one country to another are designed in Rome and then implemented by staff in the field. In the early years, there were projects to test and develop technologies across the spectrum of agriculture. For example, there was a massive global programme of projects to develop fertiliser regimes in countries that had never used much mineral or chemical fertiliser. In addition, there were credit, marketing, irrigation, horticulture, forestry, animal-production and soil-survey projects.

Not all field projects in the early years were successful, but by and large, they helped augment the normative work of the organisation, helped countries modernise their farming and helped to train nationals in specialist areas. Today, in the third decade of the 21st century, there is much less need for such an agency as, with few exceptions, most countries have developed their own agricultural expertise and institutions. Furthermore, almost everywhere, the private sector now drives the agricultural sector worldwide and develops most of the new technologies, albeit within a nationally approved regulatory-policy framework.

It is also the case that, with some important exceptions, most countries can now feed themselves – the food shortages and hunger associated with the Second World War years are thankfully a thing of the past. With these changes, the role of governments and organisations such as the FAO have also changed, with governments largely playing a regulatory role rather than being directly involved with production. To a considerable extent, however, the FAO has failed to adjust to these developments; instead, it has metamorphosed into a political talk shop that seems to have its own self-preservation as a main objective.

Recognising this situation, a group of donor countries financed an extensive and expensive (US$4.0 million) IEE of the agency, which reported its findings in September 2007 (FAO, 2007A). The aim of the IEE was to review the achievements of the FAO to date and suggest where its focus should be in the future. The emerging-issues paper of the IEE (FAO, 2007B) was highly critical; although written in fairly diplomatic language to avoid absolute rejection by FAO management, the overall conclusions were pretty negative. Paragraph 42, for example, starts off as follows: 'FAO is not maximising its comparative strengths for technical cooperation nor meeting adequately the priority needs of its members.' It goes on to list eight areas of considerable concern, which include a failure to set priorities; a headquarters-centric culture (too much internal politicking); a disconnect between the country, regional and headquarters offices; and a lack of strategy at country levels. Paragraph 43 suggests that there was no agreed strategy on how the FAO should provide its services, what its priorities should be and on the resource needs to meet any such priorities. It goes on to say that an inappropriately large amount of staff time is spent seeking funding for the very survival of operations.

To say that the IEE report ruffled feathers would be an understatement. The then DG (Jacques Diouf) was very upset, but he was wise enough not to rubbish the report, as to have done so would have given the donor nations good reason to walk away altogether. Instead, management agreed to address the main concerns raised and start again on a different tack. In fact, all they did was to wait for the IEE to become history, and business has continued much as before.

The politics of the FAO, which may or may not be similar in other UN agencies, is epitomised by the ways in which the recent DGs of the FAO have held on to power. The first DG of the FAO was Lord Boyd Orr (1945–48), a leading British animal-production scientist. He did not see out his full term for reasons that have never really been explained. He was followed by two US nationals: Norris Dodd (1948–53) and Philip Cardon (1954–56). They were followed by an Indian, Binay Ranjan Sen (1956–67). Since then, with the exception of a Dutch national, Addeke Hendrik Boerma, the position has been seen as belonging to the countries of the developing world. He was followed by a wily Lebanese, Edouard Saouma (1976–93), who had been the FAO's man in India and used his contacts there to secure his election when Boerma's years were up.

Saouma got himself re-elected twice, serving for a total of 18 years. He managed to avoid the standard two four-year terms by having the constitution of the agency changed. He had three other main achievements. Firstly, he managed to upset the Americans big time, which led to a lot of financial problems with late assessment payments. Secondly, he established an almost unbeatable system for getting re-elected. This was done by the simple expedient of creating an FAO country office or representation in as many countries as possible. Previously, the agency had retained a technical officer as the UN country representation.[26] With his own flag-waving representative in each country, he could now secure direct access (rather than going through the UN country officer) to the minister of agriculture, who would be responsible for his re-election. Thirdly, he now could – and, no doubt, did on occasion – pay the travel costs of any poor country minister to enable him or her to attend the important election conference every six years. He showed just how an incumbent UN DG could rig any election by a simple system of patronage and funding.

Saouma was followed by Jacques Diouf from Senegal. He easily got a second six-year term by cleverly manipulating the rules associated with the number of international posts member nations can expect. The change meant that, instead of simply using the size of a country's economy to assess its financial contributions, the new formula also took into consideration the size of a country's population. He manipulated the system even further by ensuring that all FAO representatives owes their allegiance to him and him alone. They, in turn, were expected to ensure that the loyalty of any minister or senior civil servant visiting the FAO was unquestioned.

---

26. There is a bit of history here in that the FAO's annual budget at the time was larger than that of the UNDP, and the UNDP considered that the FAO should pay all the costs of the office it shared with the UNDP country office. The FAO's position was that if it was going to pay the full office costs, it might just as well have its own office.

This clearly favoured a number of large emerging nations, and he was clearly hoping for a third term. This was done by the simple expedient of carrying out favours for the incumbent minister,[27] by either giving out small consultancy assignments to chosen national experts or by supplying tickets for favoured individuals to attend international meetings, etc.

Just before his third term of office and soon after Hurricane Ivan, I was in Grenada and happened to meet the person who represented Grenada in Europe, who was charged with delivering Grenada's vote. I was dutifully tactful in my discussions with her, but it was clear that she (who knew nothing at all about the FAO) was convinced that Diouf was the man to vote for. I did not ask who would be paying her fare from the island to the Eternal City, but she was clearly grateful for something the FAO had done or was about to do for her.

The next DG was José Graziano da Silva, a Brazilian, who also said he would only do one four-year term but managed to secure a re-election in 2014. Graziano will probably be remembered as the DG who did more than anyone else to hasten the agency's demise. He did this by poisoning the well as far as the as the Western powers are concerned, and handing it over to China and the developing countries. Like his predecessors, he used his position for political advantage. But unlike his predecessors, he has tried to use his position to protect fellow politicians from Latin America from corruption charges, rather than providing political support for the interests of politicians from the developing world in Africa and the Middle East. In 2017, he gave Nadine Heredia, the wife of the former Peruvian head of state, the job as head of the FAO liaison office in Geneva. This was to provide her with protection from corruption charges associated with money laundering. In the event, the protection scheme failed as she renounced her post and gave herself up after arrest warrants were issued by Peruvian magistrates.

It has also become the butt of various jokes, the best of which concerns a weird libel action brought by a senior staff member against *The Italian Insider*, a weekly English-language newspaper. The newspaper had apparently slandered a senior staff member by describing his performance as being 'piss poor'. In the Italian court hearing the libel case, the translation of 'piss poor' was given as incontinent. The

---

27. In 1999, I was in Lesotho, helping to put together a small irrigation project. I was joined by a Ugandan colleague based in Harare, who was carrying out an audit of a project under the Special Programme for Food Security (SPFS). Fred asked to have a word with me one evening. He said the project he was auditing was supposed to have had a report produced locally, for which some US$10,000 had been budgeted. He told me the money had been spent, but there was no evidence of a report. Furthermore, he said he was convinced that the FAO representative who was about to retire from the FAO had, in his desperation to continue in a job, used the money to try to secure a juicy consultancy from the Ministry of Agriculture. He asked me what he should do with his findings. My answer was that he needed to be very careful. If he went public with his findings, it could cause a lot of difficulty for the DG, whose special programme was being heavily criticised by many donors. I said he should tell his boss what he had found, and then leave it up to his boss to take action or ignore the information. As I suspected, his boss did nothing.

magistrate suspended the session to obtain a better translation, but not before a good laugh was had by many in the court.

The election of Graziano's replacement in 2019 looked to be a classic case of politics. He tried to secure the job by suggesting that the three UN agencies in Rome (the FAO, WFP and IFAD) should be merged, and that, as the boss of the largest agency, he should be the head of the merged body. Fortunately, this idea did not fly. The long list of candidates or contenders originally included a serving FAO staff member and one of the sons of a previous senior Indian staff member.[28] One of the other early candidates was also of Indian origin and a UN staff member (WFP) in Rome. However, a candidate has to be nominated by their country of birth, and in mid-2018, it was not clear whether India wished to endorse either Indian candidate, as there were reports that at least one of the candidates was not actually born in India. Later, France put forward a strong candidate (Catherine Geslain-Lanéelle), a technically highly qualified woman – the hope being that she would bring about the necessary reforms of the agency. However, she had stiff competition, as China was also considering putting up a candidate as part of its strategy of playing a bigger role in the UN system.

Some well-connected observers considered China's candidate to be the favourite, if only because of China's close relations with the heads of most African countries. In the event, they were proved right as Qu Dongyu of China secured 108 votes to Catherine's 71 and Georgian candidate Davit Kirvalidze's 12 votes. The voting is nominally secret, but it is almost certain that Qu Dongyu received most of the votes of the 50 or so African member states.

The published curriculum vitae of Qu Dongyu – a farmer's son, with a PhD from Wageningen University & Research (the famous agricultural university in the Netherlands) and China's vice minister for agriculture and rural affairs in 2015 – is impressive. However, although no doubt a good biologist, he is also a senior member of the Chinese Communist Party (CCP), from which he will receive his ultimate guiding orders. In effect, China has replaced the US as the most important member nation of the FAO, and although the election may appear to be a win for China, the future looks rather grim for the FAO. Globally, agriculture (apart from regulatory aspects) has largely moved into the private sector, with which the FAO has no close links. Indeed, the agency took steps on at least one occasion (see 4.9.) to move away from the private sector.

It is also in danger of losing its technical reputation and competence. Thirty years ago, if there was a serious locust outbreak, the FAO's early warning system would have activated international assistance. In late 2019, when a devastating

---

28. This guy was very smart and managed to get all three of his sons jobs in Rome: one in each of the UN agencies!

plague of locusts hit East Africa, the FAO's calls for help largely fell on deaf ears. Such emergencies are always complicated, but over time, the richer member nations have lost confidence in the FAO's ability to respond responsibly to such emergencies. Too often in the past, the FAO's response has been coloured by the organisation's incompetence and tendency to grab as much emergency financing for itself as it can.

Furthermore, the agency no longer has as much political value to the West as it had during the Cold War. The feeling among FAO watchers is that few of the original member-nation supporters are ready to walk away, but they are cutting back financial support at every opportunity. Indeed, in 2018, both Germany and the US withheld their assessment contributions because of serious concerns about FAO policies. I doubt that the FAO will collapse overnight; if nothing else, Italy will keep it going for some time as it is one of the very few international institutions based in Italy. Furthermore, Italy maintains the FAO complex of buildings as a major part of its membership assessment, which it would have to continue to meet whether or not the FAO was in residence. It also provides quite a large number of nice support staff posts for Italian nationals.

It is always risky to make predictions, but if the trends of the past 40 years or so continue, the FAO will become increasingly staffed by nationals from the developing world – many appointed for political rather than technical reasons. It will be interesting to see whether China can secure a constitutional change that would result in the US having to give up its right to appoint the senior deputy DG. I have no doubt that this change will be on China's list of things to do; however, it will not be done too soon, but quietly, when the Western world is focused on bigger issues.

2.3.   International Civil Aviation Organization (ICAO)

The ICAO is one of the oldest and smallest UN agencies. It was founded in 1944 and is headquartered in Montreal, Canada. It has 193 member nations (all UN-recognised independent nations), an annual budget of some US$80 million (2019) and 900 staff. The current (sixth) council president is a Chinese national, Fang Liu, who will serve until his retirement (scheduled for August 2021).

The main functions of the ICAO are to develop a consensus on international civil aviation standards and recommended practices. It also provides member states with assistance and capacity building in regard to aviation development objectives, and it keeps aviation data, such as passenger miles flown per year. Though not an aid agency, it is nevertheless an excellent example of good cooperation between nations in a vital area of common interest – almost a perfect example of the what the economist Elinor Ostrom would have considered the benefit of 'collective ownership' – in this case, of knowledge and its use rather than an asset. Few doubt its value to mankind and I am sure it will survive, whatever happens to other UN agencies.

2.4.   International Fund for Agricultural Development (IFAD)

One of the youngest of the UN specialist agencies, the IFAD was born in 1976 and became operational in Rome in 1977, following the so-called 'oil crisis' of 1973. The IFAD has always been a bit of an orphan in many ways. Its parents are, on the one hand, an unholy alliance of donors (i.e. OECD and OPEC) and, on the other hand, the beneficiary or developing countries. Its conception was hasty, with little in the way of prenuptials, and while its delivery was fairly natural, some use of forceps was necessary to squeeze sufficient contributions from some of the OPEC members, in particular Iran, which was going through an exceptionally turbulent period. The IFAD's early years were full of promise; as it matured, however, signs of congenital weakness – if not deformity – have become more than a little apparent.

At the World Food Conference, hosted by the FAO in Rome in November 1974, a key issue raised was the effect of rising oil prices on the poorest oil-importing countries. Given that rising oil prices directly and indirectly affect food prices – through the cost of transport and inputs, especially fertiliser – it was felt that one way of assisting poor countries affected by higher oil prices was to help them improve their domestic agricultural output. It was also felt that the rich oil-exporting countries in particular should do something to mitigate or minimise the effect of the price rises, and it was eventually agreed to set up the IFAD, with contributions from OPEC member states and OECD countries. The IFAD would lend money at concessional rates to poor countries for agricultural and rural development only. The IFAD's mission is very simple and direct: 'it is to enable the rural poor to overcome poverty'.

The IFAD was set up as a fund, partly to distinguish it from the existing development banks and partly for administrative simplicity. The donors contribute, and the IFAD manages what it has received. The IFAD is, in effect, what is known in financial circles as a 'revolving fund' – it recycles capital, and it uses the spread on its loans and investment income earned to cover its operating costs. Whatever its origins, the IFAD is unusual in the UN family in so far as it has a single mandate or role: rural poverty reduction. A noble idea but a tough one to execute, especially when most of its target group have little or no idea of conventional investment and financial practices, and for which much of the credit needed is for consumption purposes, not production.

Being mindful of the problems of equitable member-country representation and the ease with which UN agencies can become employment havens, considerable thought was given to the constitution and structure of the new agency. Instead of the traditional 'one country, one vote' system that is common to most UN organisations, the IFAD's membership structure is more weighted towards economic power and influence. There are three types of membership: Lists A and B are donor countries, OECD and OPEC, respectively; and List C countries are recipient poor countries, or 'partner countries' as they prefer to be called. There is some overlap as a number of recipient countries (e.g. Nigeria and Indonesia) are also members of OPEC.

Membership is open to any member of the UN. In 2019, there were 176 member countries. The governing council, consisting of representatives from all member states, is the fund's principle governing body and meets once a year, usually in January in Rome. The governing council, in turn, elects an executive board consisting of representatives and alternates from 18 member states (eight List A members and eight alternates; four List B members and four alternates; and six List C members and six alternates).

The executive board is responsible for overseeing the general operations of the IFAD and approving its programme of work. The chairman of the executive board is the president of the IFAD. The executive board meets three times a year, at which time it approves projects, programmes and grants. Day-to-day operations are the responsibility of the president and his vice president, assisted by the office of internal audit and the general counsel. In 2017, Gilbert Houngbo from Togo became the president for his first four-year term of office. The four previous presidents were Idriss Jazairy from Algeria, Fawzi Hamad Al-Sultan from Kuwait, Lennart Boge from Sweden and Kanayo F. Nwanze from Nigeria.

The president or senior officer of the IFAD is elected by the membership, and although he or she could be presented from any of the three categories, only List A and B country nationals were elected until 2017. Houngbo is the first List C member to become president. The period of office of the president, like that of the president of the US, is limited to two four-year terms.

As far as staffing is concerned, the initial emphasis was on efficiency and flexibility with a minimum dependence on permanent staff and the maximum use of short-term consultants. The idea was to have a small cadre of administrative staff and a core of technical staff to oversee the loan portfolios from inception to resurrection. Hired service providers and consultants would be used to design and supervise projects, and to undertake routine work such as preparing annual reports. The original intention was for the agency to have some 180 full-time permanent staff, all of whom would be based in Rome. In 2019, the staff numbers had risen to 627. This reflects the sad tendency of UN agencies to put their own interests ahead of their official responsibilities.

Each country portfolio manager has a country or cluster of countries for which he/she is responsible. His/her main task is to ensure a steady stream of investment projects are prepared, implemented and, finally, evaluated. It is a remarkably responsible job. Typically, a country such as Bangladesh will sign one project a year with an average value of US$25 million. Thus, the country portfolio manager will typically be responsible for a portfolio of US$150 million. In return, he/she will almost certainly occupy a middle-ranking UN post with a gross salary of around US$90,000 per annum – not exactly a king's ransom, given the size of the portfolio.

The country portfolio managers have almost total freedom to select the projects, the consultants to prepare them and the implementing arrangements. There are a few checks and balances. There is a system of technical and financial evaluation before a project is sent to the IFAD board for approval. All projects are supposed to be vetted by a technical review committee (TRC) at critical stages of preparation. However, the TRC is understaffed and overworked. In practice, the TRC is a paper tiger that can at best delay a project slightly while its worst faults are addressed.

Originally, it was envisaged that the OPEC countries would chip in 60% of the fund's capital, and the OECD countries would chip in the balance. In the event, OPEC never met its target. Every three years or so, there is a new pledging session and donors are invited to make contributions. Unlike the membership assessments of other UN agencies, these are voluntary and do not directly reflect the size and strength of a country's own national economy. Actual pledges and contributions have generally been less than those requested by the IFAD, in part because the IFAD has never managed to commit its existing resources fully, and with repayments and interest income, its capital base seems fairly secure. However, in the future, if the IFAD moves towards giving more grants and forgiving loans, this situation could change rapidly. In a press release on 20 April 2007, the IFAD announced a new debt sustainability framework under which the countries deemed least able to sustain debt will receive 100% grant assistance from the IFAD, and those with medium debt sustainability will receive 50% grant assistance and 50% loan assistance.

The IFAD keeps accurate records of its disbursements, so it is known with some certainty how much of its money has been spent. The information tends to be provided according to replenishment. For replenishment 10 (2016–18), broken down by type of country (low income, middle income or upper–middle income) and by type of disbursement (loan, grant or blend) the total approved disbursement was US$3.2 billion, which is roughly US$1.0 billion a year. The total value of its ongoing loan portfolio was reported to be US$6.25 billion, covering 151 projects in 92 countries. This works out at an average of US$43.3 million per project. In practice, project funding ranges from US$7 million to more than US$50 million, and things are further complicated as there is often co-financing from other sources in addition. This makes direct comparison with other funding agencies difficult.

It is much more difficult to assess the impact of this expenditure. All its projects are subjected to a project completion review on closure, and every 10 years or so, a country portfolio evaluation is undertaken, which looks at all the previous loans. These documents are not, however, in the public domain – at least not permanently. If you go to the IFAD website, unlike other international financial institutions, you cannot download even the executive summary of any evaluation report. An evaluation summary or 'profile' is available on the web, but it only shows what the IFAD wants to show. It is therefore virtually impossible for an outsider to assess how well an individual project or a country portfolio has performed.

As far as achievement is concerned, its own reports are pretty dire. The Annual Report on Results and Impact (ARRI), conducted for the IFAD in 2017 by independent consultants, undertook 320 evaluations (International Fund for Agricultural Development [IFAD], 2018). Over the review period of 2006–17, only 76% of interventions were moderately satisfactory or better. The term 'moderately satisfactory' is not defined in the ARRI, but hints that things could have been much better. What is more, the ARRI states that the trends in terms of project efficiency and sustainability were flat or not improving. The IFAD claims its projects are as good as those of the other main lenders to the rural sector in the countries where the projects were undertaken. But all this does is underline or confirm that the rural poor are the most difficult sector for aid. Furthermore, it suggests that the IFAD, which was set up specifically to develop a better way to help the rural poor, has failed in this respect. For any agency to have to admit publicly that so many of its projects have failed to live up to expectations is dynamite. In the commercial world, shareholders would have sacked the CEO and closed the business years ago.

The agency was subject to an independent external review (IFAD, 2005), which was highly critical of some aspects of the agency. Lip service was paid to the key recommendation of the review, but nothing substantial appears to have changed since then. What does all this mean for the future? Nothing too drastic anytime soon, I suspect. The IFAD is very popular with its donor countries, despite its weaknesses. This is due to its focus on the rural poor and because its replenishment funding needs are convenient for donor budgets looking for somewhere to place their aid funds. I think the fact that a List C country national became the president of the IFAD for the first time in 2017 suggests that List A and B countries are not that interested in the agency any longer.

2.5.   International Labour Organisation (ILO)

This is one of the oldest UN agencies, founded at the Treaty of Versailles in 1919 and supported by nine member states. It moved to Geneva in 1920 and became a UN specialist agency in 1946. It has a staff of 2,700, located in Geneva and 40 field offices around the world. The ILO has 187 member nations and a total biennial budget (2018/19) of around US$1.0 billion. This is made up of regular assessments (member-country contributions) and additional voluntary core funding provided by some countries. The current DG is Guy Ryder, a UK national.

The aims of the agency are to promote rights at work, encourage decent employment opportunities, strengthen dialogue on work-related issues and fight against poverty. It has a special role in negotiating international treaties relating to employment by providing an appropriate venue and conference facilities. The work of the ILO covers all nations, but given that most developed countries have their own robust employment legislation, its work in the developing world is particularly significant. In this context, it can be seen to have an important aid-supporting role.

2.6.   International Maritime Organisation (IMO)

The IMO is based in London, which was once one of the major global shipping ports. It started life at an international conference in Geneva in 1948, which agreed to establish the Inter-Governmental Maritime Consultative Organisation. The name was changed in 1958 when the agency moved to London. It is one of the smaller UN specialist agencies with some 300 staff, almost all based at headquarters.

The IMO has an annual budget of US$60–65 million. Two-thirds of this is met from annual member assessments, of which over 98% are paid on time, and the balance comes from other sources of income. The current (at time of writing) secretary general, Kitack Lim, a Korean national, was elected for a four-year term in 2016. An unusual feature of the IMO is that, unlike most UN agencies, it actually owns the building in which it operates. It was given the building on the Albert Embankment of the River Thames in London in order to reduce long-term UK responsibility for the building's upkeep.

The mandate of the agency is as a standard-setting body for the safety, security and environmental protection of the seas. It aims to provide a regulatory framework for international shipping that is fair and effective. As in the case of the ICAO, the agency is not directly involved in aid but is an organisation that benefits all of the world's people, rich and poor alike, who depend upon safe and reliable shipping. It has played an important role in minimising pollution, especially oil pollution at sea, by introducing standards for oil tanker construction and maintenance.

2.7.   International Monetary Fund (IMF)

The IMF is a sister organisation to the World Bank, and was also the brainchild of John Maynard Keynes and Harry Dexter White. Folklore has it that White saw the IMF as having similar functions to the New Deal that had helped the US get over the depression in the 1930s, but with an international focus. Keynes was concerned that the IMF resources would be too expensive for many of the world's shattered economies, and he was only going to agree to the IMF if White supported the World Bank, which would provide more concessional lending.

The IMF is not usually seen as a development agency, as such, but by supporting countries in times of financial crisis, it prevents economies collapsing, thereby helping prevent poverty. Its articles of agreement are to promote international monetary cooperation, international trade, high employment, exchange-rate stability, sustainable economic growth and the provision of financial resources. It works to foster global growth and economic stability. It achieves this by providing policy advice and financing to member nations to help them achieve macroeconomic stability and reduce poverty.

The rationale for the IMF was, and is, that private capital markets do not work perfectly and, in particular, do not provide support to countries with weak economies. The IMF provides an alternative source of funding to countries unable to access private capital markets. It sources its funds from member-country quotas paid into the fund. To be able to lend to countries in financial distress, the IMF requires borrowing countries to meet certain conditions – in particular, the provision of some form of collateral – and it requires governments seeking assistance to correct macroeconomic imbalances. This means making key macroeconomic indicators available to the IMF, and agreeing to make essential changes to ensure such things as balanced budgets, appropriate exchange rates, improving governance, etc. The list is quite long, and many borrowers find the terms invasive and onerous; however, they usually have no option but to agree. The IMF has a range of lending options, including concessional loans with a period of no interest payment, but most loans have to be serviced with interest that is close to market rates. The actual interest shared is based on a complicated formula closely linked to the current global market interest rates.[29]

The IMF, like the World Bank, is based in Washington, DC; its president is always a European. In 2020, the IMF had 189 member countries. Membership of the IMF is a precondition for a country to be a member of the World Bank. The IMF and

---

29. IMF loans are provided in special drawing rights (SDRs) that are made up of a mix of currencies. SDR interest rates depend on a blend of the market interest rates for the constituent currencies and current exchange rates. The rates are checked weekly.

the World Bank differ from other UN organisations in that they do not depend on regular member-nation contributions. Instead, they are able to invest member-country quota contributions and retain the accumulated funds for future needs. As of 2016, the IMF fund had some US$666 billion of reserves. It is a highly respected agency and a vital component of the world's financial and economic systems.

A particular feature that may cause problems in the near future is that the charter of the IMF calls for it to be based in the country with the world's largest economy. It is not entirely clear what metric or metrics are used to assess the size of an economy. Until the middle of the second decade of the 21st century, no one questioned that the US was the largest economy; however, by the end of the decade, there was much media speculation about China overtaking the US in this matter.

2.8.   International Telecommunications Union (ITU)

The ITU is the oldest international organisation. It was founded in Paris in 1865 when representatives from 20 European countries met and decided they needed to agree standards for the new telegraph systems they were all constructing at the time. It became a UN agency in 1949. Today, it is based in Geneva, where it has a staff of some 700 (professionals and support staff). It has an annual budget of around US$170 million, which is met by 193 member-country assessments, together with some cost recovery from over 900 companies and other organisations that are members. The current secretary general is Houlin Zhao, a Chinese national who began his second four-year term on 1 January 2019. This makes him the fourth Chinese national to be in charge of a UN specialist agency.

The ITU has three main functions or sectors:

1. Radio communications; in particular, deciding on satellite orbits and radio frequencies.
2. It advises on standards for telephones, the internet, etc. In any given year, it updates or revises more than 150 such standards.
3. It has an important development role: 'bridging the digital divide' between richer and poorer nations. As with a number of other UN agencies, it is a common-good organisation, largely funded by the richer world but of vital importance to all nations. The ITU, as might be expected, has an impressive website.

2.9.   United Nations Education, Scientific and Cultural Organization (UNESCO)

UNESCO has its headquarters in Paris. It was formally established on 16 November 1946, building on the foundations of the League of Nations International Committee on Intellectual Cooperation.

It has five areas of responsibility:

1. Education
2. Natural science
3. Social and human sciences
4. Culture and communication
5. Information

A medium-sized agency, with 170 member nations and 2,225 employees, it had an annual budget of a little over US$650 million in 2017. It is best known for its designation of World Heritage Sites, and it played a vital role in saving the Egyptian archaeological remains at Abu Simbel that would otherwise have been flooded by the Aswan High Dam.

UNESCO's other main claim to fame is its attempt to organise a 'New International Information and Communication Order' when Amadou-Mahtar M'Bow was the DG (1974–87). The objective of this order was to corral the international media within certain guidelines. The order was seen by the US, the UK and Singapore as an attempt by the communist countries to curb global press freedom, and they withdrew their membership for some years. Since then, there have been problems associated with Israeli and Palestinian issues, and the US withdrew again in 2018.

The agency has suffered massively from budget problems, largely due to the reluctance of the US to pay its membership assessments. When I visited the agency in 1991, I was struck by how shabby UNESCO's premises were. Things might have improved since then, but I rather doubt it. It has one of the least informative and helpful websites of all the agencies, suggesting that it has relatively little to be proud of.

2.10. United Nations Industrial Development Organization (UNIDO)

UNIDO is a relatively recent UN specialist agency and is based in Vienna. The agency was founded in 1966, 20 years after many of the early agencies, and is moderately sized with some 700 staff in its headquarters and 47 field offices around the world. In 2013, Li Yong from China was elected DG. It has an annual budget of US$500 million, which is made up of the assessments paid by its 170 members and trust funds (additional voluntary contributions).

The objectives of UNIDO are the promotion of industrial development for poverty reduction, inclusive globalisation and environmental sustainability. It has four basic priorities:

1. Creating shared prosperity
2. Advancing economic competitiveness
3. Safeguarding the environment
4. Strengthening knowledge and institutions

A cynic might wonder why such an agency really needs to exist. Almost by definition, civil servants – national or international – have no comparative advantage when it comes to developing industrial projects. I suspect the rationale for UNIDO is suggested by its date of foundation and its location. In 1966, the Cold War was raging, following the Cuban Missile Crisis in 1962 (the USSR tried but failed to place missiles, facing the US, in Cuba). A soft-power weapon of the West during the Cold War was to build up the UN as a way of sharing knowledge and technology globally through neutral institutions. Vienna was an ideal location as it was politically neutral as far as the West and the USSR were concerned at the time. It was also before the onset of the monetary policies encouraged by the Chicago School of Economics that seriously questioned the government's role in industrial development. It is doubtful whether such an organisation would be started by the UN today, and it is fairly clear that the Western powers do not have any serious interest in UNIDO. In contrast to current Western indifference to the objectives of UNIDO, these would seem to have considerable appeal to China as they align nicely with its statism and the Belt and Road Initiative (BRI) in particular (see 6.6.).

2.11. Universal Postal Union (UPU)

UPU is the second-oldest specialist agency of the UN, founded in 1874 in Berne, Switzerland, following a meeting of representatives of 21 countries. Most of the representatives were from European countries, but the US played a major role in the initiative. Headquartered in Berne, the UPU had 190 member countries, plus the Vatican City in 2020, when the DG was Bishar A. Hussein from Kenya. The UPU is one of the smallest specialist agencies, with some 250 staff and an annual budget of around US$65 million. Its main function is to regulate international postal rates for letters and parcels. It played an important role in resolving the discrepancy between US and Chinese postal charges for international mail in 2018. Failure to have resolved this would have led to the US withdrawing from UPU.

2.12. World Intellectual Property Organization (WIPO)

A relatively young UN specialist agency, the WIPO was founded in 1967. It has headquarters in Geneva, and the current CEO is Francis Gurry from Australia. The WIPO mandate is to ensure a balanced and effective global intellectual property system. Not of immediate concern to development and aid perhaps, but insofar as ensuring that innovation from all countries – rich and poor – is recognised and protected, it is of importance to all.

WIPO is unique in the UN system as it is self-financing from fee-paying services provided by businesses. In 2020, it had 192 member states, confirming its value to all countries. For the biennium 2020/21 (current at time of writing), it has a budget of US$900 million. The WIPO employs a total of 1,500 staff in Geneva, and it has regional offices in Rio, Beijing, Tokyo, Moscow and Singapore. In 2020, China tried but failed to secure the DG position for a Chinese national.

2.13. The World Bank

The World Bank is more correctly known as the International Bank for Reconstruction and Development (IBRD). It is clear that, for the US, the Bretton Woods Conference in New Hampshire was mainly concerned with currency stabilisation and the formation of the IMF, and it was up to Keynes to promote the ideas for the World Bank. He saw it as a continuation of the Tennessee Valley Authority policy that had primed the pump for economic regeneration in that state by providing capital for infrastructure and the creation of jobs.

It is reported in the book *The World's Banker* (Mallaby, 2005) that Keynes had expected the Americans to continue to lend to war-torn Europe for its reconstruction. He only picked up the World Bank baton when he believed the Americans were not about to lend any more to Europe.[30] Keynes had a heart attack on his way back from the US and never really recovered from the strain of the meetings. Nevertheless, he headed the commission charged with designing the World Bank, which he saw primarily as an agency to help rebuild Europe after the war, and perhaps also India and Latin America. Its main function was to provide financial resources to the devastated countries of Europe whose credit ratings were

---

30. In fact, a bit later (1948), along came the Marshall Plan.

so poor that they could not borrow on the world markets, and in particular, the US financial markets. In fact, the first loan was to France.

However, things did not work out entirely as planned. First, there was the Marshall Plan, which did much to help get Europe back on its feet through providing soft loans (the UK finally repaid its last Marshall Plan loan instalment of US$55 million in 2006).[31] Second, there was the emergence of new nations, following the independence of many ex-colonies, which needed funds. Third, there came the beginning of the Cold War and the need for the West to find benign ways to counter the influence of the USSR. These developments allowed the World Bank and its sister agency, the IDA, to come of age in the 1950s and 1960s. In fact, it was when the larger-than-life Robert McNamara became president of the World Bank, after having been US Secretary of Defense during the Vietnam war, that World Bank lending took off big time.

For many years, the World Bank was the largest single supplier of development finance and was seen as the premier development agency. Its systems also provide the basic model for the regional development banks, such as the ADB and AfDB, and other funding agencies. Housed in sumptuous offices in the centre of Washington, DC (the headquarters address is 1818 H Street), and with classy offices in most countries of the developing world, the World Bank has been the largest development aid employer by far, with some 10,000 people on its payroll at its peak. It also paid well.

Although nominally owned by all its member countries, the US – which has the largest single share (some 16%) – tends to dominate policy, personnel and procedure. The president of the World Bank is always an American,[32] who is appointed directly by the president of the US. The president reports to a board of directors who represent the member countries. Large countries have a full-time board director, while smaller countries tend to pool the responsibility. The main function of the board, apart from overseeing the president, is to approve loans and grants. In theory, a majority vote is all that is needed for approval, but nothing ever gets through if Uncle Sam does not like it for any reason. The UK share of voting rights and capital liability was 3.61% in 2018.

Although usually referred to as a bank, the World Bank is really little more than a virtual organisation. Like most banks, it does not lend its own capital; instead, it borrows on the world's money markets and only lends to sovereign governments, with the liability being secured by the World Bank's own nominal capital and a complex system devised by Lord Keynes. Typically, the World Bank lends the

---

31. The UK borrowed US$4.34 billion from the US and Canada in 1945, which is equivalent to more than US$27 billion in 2006.
32. Jim Wolfensohn is an Australian, although one with strong US financial connections.

money it has borrowed at a premium of 2% to cover its operational costs. The nominal capital of the World Bank is the amount of paid-up capital stumped up by the member nations, plus their call-up capital. An important departure from normal banking practice is that members do not pay all their capital liabilities upfront but only pay a percentage usually (5 or 6%). The unpaid balance is 'on call' and would be paid by members in the event that the World Bank could not service its money-market borrowings. Following a share capital increase in October 2018, the World Bank's total paid-up capital was US$329 billion, of which the UK share was some US$11.8 billion (US$1.05 billion was paid up and US$10.75 billion was on call).

Unlike a normal bank, which lends on the basis of a borrower's credit rating, the World Bank lends to sovereign governments that did not – and/or still do not – have a credit rating. To address this issue, Keynes devised a means – known as 'preferred creditor status' – whereby the risks associated with lending to the poor countries are shared by a complicated and somewhat artificial pooling arrangement. Preferred creditor status refers to loans from the World Bank being top priority for repayment above all other loans to a government. Failure to repay a World Bank loan results in a borrower being blacklisted by all Western/OECD financial institutions. This also means there is no need for the members to pay all their capital liabilities upfront.

Until now, the World Bank has held an AAA credit rating from the likes of Moody's, so clearly, no one expects it to go belly-up. However, a few countries – notably Sudan and Zimbabwe – have been blacklisted (non-accrual status) because of non-repayment of World Bank loans. In 2018, the only country with non-accrual status was Zimbabwe, which had total external debts in arrears of US$2.2 billion.

When the World Bank was established, it was thought that most borrowers would be the poor countries of Europe, and no one really thought that there were alternative sources of funding to the Western financial institutions, so preferred creditor status made good sense as an insurance mechanism. Soon after it was established, along came the Marshall Plan, and the World Bank started to look for new clients in the developing world, notably in Latin America and, later, almost anywhere. Seventy years later, things are not so simple. Oil-rich countries – China and Russia – have, on a number of occasions, lent to countries unable to secure funds from the World Bank, so the value of preferred credit status no longer provides the same degree of protection to the World Bank.

In the good times, while lending was expanding, the 2% premium meant the World Bank was able to grow continually. Its clients (poor countries) liked its money because it was much cheaper and easier to access than money from other sources. The World Bank was also not too fussy about what the money was for, as its main criterion for success was getting the money out of the door. More lending meant a bigger World Bank, and a bigger World Bank meant more power – something its bureaucrats and their masters were very keen on.

The World Bank also saw itself as an ideal training ground for senior politicians and administrators in developing countries, and it did not blush to see its protégés in post. In 2008, it could claim at least two African presidents as past staff members: Ellen Johnson Sirleaf of Liberia and Bingu wa Mutharika of Malawi. Its alumni also included the minister of finance for Lesotho (Timothy Thahane) and, for a while, the minister of finance for Nigeria (Ngozi Okonjo-Iweala). Whether this is entirely a good thing depends on your perspective.

There is another important political dimension to the World Bank that it does not trumpet, which is its strong links to US/Western policy globally. McNamara, who became president of the World Bank for the period 1968–81, shaped it as no other president has ever done.

I saw this dimension myself in a small way when I queried a project proposal I was involved in preparing in Pakistan (see 3.9.) in 1986. I ran into quite a storm when I questioned the viability of an agricultural loan, only to realise that the loan was not really meant to help poor farmers, but was to support the Pakistan government in containing the USSR advance in neighbouring Afghanistan. On closer inspection, I suspect many World Bank loans have political dimensions. This used to worry me, but post-1989, I have come to believe that all peaceful measures to contain the USSR were justified; subsequently, similar arguments can be used to contain extreme anti-Western political and religious ideologies, or indeed to compete with China and other emerging large economies.

The World Bank's processes vary somewhat from discipline to discipline and region to region, and they change with development fashions. The basic methodologies, however, have remained reasonably constant. Experts – mainly economists from the World Bank – visit a potential borrower and discuss priorities for funding with government officials. These discussions result in the preparation of a country assistance strategy (CAS), which forms the framework for subsequent project lending within the different sectors. This conforms with the thinking of Myrdal (see 1.3.).

Initially, the World Bank and IDA only lent for specific projects. Projects are prepared by teams of specialists from different sectors, who visit the borrowing country and, together with local experts, put together an investment project or programme. These vary enormously in size from $10–$150 million or more, depending on the country and sector. I once helped to prepare a US$10 million silk development project in Bangladesh, but such small loans are very rare. In general, the larger the better, as far as the World Bank is concerned, as it minimises transaction costs. Full project preparation and approval (including the legal agreements drawn up after board approval) usually takes 12–18 months.

In the early days, it was keenest on large infrastructure projects (dams, roads, harbours, etc). In the 1970s, it broadened its scope, and for a while in the 1980s, agriculture and natural resources accounted for nearly 30% of its portfolio, in an attempt to shift resources into poorer rural areas. Then, in the late 1980s and 1990s, it moved into social sectors (health and education) in a big way, with agriculture and natural resources falling back to less than 10% of the portfolio.

It is difficult to know whether the main driving force for these changes is economic theory, opportunism or politics. For example, it is well known that World Bank lending for hydropower dams almost stopped worldwide following all the fuss made by environmentalists and sociologists in India over the Sardar Sarovar Dam on the Narmada River. And one of the first things Jim Wolfensohn did when he became president was to stop the Arun II hydro-barrage in Nepal, as a way of convincing NGOs that the World Bank was concerned about the environment. It was also suggested that he also knew the scheme was a big headache. It was common knowledge at the time that the politicians in Nepal could never seem to work out who would get the best kickbacks, so kept delaying important decisions about the dam's location. Jim simply called their bluff.

Typically, a project is implemented over a period of five years, with repayment over anything up to 30 or even 50 years, following a five-year grace period. Most projects are subject to a formal financial and economic analysis, which is designed to weed out projects that do not meet the generally agreed opportunity cost of capital (typically 10–12%). In other words, all World Bank-financed projects are supposed to pay for themselves through increased output and/or productivity. That is the theory, and to be fair, it does apply to quite a number of projects. I remember visiting a number of successful oil palm plantations in Indonesia in the mid-1980s that had been started by the World Bank, bringing in expertise from the oil palm industry in Malaysia. Other notably successful projects include the huge bridge over the Brahmaputra River in Bangladesh, and hydropower plants in Bhutan and Lesotho. Sadly, many more projects than the World Bank would care to admit are classified on evaluation as having had mixed success.

During project implementation, the World Bank sends a small team to 'supervise' the project every six months. The idea is that if things are not going well, problems can be addressed sooner rather than later. In practice, supervision missions have little or no power, only influence, as once lent, the money is no longer the World Bank's, but it belongs to the borrower. A project can be halted or closed, but this requires very senior executive approval and happens very rarely. Some six months after project closure it is subject to a 'completion report' organised by the World Bank's evaluation unit. In theory, an objective technical and economic evaluation of a project is undertaken. In practice, the game continues, with lots of qualifying terms that mean the word 'failed' is hardly ever used.

I led such a mission for quite a big project in Zambia (see 3.14.). We had our report cleared by colleagues in Rome and sent it to Washington, DC. There, our findings were challenged, and our ratings or assessments were upgraded by the World Bank project task manager. Subsequently, a report (project ID P003218, dated 06/23/2003) produced by the operations evaluation department (OED) (in-house evaluation unit) of the World Bank agreed with my findings. The task manager's version was withdrawn, and the final version retains my assessments. Another interesting completion-report story is outlined in section 3.7.

The IDA, which came into existence in 1960, is a section of the World Bank that lends soft or concessional funds to the poorest countries – typically, those with a per capita income of US$2.0 a day or less. The money is lent at very low interest rates (1–2%), often over 50 years and with grace periods of up to 10 years. To all intents and purposes, these funds are virtually free once you allow for inflation. IDA funds come from two main sources. The first is 'profits' on regular World Bank lending. From the start, it was recognised that it would not be morally acceptable for the richer-country members of the World Bank to make a profit as a normal bank might, so, it was agreed that any notional surplus would be used for concessional lending. Secondly, every two years, the rich countries are invited to pledge funds to the IDA for loans and grants to the poorest member countries. For example, in financial year 2017, the US contributed US$1.85 billion to multilateral development institutions such as the IDA, which almost certainly received the lion's share of these grants. Apart from the cost of the money, World Bank and IDA processes, staffing and procedures are indistinguishable, and indeed, it is possible to find loans in middle-income countries that are a blend of both IDA and World Bank funds.

The World Bank and IDA systems worked well for the first 40 years or so after 1944, but at the time of the World Bank's creation, nobody foresaw the debt problem that began to emerge in the 1970s, particularly in sub-Saharan Africa. Profligate lending, borrowing or both had led to many countries needing to borrow more and more from the World Bank to service existing loans. Their economies simply had not grown fast enough to generate the extra resources needed to service their loans and meet other expenditure.

The first solution tried was structural adjustment loans (SALs). These were quite big loans provided by the World Bank as budget support. The first SALs were lent in 1979. In fact, they were really a device to enable earlier loans to be serviced, and all they did was provide a bit of time for all concerned. The World Bank's shareholders' problem is that they cannot allow the World Bank to forgive its loans, as they would then be called upon to pay up some or all of their unpaid capital.

To a greater or lesser extent, the debt mess that first appeared in the 1970s can be attributed to a number of unforeseen events that occurred after the World Bank's establishment and to its response to these events. In the early days of lending to war-torn Europe, things worked more or less as planned, and Europe was soon able to raise capital in more conventional ways through selling bonds and private capital flows. However, the demand for World Bank funding in Europe was massively curtailed by the Marshall Plan. Undaunted and encouraged by the apparent success of public sector investment programmes (SIPs) in the US (notably the Tennessee Valley Authority), the World Bank looked further afield and embarked on lending to emerging economies in South America and Asia, notably in India and Pakistan.

One of the most successful early initiatives was to help sort out the water rights between Pakistan and India, created by the partition of India in 1947. It is also important to bear in mind that in the middle of the 20th century, few argued against public sector investment (priming the pump, according to Keynes) to provide jobs and kick-start economic growth. It was considered that this had worked in Europe and the US, and so should also work in newly independent countries.

In the late 1960s and early 1970s, a large number of the countries in Asia, Africa and the Caribbean that had gained independence were soon knocking at the World Bank's door for 'development assistance'. For the World Bank, and more specifically, for the poorest countries, the IDA seemed like magic from heaven. Want to build a new road or port to help export your primary products? Call up the men from Washington, DC, who – after you've answered a few questions – will hand over the cash you need. Indeed, it was a mutual win-win situation, in theory. The borrowing country would get money and infrastructure, and the World Bank's creditor nations would provide most of the goods and services, as well as the money. Quite a number of these early projects did make a positive contribution and helped to accelerate economic growth.

However, the post-independence period was also the period of the Cold War, and there is no doubt that, all of a sudden, both the political and economic value of the World Bank became obvious to the strategists in Washington, Tokyo, Paris and London. Not only were the borrowing countries committed to paying back the money lent, so there was no drain on rich-country exchequers, but the more they borrowed, the more they were in hock to the West rather than the command economies. The trouble was that the policy only worked if the economies of the borrowing countries grew sufficiently.

The most egregious example of such realpolitik is probably the DRC, or Zaire as it was called for a while, when it was run by Mobutu Sese Seko, an ex-army officer. The Western nations and the World Bank in particular were persuaded to shell out buckets of money to keep him supplied with pink champagne and to fly to and from Europe in Concorde, while in turn he kept the Soviet Block at bay in his part of Central Africa. It may also be important to remind the reader that the DRC is one of the largest countries in Africa and has some of the richest mineral resources, including the richest seams of uranium found anywhere in the world. It was a prize worth holding on to, and no one seemed worried when its borrowing exceeded US$600 million in the 1970s. Not all World Bank lending during the Cold War was strategic, but a fair amount was.

When the developing-country debt crisis first appeared, the World Bank remained optimistic that, with SALs, things would sort themselves out, but it became clear before long that something more had to be done. Jim Wolfensohn, to his credit, recognised this when he was president of the World Bank, and he initiated the HIPC programmes, together with the IMF, in 1996. The aim of HIPCs was ostensibly to ensure that no poor country would face a debt burden it could not manage. As of 2018, some 39 countries had been identified as needing HIPC assistance, and 36 had received assistance totalling US$77 billion. Most of the funding for HIPC debt forgiveness has come from the IMF and rich-country donor budgets, with a modest amount from the World Bank and the IDA. In other words, the World Bank and the IDA have technically not had to forgive their loans.

It is also encouraging that IDA lending over the past 20 years has increased much faster than World Bank lending, as indicated in Table 2.

Table 2 Lending by Fiscal Year: 1999–2019

Year	WB Lending US$ billion	IDA Lending US$ billion
1999	22.1	6.8
2019	23.2	21.9
Since 1945	727.5	391.5

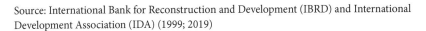

Source: International Bank for Reconstruction and Development (IBRD) and International Development Association (IDA) (1999; 2019)

These figures show that there has been a major change in the profiles of World Bank and IDA lending over the last 20 years, which tells us two things. Firstly, in real terms and allowing for inflation, World Bank lending is static or even declining. Secondly, and probably of greater significance, is the massive increase in IDA lending and grants, much of which is to poorer countries to help them balance their books and, above all, to enable them to service earlier loans that they are having problems repaying.

Around the turn of the 21st century, a number of experts began to question the whole concept of the World Bank, and since the end of the Cold War, it has been looking for a new *raison d'être*. It is more than a little ironic that the organisation whose motto 'Our dream is a world free of poverty' is carved into the brickwork of the lobby in its headquarters in 1818 H Street, Washington, DC, has actually made a lot of countries poorer. A good starting point for those interested in criticism of the World Bank is the collection of papers from the Center for Global Development (Birdsall and Kapur, 2005). Also highly recommended is a paper by Jessica Einhorn in *Foreign Affairs*, Vol. 85 (2006). (Einhorn retired from the World Bank as managing director in 1998.)

People outside the World Bank have less difficulty in being critical, but then few outsiders have access to the real facts, and the World Bank is a master at self-aggrandisement and, not infrequently, stamps heavily on bad publicity. Teresa Hayter found this out the hard way years ago when working for the UK Overseas Development Institute (ODI). She was assigned to review the World Bank's programme in Latin America. She found rampant capitalistic opportunism, rather than serious efforts to help the poor, and her report – although initially accepted by ODI – was suppressed by the World Bank. She then lost her job, and the ODI has never really recovered its reputation for integrity. She wrote up her story after she left the ODI in *Aid as Imperialism* (Hayter, 1971).

I experienced something similar soon after I joined the FAO/CP as an agronomist. I wrote a long report on upland farming on the acidic soils of Indonesia's outer islands. It was very critical of a major programme[33] to settle people on these islands. Ten years after I wrote my report, I had a call one day from a man in the OED of the World Bank who was undertaking an audit of the World Bank's support for the transmigration programme. He wanted to know if I had, in fact, written a report about my visit, and I said I had. He then said something along the lines of, 'Your report must have been suppressed' (see 3.8.).

The World Bank is also very careful to keep the academic world – particularly the US academic world – happy. The World Bank hires a lot of academics, either as short-term consultants or to undertake research on development. It is probably the largest generator of academic research treatises and reports on almost all aspects of development. Typically, they are so erudite and arcane that all they really achieve is to fill up shelves and provide an excuse to do more research. Occasionally, someone steps out of line. William Easterly used to work for the World Bank. He found failure on a large scale, and he began to question a number of the World Bank's fundamental precepts. He left to work for New York University, and his book *The*

---

33. The Transmigration Programme aimed at settling farmers from Java on the outer islands of the Indonesian archipelago. The rationale was that Java was too crowded, and the outer islands were underpopulated. There was a good reason for this. The soils and topography of Java is ideal for intensive paddy-field rice cultivation. The soils of the outer islands are very infertile and are not suitable for paddy-field rice production. The World Bank had allowed itself to be persuaded that, by providing fertiliser to the settlers, they could start afresh on the poor soils of the outer islands. No one, however, had really worked out how to get the fertiliser to the farmers every season, as most of the settlements were miles and miles from any surfaced roads.

White Man's Burden (Easterly, 2006) provides an excoriating analysis of the World Bank's failures.

One or two international publications do publish deprecating articles now and again. *The Economist* and the *Financial Times*, in particular, are always ready to highlight World Bank difficulties. One of the *Financial Times'* correspondents, Martin Wolf, used to work for the World Bank and has insider knowledge. In a special *The Economist* (2002A) feature article on banking, there was a paragraph on the World Bank that said there was little to show for the US$500 billion it had lent in loans and credits over the past 50 years. Something similar was said by Kenneth Rogoff of Harvard, speaking on the BBC World Service (Rogoff, 2007). He contended that there is really very little evidence that aid helps countries develop economically.

There is no doubt that the World Bank was started with good intentions: to rebuild the Europe destroyed by the Second World War. However, it is now clear that, buried within these good intentions, the seeds of its own ultimate destruction lay, namely the assumption that the integrity and efficacy of the key institutions of state (legal and financial systems, stability, security, and governance) are common, or would be, everywhere. It is important to realise that when the World Bank was founded – with a few notable exceptions such as Russia and much of East Asia – Western ideas of government were paramount. You only have to look at all the little 'Westminsters' set up in the ex-British territories of Africa to see how overwhelming Western ideas were.

I do not think one can entirely blame the founders – they were simply building on what they knew and understood to be the roles and responsibilities of government and the public sector. And to be fair, many of the early loans to countries such as France, Chile, Japan, South Korea and Portugal worked very much as planned. Infrastructure was rebuilt or created, which helped get the economies going again, and the loans have all been serviced in full. It is not coincidental, however, that these countries had relatively stable governments and robust state institutions at the time they took World Bank loans. With hindsight, it seems it was political expediency (based on overoptimistic belief in the competence of developing nations' governments) during the Cold War that has led to many of the organisation's problems.

There have been several major reviews of the agency, notably reports by Professor Allan Meltzer (2000) and Senator Richard Lugar (2010). Both these reports identified many issues and made recommendations for changes. However, they both realised that it was almost impossible to change the organisation, as it is effectively an independent agency that would require most – if not all – shareholders to agree to any serious changes.

The World Bank and IDA websites and annual reports provide a considerable amount of information about their lending programmes, and the DAC of the OECD keeps statistics on global aid programmes, including those of the World Bank and IDA. There are numerous books on the World Bank, including *A Guide to The World Bank* (World Bank, 2003). As might be expected, it is not a warts-and-all guide, but it sets out the basic concepts and practices of the organisation. There is also quite a long list of critical books, including books by Tendler (1975), Hayter (1971), Caufield (1997), George and Sabelli (1994), Mallaby (2004), Calderisi (2007), Berkman (2008), Easterly (2006), and Moyo (2009).

The IFC is a special window of the World Bank that was created to promote economic development through the private sector. It was established in 1956, and it had 185 member countries in 2020. The World Bank and IDA can, according to their articles of agreement, only lend to sovereign governments. The IFC provides equity, loans and other financial support services to business clients. It charges market rates for its money, which can vary from as little as US$1 million to US$100 million. As of 2020, IFC equity investments totalled US$12.9 billion, representing 30% of its total disbursements (World Bank Group, 2020). Together with the IDA, the IFC would appear to be becoming a more important development organisation than their World Bank parent. In many ways, this reflects a major change in aid policy in recent years that has seen an increase in the importance of assisting the private sector, rather than governments.

IFC rules limit its investment in an enterprise to 25–35%, except in special circumstances; the balance having to come from private sector lenders. Funds may be used for working capital or expenditures in any World Bank member country. IFC participation calls for it to make a special contribution, complementing the role of market operators. This is to ensure that it does not distort the private market. Typically, it syndicates loans with international commercial banks and by underwriting investment funds and corporate security issues. It also provides advice to businesses in developing countries. In the past decade, it has supported a number of climate change mitigation initiatives in Latin America and Africa.

2.14. World Health Organization (WHO)

The charter of the WHO was drawn up in 1946, and the agency was formally established in April 1948. It is headquartered in Geneva, and has six regional offices in Brazzaville, Cairo, Copenhagen, Manila, New Delhi and Washington, DC. As of 2020, the WHO had 194 member countries and was operational in 150 (mainly developing) countries. It has a total staff of some 7,000 and an annual budget of

US$2.0 billion. Half of the WHO staff are based in Geneva, and half in regional and country offices. The DG in 2020 was Dr T.A. Ghebreyesus, a national of Ethiopia. He succeeded Margaret Chan from China, who was WHO DG from 2006–17.

The current annual WHO budget contributions from member states (US$2.2 billion) covers only 50% of its costs and has to be topped up by donations from foundations and special contributions from rich countries. This dependence on external funding reduces the WHO's responsibility and decision-making powers. To make matters worse, in 2020, the US was two years in arrears with its contributions, and Donald Trump temporarily withdrew the US from the WHO, making the agency increasingly dependent on China and other donors during the Covid-19 pandemic.

The mandate of the WHO calls for universal health coverage for some 1 billion people not presently covered. Its priorities are primary health care, sustainable health financing, improved access to medication, training of health workers, national health policies, data and information monitoring, and communication about disease globally. The WHO plays a vital role in assessing whether or not disease outbreaks are international crises that need an emergency response. In January 2020, it was four weeks before the WHO declared the Wuhan Coronavirus (Covid-19 or SARS-CoV-2) a global health emergency, and it was more than another month before the agency acknowledged that it was a pandemic on 11 March 2020.

When a global emergency is declared by the WHO, countries are able to prevent travel from an infected country and are obliged to strengthen their medical services accordingly. There is little difference between a global health emergency and a pandemic, but the declaration of a pandemic means the disease is very likely to spread to a large number of countries, and therefore puts health services globally on full alert. This was certainly the case by April 2020 when nearly 1 million people had become infected in some 175 countries and more than 40,000 had died as a result of catching the disease. By May 2021, more than 3.2 million people worldwide had died and 155 million cases had been reported. If the WHO had declared a pandemic earlier, many lives might have been saved.

Some observers consider that China might have used its influence on the WHO to delay the emergency announcement for fear that such an announcement would hit the Chinese economy heavily. It may just be a coincidence, but the previous DG of the WHO, Margaret Chan, was Chinese and would have had some influence over who filled any vacant senior posts while she was in charge. It is quite possible that the WHO encouraged a delay in declaring the outbreak a pandemic. The Chinese authorities must have hoped that the virus would not leave China and/or would not be so infectious. In fact, the Chinese authorities almost certainly made a big mistake in how they handled the outbreak and will pay a very heavy price economically and in terms of a loss of trust in their integrity.[34]

On a more positive note, the WHO played a large role in the eradication of smallpox. The agency is involved in a consortium of NGOs and private foundations (e.g. the Bill & Melinda Gates Foundation) working to eliminate yellow fever. It is also active in campaigns to control HIV/AIDS, malaria, polio, Ebola and tuberculosis. It is clearly an agency with a large – but by no means exclusive – focus on developing countries.

2.15. World Meteorological Organization (WMO)

The WMO is one of the more important technical specialist agencies. It is also one of the oldest, as its roots go back to 1873 and the International Meteorological Congress held in Vienna that year. It became a UN specialist agency in 1950. The WMO is based in Geneva, where it is headed by a secretary general – an elected position that may be held by an individual for up to two four-year terms. The current secretary general is Petteri Taalas, a national of Finland, who was appointed in 2015. The agency operates six regional associations: Africa, Asia, South America, North America, Central America and the Caribbean, South-West Pacific, and Europe. It employs just over 300 staff and has an annual budget of around US$65 million. It has 187 member countries plus six member territories.

The WMO provides leadership for international cooperation in the delivery and use of high-quality weather, climate, hydrological and environmental services. Much of the work of the WMO is the coordination and networking of weather and climate data, based on the observations of national meteorological services. This information is networked by the six regional associations. Globally, this information is collected from 15 satellites, 700 buoys, 3,000 aircraft, 7,300 ships and over 10,000 land-based observation stations. It is difficult to envisage the modern world functioning without an effective WMO.

2.16. United Nations World Tourist Organisation (UNWTO)

The UNWTO ('UN' is included in the full acronym to distinguish it from the World Trade Organisation) is one of the youngest and smallest specialist agencies,

---

34. The way the authorities challenged Dr Li Wenliang when he first alerted the health authorities in Wuhan to what he suspected was a new virus, and his subsequent death from the virus, have done enormous damage to the reputation of the CCP. It has shown once again how the interests of the party are paramount over and above the interests of the people.

although its origins go back to 1934 when the International Union of Official Tourist Publicity Organisation (IUOTPO) was established. The IUOTPO became a specialist agency in 2003, with the ECOSOC of the UN as its governing body. The secretariat is in Madrid. The current head of the UNWTO is Zurab Pololikashvili from Georgia. He took over from Taleb Rifai, of Jordan, in 2018. The agency currently employs some 650 staff and has an annual budget of around US$200 million.

The UNWTO is funded by 158 member countries, whose contributions are based on their share of international trade rather than their GDP. It also has some 500 affiliate members, which include companies, research institutions and NGOs. Uniquely within the UN system, some of these private sector bodies play an active role in fulfilling the mandate of the UNWTO, which is to promote responsible, sustained and universally acceptable tourism (classic UN jargon that means almost nothing) as a driver of economic growth. To this effect, it has an aid focus, although most of its work is, in fact, for the richer countries.

2.17. International Atomic Energy Authority (IAEA)

The IAEA is based in Vienna. It was set up in 1957, largely due to a US initiative in response to concerns about nuclear weapons. The agency has no powers as such, and it functions mainly as a monitoring organisation and a forum for debate. It plays a vital role in the monitoring and implementation of the Treaty on the Non-Proliferation of Nuclear Weapons. It reports to the General Assembly and the Security Council.

The IAEA has three basic functions:

1. Nuclear verification and security
2. Nuclear safety
3. Nuclear technology transfer

The agency also plays an important role in the use of nuclear technology for peaceful purposes, especially in medicinal uses.

In 2019, the IAEA had 171 member states. The Democratic Republic of North Korea withdrew its membership in 1994. Although one of the smaller UN agencies, with a total staff of 2,500 (almost all in Vienna) and an annual budget of around US$500 million, it is also one of the most respected. At the time the IAEA was established, Austria was technically 'neutral' as far as the West and the USSR were concerned, making it the ideal country to host such an organisation.

At the time of writing, one of the most important roles of the IAEA is monitoring the Joint Comprehensive Plan of Action. Under this plan, in 2015, the US, UK,

France, Germany, Russia and China agreed with Iran to lift economic sanctions and release tens of billions of dollars of withheld assets in return for Iran scaling back its nuclear ambitions. In particular, it called for the cessation of uranium enrichment. In 2018, President Trump withdrew the US from the consortium, saying that the agreement was not robust enough and did not prevent Iran from acquiring nuclear weapons at some time in the future. In 2021, President Biden signalled that he intends to reverse this decision.

Although the agency is not an aid issue, the end of peace that would result in a nuclear war would be devastating for all and would make aid irrelevant. In this sense, it should be seen as part of the peace-making efforts of the rich world that facilitate the potential achievements.

2.18. Regional Development Banks

In addition to the World Bank, there are a number of regional development banks. The more important ones include the IADB, ADB, AfDB, Caribbean Development Bank (CDB) and European Bank for Reconstruction and Development (EBRD). Like the World Bank, most have concessional windows – usually called 'funds' – which are contributed to by donor nations.

The IADB, which covers Latin America, is based in Washington, DC. It is based here as no Latin American country offered to house it, and so – being the largest shareholder (30%) – that responsibility was taken by the US. The ADB is a big player in Asia. It is based in Manila and is traditionally headed by a Japanese national. In 2018, its lending and grants totalled US$21.6 billion, making it by far the largest regional bank. The AfDB, based in Abidjan in the Côte d'Ivoire, is much smaller. In its first 50 years (1964–2014), it lent a total of US$47.5 billion. The AfDB has had a chequered existence, having needed to be 'rescued' in 1995. The CDB is very small, based in Barbados and started about the same time as the other regional banks (1969). In 2018, it disbursed US$280 million. The EBRD, based in London, is the youngest of these development banks and is heavily involved in the ex-Soviet republics. In fact, it started life in 1991, soon after the fall of the Berlin Wall. The EBRD is one of the best regional banks. Over the five years to 2018, it disbursed an average of over €9.0 billion (equivalent in early 2020 to US$9.70 billion).

The overall structure, objectives, funding mechanisms and working ways of these banks are very similar to the World Bank, but they only lend within their own geographical region. They are staffed by qualified nationals from all their member countries, but they prefer to hire staff and consultants regionally. Because so few rigorous evaluations have been undertaken, it is difficult to assess the achievements of most regional bank loans, many of which were made for political (not economic) reasons. The best regional bank loans have been used for big infrastructure projects, such as the Jamuna Multipurpose Bridge in Bangladesh. In the late 1980s and 1990s, when it became clear that many borrowers could not service all their loans, the Western powers decided to forgive a number of loans. In total, more than $100 billion has been forgiven.

The newest development bank is the Asian Infrastructure Investment Bank (AIIB) in Beijing, which was established in 2015. By mid-2019, the AIIB had some 75 accredited member nations, but these did not include the US or Japan. Ostensibly, the purpose of the bank is to speed up the creation of sustainable infrastructure in developing countries in Asia – something that fits in very well with the BRI that is supported by China (see 6.6.). Another major objective is to increase the clout of China in a major development agency. China is by far the largest shareholder, with some 30% of the shares and capital invested. In comparison, China has less than 10% of the capital or shares in each of the World Bank and the ADB. The UK, France and Germany are members. Its structure is very similar to the other development banks. That is, it has a total capital base of US$100 billion, of which 20% is paid up and the balance is on call. By July 2019, it had committed some US$8.5 billion to countries in Asia, including Turkey, for around 500 projects. It is too early to know whether the AIIB will be successful. Initial indications are that its lending has slowed since 2018. Whether this is because of a general slowdown in the global economy, the trade conflict with the US or a lack of demand is not clear.

The AIIB should not be confused with the New Development Bank (previously known as the 'BRICS bank') also established in 2015, but in Shanghai, with a total share capital of US$100 billion. The founding members of this bank were the five BRICS countries: Brazil, Russia, India, China and South Africa. Each member had a 20% initial shareholding. This is to be reduced proportionately if and when other countries join. Its objectives are similar to those of the AIIB, although its priorities are to provide loans for renewable-energy projects in member countries. As of March 2019, it had lent funds for some 30 projects with a loan value of US$8 billion. Frankly, it has not really lived up to expectations.

2.19. Bilateral Aid Agencies

Most of the 36 OECD member countries[35] have a bilateral aid agency. Typically, this is a department or section of the Ministry of Foreign Affairs, although some of the larger countries have a fully fledged and independently funded aid agency. Very

---

35. Austria, Australia, Belgium, Canada, Chile, Czech Republic, Denmark, Estonia, Finland, France, Germany, Greece, Hungary, Iceland, Ireland, Israel, Italy, Japan, South Korea, Latvia, Lithuania, Luxembourg, Mexico, Netherlands, New Zealand, Norway, Poland, Portugal, Slovakia, Slovenia, Spain, Sweden, Switzerland, Turkey, the US and the UK.

few of these agencies have a total allocation of more than 0.25% of the national GNI, and much of this goes towards contributions to international agencies, such as the UN, its specialist agencies and other organisations (e.g. the big international charities). In addition to aid provided by their bilateral agencies, most members of the European Union (EU) also contribute to EU trust funds for aid purposes, notably for climate change. Trust funds are pools of donor money used for specific international development initiatives. The EU claims to be the world's largest donor of aid funds, but this is a bit misleading as the total claimed for ($70 billion in 2018) is, in fact, mainly the sum of individual EU countries' bilateral aid.

Most agencies have a geographical focus, often based on countries that were previously colonies and/or for which they have a particular interest in helping for political and other reasons. Iceland, as a small donor, has identified four development institutions that it gives priority to: the World Bank, UN Women,[36] UNICEF and the UN University in Japan. It provides TA in the fields in which it has specialist expertise: fisheries and renewable energy.

Some countries have policies that tie their aid to goods and services from the donor country; others do not. Almost all have a political reason behind some of their aid, and most have a supporting policy or policies for their aid. For example, the UK announced in January 2020 that half of the £98 million allocated for India would not go the government, but to private enterprises, and the rest would be for TA. In this section, I provide a thumbnail sketch of some of the larger or better-known bilateral agencies.

United States Agency for International Development (USAID)

The USAID is one of the largest bilateral agencies in terms of its overall resources, but its annual budget is small: just 0.25% of the overall national budget of the US government. In 2017, US foreign assistance was just under US$50 billion, making it the largest single aid donor. However, it should be recalled that some 35% of that total was for military aid and non-military security assistance. US aid policy in the past decade or so has seen a growth in global health programmes, increased security assistance (anti-terrorism) and humanitarian assistance to address a range of crises.

US aid has three basic rationales:

1. National security
2. Commercial interests
3. Humanitarian concerns

36. UN Women is a UN entity founded in 2011 that works for the empowerment of women globally. It has headquarters in New York and reports to the General Assembly, ECOSOC and the Commission on the Status of Women. The current ED is Phumzile Mlambo-Ngcuka.

Broadly speaking, these are common to most bilateral agencies, although the emphasis varies from country to county. Most US aid is now provided as grants, rather than loans – typically, in the form of project-based assistance.

For over 50 years, the bulk of US aid was implemented by the USAID. The agency was founded in 1961 under the Foreign Assistance Act, when John F. Kennedy was president of the US. It was based on the success of the Marshall Plan, which helped rebuild Europe in 1949 after the Second World War. Based in Washington, DC, it is an independent agency of the US government that reports to the president, the secretary of state and the National Security Council. The USAID has some 100 missions in developing countries and had a staff of just under 10,000 in 2018 – of which 70% were working overseas, many as locally contracted staff – whose main task is overseeing the hundreds of projects undertaken by private sector contractors, consultants and NGOs.

Millennium Challenge Corporation (MCC)

The MCC is one of the newest bilateral aid agencies. It was established by the US Congress in 2004 as an innovative and independent aid agency. Its distinguishing features are that it forms development partnerships with poor countries, but only with countries that are committed to good governance (such as democratic governance and sound economic and social policies). The partnerships are in the form of a compact agreed by the MCC and the recipient country. MCC grants are transferred to a special account in the recipient country, which is used for compact implementation and is rigorously monitored.

By 2019, the MCC had drawn up 33 grant agreements with 29 developing countries, and it has granted a total of US$5.2 billion. Its annual budget was just over US$900 million until it was reduced to US$800 million by President Trump in 2019. Although relatively small compared to the size of lending by the World Bank and IDA, nevertheless, it can be seen as a challenge to the more established aid institutions. Almost certainly, the MCC was established by the US Congress as it was losing confidence in more traditional aid approaches. Although not stated, it is pretty clear that the aim of the MCC is to provide aid in a more controlled or directed way to countries sympathetic to the US. It remains to be seen whether its aid is actually used more effectively than more traditional forms of aid.

Department for International Development (DFID)

The UK bilateral aid agency was one of the largest of such agencies. In 2019, the DFID's total budget was £14 billion (US$18 billion), equal to 0.7% of the total UK GNI. The UK is one of the six countries that has committed in law to spending a fixed percentage of its taxed income on aid. It is, however, important to realise that the total figure includes existing commitments to multilateral agencies, as well as specific projects and programmes in developing countries. In late 2020, the UK government subsumed the DFID into the Foreign Office, and 'temporarily' cut its annual budget by £4 billion due to Covid-19.

The DFID has staff in London, Glasgow and a number of capitals in the developing world. Its total staffing in 2020 was just over 3,500. To some extent, the DFID's own history reflects the changing policies and philosophies of the aid business over the last 75 years or so.

Overall, the UK's aid policy is poverty reduction. Policy details are subject to a fairly regular review. The most recent in-depth review was in 2015 when a joint Treasury and DFID paper 'Tackling global challenges in the national interest' (Greening, 2015) was produced, emphasising that UK aid should be spent in ways that are clearly in the UK's national interests. It identified four basic strategic objectives:

1. Global peace
2. Response to crises
3. Promoting global prosperity
4. Tackling extreme poverty

Within these four objectives, some new approaches were highlighted. In particular, 50% of all DFID spending was to be in fragile states and regions, an end was to come to providing general budget support to developing countries and expanding cross-government support (i.e. endorsing the use of the UK military), an emergency fund of £500 million was to be created, a £1 billion fund was to be designated to support global public health (notably, the control of infectious diseases), and a cross-government prosperity fund was to be used to promote global prosperity. Reading between the lines, the policy provides for allocating funds for the poorest, for emergencies (including conflict resolution), for disease control and for promoting the private sector (the latter being a theme common to many bilateral agencies that have experienced disappointment with aid given to developing-country governments). For more details about UK aid policy, the reader is directed to the House of Commons Briefing Paper no. 7996 (Lunn et al., 2020).

Other Bilateral Agencies

Almost all OECD countries have recently reviewed their aid policies and quite a number have restructured their aid agencies, reflecting concerns that aid funds have often not achieved as much as had been hoped. If there are themes that emerge from these reviews, they are that much more emphasis is being put on the private sector rather than government-to-government aid; a narrower geographical perspective; and a focus on fragile states and countries with some, albeit rudimentary, democratic governance. There is also more emphasis on issues of global concern, such as climate change, rather than economic growth.

Almost all bilateral agencies fall within the remit of the Ministry of Foreign Affairs; the big exceptions to this are the UK (until 2020) and the US. Most agencies have good websites that provide a considerable amount of detail about the country's aid policies and programmes. Some promote their own interests above international policies; for example, by insisting that goods and services are supplied by the host country's companies. A brief summary of the better-known OECD agencies follows.

While the individual bilateral aid contributions may not seem notable, they are highly significant in total. According to the DAC of the OECD, the total bilateral aid in 2018 amounted to US$153 billion. This is nine times more than the US$17 billion disbursed by the World Bank that year. Clearly, bilateral aid is very important.

Australia

The Australian Department of Foreign Affairs and Trade, previously AusAID, reports to both the Ministry of Foreign Affairs and the Ministry of Trade. This appears to be the result of a number of significant aid policy changes and reductions in aid spending by Australia in recent years. Australian aid is predominantly focused on the Indo-Pacific region. In 2014, a new policy stated that Australia's aid policy was designed to promote Australia's interests and its priorities would be as follows:

- Support for private sector development
- Strengthening human development (education and training)

Belgium

Belgian aid is handled by the Enabel development agency on behalf of the Directorate-General for Development Cooperation and Humanitarian Aid, which lies within the Ministry of Foreign Affairs. It has identified three main policy arenas as its focus:

1. Peace and security
2. Human rights
3. Global solidarity

It works specifically in the following areas or sectors (interestingly, it does not mention economic growth as a key area or sector):

- Agriculture and rural development
- Energy and climate
- Gender
- Governance
- Health
- The private sector
- Water and sanitation

It operates in 14 countries predominantly, the majority of which are in Africa. In 2012, it spent 0.63% of GNI on aid. If that figure had been maintained, this would have meant an annual budget of nearly US$3 billion, which for its size would make Belgium one of the largest per capita bilateral donors.

Canada

In 2013, the independent Canadian International Development Agency was folded into the Department of Foreign Affairs, and is now known as the Canadian International Development Platform. It seems likely that this change was to ensure the greater alignment of aid with foreign policy. In fact, Canada is one of the meanest donor nations, providing less than 0.3% of GNI for aid. In 2018, the total aid budget was US$4.3 billion (CAD$6.1 billion). Some 40% of Canadian aid was spent in Africa and 30% in Asia.

As far as priorities are concerned, 90% of Canadian aid goes to the top five SDGs:

1. Ending poverty
2. Ending hunger
3. Ensuring healthy lives
4. Quality education
5. Gender equality

Denmark

Danida, the Danish aid agency, is one of the oldest bilateral agencies, coming into existence in 1962. Before this, most Danish aid went directly into the UN system. In 1990, it was brought into the Ministry of Foreign Affairs as a freestanding unit.

Danida has four core strategies guiding its aid funding:

1. Human rights
2. Democracy

3. Sustainable development
4. Peace and stability

It also embraces the SDGs. Denmark is one of only six OECD countries that budgets 0.7% of GNI for aid. In 2016, this was US$2.34 billion.

France

The main French aid agency is Agence Française de Développement (AFD). It can trace its origins back to 1941 when Charles De Gaulle was in London and established an agency to provide credit and help to countries that had helped France in the Second World War. In 2017, it became a financing company.

AFD is one of the largest donors. In 2018, it had a budget of US$12.2 billion, equal to some 0.43% of French GNI. It envisages increasing this to 0.55% of GNI by 2022. In any given year, AFD supports around 4,000 projects globally, mainly in some 115 countries and French overseas departments.

Its priorities for support are similar to those of most bilateral agencies, including the following:

- Global health, climate change and biodiversity
- Gender equality, education and international stability (peace)

In addition, the 17 SDGs are also prioritised. The work of AFD is overseen by the Inter-ministerial Committee for International Cooperation and Development, which represents the Ministries of Foreign Affairs and Finance. An important subsidiary of AFD is Proparco, which provides aid to the private sector. AFD has come in for considerable criticism for being one of the least ethical donor agencies.

Germany

Germany has two large aid institutions: Deutsche Gesellschaft für Internationale Zusammenarbeit (GIZ) and KfW (formerly Kreditanstalt für Wiederaufbau). GIZ was established in 2011 by the merger of three German aid organisations: Deutscher Entwicklungsdienst, Gesellschaft für Technische Zusammenarbeit and Internationale Weiterbildung und Entwicklung. It has offices in Bonn and Eschborn, had a budget of €2.4 billion (US$2 billion) in 2016, and has a total of 19,000 employees who are spread over more than 120 countries.

GIZ implements projects on behalf of the German Federal Foreign Office. The main focus of GIZ is to foster private sector development, and it cooperates closely with business chambers and associations in developing countries. It considers capacity development to be its core competence. It has identified eight so-called 'project areas':

1. Methods
2. Rural development
3. Sustainable infrastructure
4. Security and peace
5. Social development
6. Governance and democracy
7. Environment and climate change
8. Economic development

It is notable that the latter project area does not specifically include economic growth per se, but it does include economic policy and private sector development.

KfW is a special state-owned development bank, based in Frankfurt, that is a corporation under public legislation. It was started in 1948 under the Marshall Plan, and is now Germany's third-largest bank. It has some 6,350 employees and offices in more than 60 countries. In 2018, it lent a total of €75.5 billion (US$81.5 billion), of which some $11 billion was for projects in developing countries. Most of these were for climate change and environmental protection.

Ireland

Irish aid is handled by the Development Cooperation Division of the Department of Foreign Affairs and Trade. In 2017, it had a budget of €650 million (US$700 million), making it one of the smaller donors. Ireland has a policy to increase aid funding to 0.7% GNI by 2030. Most Irish aid goes to Africa. Key aid policies are similar to those of other donors, as well as the SDGs, they include the following:

- Hunger
- Education
- Health
- Humanitarian assistance
- The environment (climate change)
- Gender equality
- Governance

Italy

Italy is one of the larger aid donors. In 2018, its total budget was US$5 billion, making it the eighth-largest bilateral donor. However, this was equivalent to only 0.24% of GNI, making Italy one of the meanest donor countries on a per capita basis.

The Italian Agency for Development Cooperation (Agenzia Italiana per la Cooperazione allo Sviluppo [AICS]) is a relatively new organisation within the Ministry of Foreign Affairs and was established in 2016. It is a small unit with 240 staff, located in Rome, which oversees aid interventions undertaken by a wide range of central and local government administrations. As with the French agency, it is overseen by an inter-ministerial committee that represents the Ministries of Foreign Affairs, the Interior, Economic Development and Culture.

AICS has much the same policy priorities as the other bilateral agencies, but with the significant difference that it also responsible for migration and refugees. Its geographical focus is on Africa. It replaces a previous organisation and is intended to ensure that Italian aid is aligned with its European partners.

Japan

Japan has one of the longest histories of aid, which began in 1954 under the Colombo Plan.[37] The Japanese International Cooperation Agency (JICA) was founded in 1974 and reformulated in 2008. It is an independent administrative authority within the Ministry of Foreign Affairs. In 2018, the value of JICA's aid was US$14.2 billion, equivalent to 0.28% of GNI, making it the fourth-largest donor nation. Most of its aid (70%) is spent in Asia, although aid to Africa is growing. JICA has the same basic priorities as the other bilateral agencies, but it also has a large investment loan window.

South Korea

South Korean aid is handled by the Korean International Cooperation Agency (KOICA), a unit formed in 1991 within the Ministry of Foreign Affairs. In 2018, it had a budget of US$2.4 billion, making it the 15th-largest donor country.

Key themes for support include these:

- Health
- Education
- Information technology (IT)
- Water and sanitation

37. The Colombo Plan was formed in 1950 by a group of seven UK Commonwealth foreign secretaries in Colombo, Ceylon (now Sri Lanka). The basic idea was to challenge the threat of communism in Asia by providing technical and economic assistance to non-communist countries. An early initiative was help for the sericulture industry in Bangladesh. Today, the Columbo Plan has 27 member countries, including Japan and the US. It has a secretariat in Colombo that is funded by equal contributions from all member countries. Active programmes, mainly scholarships, are funded by voluntary member contributions. The Columbo Plan has a primary focus of drug (opium) reduction in the region. At time of writing, the Columbo Plan is a shadow of its former self, but it shows how difficult it is to phase out an international body.

It has a focus on providing loans for infrastructure investment in Asia, but it has projects in many countries throughout the world.

What makes South Korea especially interesting from an aid perspective is that it was a recipient of aid itself until the end of the 20th century. It became a member of the DAC as recently as 2010. South Korean economists consider that aid played an important role in the country's economic development and that the country's use and experiences of economic transition can be useful in the design of its aid programmes.

The Netherlands

The Netherlands' aid falls within the remit of the Ministry of Foreign Affairs and is coordinated by the Directorate-General for International Cooperation (Directoraat Generaal Internationale Samenwerking [DGIS]). The priorities for Dutch aid are similar to those of the other bilateral agencies, with perhaps the addition of the support for refugees.

Dutch aid appears to be implemented by a range of organisations, rather than one dedicated agency. One of the best known is Stichting Nederlandse Vrijwilligers (SNV), which was set up in 1965 and provides Dutch volunteers to work in developing countries. It was a unit within the Ministry of Foreign Affairs until 2002 when it became a not-for-profit international development organisation.

The Netherlands' aid organisation and policy has changed over the years in response to the political complexion of the national government. The Dutch have been wandering – some would say, plundering – the world for centuries; they therefore collectively know as much as any other nation about the issues and potential of other countries. They are also a remarkably pragmatic people, and where they lead, I am sure others will follow.

Since 2018, there has been an increase in aid funding and a geographical refocus towards unstable regions near Europe, in particular West Africa (Sahel), the Horn of Africa, the Middle East and North Africa. This policy is based on the need to address the root causes of poverty in these regions, seen as the key to resolving conflicts. Whether or not this is convenient political rhetoric, it underlines the fact that that much aid has a political – in this case, security – rationale. The Dutch can see that if the problems in these regions are not addressed satisfactorily, they are likely to become problems in the Netherlands. In 2018, the Netherlands' aid was worth US$5.6 billion, equivalent to 0.6% of GNI, making it one of the largest donors per capita of the national population. Before Covid-19, this was expected to increase to a target of 1% of GNI.

New Zealand

Like most other bilateral aid agencies, New Zealand's agency resides in the Ministry of Foreign Affairs and Trade. It delivers its aid principally (60%) in the Pacific Islands region. The priorities of New Zealand aid are very similar to those of the other bilateral donors, with the addition of specific reference to fisheries, tourism and IT. It also embraces the SDGs. New Zealand is a relatively small donor. In 2017, the budget was NZ$613 million (US$387 million), equivalent to only 0.24% of GNI.

Norway

Norway is the only OECD country that aims to spend 1% of GNI on aid. In 2018, its budget was US$4.3 billion, making it one of the largest per capita OECD donors. The Norwegian Agency for Development Corporation is a directorate in the Ministry of Foreign Affairs. It is also one of the oldest agencies as it can trace its origins back to 1939. It has similar aid themes to the other bilateral agencies, with the addition of a theme to help developing countries use their oil resources sustainably. It is active in 20 countries in Africa, 10 in Asia, three in Latin America and the Caribbean, and three in the Middle East, and is one of the six countries that spends 0.7% of GNI on aid.

Spain

Spanish aid closely resembles that of the other OECD countries discussed previously. Aid is handled by the Agencia Espanola de Cooperacion Internationale, a unit within the Ministry of Foreign Affairs, and it is headquartered in Madrid. Its priorities are identical to the other countries. However, it has retained a much more limited geographical focus in which Latin America and the Caribbean dominate. It has some activities in Africa, notably those nearest to Spain or where Latin languages are spoken. In 2018, the value of its ODA for projects and debt relief was US$2.9 billion, equal to 0.21% of GNI.

Sweden

The Swedish aid agency, Swedish International Development Cooperation Agency, was founded in 1995. It is an agency of the Ministry of Foreign Affairs. It has six main thematic areas:

1. Democracy and human rights
2. The environment and climate change
3. Gender equality
4. Economic growth

5. Social development
6. Peace and security

If these are in line with the other bilateral aid agencies, the amount it budgets for aid is exceptional, as it is around 1% of GNI. In 2018, its budget was US$5.8 billion, making it the largest donor in proportion to the size of its population.

Switzerland

The Swiss Agency for Development Cooperation (SDC) is an agency of the Federal Department of Foreign Affairs. It is responsible for coordinating all Swiss aid. The SDC is charged with implementing the following aspects of the Swiss constitution:

- Alleviation of hardship poverty and hunger
- Human rights
- Promotion of democracy and peaceful coexistence

It has traditionally focused its work on some of the world's poorest countries in Africa, Asia and Latin America, and recent policy indicates that fragile estates will receive the bulk of Swiss aid in the years to come. A lot of Swiss aid is implemented by SWISSAID, a not-for-profit organisation based in Bern. In total, Swiss aid has averaged US$3.0 billion a year since 2012; in 2017, this was equivalent to 0.5% of GNI.

2.20. Consultative Group for International Agricultural Research (CGIAR)

For many years after the Second World War, raising global food production was seen as a priority by most governments, and the development and use of new agricultural technology was seen as one of the most cost-effective ways to do this. The problem for the developing world was a shortage of research capability for developing and/or adapting new technologies suitable for tropical and subtropical ecologies.

Aware of the gap created by the demise of the colonial influence, two of the larger US foundations (the Rockefeller Foundation and the Ford Foundation) put forward considerable sums of money to develop international research institutes for rice and wheat,[38] which subsequently became the founding centres of the multilaterally funded CGIAR system. As the system grew, however, these foundations partially

---

38. The wheat breeder Norman Borlaug, who bred the famous dwarf wheats that saved India from famine, undertook his work (sponsored by the Ford Foundation and Rockefeller Foundation) in Mexico.

withdrew, and the centres became more dependent on donor funding from both bilateral sources and multilateral sources, such as the UNDP, the World Bank and the FAO.

The basic concepts were to use public funds to develop new technologies for all to use, and to establish research capabilities for the more important crops, which were to be located as near as possible to the 'centres of origin'[39] of the concerned commodity. For example, Mexico was ideal for maize, Peru for potatoes and the Philippines for rice. The thinking behind this was to locate the research institutes as geographically close to as many landraces (naturally occurring varieties) as possible. These would be collected and studied, and their seeds saved and stored as possible sources of new genes for transfer, through breeding, to recognised commercial varieties.

The early results were very encouraging. The so-called 'green revolution' owes much of its success to the semi-dwarf wheat and rice varieties bred at the International Maize and Wheat Improvement Center (CIMMYT) in Mexico and the International Rice Research Institute (IRRI) in the Philippines. The centres – as they soon became called after the system was formally established in 1972 – attracted dedicated, competent scientists, and jobs at the centres became much sought after by agricultural scientists from all over the world in the 1970s and 1980s. Spending increased from US$14.8 million in 1970 to over US$305 million (in nominal terms) by 1990.

At its peak in the mid-1990s, there were 18 centres (see *Appendix F*), covering most annual crops, and two livestock centres; while the overall funding was higher, at some US$350 million (in nominal terms), funding per institute – especially at the older institutes – was in decline throughout the 1990s. It is difficult to find a single major cause of the decline. What is not in doubt is that governments in the West were no longer worried about food security, either for their own populations or for others less fortunate. It was also the time of the WC, which basically said 'leave things to the private sector and the market'. Again, to a large extent, this seemed sensible. The private sector, for example, jumped on the genetically modified organism (GMO) technology. It seemed that there was no longer any great need for public investment in agricultural research.

These were the main reasons for the cutbacks in core funding for the centres at the end of the 20th century. There was also a sense that some of the centres needed to show more value for money. While it is the case that many of the centres were developing commercially viable new production technologies, nothing compared with the scale of the green revolution. As well as reviewing the financing

---

39. In the 1920s, the Russian scientist Nicolai Vavilov had convincingly shown that the main crops grown by farmers had originated in specific parts of the world. Wheat, for example, was determined to have originated in the Middle East.

of the centres, there were moves to streamline their overall administration and management. Each centre had become a little empire in its own right, with its own DG and administrative staff – guided, in theory, by an international board of governors and subject to an independent review every five years or so. With so many centres, it was becoming difficult to find competent board members and, more and more, the reviews became a formality only. There is little doubt that the CGIAR system has suffered from far too much politics.

That said, there is no doubt that the CGIAR system has contributed to technology development, and the benefits to mankind of the semi-dwarf wheat and rice varieties alone have probably justified all the CGIAR investment made. The centres have also made significant genetic improvements to crops, including maize, sorghum, millet, barley, lentils, beans, cassava and potatoes. An evaluation of the results between 1965 and 1998 shows that 60% of the global area planted with these crops was sown with varieties that had CGIAR ancestry. Clearly, the monetary value of the CGIAR investment runs into billions of dollars. It also is important to recognise the value of some of the livestock disease research done at the International Livestock Research Institute (ILRI), notably the work on rinderpest eradication.

However, like so many aid initiatives, the system had become too self-serving and had lost sight of its original objectives. Few really important technological breakthroughs have been achieved within the past two decades. The crop centres have continued their valuable work in breeding new varieties and strains, which they pass on to national breeding programmes for local evaluation and crossing, and the collection of germplasm at the crop centres is an invaluable global resource that needs careful husbandry. Quite a number of national cereal-breeding programmes in Asia depend very heavily on the germplasm supplied by CGIAR centres. The centres have also suffered competition from the National Agricultural Research System (NARS), especially in larger countries such as India, China and Brazil, which now have competent public and private agricultural research capacity. Over the years, there has been some consolidation and the number of centres was reduced to 15 (see *Appendix F*).

Aware of the overall weaknesses and, in particular, funding difficulties in 2010, the donor community stepped in and engineered some major transformations. But these were only partially successful, and in 2014, discussion began on further reforms (Hawtin, 2017). This led *inter alia*, to an agreement on eight research priorities aligned with the UN SDGs and to a modified organisational framework in 2016. This was subject to further review in November 2019 at a meeting of the system council in Chengdu, China.

Reading between the lines, it seems clear that the enthusiasm of Western governments and foundations for supporting international agricultural research is waning, for the following reasons:

- The system as a whole has failed to develop a sufficient number of green revolution technologies.
- Many of the larger NARSs are now able to develop their own improved varieties, together with the private sector.
- Many funders have the desire to invest more of their funds in their own national research institutions.
- Funding climate change adaptation and mitigation measures is becoming a priority (over agriculture) for donor funds.

The key remaining value of the centres is largely their germplasm collections, and these do need to be maintained. In 2008, the Svalbard Global Seed Vault, operated by the Nordic Genetic Resource Center (NordGen), started operations. NordGen is located on the island of Spitsbergen, near the North Pole, and provides very low temperature storage (-18°C) for a second copy of all the varieties bred and kept at the centres and/or other sources. It has already 'saved' the varieties of crops bred and kept at the International Center for Agricultural Research in the Dry Areas (ICARDA) in Aleppo, Syria, which were destroyed in the recent conflict in that country. Seed from Svalbard has been sent to the new ICARDA facility in Lebanon, where it has now germinated and replaced the old collection. NordGen is funded by the Norwegian government, the Bill & Melinda Gates Foundation, and other supporters. Stored seed belongs to the depositor and is only stored by Norway; an international advisory council provides guidance. The FAO and the CGIAR system have representatives on the council.

In 2021, it was too soon after these changes were made to know how successful they will prove to be. It seems probable that one or two of the weaker centres may struggle to secure enough funding and will, almost certainly, merge some or all of their activities with other centres, as has happened in the past.

The big unknown that may prove me wrong is what China decides to do with the centres. China has a very sophisticated agricultural research system and does not really need the CGIAR, but it might decide that having a major influence on the system might be a good political investment. To be able to dictate who gets which new crop varieties in the future could be a useful lever. However, it would be a risky game to play, as withholding the better varieties would not make friends, and it would give wonderful verbal ammunition to China's enemies. The other big plus for China is the fact that quite a number of the CGIAR centres are in strategically important countries, such as Lebanon, India, Peru and the Philippines. To have the diplomatic right to post Chinese nationals to these countries might be too tempting an opportunity to forgo. My guess is that the West will maintain a large foothold in the CGIAR system in the future, if only to keep an eye on what China is up to.

As an ex-director of one of the centres has helpfully pointed out, by 2020, the CGIAR system had come full circle in many ways: a major impetus for its initiation during the Cold War was to counter Soviet influence, and post 2020, it could play a similar role with China in the anticipated competition for global influence. As with so much aid, even that related to high-tech science, it is difficult to ignore the politics.

2.21. Organization of the Petroleum Exporting Countries (OPEC) Fund

The OPEC Fund for International Development provides development finance for economic growth in developing countries other than OPEC member countries. Based in Vienna, it was founded in 1976, some three years after the 1973 oil crisis. To date, the fund has disbursed US$25 billion in 134 countries. This is equivalent to just over US$600 million a year since it was founded, making it one of the smallest aid agencies. Given the massive wealth of the OPEC countries, it is really little more than petty cash. In 2020, there were signs (an increase in staffing) that the fund was planning to expand its activities considerably.

2.22. The Private Sector

Private Foundations

In addition to publicly funded aid agencies, there are a large number of privately funded organisations involved in aid work. Most, but not all, are based in the US. Perhaps the best known are the Ford and Rockefeller Foundations, which have been around for many years, but catching up fast, and by far and away the largest, is the Bill & Melinda Gates Foundation,

The Bill & Melinda Gates Foundation, which has an endowment of US$50.7 billion, is active across a wide range of activities under the broad heading of 'venture philanthropy'. In the developing world, it has important programmes in agriculture, water and sanitation, health (notably the control and elimination of diseases, especially polio), and the provision of scholarships.

The Ford Foundation has an endowment of US$12.4 billion. Its focus is on improving human welfare, and it provides active support for economic empowerment, education, human rights, democracy, the arts and developing world development. Typically, it provides grants worth a total of some US$500 million a year.

The Rockefeller Foundation, which was based on the wealth of Standard Oil (now Esso), was founded in 1913 and has an endowment of US$4.1 billion today, which actually makes it one of the smallest foundations (39th in the US). It has a similar focus to the Ford Foundation, providing support for public health, agriculture and natural resources, arts and the humanities, social science, and international relations.

Other important private foundations include The END Fund, funded by the Legatum investment firm and founded in 2012, which has a focus on neglected tropical diseases; and the Margaret A. Cargill Philanthropies, which had a bequest of US$5.0 billion and has a focus on improving lives and the environment.

A small but interesting and fairly new foundation is the Acumen Fund. This was founded in 2001 by Jacqueline Novogratz, with financial support from the Rockefeller Foundation, Cisco Foundation and three private philanthropists. Acumen's approach to poverty alleviation is based on a belief in the value of 'patient capital' – capital that is best understood as a hybrid between traditional capital (with clear rates of return and return periods) and pure philanthropy or gifted money. The big difference between traditional capital and patient capital is a willingness to take bigger risks and to allow for long periods of return. It is, however, not simply gifted, as rigorous evaluations are part of the mix. By 2020, Acumen had invested some US$126 million in 14 developing countries. It is headed by its founder, who left Wall Street to found a microfinance organisation in Rwanda in 1986. She is someone who knows how both traditional and non-traditional capital investment works. Acumen focuses its investments on health, agriculture, water supply, housing and innovative energy supply – it is big in rural electricity systems.

In Europe, the largest and best-known foundations are the Wellcome Trust and the Novo Nordisk Foundation. The Wellcome Trust was founded by the pharmacologist Henry Wellcome in 1936. It has an endowment of £29.5 billion, making it the fourth-largest in the world. The trust supports biomedical and healthcare research, and it has a number of projects in Africa. It was involved in helping to develop a rapid response to the Ebola outbreak in West Africa. The Novo Nordisk Foundation, based in Denmark, is one of the largest foundations, with an endowment of US$50 billion. The foundation supports medical research into diabetes and some other diseases. It would not appear to have a particularly large footprint, focusing on developing-country health and disease. The foundation is the owner of Novo Nordisk, the pharmaceutical company responsible for much of the insulin produced in the world.

The big advantage of private foundations is that they are not bound by the protocol rules and regulations found in public sector aid agencies, and they also tend to be apolitical. This means they can often respond to needs very rapidly, and they can work in any country, even those that are not acceptable to Western donors for political reasons. Foundations usually provide grants, not loans, making for simpler financial systems. That said, any support has to fall within the foundation's overall mandate, although they can be remarkably flexible in responding to unforeseen crises or emerging opportunities.

Alliances

These are a relatively new type of institution or organisation with a specific mandate or purpose, formed from a consortium of private and public sector partners. The most well-known is probably Gavi, the Vaccine Alliance (originally named the Global Alliance for Vaccines and Immunizations). This is a consortium formed of international agencies (such as UNICEF, the WHO, the World Bank and the Bill & Melinda Gates Foundation), vaccine manufacturers, private companies, NGOs and national governments. Its objective is to improve primary healthcare in poor countries through vaccination campaigns. Gavi is operational in 73 countries and has inoculated nearly 500 million children with a pentavalent vaccine against diphtheria, pertussis, tetanus, hepatitis B and haemophilus influenza. It has also vaccinated more than 100 million children against polio.

Gavi was founded by the Bill & Melinda Gates Foundation in 2000 in order bring together the strengths of public and private health providers. It is headquartered in Geneva, alongside the WHO. While there is no doubt that Gavi has achieved a great deal in a short period of time, it has also highlighted the failure of some of its partners to achieve their mandates fully. I think the achievements of Gavi show that public sector agencies are often held back from achieving their mandates because of protocols that require consent at many levels. An alliance can work more effectively with the thrust of the private sector, which does not have to get approval for every stage of fund sourcing and release.

Although Gavi has a staffed secretariat in Geneva and offers careers to its staff, its structure is less permanent than that of its individual members, and this should make it easier to close it down if and when its work is done. Closure is one of the biggest problems associated with international bodies, which become rapidly hijacked by the career interests of their staff. The Colombo Plan, for example, began life in 1950 and, although still functioning, has essentially been done out of a job by bigger and better-funded agencies, but has no way to shut up shop (see footnote 37).

The Global Fund to Fight AIDS, Tuberculosis and Malaria (the Global Fund) is a partnership of international and national organisations that finances the treatment and care of people with one of these three diseases. It was set up in 2002. Its key founders were the Bill & Melinda Gates Foundation, Kofi Annan, Jeffery Sachs and Amir Attaran. It was initially hosted by the WHO, but it became autonomous in 2009, with a secretariat in Geneva employing some 700 staff. It monitors implementation programmes undertaken by in-country stakeholders from the public and private sectors. It began life in 2001 following a series of discussions led by the then Secretary-General of the UN, Kofi Annan, about the need to initiate a new funding mechanism to fight these diseases.

The Global Fund has received some 95% of its funding from over 60 governments. The largest donors to date are the US, the UK, France, Germany and Japan. Of the private sector donors, the Bill & Melinda Gates Foundation has been the largest donor, and by 2020 had contributed US$2.24 billion. By 2018, the total funding received by the Global Fund was US$45.8 billion.

The Global Fund has achieved considerable success. By the end of 2018, it had saved 32 million lives in the countries in which it invests. It had provided retroviral therapy for 19 million people with HIV, treated 5.3 million people with tuberculosis and supplied 131 million bed nets. It has not all been plain sailing, though, as it has experienced a number of problems with the misuse of funds, both at headquarters and in participating countries.

Originally seen as a new and better way of helping national ministries of health improve treatment and care programmes, the Global Fund initially limited its role largely to monitoring and releasing funding on the basis of performance. In other words, it was an attempt to circumnavigate the shortcomings of existing aid and development agencies working in the health sector. However, difficulties in measuring actual performance in the field and a realisation that it needed to provide technical expertise as well as just a pure funding role has resulted in a growing dependence on agencies such as the WHO and UNDP.

Today, the Global Fund is best seen as a financial supplement to the existing global health architecture. While this devalues the Global Fund's early intentions of independence to some extent, it does allow it to retain control of its funds. In particular, it ensures that its funds are used for disease control and treatment, and not for the administrative costs of the older, established agencies. To this extent, it reflects aid agencies' growing focus on delivery through the most efficient means, rather than simply giving money to national governments.

It is perhaps too early to assess the overall value of the Global Fund, but there have been numerous reports of corruption and misuse of funds in a number of African countries, and some European countries have temporarily withheld contributions. If nothing else, the experience of the Global Fund underlines yet again the difficulties of basing help given to poor countries on culturally different

Western values. It is, however, the case that its programmes of distributing insecticide-treated mosquito bed nets and the distribution of retroviral medication for use against HIV/AIDS has saved thousands of lives. It has also made a significant contribution to containing the spread of tuberculosis.

2.23. Non-Governmental Organisations (NGOs)

Statistics about the number of NGOs in the world are incomplete. According to the Union of International Associations (2020), there are estimated to be some 42,000 such organisations globally. To summarise such a number would require an entire book, let alone a section of a chapter in a book. Furthermore, it is important to realise that many, if not most, are not involved in development. NGOs play an important role in aid for a number of reasons. Almost by definition, they are much more flexible in how they work than government departments. They are very often the first on the scene after emergencies, as they are able to recruit and send people quickly to remote parts of the world. This is partly because they have dedicated staff willing to take the risks of going into difficult and dangerous areas. They often provide good value for money when hired to execute projects, as they do not have to make a profit and many of their overheads are met by donor contributions. Probably the best-known development NGOs are Oxfam and Cooperative for Assistance and Relief Everywhere (CARE) International (formerly Cooperative American Remittances for Europe).

In total, the expenditure of the eight organisations outlined in the following sections was US$11.6 billion in 2018, equal to more than 50% of the World Bank's loan disbursements in that year. Not all of the best-known aid NGOs started in the West. Two, BRAC and Grameen, were born and are headquartered in Dhaka, Bangladesh.

Oxfam International (Oxfam)

Oxfam – or to give it its original full name, the Oxford Committee for Famine Relief – was founded in Oxford, UK, in 1942. It was founded by a group of Quakers, social activists and academics who managed to persuade the British government to allow food through a military blockade to reach starving Greek victims of the Axis powers. It raised funds by selling donated clothes in a shop in Broad Street, Oxford.

Oxfam has continued to raise some of its funds from a global network of 1,200 shops staffed by volunteers selling donated items, notably books. It also raises funds from regular donations, sponsored events and contracts with aid agencies. In the 21st century, it has grown into an international confederation of 19 independent charitable organisations headquartered in Nairobi, Kenya. Its focus is on the alleviation of global poverty, but it also provides rapid resources after natural and man-made emergencies. Oxfam is large: it employs more than 10,000 people and had total expenditure in 2018/19 of more than US$1.0 billion.

CARE International

CARE International was founded by 22 US charities in 1945 to provide food packages to the starving millions in Europe after the Second World War. In the 1960s, it broadened its activities to include primary healthcare, and in later years, it has developed a rights-based approach to much of its work.

CARE is large, with some 14 independent national operations, 9,000 staff worldwide (most in developing countries) and poverty-relief projects in 85 countries. It is funded by a combination of donations from individuals and contracts from multilateral and bilateral aid organisations (such as the USAID and DFID), private companies, corporations, foundations and trusts. In 2017, the total expenditure of CARE international was some US$800 million.

Other Important Development Non-governmental Organisations (NGOs)

Action Aid International

This is a non-denominational charity that works mainly with girls and women living in poverty. It was founded in the UK in 1972, but moved its international headquarters to Johannesburg in South Africa to be nearer to the people it mainly aims to help. It started with a child sponsorship programme, which together with individual contributions accounts for 50% of its income. It also raises money from fundraising activities and gets some 40% of its income from bilateral and multilateral agencies.

Action Aid's expenditure in 2018 was US$225 million, making it one of the smaller international NGOs. But it is no minnow – in 2018 it had a footprint in 46 countries (20 in Africa), reached 6 million poor people and employed 4,000 people worldwide.

Caritas Internationalis

The first Caritas (which is Latin for love and compassion) organisation was set up in Germany in 1897, making it the oldest of the aid NGOs. Caritas Internationalis, with its headquarters in the Vatican City, was recognised in 1954 under Pope Paul VI.

Today, Caritas Internationalis is a confederation of 165 national organisations that provides humanitarian assistance (emergency response) and human development programmes alongside other church agencies. It is formally non-denominational in its programmes, which can be found throughout the world, but it has a clear bias towards the Catholic faith. Financially, it is one of the largest such organisations, with expenditure of US$ 5.1 billion in 2018.

Médecins Sans Frontières (Doctors Without Borders) (MSF)

This is an independent international medical humanitarian organisation, which was founded in Paris in 1971. Since 2011, it has become a confederation of movements based in Switzerland. Most but not all staff are medically qualified.

MSF provides assistance to populations in distress and to victims of natural and man-made disasters. In 2018, it provided medical help to people of all races, religions and creeds in more than 70 countries. It is essentially an emergency-response agency, rather than a traditional development organisation. In 2018, its expenditure was US$1.7 billion.

Plan International

One of the older aid NGOs, Plan International was founded in the UK in 1937 to help children affected by the Spanish Civil War. It is a development and humanitarian organisation that has a special focus on education for young people and gender equality.

By 2020, it was operational in 70 countries worldwide, and it has helped more than 30 million young boys and girls. It differs from other aid NGOs in that it relies heavily on sponsorships of individual children by individual donors. It had an expenditure of £870 million in 2018, some 50% of which was used to provide emergency relief.

Save the Children

One of the oldest aid organisations, Save the Children was founded by Eglantyne Jebb in 1919. Today, it is a federation of national charities, headquartered in London. The focus of its work is on providing children with primary healthcare, food and education. It also has a large commitment to humanitarian emergencies. In 2018, it was very active in helping Rohingya refugees from Myanmar who have settled in Bangladesh.

It is a big organisation whose income and expenditure in 2018 was US$1.2 billion. Of this, 55% was spent on development activities and 45% on emergency relief. About 50% of its income came from bilateral and multilateral aid agencies such as DFID, and the balance from donations and fundraising activities. In 2018, it helped 39 million children in 61 countries.

World Vision International

This is probably the largest aid NGO. It was founded in 1950 in Korea, but today, it has headquarters in London and administrative offices in Monrovia, California. It has independent, federated World Vision organisations in over 12 countries and employs a total of 39,000 people in 100 countries. Its primary interventions, like most aid NGOs, are in education and health, using a sponsorship approach.

World Vision differs from most other aid NGOs as it is proudly an evangelical Christian organisation, and some critics consider it to be too close to the US State Department. It has experienced quite a number of problems with staff corruption in some African countries. In 2018, the US section of World Vision International reported expenditure of over US$1.1 billion, and £55 million was reported by the UK branch.

BRAC

Now known simply as BRAC, this NGO started life as the Bangladesh Rehabilitation Assistance Committee. It was founded in 1972 by Sir Fazle Hasan Abed, soon after Bangladesh's independence in 1971, when there was effectively no government administration in the country. It was founded to help provide essential supplies to returning refugees whose homes and livelihoods had been destroyed by the war of liberation from West Pakistan.

From a small start in one *upazila* (administrative subdistrict), BRAC soon became active in a wide range of community activities, health and education, microfinance, and agriculture in almost all of the 500 *upazilas* in the country. It constructed a large tower-block headquarters in Dhaka and has received much support from multi and bilateral donor agencies. Today, it is the largest NGO in the world, employing more than 90,000 people, and in addition to its work in Bangladesh, it operates in a number of other Asian and African countries. Its income in 2018 was U$114 million. This was made up of grants and income from commercial activities (e.g. dairy, poultry, food products, handicrafts, microfinance and a university.)

Grameen Bank

Grameen (a Bengali word for rural) Bank is not a typical NGO. It is an NGO, but as a bank, it has to make a surplus in order to continue operations and to accumulate additional funds for on-lending.

It was founded in 1976 by Muhammad Yunis, a lecturer at the University of Chittagong. During the famine in Bangladesh in 1974, he had made a small personal loan to destitute villagers to enable them to buy materials to make simple goods for sale. At the time, a formal bank loan would have been out of the question, as interest rates were very high for landless poor people with no collateral. His loan was repaid, and he began to think about whether his experience could be replicated. The key was finding a form of collateral that would enable interest rates to be kept as low as possible. After some practical research, he found that lending to a village group that on-lent to individuals seemed to work. If an individual failed to repay, he/she would be ostracised by the group. Based with a group microfinance model, he then secured guarantee capital of US$800,000 from the Ford Foundation and a loan of US$3.4 million from the IFAD. The rest, as they say, is history.

By the end of the second decade of the 21st century, Grameen had nearly 10 million borrowers in Bangladesh with a 99% repayment rate. An important feature of Grameen – and, indeed, of other microfinance lending – is that it works best with women. Grameen is now operational in 64 other countries. Yunis and his bank shared the Nobel Peace Prize in 2006.

2.24. Aid Workers

Jock Stirrat (2008) wrote a splendid anthropological paper that identifies aid workers broadly as either 'missionaries' working for a cause, 'mercenaries' working for money or 'misfits'. As far as missionaries are concerned, they typically stay in one country or part of the world for much of their working life, learn the local languages and almost become 'native'. The key thing about missionaries is that, while they are motivated to change and improve the world, they are not motivated by money.

As for the mercenaries – of whom I was one – there is no doubt that the relatively attractive salaries of many aid jobs are, or were, the draw to lead some of my generation into aid work, coupled with an interest in helping others who are less fortunate and an interest in having a bit of an adventure. Among aid workers, there are a few who are, or were, only in it for the money. According to Stirrat (2008), they were the ones pilloried by some commentators who accuse aid workers of being grossly overpaid. Quite a few mercenaries started as volunteers with organisations such as the UK Voluntary Service Organisation or the US equivalent, the Peace Corps. Finding the lifestyle and its challenges attractive, they moved on to more permanent jobs with national or multilateral aid agencies, or companies working for such agencies. Quite a few dropped out along the way, as partners and young families mitigate against posts in remote areas, but the more determined and lucky ones got a nice job with the UN, a development bank or in a home-based organisation with travel to and from developing countries.

When I started out as a starry-eyed young man in 1972, hoping to do my bit for mankind, as well as for myself and my family, it must be said that things were very different to how they are today. In particular, there was a general belief that if we all (the helped and the helpers) pulled together in the right direction, living standards would improve in the newly independent developing countries sooner rather than later. Of course, we had long and heated debates about how best to help. Some of the older folk among the aid community seemed to be more interested in their golf handicaps or their pension prospects than how to help improve the functioning of the department they were attached to, but despite their frequent cynical remarks, they too were really trying their best to help transfer their skills and experience.

Anyone who questioned what they had been asked to do was considered a bit of a traitor (see 3.8.). It is always a bit distasteful, not to say risky, to bite the hand that feeds one, and I am pretty sure this is the main reason why so few World Bank staffers and ex-World Bank staffers ever said anything too critical about the organisation. A notable recent exception is Robert Calderisi (2006).[40] Other notable ex-staffers who have written about this critically and informatively are William Easterly (2002; 2006; 2013) and Berkman (2008).

It is also the case that, ideologically, many staffers have convinced themselves that they really are (or were) making a contribution to development as well as drawing a handsome salary. I have had many conversations with World Bank staff over the years, and it is weird how they will all accept and agree on many of the World Bank's shortcomings, but invariably, when the deeper issue of the agency's overall relevance is discussed, their sense of loyalty gets the better of them. As I saw it, this was very much like losing confidence in something they had been encouraged to believe in, and picking holes in the fundamentals was too painful emotionally.

It might also have something to do with the sentiments of Tom Clausen; when president of the World Bank in the early 1980s, he said: 'Any staffer criticising the [World] Bank publicly is looking for a new job.' It is also the case that admitting much of what they have spent their lives doing was of marginal value in the fight against poverty must be a bit like a priest losing faith in God. It happens, but almost always very privately, and with considerable collateral damage when and if it becomes public. In a very small way, I had my own experience of challenging the titans of 1818 H Street, as related in my stories of visits to Pakistan in 1986 (see 3.9.) and later to Bhutan in 2007 (see 3.15.).

---

40. Calderisi worked in development for some 30 years, much of it for the World Bank. His 2007 book, *The Trouble with Africa: Why Foreign Aid Isn't Working,* is an eye-opener.

The typical aid worker in the early days was a technical expert, such as a civil engineer, an agriculturalist or a plant breeder. There were also any number of economists and sociologists. Almost all the aid workers I have met had good qualifications and were good communicators – both in the spoken and written word. They worked alongside nationals on specific projects, and moved on from one project to another and/or from one country to another. They left behind a new variety of cotton, a completed road or an irrigation dam, as well as helping to train national experts in their field.

Misfits form the smallest group. They are often sad folk who have typically grown apart from their own roots and culture, but have not fully embraced the culture of the country where they worked. They were big fish in a little pond in the development business – far bigger than they were at home. As time went on, however, they began to realise that they were no longer important as development workers, but by then, they had no roots, had limited job prospects back home and had become addicted to the expatriate lifestyle. They were distinguished from the other two categories, according to Stirrat (2008), in that that they did not really believe in transforming the developing world and often considered the most important thing to be helping to preserve indigenous culture. They were more likely to be found working for an NGO than a large public sector donor agency. Rather like the whisky priests of old who lost their faith, they could become cynical yet unable to escape from the way of life that had effectively trapped them.

An unpleasant side effect of the whole event was the naked grab for resources and publicity by agencies such as the WHO, the FAO and UNICEF. The UN agencies were quite open about how they hoped to get large slices of the World Bank project credits to fund their TA efforts. They even competed with one another.

In many ways, the whole exercise demonstrated yet again the dreadful hypocrisy of much of the aid world, which is more interested in its own immediate future than the longer-term benefits of well-thought-out and well-financed support. The UN agencies and the bilateral agencies involved were shameless in their attempts to secure funding and kudos. As far as the World Bank was concerned, they made little secret of the fact that they saw the avian influenza or bird flu as a golden opportunity to get back into the veterinary world.

3.
Case Studies

If there are themes to these case histories, the first is that what we foot soldiers found on the ground in the countries we were sent to was rarely what we had been told to expect. To be fair to our bosses, they were, more often than not, simply doing what their bosses had told them. The net effect was often that, in the case of loans, the pressure to lend was frequently far greater than the wishes of the recipient to borrow.

The second, if more subtle, theme is the change in aid thinking over the years. As far as agriculture is concerned, the main change has been the recognition that the more complex a project, the more likely it is to fail. The best case study examples I can think of are the ADPs in Nigeria (see 3.7.) and Brazil (see 3.12.). To some extent, the changes in aid thinking reflect a growing awareness that simply throwing money at projects and programmes is insufficient, and that successful aid needs to be very carefully tailored to the local conditions and cultures. In the early days, the simple idea was that – with a bit of training from Western experts, linked to some investment in essential infrastructure and in initial operational budget support – the newly independent countries would soon be self-reliant and economically independent. This was at best naïve but, more likely, hypocritical wishful thinking. At least that lesson has now been learnt, and some aid is now more carefully targeted. The case study histories are mainly country based and are reported in loose chronological order. For most of the stories, I was either the mission leader or a key team member. In one or two of the case studies, I was involved only tangentially, rather than as a main participant.

3.1.   Israel: Farming at Height

An early insight into agricultural development came during a course I attended in Israel in the summer of 1971. One day, we were taken to Mount Herman on the Golan Heights – the strip of land seized by Israel from Syria in the six-day war of 1967.

What we visited was a sophisticated vegetable farm. We were driven around, having various technical things pointed out and explained to us. It was not explained what the difference was between the area being farmed on the 'Israeli' side of the border fence, and the land on the other side belonging to Arabic-speaking Syrian Druze. The Israeli field was a highly productive field, producing probably 50 or more tonnes per hectare of plump carrots. On the other side of the fence was dry grassland. Leaving aside the politics or the system of land tenure, the two fields were an amazing demonstration of how management is as important as the intrinsic capability of an area, in terms of the factor leading to more productive exploitation. Clearly, the land on both sides of the fence had considerable potential. All that it needed was finance to invest in a suitable irrigation system, good farm managers and a market for the produce. To me, what the visit underlined was the importance of human aspiration or 'culture' in exploiting and managing land potential.

When I got back to England to finish my master's degree studies, there was an essay competition being organised by the college. I wrote an essay entitled 'The Technology on the Other Side of the Fence'. It was an attempt to underline the importance of factors other than finance or technology in agricultural production. My essay did not even merit a commendation from the judges. I was not really surprised as the college was very dependent on providing training to students from the developing world. My essay could easily have caused offence to some of the more sensitive students if it had been endorsed by the authorities in any way. And at the time, the official view about development was that it was a lack of knowledge and capital, rather than culture or anything else that was keeping countries undeveloped. Any talk of cultural inferiority or the superiority of political, social and psychological factors was discouraged. Some 50 years later, thinking has changed (see *Chapter 6*).

The strange thing is that my observations were, in fact, quite prescient in many ways. If you look at agriculture in a number of countries today, one of the most interesting developments is the expansion of large-scale modern farming – often by expatriate companies that have the finance, technology, and – above all – the determination to exploit the potential of the land and people more efficiently than is done by traditional subsistence farmers.

3.2.   Lesotho – Pastures New

Irrigation One

My first real job was as a TA adviser on a small three-man team looking at ways to improve irrigated crop production in Lesotho. The team was entirely financed by the UK Overseas Development Ministry (ODM). The original thinking behind the irrigation research team has long since been lost in the archives of Whitehall, if it was ever fully documented, but I think it is fair to assume that, as part of the independence handover agreement, the British government agreed to provide the new Lesotho government with TA until such time as enough nationals had been trained. I was one of about a dozen experts in various fields – including medicine, teacher training, radio and general government administration – funded by the UK.

Agriculture, or rather crop production, had never been important in the economy of Lesotho, which was generally regarded as a pastoral country that provided migrant labour to the gold mines in South Africa. To reduce dependence on these mines, other economic activity was being encouraged, and one small bit of this was irrigated farming. There was little tradition of irrigation in Lesotho, and the promotion of new irrigation practices seemed as good a way to help as any other. That would have been a plausible and sufficient official rationale anyway.

Other more speculative reasons for our project also come to mind. The first might have been the need to create a job for a member of the so-called Corps of Specialists. At the time, the ODM retained a cadre of experts in agriculture and natural resources, who were supposed to be available to provide technical advice to newly independent countries. It was a neat way of providing such expertise and, at the same time, giving jobs to ex-colonial civil servants who were too young to be pensioned off. The team leader of our irrigation research group was one such lucky fellow. The problem was that he only had African experience, and although he was a British national, he had been born in South Africa, and there were few newly independent countries in Africa where he could be posted easily. The post in Lesotho was almost tailor-made for him.

A second and somewhat related reason was the whole apartheid issue and the UK's relations with South Africa. As was so often the case, the UK's position was of purposeful ambivalence, as it tried to support majority rule and independence in the ex-colonies of southern Africa, while at the same time supporting minority rule in white-run South Africa. One way of squaring such an oval circle was to pump aid into places like Lesotho, Swaziland and Botswana, in the hope that this would at the least persuade the politicians there that it was in their interests not to rock the boat too much with regard to the UK's involvement with South Africa.

Hopefully, it would also prevent Lesotho from offering itself as a staging post for armed aggression by the African National Congress, which was mainly holed up in Lusaka, Zambia, at the time. For those unfamiliar with the geography of southern Africa, it is important to realise that the mountainous little country of Lesotho is an island surrounded by South Africa, but in theory, as an independent nation, it could invite anyone from all over the world to come and look over the border at the horrors of South Africa from right within the bowels, as it were, of the wretched regime. Indeed, at the time, Lesotho was like an aircraft carrier supporting aid agencies and worthy missions from all over the world, all trying to defy South Africa and demonstrate support for independent black Africa and Africans.

There was also a bit of history, as there is so often in these things. Lesotho's place in the old British Empire was one of the more unusual.[41] The country has few natural resources, has very limited agricultural potential and is a long way from any port. In short, its economic value to the British was minimal; in fact, it became a protectorate at the request of the nation's founder, King Moshoeshoe I. For nearly 30 years, his people – the Basuto – had been squabbling (with hot lead and spears) with the Boers in the neighbouring Orange Free State (OFS) over land and resources. At the Convention of Aliwal North in 1869, a peace treaty was signed between Basutoland (today's Lesotho) and the OFS, under which the security of Lesotho was secured by the country coming under the sovereignty of Queen Victoria and being administered by the government of the Cape Colony. The interest of the British had little to do with economics or resource exploitation; they simply wanted to avoid having to deal with Basuto refugees fleeing their oppressors in the OFS and the expansion of the OFS. Given that its new colony had very modest economic value to the UK, the resources put into administering the country were equally modest, right up until independence in October 1966.

Mrs Thatcher was the UK prime minister when I arrived in Lesotho, and she had made it clear that she was not going to dump South Africa on the altar of black consciousness, if only for economic and security reasons. She was also persuaded by the arguments that the bigger menace to all in the short run was communism rather than white racism, and I think she may well have been right in this. After all, both have now faded somewhat, but might not have done so as quickly as they did if the Anglo-Saxons in the West had not been as ambiguous as they were. As for trade, I do not recall the exact figures, but at the time, the UK was South Africa's largest trading partner, and with the UK still recovering from Mr Heath's three-day week and the miners' strike, there was no way she was going to sacrifice the UK jobs associated with this trade. Finally, there was national security. This issue was perhaps less important, but Simon's Town, just outside Cape Town, had been one of the largest UK naval bases outside the UK.

The opportunities for developing irrigation in Lesotho were – and are – very limited because of a shortage of good soil on the one hand and limited available water supplies on the other. What few opportunities that do exist are in the lowlands (at around 1,500 metres above sea level). There are, however, very few opportunities for surface or gravity water supply, and what potential there is requires pumping from rivers or storage dams. Such irrigation is expensive, in terms of both capital and operational running costs, and is only viable when the crops grown have high value. Our job was to try to find crops that would pay for the costs of irrigation and

---

41. For details of the history, see Gill (1993) or Becker (1966).

to see if there were irrigation technologies that could be used to grow crops on the more common poorer soils.

My own terms of reference called for me to see whether it made sense to use irrigation to produce fodder crops. This might seem odd, but as I have already said, the country was predominantly pastoral and there was always a good demand for hay during the cold winters when the grass stopped growing. In fact, then and 40 years later, large quantities of Lucerne (alfalfa) hay were imported from South Africa every winter to feed the large national herd of cattle and goats. If this could be replaced with home-grown feed, there might be considerable savings, as the transport costs of bringing the Lucerne hay from the Eastern Cape, where it was grown, were not inconsiderable. I had a blank slate on which to draw, as there had been little or no work done on irrigated fodder crops previously, and the South African experience was not relevant because of climatic and edaphic differences between the lowlands of Lesotho and the fodder-growing areas of South Africa.

In the tea room that doubled up as a research station library, I read what I could find about fodder production in the region, and I made a few contacts with other pasture experts in southern Africa. I even got some legume and grass seeds from the South African Ministry of Agriculture in Pretoria. I had long discussions with my two colleagues, but it became increasingly clear that I would have to work out my own research programme. I also knew that I could waste a lot of time and money if my programme was poorly designed. So, I decided to contact ODM, and to seek some professional advice through them. I wrote up my proposed programme in some detail and sent a copy off to London, asking the natural-resources adviser who had interviewed me for the post to get the programme looked at by one of the researchers at the UK Grassland Research Institute in Hurley. In those days, the ODM maintained liaison units with most of the national agricultural institutes in the UK for just this kind of oversight and technical advice. I waited and waited for an answer to my letter, but nothing came. Of course, I was a bit dejected, as I had put a lot of thought into the programme, and I wanted it to be blessed in order to have confidence in my approach and to ensure I could access the necessary funds from the overall project budget for inputs and labour.

After a while, I began to realise that I was not going to get a reply for the simple reason that what I did or did not do mattered not a jot to the adviser and his colleagues in London. Around this time, we'd had a kind of supervisory visit from the scientist who later took over as the natural-resources adviser, and we tried to get him interested in all sorts of our team's problems, large and small. He made supportive clucking noises and a few notes, but all he really wanted to do was be shown the famous dinosaur footprints in Lesotho, so that he could take pictures with his new toy – the latest kind of movie camera. He never bothered to contact us again after he got back to London, and it was becoming clear to me that, as far as ODM was concerned, once they had sanctioned a project or programme and got it staffed and operational, they had done their job.

I went ahead and started some simple grow-out trials to see what grasses and legumes would grow under irrigation during the various seasons. I managed to get some seed of Egyptian clover or berseem, which I thought might do well in the cooler parts of the year, and also kikuyu grass (*Pennisetum clandestinum*), which is normally propagated only from cuttings. I planted quite large areas of a quick-growing annual grass called teff (*Eragrostis tef*), some Italian ryegrass (*Lolium perenne*) mixed with clover from New Zealand, and of course, some Lucerne/alfalfa (*Medicago sativa*) to see whether we could make good hay. Some of the results were encouraging, but we had great problems with keeping stock off the fields and keeping the irrigation systems running at the out stations.

I decided to concentrate on some trials at the main station and managed to persuade some livestock colleagues to let me have access to some young stock to feed with silage over one winter season. We duly planted some fodder maize and made a nice silage pit. When the maize was ready, we cut it and placed it in layers in the pit, before crushing it with a tractor. When the pit was full, we covered it with a plastic seal and allowed it to ferment. When it was ready, we weighed the young calves and allowed them ad lib silage, but they received nothing else apart from water and a cattle lick for salt and minerals.

Every week, I weighed the animals, but to my chagrin, I found little or no gain in weight. They looked in good condition and did not lose weight, but something was clearly not right. Eventually, I came across a paper on maize silage, which provided a nutritional analysis. To my horror and shame, it turned out that maize silage only provides the energy food needed by cattle and has to be used along with a protein supplement. Had the natural-resources adviser seen fit to provide me with a mentor at Hurley, I suspect I would not have made such a simple error. But these were the days before the internet, and as I said earlier, we were conveniently out of sight and nearly out of mind.

So, on reflection, what did I learn from my three years in Lesotho? The clearest lesson was the disconnect between the specific objectives of a development aid project and its achievement. Even allowing for specific political and personal overtones, the basic idea of our little project was to use British resources (money and men) to help the people of Lesotho. Did it do this? Well, the simple answer is no. We did not develop any new technologies that have been adopted and have benefitted farmers in Lesotho. However, if one takes a broader and perhaps more pragmatic view, I think it was not a total waste of money. I say this as, between 1972 and 1990, the political situation in southern Africa changed dramatically, both from a global perspective (notably the fall of the Berlin Wall) and regionally (the release of Nelson Mandela). No one knew if and when the Cold War would end, but until it ended, the West was morally right to do as much as possible to weaken the influence of the USSR, ideally using as little hot lead as possible. If this meant throwing money at odd projects in Lesotho that resulted, albeit tangentially and intermittently, in a dialogue between the leaders in Lesotho and South Africa and the West, this was no bad thing. I would say it was actually the best way of keeping open options that could subsequently be built on more constructively.

On a more philosophical note, I think it made me aware that nation building is a slow and complex process, and that simply gaining 'independence' from a colonial master was, in many ways, a step into the dark and even perhaps a step back as far as many independent nationals were concerned. One that, like parenthood, had to be learnt the hard, painful way through experience. Sure, a few politicians and well-connected advisers did well – albeit for short periods – as they took over the reins of power, but the man in the street saw little material change or benefit. Indeed, ironically, the men in the street that benefitted most from the disposal of empire were the citizens of the mother country whose taxes were no longer needed to pay for colonial administration. This is not supposed to be an apology for empire or a call for its reintroduction – far from it. It needs to be recognised that long periods of hand-holding are essential until previous colonies can stand on their own feet. This does seem to have been the case in many countries in Asia that have been freed from colonial bondage.

Irrigation Two

Some 20 years after I left Lesotho, I found myself back there on a mission for the FAO, and I came across quite a few more hopeless aid projects. One of the worst was another irrigation story. In its own way, this was a devastating exposé of the callous attitudes of both donors and national politicians. Around 1990, the Bauer Irrigation Company of Austria found itself with a large stock of unsold irrigation equipment at the end of the European summer. Some clever company executive hit on the idea of getting an export credit subsidy from the Austrian government and thereby selling the old stock off cheaply to some unsuspecting African country. For reasons lost in the mists of time, Lesotho was picked as the lucky beneficiary. The necessary encouragement was transferred to the then minister of agriculture and work began.

No one, it seems, took the trouble to look into the history of irrigation in Lesotho or the kind of irrigation technology that would be most suitable. If they had, the whole thing might just not have happened, because the Bauer equipment was and is totally unsuitable. Anyone who knows anything about irrigation would have known this. The basic problem is that the Bauer equipment is designed for the very-high-pressure overhead (sprinkler) application of water to large areas; the key piece of equipment being large semi-automatic, hose-reel irrigators of the kind you see all over Europe in the summer months, irrigating large, flat fields. Typically, the water is pumped down a buried main line from a purpose-built farm reservoir or perennial stream. The conditions in Lesotho could hardly be more different. The landscape is, at best, gently undulating; the fields are all small; and there are no reservoirs. Furthermore, the rivers are mostly seasonal, flowing mainly during the rainy season, when irrigation is not needed. The rivers also have an annoying habit of rising and falling very rapidly and, consequently, can only be pumped from by using sophisticated systems that allow the pumps to be raised and lowered quickly.

Undaunted, the Bauer people set to work modifying their systems. At one infamous site in the middle of the country, a massive slipway was built, allowing three huge pumps to be raised and lowered as the river level changed. The pumps were used to fill a purpose-built storage structure from which a network of buried pipes fed hydrants at the field boundaries. From the hydrants, portable aluminium pipes delivered water to lines of sprinklers placed at strategic points across the fields. It was potentially an ingenious engineering solution, but one that was never used because the 'owners' of the fields could not agree on how to realign their lands to accommodate the sprinkler lines, and anyway, there was not enough stored water during the dry season to irrigate the maize they all wanted to grow. Twenty years later all you could see was the remains of the pump slipway and a mountain of unused aluminium pipes stacked at random in the yard around the storage tank. In other parts of Lesotho, there are similar stockpiles of aluminium pipes and a handful of huge hose-reel machines, none of which has ever worked.

Meanwhile, for many years, the poor Lesotho taxpayer had to service a loan taken out to buy the wretched equipment. It was not a big loan – US$8.0 million, if I recall correctly – but the interest rate of 8% was not concessional, and for an investment that has never delivered any benefit, it seems scandalous. When I visited Lesotho in 2001, serious efforts were being made to have the loan written off, but by then, it had already cost the citizens of one of the world's poorest countries a large amount that they could not afford (the minister and perhaps a few cronies being notable exceptions, as they'd no doubt had their palms crossed).

3.3.   Sudan: Just Deserts

This story is about trust, or more specifically, about how a company or a government knows when to trust professional advisers – a key consideration when trying to develop new ventures in out-of-the-way places. It is also an example of the false optimism associated with many development initiatives pursued in the late 20th century by both the public and private sectors; the naïve optimism associated with what looked from the outside like good investment ideas, but were not really thought through in terms of national capacity, commitment or (dare I say it?) integrity. This particular initiative was heavily promoted by the wife of a leading politician who presumably expected to get some financial reward from the investors for her help. What is more, this help would come early in the process before any problems became obvious.

This was my first substantial assignment for the consultancy company I worked for after I left Lesotho. I was the agronomist on quite a large team doing a pre-feasibility study of a large irrigation and animal-fattening project for the Sudanese Kuwaiti Animal Production Company (SKAPCO) in 1975. Sudan was new to me, but my old professor at Cambridge – Sir Joseph Hutchinson, FRS – had been the senior cotton breeder on the Gezira Research Station, south of Khartoum, so I knew a bit about the Gezira scheme and I looked forward to a chance to make a pilgrimage to the famous research station at Wad Medani. In its heyday, the Gezira and Managil Extension was the largest man-made irrigation scheme in the world, with over 0.5 million hectares under command.

Our task was to calculate the costs and benefits of a proposed animal-fattening lot that was to be established on 8,000 hectares of unused land on the east bank of the Blue Nile, some 50 kilometres south of Khartoum. The basic idea was to buy animals (mainly cattle and sheep) in the far west of the country and trek them to Khartoum, where they would be fattened before exporting them to the Gulf states. It was a massive investment involving the construction of a huge pumping station on the banks of the Blue Nile and a network of canals to distribute water to the fields, together with providing all the necessary farm machinery and associated buildings. We had to cost all of this, along with estimating the costs of purchasing and trekking the animals to the feedlot, producing the necessary feed, and transporting the finished animals to the Gulf. It was quite a tough task as there was very little hard data available, but we had a strong team of engineers, agriculturalists, livestock experts and economists who knew all about costing agricultural enterprises in the UK, and most of us had also experience of agriculture overseas.

We had a couple of little adventures in the air. To assess the viability of the stock-trekking idea, we decided to hire a plane to fly over the possible route and also to make some kind of estimate of what sort of take-off in terms of animal numbers might be available. We duly set off from the airport in Khartoum one morning in a little Piper Aztec. I ended up sitting in the co-pilot's seat with a couple of colleagues and a Sudanese counterpart in the back. After about half an hour, I noticed a red light had come on in the cockpit instrument panel. I pointed this out to the pilot, who started flicking up and down a switch by the side of the light, but to no avail. He then asked me to reach under my seat and pull out the plane's technical manual. We eventually found the relevant section, which basically told us one of the electrical power generators had failed. The pilot said we had two options: either return to Khartoum or fly on to El Fasher and wait for the parts to be sent up. By now, the sun was up, and the heat of the day had created some fairly aggressive air pockets. This was too much for the international livestock expert, who had started throwing up his breakfast. I think the thought of having a sick passenger as well as a sick plane was enough to convince the mission leader that we should return to Khartoum.

The next day, we set off once again – only this time without the international livestock expert – and made it to Nyala in Darfur with no further problems. The flight had given us a great opportunity to confirm what we had been told, namely that stocking rates were very, very low – if I recall correctly something like 40 hectares for one livestock unit – and that rounding up sufficient numbers would be an immense task. It was also becoming clear that expensive watering points would have to be constructed along the trekking route if the animals were to make it to Khartoum – a journey of some 2,000 kilometres.

My job was to look at the cropping prospects for the irrigated feedlot on the east bank of the Blue Nile, and I was in luck. In 1975, a well-known agronomist, Herbert Farbrother, was still working at the research station at Wad Medani in the middle of the Gezira. Between puffs of his pipe and chats in broken Arabic to his Sudanese colleagues, he gave me a wonderful introduction to the ins and outs of growing crops on the heavy black-cotton soils of the central plains of Sudan. This was useful information that I used to predict what our client could expect to produce on the land they had been promised on the east bank of the Blue Nile.

A few days later, I wandered over the area and confirmed that the soils were predominantly heavy montmorillonite – swelling or cracking clay. This is quite fertile soil, but it is difficult to work. When dry, it develops deep cracks, sometimes well over a metre deep, but when wet, it swells up. This means that the land, if used for surface irrigation, has to be relevelled almost every season at considerable cost. Farbrother helped me to develop a cropping pattern for the new farm, based largely on the production of fodder: mainly quick-growing Sudanese grass, some legumes such as *Dolichos lablab*, and alfalfa or Lucerne. I also incorporated some cereal production, mainly wheat, into the crop mix. I took quite a lot of trouble to get realistic cropping costs and yields. After all, our company's reputation was built on providing accurate farm-management advice, and we were not going to oversell the project. I fed my information to the team economists, and they crunched the input costs and output benefits for the whole project.

By now, we were coming towards the end of our field work, and after a few more enquiries, we set off for our home base in Warwick, England, where we wrote up the report. After much number crunching, we came to the conclusion that the proposed venture would lose a lot of money. The client was not best pleased, and although we were paid for our work, unsurprisingly, we did not get the follow-up contract to do the detailed feasibility study. Instead, this went to a French consultancy company. They massaged some of our numbers, and lo and behold, the venture was profitable all of a sudden – on paper anyway. This greatly pleased the SKAPCO people, as they had already ordered the irrigation pumps needed for the feedlot. If I remember well, some bigwig (perhaps even the then president's wife) was a shareholder in the company that imported the pumps, and the lease of the land was linked in some way to the pumps being purchased and shareholders being adequately rewarded.

We heard nothing more about SKAPCO for nearly eight years, until out of the blue, they came back to us, somewhat contrite, and asked us to see if we could come up with some proposals to rehabilitate the project. Having ignored our advice, SKAPCO had invested masses of money in the crazy venture, had lost most of it, and were at their wits' end to know what to do. As we had predicted, there were not enough animals to buy in and fatten up, and the crop yields the French had predicted were nowhere near being achieved. In view of the calculated shortfall in the number of animals to fatten, not all the farm was going to be needed for fodder production, and we had done our calculations on the basis that other crops as well as fodder would be grown.

In particular, we considered that wheat – for which there was a good market – would be one of the main outputs of the farm. I had estimated wheat yields of about 1.5 tonnes per acre, as it is well known that wheat requires a cool spell before flowering if it is to yield well, and such cold spells do not occur in Khartoum. Anyway, the French guys had raised my wheat yield estimates substantially to 4.0 tonnes per acre. It was this kind of overoptimistic forecasting that had enabled the French team to suggest that the venture was viable. I have no idea where the French got their estimates from, but mine were based on actual results obtained from better land in the Gezira.

We were unable to come up with any brilliant ways of rehabilitating the farm, and in the end, all we could recommend was that the company wind up the farm and set the losses against the tax liabilities accumulated from the company's more profitable transport ventures in the country. With hindsight, it is easy to think that the SKAPCO farm venture simply got its just deserts, as if they had taken our initial advice, millions of dollars would not have been lost. But I think there are broader issues of trust involved here. In the first place, why did SKAPCO hire international consultants rather than local experts? After all, by 1975, Sudan was nearly half a generation into independence, and most of the large agricultural operations were being managed by Sudanese technicians. The country also seemed to have more than enough veterinarians – surely some of whom would have been able to tell the company how to fatten livestock, what crops to grow and what yields to expect. Perhaps SKAPCO was not sure that it could trust Sudanese technicians to give entirely objective advice? Perhaps they suspected interference from vested interests, such as the president's wife? Then again, how were they to know which international company to trust? How were they to know that our predictions were any better than the French ones?

Of course, what they should have done was ask us or a third party to run a critical check or appraisal on the French numbers as a kind of insurance against mistaken advice, designed specifically to reduce risks. These are risks that are always there because, ex ante, you can never really be sure who to trust. Leaving aside the mechanics of risk minimisation, the story shows how difficult it is for investors to assess the wisdom or profitability of productive – as opposed to extractive – ventures in much of the developing world. There is simply not enough hard data easily available, and it is too easy for convenient guestimates to replace real numbers.

3.4.   The Philippines: *Noli Me Tangere*

In 1988, I was part of a three-person mission helping a national team of experts design a training and research project for agricultural support services. The national team was headed by a nice, competent staff member from the Ministry of Agriculture. Our team was headed up by a senior FAO/CP staff member. The two team leaders got on well at our first meeting, and a field programme for the mission visit was drawn up.

Soon afterwards, things began to go backwards. We were summoned to the Ministry of Agriculture and informed that the national team leader was to be changed and a meeting had been set up for us with the new guy. He turned out to be an anthropologist member of staff with no special expertise in agricultural support services, but was clearly close to the minister. We met the new guy as instructed, but it was not a good meeting.

I was sent on a field trip to look at the needs of various agricultural research stations, and the other junior member of the team did something similar for farmer training. We spent a week drafting a series of outline working papers as guides for the national team. It was, without doubt, the most soulless project I was ever associated with.

At the end of the trip, we secured a meeting with the minister. We briefed him on what we had done and what still needed to be done. At the end of the meeting, our team leader implored him to reinstate the original national team leader. The minister registered the request, but would not be drawn. I was a little shaken by the meeting as our mission leader had not let the two technical members of our team say anything, and he had not briefed us on his final request.

A few days after our arrival back in Rome, there was a final twist to the mission. Our mission leader called me to his office and showed me a telex from Manila, in which he had been formally advised by the Ministry of Agriculture that he would not be welcomed back to the Philippines. It seems that, during our last night in Manila, he had handwritten a letter to the minister reiterating his request for the original national team leader to be reinstated. The letter had been delivered to the ministry, but it had been widely read before the minister saw it. When the minister did see it, he considered it an affront to his authority and went ballistic.

Leaving aside the possible murky aspects of the appointment of the new national team leader, it is never wise to challenge senior politicians anywhere. By definition, any successful politician is driven in part by a lust for power and loves the opportunity to exercise such power. Our mission leader had failed to realise the financial importance to the minister of keeping as close as possible to the project from day one. Development bank loans were mana from heaven to emerging government politicians. They could use the funds to hire their mates for local consultancy assignments, and they could make sure the money for infrastructure went to places where it was politically helpful to them or their fellow politicians. I suspect my team leader was well aware of this and was trying to minimise any such abuse of funds. What he should have done was accept the reality on the ground in Manila, keep us involved in the project design phase and use his influence in Washington, DC, to shine a light on things in the Philippines.

3.5. Egypt: Sugar and Silt

Sugar

In 1977, the company I worked for at the time secured a contract from the UK ODM to undertake a pre-feasibility study for a sugar beet project on the western edge of the Nile Delta. At the time, we were told it was all about helping Egypt increase its domestic production of sugar to reduce imports. I remember thinking this was not a very convincing argument, as there was huge scope to improve sugar output more cheaply and quickly by improving the harvesting of sugar cane, which was grown in the hot south of the country. However, the real reason for our work soon became clear, and as is so often the case in development, it was a small piece of the Cold War jigsaw puzzle and perhaps a few confidence tricks.

The Aswan High Dam in Upper Egypt was originally going to be built jointly with Western and Soviet support and expertise, but after the coup that led to Nasser taking over in Egypt and his nationalisation of the Suez Canal in 1956, relations with the West went west, and the Russians stepped in and agreed to build the Aswan High Dam. They also started to construct a long canal to take water from the Rosetta Branch of the Nile up into the western edge of the delta to feed the so-called New Lands around Nubariya. The dam and associated works were built on credit (US$1.12 billion at 2%) supplied by the USSR.

The Aswan High Dam has actually been a great success, but the irrigation scheme little more than a confidence trick. That is really where the first confidence trick gets exposed and the story starts, as one of the things the Soviets left behind was the unfinished canal system. It was another of those crazy command economy schemes based on engineering solutions with no thought to finance or economics. The canal itself runs largely through light, sandy land and had to be lined at great expense. More important, perhaps, was the Soviet notion that energy is free or almost free and can be used to pump water anywhere at any time. If I'm not mistaken, the canal calls for eight large pumping stations to lift water to the final section before distribution to the fields. Anyway, the Soviets left, leaving the half-finished monster and no viable plans as to how the water would be put to any good economic use.

By the time Anwar Sadat became president of Egypt in 1970, the country was having difficulty servicing the debt to the USSR, and Sadat needed little persuasion to drop the USSR and ride off on a Western pony.

The second confidence trick was, however, not far behind, as the World Bank saw a great opportunity to invest in Egypt by offering to provide the finance to finish the project, providing something of high value could be grown using the pumped water. This was our entry point.

The company assembled quite a large team of experts, which included a soil scientist, an irrigation engineer, a general agriculturalist (me), a sugar beet expert and a couple of economists. It was technically a strong team, and we immediately began to see problems. The soil scientist took a pee in one of the proposed project areas one day, and he concluded that the calcareous soils of the area capped very easily, as his offering stayed on the surface for some while before infiltration. This was likely to make ingress of the irrigation water difficult. The engineer calculated that the cost of pumping water up to the end of the canal would be very expensive and could only be justified if a very valuable crop could be grown. He was also worried about whether the area could be irrigated anyway, as the poor infiltration rate of the soils seemed to counsel against flood or surface irrigation, and sprinkler or overhead irrigation also looked risky as the area is subject to frequent strong winds.

As the agronomist, I found it very difficult to predict what was going to happen if the land were irrigated, but it was fairly clear from what little development there was already at the lower ends of the canal that most settlers would probably want to grow vegetables and fodder, for which they could see a ready market. My most difficult problem was getting reliable information about the costs and return to any cropping. With no history of growing sugar beet in the area, we had no reliable information, only guesswork on which to base our calculations of the costs and returns to sugar beet production.

The honest thing would have been to admit that there were simply too many unknowns and risks. In particular, there were huge risks associated with building a sugar beet factory, unless the supplies of sugar beet could be assured, which could not be on the basis of the pre-feasibility study. At this point, a mini-confidence trick conveniently suggested itself in the form of a recommendation to do some grow-out trials and more intensive soil-survey work. This had a number of advantages for all concerned. It kept alive the idea of a sugar beet industry, it gave our company a nice new contract, and it gave the men from the ministry something useful to do in supervising it all.

It is also quite possible that this was a classic case of 'trade and aid'. I recall that a UK company secured quite a large contract to supply the Egyptians with military helicopters around this time. As everybody knows, military equipment prices are the subject of negotiation, and it is more than likely that, as a sweetener for the deal, the UK was only too happy to pay for the sugar beet project feasibility work. Although I was unaware of it at the time, this UK-supported aid initiative was almost certainly in line with the 'aid and trade provision' of the government, formally introduced a little later by Judith Hart when she was aid minister in 1977. It was a policy to support UK jobs by linking aid to the supply of British goods and services that silently allowed the linking of aid projects ostensibly designed to help commercial business – in this case, manufacturers of sugar beet processing facilities with arms manufacturers. This process is well described in Tim Lankester's book about the Pergau Dam Affair in Malaysia (Lankester, 2012). The policy was revoked by Clare Short when she was aid minister a few years later.

Back at our headquarters in Warwick, England, the economists massaged the numbers and made it look like the investment was viable if sugar beet could be grown successfully in the area. The company then put together a proposal to carry out some field trials, and they got the go-ahead. Along with three colleagues from the company, I spent the best part of a year trying to grow sugar beet on the silty-clay calcareous soils of West Nubariya. We lived in Alexandria and drove out to the site almost every day. We imported a sugar beet seed-sowing machine, pelleted sugar beet seed and portable sprinkler irrigation sets. One of the sugar beet experts came back with us and helped us plant the wretched stuff. My job was to keep it wet. I did this largely by shouting in pidgin Arabic to day labourers hired to move the pumps and sprinkler stand pipes up and down the fields. To try to ensure an even distribution of water, I installed a series of collection jars in the field in a predetermined grid pattern. After every irrigation, I would measure the quantity in each bottle and see whether we had achieved an even spread. We rarely did. The winds were simply too strong and gusty.

There was another major technical problem: almost half the wretched sugar beet seedlings decided they did not think too much of their new habitat and promptly keeled over and died after germination. The soils were not uniformly saline, but there were large patches that were really quite saline. While the textbooks say sugar beet is a salt-tolerant crop, they generally forget to mention that sugar beet seedlings are quite sensitive to salt. So, if the salt is below the surface, the seedlings get away and the crop survives. Our problem was salt on the surface. In addition, there were patches that dried hard after wetting, and the poor little seedlings simply could not push their way through the crust. We did manage to produce a few sacks of beet, which went off for some kind of analysis, but the clear overall conclusion was that the land simply was not suitable for sugar beet unless it could be leached first, and that was going to be difficult because of the poor infiltration.

I left the project around this time, but I followed it from a distance. Despite the difficulties experienced during the field trials, the consultancy managed to persuade the ODM to finance a full feasibility study. I am pretty sure they did this by another little trick; that is to say, only showing the results from the few plots, where the beet grew well. In addition, I suspect ODM was keen to go ahead because the World Bank was well and truly hooked by then, and it had agreed to finance the massively expensive irrigation system. I never saw the World Bank documents, but it is fair to assume that they too played a few little tricks. One of which would almost certainly have been to consider all the USSR investment to be sunk costs that could conveniently be left out of their calculations for the field system and the finalisation of the pump stations. In other words, the declared cost of the scheme would have assumed no cost for the 80% of the canal system already constructed. Whether Egypt ever paid back the USSR for these canals I have no idea, but I suspect not. The ODM's thinking was straightforward. If the World Bank and the government of Egypt pay for the irrigation development, we can chip in for a sugar beet factory and get maximum kudos at minimum cost to the UK taxpayer.

I went back to West Nubariya 25 years later, while on another assignment in Egypt. The irrigation scheme had been constructed but was only partially operational. About 50% of the canals were leaking badly, and less than 50% of the area was under reliable command. There was no sugar beet being produced. Instead, as I had predicted, most of the area was being used to produce fodder and vegetables – some of which I think finds its way onto the shelves of UK supermarkets these days.

It is, of course, easy to be wise after the event and reflect on what might have been saved if we had killed the project off at the start. However, there is perhaps a little more to this story. Indeed, I think I would go so far as to say that, without the various confidence tricks, there would have been no irrigation development in the area at all, and although almost certainly not economical, the development has benefitted a considerable number of farmers in West Nubariya. My analysis is as follows: without the promise of a high-value crop such as sugar beet, the World Bank would probably not have financed the irrigation scheme, even with all the sunk costs. The government of Egypt almost certainly got a concessional loan from the World Bank for the project, so they got the scheme finished on the cheap. The ODM scored a few brownie points for the UK at very little cost, and above all, the West was seen to be taking Egypt's transfer of allegiance seriously. Yet again, the whole exercise was an example of the inseparability of politics and aid.

Silt

This is another story with a technical twist that serves to confirm the lack of integrity among some of those involved in the aid business. It is also another tale from West Nubariya – one that took place almost exactly 25 years after my first visit there in 1976 – and it also involves the development of the so-called New Lands along the desert road to Alexandria from Cairo.

One of the daft but understandable policies of the Egyptian government was to promise jobs to university graduates. For years, this meant rows and rows of people doing nothing, other than reading newspapers while sitting in government offices. When they ran out of office space, the government started to look for other possibilities, and for agricultural graduates, they hit upon the idea of giving them land to farm. Initially, they were supposed to be given land in the New Lands, but things somehow got a bit muddled, and in the end, they got land in the soil-rich delta, and the folk displaced to make way for them were given land in the New Lands. To sugar-coat the pill a little, the New Lands settlers were provided with a simple house in a purpose-built village and were given training in how to farm the New Lands. It all looked okay on paper. Jobs (or at any rate an income-generating activity) and accommodation, plus community facilities and access roads were provided for families with nothing or, at best, very little other than fertile Nile Delta soil in their original lands.

Of course, not enough money had been allocated to do the job properly, so the IFAD kindly offered to help out with some low-cost loans. We came in at the time of the appraisal of a second-phase loan, ostensibly building on the achievements of the earlier loan. In fact, there was not much to see or build on, so we virtually had to start from scratch.

My job was to look at the technical aspects of crop production and farmer training. What I saw – and was being asked to bless – in the way of project activities made me want to weep. The land in question was effectively sand (98% pure quartz, according to mechanical soil analysis data) with no natural fertility and/or water-holding capacity. It was only possible to grow anything by using sprinkler or drip irrigation, and by applying fertiliser every two weeks. In effect, it was hydroponics.

The trouble with sprinklers is that they need considerable water pressure to work, and that means pumping and pumping using large amounts of fuel. A very quick calculation showed that the costs of applying the water needed to grow the main crop, wheat, far exceeded the income from the sale of the harvested grain. What is more, that part of Egypt suffers from strong winds in the wheat-growing season, which play havoc with the uniformity of water distribution applied by sprinklers – most of it ends up on a neighbour's field or on wasteland. The technology simply was not appropriate for field crops. In recognition of this, smallholders were being encouraged to plant part of their land with fruit trees (oranges, apricots, etc.) and use much simpler low-pressure drip-irrigation systems. The trouble with orchard crops, however, is that they do not bear fruit until the fourth or fifth year, if they manage to survive at all.

My other main concern about the agricultural proposals for this project was regarding farmer training. As I said earlier, the settlers were used to farming the rich alluvial soils of the Nile Delta using surface- or flood-irrigation techniques. If they were to make a living in the New Lands, they had to be shown how to farm using completely new techniques. Under the project, it was envisaged that these poor souls were going to be trained by taking them in buses, bought by the project, to a community centre every two weeks, where they would be given lectures on crop production by lecturers hired by the project from the University of Alexandria.

Anyone who knows anything about vocational training knows that it is best done in the field or on the bench, not in the classroom. Thus, rather than buying buses to transport the farmers, the project should have bought motorbikes so the extension staff could travel into the fields. , However, this would have required the establishment of a cadre of extension agents who were trained and able to visit the fields on a regular basis. Much easier, and with minimum long-term commitments, was the idea of hiring experts – in this case university lecturers – even if few had relevant training expertise.

The project manager of the first IFAD-supported projects had not managed things very well, and in fact, when we arrived, he had been suspended and instructed not to assist or participate in the mission in any way by the responsible authorities in Cairo – an instruction he carried out to the letter, if not in spirit. Thus, he never appeared at any meetings or helped with mission arrangement meetings and schedules, but he did invite us all to a lavish meal at his luxury flat in Alexandria. Then, to my surprise, he turned up in Rome while we were writing up the project document. Thankfully, I was not the mission leader, so I have no idea how he managed to get reinstated, but if I were asked to guess, I would think it possible that he had promised his superiors in Cairo a larger slice of his project management fee in the second phase of the project.

When you put the two key technical considerations together – namely the very poor soils and the hopeless training proposed – it seemed to me to be a disaster waiting to happen. But when I raised these concerns with the IFAD country programme manager, he simply told me not to worry as, in a few years, the sandy soils would have become as fertile and easy to manage as the silt land of the Nile Delta. As far as the soils are concerned, his remarks reminded me of the alchemist's promises in the Middle Ages of being able to turn lead into gold. It simply is not possible to alter the physical structure of a soil. Sure, you can add organic matter and temporarily improve its qualities; at the extreme, you can mix sand and clay to produce a better soil mix. What you cannot do simply by farming is turn sand into the kind of magnificent silt soil of the Nile Delta, which is the result of thousands of years of natural processes – flooding and the deposition of silt particles as the floods recede. As for the extension, that was what they had done during the first phase of the project, so that was what they were going to do again.

I was too staggered to challenge him, especially as the IFAD technical adviser seemed to be on his side. I just bit my tongue and thought to myself, yet again, that the aim of the aid game is to get the money out, not to worry about how it is used! If I had made a fuss, I would simply have been treated as a leper or a spoilsport, who would never be invited to the party in future. I resolved to get my revenge in a more useful way and to share the experience in print somehow later on, when all the *dramatis personae* had moved on to other things, and I ran no risks of upsetting any individuals. After all, it is a game, and most of the players are well aware of the deceits that have to be tolerated at times.

3.6.   Zanzibar: Dam Trouble

In 1979, I went on a mission to Zanzibar to join an economist on a review of a proposed irrigation project. It was at a time when one of the key thrusts of the aid business was for the UNDP to send multidisciplinary teams to developing countries to undertake field studies to assess and design development projects for subsequent funding by the development banks, such as the World Bank.

One of the objectives of using the UNDP was to involve nationals from as many countries as possible, notably from the Eastern bloc. This was done in order to emphasise the technical aspects of a project and to provide a veneer of political neutrality. It also encouraged a rapprochement between the citizens, if not the politicians, of the two Cold War protagonists.

The basic idea of the scheme was to provide for double cropping of rice in a part of the island where there was the possibility of damming a river to create storage for irrigation in the dry season. As soon as we arrived, we set about talking to the

UNDP team members, trying to find out where the dam would be sited, what it might cost to build, how many hectares the stored water would irrigate, how much extra rice would be produced and how the whole project would be managed. Our questions seemed to fall on deaf ears, as we went round and round in circles trying to pin down the numbers. To make matters worse, the UNDP team leader – a rather eccentric Englishman – was never available, and for no obvious reason, he had told all his team not to cooperate with us.

It was surreal, but we persisted and, eventually, began to unravel the puzzle. This began when the Serbian engineer asked me to come with him and inspect the prospective dam site. It turned out to be a rocky outcrop with a stream running through it. Ideal, one might have thought. When we got back to the office, the engineer drew my attention to the fact that the rocks we had seen were made of karstic limestone and were full of fissures. What he did not say outright but allowed me to work out for myself was that any water stored on such rocks would simply leak away. The dam site was a dud. The next revelation came when I looked into the rainfall records. It soon became clear that rice could easily be double cropped from rainfall alone, providing the right varieties were planted and care was taken to plant at the right time. In other words, there was no technical or economic case for the dam at all.

At this point, the behaviour of the team leader made sense. He had been promoting a dud project, and he did not want us to expose the nonsense. Quite why he was doing so never became clear, but I suspect it was because he hoped there would be another phase of field work, and so he would keep his job. Once the UNDP knew the proposed project was a dud, the agency would have to pull the team out. Our work was almost finished at this point, and we flew back to Rome and wrote up our findings, saying there was no scope for an investment. That was the end of the story as far as irrigation dams in Zanzibar were concerned.

3.7.   Nigeria: Harvest Failures

Agricultural Development Projects (ADPs)

I was not directly involved in this case, but I think it was and is an important example of bad aid. In the 1970s, the World Bank was very keen on complex rural development projects that had a bit of everything: health, education, infrastructure, agriculture, etc. Typically called ADPs, Nigeria had quite a few of these in the central belt of the country. The basic idea was that, by investing in the rural space, the increased agricultural output would pay for the investment.

Around the time I joined the FAO, a handful of these Nigerian projects came to an end and project completion reports were called for. A small FAO team visited

Nigeria and gathered what data they could about several ADPs. Back in Rome, they crunched the numbers and sent their reports over to Washington. They were not well received, as their figures suggested the economic rate of return was much lower than had been anticipated when the projects were prepared in the mid-1970s. Our senior management got involved and agreed to rework the calculations at no cost. It was little more than a gesture, really, as the revised figures were still much lower than the World Bank expected. They still could not believe our figures, as the six-monthly project supervision reports prepared by World Bank staff based in Nigeria during the implementation were all positive.

The World Bank's vice president for West Africa at the time, Willy Wappenhams, was reported to be furious. He dismissed the FAO team and hired a German consultancy company to redo the whole exercise. The report of the Germans began with a simple statement to the effect that there was no evidence the ADPs had taken place at all. At this point, everything went very quiet, in more ways than one. According to World Bank policy, all implementation completion reports (ICRs) for projects are supposed to be in the common domain and can be assessed on the World Bank website. However, if you look on the website, you will find that there are no available completion reports for the Nigeria ADPs and no explanation why this is the case!

So, what is the back story? It is quite simply one of deliberate deception. The Nigeria-based World Bank staff were mainly from Asia and not inclined to pass on bad news. They considered they were doing themselves, Nigeria and the World Bank a favour by suggesting in their six-monthly supervision reports that all was going according to plan. After all, who could be sure that things would not turn out okay in the final analysis? No one in Washington had any idea what was really going on (or not going on), and if they had known, it could have made life very difficult. At the time, Nigeria was a massive borrower from the World Bank, and it would have been a very brave person to suggest that all was not well.

From what I have read elsewhere – in *The Trouble with Africa* (Calderisi, 2007) – there were similar problems in the energy sector in Nigeria at around the same time. The only good news to report is that, as in Brazil a few years later, the whole concept of ADPs was discarded on the grounds that inter-ministerial projects were impossible to implement effectively. I think the real reason for their discontinuation is much more serious and is because, in many developing countries, the concept of government departments cooperating is anathema. Each ministry is a kingdom of its own and has no intention of cooperating with other ministries. Empire building is bad enough in the developed world, but in the developing world, it is everything. The more aid money a minister can rake in, the more power they have, and the idea of sharing is simply anathema.

Elon, a dear American friend who knows the development business as well as anyone else I know, thinks I have been a bit hard on these ADPs. He was involved in the early days of some of the projects, and he says they were predominantly agricultural, with some access roads – they were not really multipurpose. He also thinks the designs were based on research done at the agricultural research station at Samaru. He may be right, but the trouble is that the Samaru research results were not fully field tested.[42]

Agricultural Research

This little story illustrates a number of features about World Bank lending in the late 1980s; in particular, the apparent naivety of the World Bank's senior managers, who clearly had little or no idea what they were asking their staff to do or who deliberately ignored all the signals that funds were being wasted in Nigeria. The project itself was a large US$100 million loan to modernise the agricultural research system of the country. The basic idea was to rehabilitate the country's 20 or so major agricultural research stations, to train staff, and to provide operational funding for key research programmes.

In 1988, I assembled a large team of experts who had worked in agricultural research and its administration in the UK, the US and the Philippines, and together with some FAO colleagues, we set out for Lagos and the infamous Eco Holiday Inn (infamous for various faults, including security safe boxes that had front and back doors). It was just after the real boom times, and it was possible to get rooms in Lagos, although it did not pay to be too fussy about décor and facilities.

My first task, as mission leader on such undertakings, was to arrange a field programme – in this case, to visit as many of the research stations and agricultural departments in the universities as possible. We divided the mission into two teams and worked out a schedule of visits. I then asked our counterpart in the Ministry of Agriculture if he could provide someone to accompany each team. He seemed to think this was an entirely unnecessary request. I said that if we had known it was going to be so difficult to find counterparts to travel with us, we would not have bothered to come all the way from Rome. This resulted in an outburst of fury, during which he repeatedly said he had not wanted the mission to come anyway.

In an attempt to pacify the situation, I said we would meet the costs of the local guys accompanying us, and a couple of volunteers were eventually rounded up, one of whom turned out to be very helpful and interesting. I was still fairly new and naïve in those days, and like most other people involved in development, I thought

42. At the time, an ex-FAO colleague was working in Nigeria on an agricultural-land-use survey of the central belt of Nigeria. This included actual farmer yield data for a range of crops. Ian says he offered to make their findings available to the World Bank design team, but his offer was turned down.

that the World Bank was a good institution with similarly noble intentions. I was surprised that our Nigerian counterparts did not really seem to share this view. Looking back on it now, I realise that we were there mainly because the World Bank wanted to lend the money, not because the Nigerians wanted to borrow it; an observation confirmed by the stories told in the book *The World Bank and the Gods of Lending* (Berkman, 2008). Furthermore, our investigations simply meant a lot more work for our counterparts, who were unlikely to see much direct personal benefit.

That was lesson number one. Lesson number two was a magnificent demonstration of how out of touch with reality the World Bank's management was. As stated earlier, one of the project's objectives was to train research staff. We had been told to identify opportunities for training master's and doctorate students in Nigeria rather than overseas. Two reasons for this were put forward: the first was the considerable cost savings, and the second was that the postgraduate research should be based on solving local problems. For example, it was argued that there was little point in doing a master's degree on cattle production in Montana, if the scientist was going to end up working on goats in Maiduguri. Ostensibly, both reasons made sense, but they were totally impractical and irrelevant, as not one of the laboratories we visited was equipped to teach a basic degree, let alone a postgraduate degree. At Samaru, once the best-known research station in the northern belt of the country, we could not even find a pH meter that was operational. Okay, so the project might have been able to supply working equipment, but really, the point is that all who had the capacity to use such equipment had left, so there would have been no one to train the postgraduates.

It was during a visit to the research station in Samaru that I had a rare insight into what we were really being asked to do. We were briefing a few of the remaining scientists at the research station about the project, and one of them asked us why Nigeria should borrow money from the World Bank to pay for its agricultural research service. Was there any certainty that the borrowed money would produce a positive return that would justify its cost? Having just seen the laboratories and fields where the research would be done, I found myself being more than a little economical with the truth when I said in answer that there was plenty of documented evidence showing good returns on investment in agricultural research. I quoted the famous case of hybrid maize. The returns on the investment in the research that led to the development of hybrid maize had been estimated at over 700%.

On later reflection, I asked myself the same question and had to admit that, in all honesty, the loan would almost certainly not pay for itself, and furthermore, that I could not be the only person with such doubts. Shortly after the mission, I chanced upon an article about World Bank lending that, *inter alia*, pointed out that many of the biggest borrowers were countries such as Nigeria and Indonesia, which had collateral in the form of hydrocarbon reserves. All of a sudden, it all became clearer. As Teresa Hayter has said on numerous occasions, the World Bank exists primarily for the interests of its main funders: the US and other Western countries. By saddling Nigeria with well-secured debt, it was binding the country to the West, and thereby ensuring that the West would have first call on its oil reserves! That was the basic thinking until the Chinese and Indians came along in the first years of the 21st century and offered better deals.

So much for the global politics that was being played out behind the scenes. The project we prepared was rapidly appraised and approved by the World Bank's board of directors. In essence, each of the 20 key research stations was to receive US$1 million a year for five years. I have not had the luxury of reading the evaluation or ICR for the project, and I doubt that I ever will, as contrary to World Bank policy, no evaluation has been undertaken. This is not unusual, but it strongly suggests that no one really wanted an evaluation.

Nigeria was not an easy country to work in, but there were a few opportunities for humour, reflection or even sharing the spirit of human nature. On one occasion, one of the mission members and I were stuck in Lagos traffic for over four hours. I remember getting more and more frustrated as I wondered whether we would ever get back to our hotel in one piece, only to be calmed down by my colleague who quietly remarked that, 'Nothing lasts forever.' Somehow, it seemed a most appropriate sentiment, which summed up almost all the frustrations of the mission, and I have subsequently reminded myself of that moment when faced with travelling frustrations. When there is nothing you can do but wait, the best thing to do is to stay calm, as to panic just makes things worse. In the end, we learnt that the reason for the delay was that a major bit of dual carriageway had been closed to traffic earlier in the day to let the presidential convoy speed to the airport. After he had passed, however, the traffic police were too slow in redirecting traffic, and cars and trucks started going in both directions on both carriageways until total gridlock ensued.

At the very end of the mission, I asked the Yoruba chief if I could meet the minister of agriculture in a personal capacity. I explained that the minister had been my father's first PhD student when he was a lecturer at the University College of Ibadan in the 1950s. After much protestation, he agreed and sent a messenger to see if I could be accommodated. I was, within minutes, and had a most pleasant informal chat with Emmanuel Emovon, who wanted to know how my father was and what my brothers were doing. He had known us as young boys and was clearly delighted to be reminded of old times. It made a pleasant end to what had perhaps been my most difficult mission to date. We did not talk about the proposed World Bank project.

3.8.   Indonesia: A Moving Story

Transmigrasi

One of the best stories I know about misplaced intentions concerns transmigration in Indonesia and the World Bank at the end of Robert (Bob) McNamara's reign as its president. As anyone who knows anything about McNamara[43] knows, he always did things on a big scale and his Indonesian intentions were no exception. One famous story concerns a visit to Indonesia he made in the 1970s, during which he held up a cheque book at a press conference and said, 'I have US$2 billion to lend to you guys.' What he did not say was that 'This should continue to help keep the commies away and keep the Strait of Malacca[44] open, and anyway, with all your oil and gas, you have lots of collateral.'

The problem was finding public sector investments with enough economic/financial return that would benefit the poor of the country, most of whom lived in rural areas. One approach that had worked quite well was to expand the area of tree crops, especially oil palms, rubber and tea, which grow well in the tropics and are relatively easy to manage. Indeed, the World Bank supported the development of a large number of tropical tree-crop plantations in Indonesia in the 1970s. The trouble with tree crops is that they take a long time to reach maturity, they provide limited scope for employment or resettlement, and there is a limit to how much palm oil or rubber the world can absorb. Other investment opportunities for the rural space were actively being sought.

Around the time of McNamara's visit, the government of Indonesia had announced a massive programme to resettle about 1 million landless people from Java (the main island) onto the outer islands (mainly Sumatra, Kalimantan and Sulawesi). The official justification was that it would reduce the population pressure on Java, give new economic opportunities to severely marginalised people from Java and help kick-start development in parts of the underpopulated outer islands.

Some of what follows is a bit technical, but the technical issues are vital to gaining a full understanding of the events. The outer islands of Indonesia – unlike Java, a volcanic island with very fertile and heavy clay soils that are suitable for paddy rice – consist largely of infertile, light (sandy), acidic tropical soils, and in the costal zones, deep acidic peats. In the natural state, these acidic mineral soils support tropical forests with extensive, deep root systems that are able to extract the nutrients they need. Once you cut the trees down to provide land for annual

---

43. He died in July 2009, aged 93.
44. The 800km-long strait between Malaysia and the Indonesian island of Sumatra is only 2.5km wide at the narrowest point, which is a potential choke point for shipping, especially for oil being transported from the Gulf to Japan and China.

cultivation, the problems start. For the first two years after deforestation, quite good crops can be grown on the fertility provided by decaying organic matter from the forest. Then, all of a sudden, the land turns barren and is often invaded by a pernicious weed – alang-alang (*Imperata cylindrica*) – which is very difficult to control in open crop-bearing land.

The government's view was that these technical limitations had been exaggerated by donors who were against the transmigration programme for social and political reasons, and that settlers would find a way to manage in due course. And to be fair, a few did. Those lucky enough to be near towns or close to low-lying areas suitable for paddy rice often survived. Many, however, struggled from the start and went back to Java or died.

The government dearly wanted some of Mr McNamara's dollars to help meet the high costs of transmigration and, perhaps even more significantly, to provide a seal of approval. At first, the World Bank was reluctant to get involved. The ecologists and social anthropologists seemed to have won the day. But pressure from the Suharto regime (probably promises to buy lots of Western-made goods and services, to keep the Straits of Malacca open to international shipping, and to provide lots of cheap oil to Japan, if not the US) and the opportunity to lend buckets of money caused the World Bank to reconsider.

To justify its change of heart, the World Bank came up with a simple rationale for its involvement: transmigration was a fact of life, and the World Bank could not stop it, but it could ensure that it was well planned for and implemented. There would be no more ripping out of trees – forested areas would have to be surveyed first and the trees cut in ways that minimised damage to the land; cover crops of legumes would be planted after deforestation; decent housing would be built for the settlers, each home surrounded by a garden; and every settler would have two or three hectares of cleared land ready for him and his family on his arrival. They would also receive seed and fertiliser packages for three years, plus rations to help them get established. Schools, community facilities and feeder roads into settlements would also be built. All of this, of course, added enormously to the costs for the government, but no worries, Bob's money was there for the asking.

Questions remained in some quarters about the feasibility of farming the upland soils, but much to the relief of the bureaucrats in the World Bank, it looked as though a solution to this problem had been found. Some researchers from IRRI who were working on upland rice at the Central Research Institute for Agriculture (CRIA) in Bogor, Indonesia, claimed they had developed a sustainable farming system to exploit the acidic mineral soils of the outer islands. They claimed that the so-called CRIA system, if followed correctly, could support a family of five or six from a plot of two to three hectares of upland soils. The system was not complicated, although it was very labour-intensive, but it did depend on two key factors for its success. The first was the timely availability of fertiliser, particularly phosphate. The second was an intensive extension effort to train settlers, who were used to growing irrigated paddy rice, in the techniques of upland or rain-fed farming.

This is the point at which I became involved. In January 1984, I started work with the FAO/CP and was sent on a project supervision mission to Indonesia. My terms of reference called for me to visit a number of World Bank-supported transmigration sites in Sumatra and write a working paper on the progress and problems of upland cropping. At the time, I was blissfully unaware of any of the background, and so – in many ways – I was well placed to carry out an objective evaluation.

It did not take me long to realise I had stumbled into a snake pit. The local World Bank task manager travelled to Sumatra with me, but after two days, he rushed back to Jakarta, saying he had to supervise an office move. It was very convenient, as it meant he could keep his distance from the scene of the crime. I was left to travel with a national counterpart, crammed into a short-wheel-base jeep, for a series of eight-hour journeys on unsurfaced roads to get to the project sites. Those I visited in Jambi province were probably among the best sites in the outer islands. A proper soil survey had been done to identify and select the sites, some legumes had been planted as cover to minimise erosion after deforestation, settler housing had been built, and settlers had received some of their intended rations and crop inputs. The rest had got 'lost' somewhere between Jakarta and the site. Some settlers had also been provided with a cow, under a parallel donor-funded project. However, it was obvious that the CRIA model was not being followed anywhere, because as some of my erstwhile FAO/CP colleagues had predicted, farmers simply could not access the essential fertilisers, and without this, the system was doomed.

But the World Bank did not really want to hear this. Almost as soon as I got back to Jakarta from the field, I was summoned to the Mandarin Hotel by a senior staffer from Washington.[45] Over a beer by the pool on the third floor of the hotel, he tried to bend my ear and convince me to see the logic in the CRIA model and its importance to the whole transmigration programme. I remained sceptical, not because he was French and an engineer but because his arguments seemed to be based more on what he wanted to believe than what I had seen in the field. At the time, I was a bit shocked by our discussion; later, I realised he was trapped in a system that at times called for Nelson's eye, albeit that it condoned very poor decisions and not a little corruption.

On my return to Rome, I became increasingly aware of just how big and venomous the snake pit I had fallen into was. In fact, my predecessor later told

---

45. He was a Frenchman, with a famous poet's name, who spoke extraordinarily good English, as his father had been involved in the Marshall Plan aid to France after the Second World War, and he had grown up in Washington, DC.

me a fascinating story that I think is long overdue in the telling. He was one of those with grave doubts about the CRIA upland farming model from the start. As a soil scientist, he was aware that access to fertiliser was going to be the main issue. Furthermore, if farmers were to use fertiliser, it needed to be available at the right time, and farmers needed to have the cash to buy it or access to credit at planting time.

For most of the transmigration sites, it was clear from the start that these conditions would not be met. Few, if any, were linked to urban centres with all-weather roads, so reliable supplies could not be guaranteed. However, even if supplies could have been guaranteed, few farmers would have had the cash to buy the fertiliser and there were no effective credit facilities at any of the sites. To have built-in mechanisms to ensure reliable fertiliser supplies would have increased project costs enormously without raising the estimated benefits and would almost certainly have sunk the 'economics' of the projects.

My predecessor, together with another Irishman called Kelly (an economist and World Bank staff member), had written an internal paper in which they voiced their concerns about the technical and economic viability of the settlement schemes the World Bank was proposing to support. It caused a lot of internal problems, and copies were sent right up to the president of the World Bank. He summoned the two authors and asked them if they wanted to change their positions. They both declined. Mr McNamara then turned to the economist and told him, 'You're fired.' He could not fire my predecessor as he did not employ him, but his life in the FAO/CP was not what it had been, and before long, he resigned.[46]

While this story itself is bad enough, what still shocks me when I think about it is the lack of support provided to the two men by their respective organisations. After all, they were simply trying to provide honest, objective advice, for which they got a mighty kick in the balls. In particular, it shows the desperate culture of fear that ran, and probably still runs, through the World Bank. Only a fool stands up to the wishes and whims of the president, even if the emperor has no clothes.

As the lead technical agency, I believe the FAO/CP should have had more courage too. It should have given more support to its technical experts. One or two staff members tried, but they were not senior enough to influence things. The senior officers did nothing, for the simple reason that, had they done so, the World Bank might well have walked away from the partnership agreement between the FAO and the World Bank, and left over 200 people out of a job. Instead, the FAO/CP tried to kick over the traces by organising a series of workshops, involving World

---

46. I discussed this with the late John McCartney a few years after I had visited Indonesia in 1984, and subsequently, I wrote up what he had told me about his interview with Bob in a letter I sent him. He wrote back saying all I had written to him was quite true. I still have his reply.

Bank staffers and other experts, to discuss the weaknesses and look at solutions to the CRIA model. I guess my assignment was a last gasp attempt at retaining its technical reputation and independence.

I moved on to work on other projects and thought little more about the whole exercise until nearly 10 years later when, sitting at my desk in Rome one afternoon, I got a phone call from someone in the OED of the World Bank in Washington, DC. The OED was a quasi-independent organisation that monitors the quality of the World Bank's work. The guy who called me was doing a comprehensive audit of World Bank support for transmigration, and he had come across the terms of reference for my first mission to Indonesia in February 1984. He wanted to know if I had, in fact, undertaken the work, and if so, whether I had written a report, as he could not locate a copy within the World Bank. When I replied yes to both questions and offered to send him a copy of my report, his response was, 'No need to send your report; you have just confirmed what I suspected: your report must have been suppressed.' I have not seen his audit report, but in all probability, he explained the non-existence of my report as an administrative oversight. This would have prevented any awkward questions.

When I first heard the story of the two Irishmen and McNamara, my reaction was that, in the aid business, as in many others, 'he who pays the piper chooses the tunes'. The West and its agencies have no principles, only interests. On reflection some years later, my criticism is more nuanced. It is now no secret that a lot of foreign aid during the Cold War was used to buy allegiance from governments that might have been tempted to look up to Moscow or Beijing, and I am of the opinion that the West had to win that war.

What I still find distasteful is the pretence that it was trying to help poor farmers in this instance, especially as it actually made many of them suffer even worse poverty than they left behind in Java. It is easy to be wise with hindsight, but surely it would have been easier and more honest for the World Bank to accept the technical stupidity of the project and simply give Indonesia a direct budget support loan and allow them to spend it as they wished. Indeed, this may have been considered, but it is also the case that the career of at least one young and rather ruthless unnamed World Bank staffer from the Middle East benefitted enormously from his promotion of the CRIA model.

Integrated Pest Management (IPM)

IPM is a general term used to cover a number of actions taken to control or minimise the damage to crops from pests and diseases. The actions include the selection of resistant or tolerant varieties; good husbandry; field monitoring of the intensity of pathogen or pest attacks; the production and release of parasitic species to control pests; the use of biological (medicinal plant extracts) and physical (light and other traps) control methods; and use of chemical pesticides and fungicides, but only as a last resort.

It is important to note that IPM actions and controls are often time-consuming and labour-intensive, and they work best when all farmers in an area practice them; furthermore, IPM may not be able to control all pests or diseases. Farmers should be encouraged to use IPM in those situations where it works technically and is financially attractive. It should not be promoted in situations where it is not fully effective.

However, IPM was one of the most popular movements among agricultural development workers in the 1990s, as it was said to be low cost and environmentally friendly. The origins of the movement were noble and well intentioned. Thus, the so-called 'green revolution' in Asia had brought about much greater intensification of crop production, which had in turn led to massive increases in pesticide use. Not only were such pesticides often rather nasty to humans and the environment but they were also often used as insurance rather than out of necessity. And it is also true that many of the companies selling pesticides did so in an incredibly irresponsible way, selling bottles or packets of foul poison with illegible instruction labels and no concern for the safety of users or the environment. When pressed, the Western companies involved would admit to practices they would not pursue back home, but claimed they were simply following local rules and regulations, and they could not afford to be responsible or they would lose out to the competition from even less scrupulous local or national companies. It must be said that there is more than a grain of truth in these allegations.

Some clever population dynamic studies of a major rice pest – the brown plant hopper (BPH) – in the Philippines and Indonesia in the late 1980s had shown that indiscriminate use of pesticides can actually make a pest problem worse. In essence, the work revealed that indiscriminate use of pesticides kills off not only BPHs but also all their natural enemies and predators. Subsequently, when there is a resurgence of BPHs, which reproduces very rapidly, there are no natural predators to control the pest, and what might have been a minor attack becomes devastating. The work also identified that a healthy rice crop of selected tolerant varieties can, in many situations, withstand a limited BPH attack with only minor yield loss, which in economic terms is less than, say, the cost of any pesticides that might have been used. The science was, and remains, convincing.

The next step was to get the message across to farmers and extension agents on a large scale. With generous funding from the USAID, the FAO undertook a major initiative to retrain extension staff and farmers in Indonesia on how to grow a rice crop with minimal or no use of pesticides. The project developed a method of experiential farmer training. Groups of farmers, usually called farmer field schools (FFSs), were visited regularly (weekly or fortnightly) by a specially trained field agent. The field agent would teach the farmers how to grow a healthy crop of rice (i.e. use good varieties, good seed, the right spacing and fertiliser applications), how to monitor crop growth during the growing season and how to manage the crop according to the results of the monitoring. The farmers were trained to observe and record the incidence of pests and pest predators on a routine basis. They were shown that, by only applying pesticides when the balance of pests and pest predators was beyond a certain ratio, they could minimise their use of pesticides and save a considerable amount of money. This IPM was also environmentally friendly and so had a benefit to the whole community, not just to the individual farmers involved.

My first exposure to IPM was in Indonesia in 1992 when I led a team developing an IPM project for World Bank financing, based on the work of the aforementioned USAID/FAO project. For reasons that I do not fully recall, my unit had agreed to work in Indonesia for an extended period and to complete the write-up of our report in-country, rather than back in Rome. I suspect it was felt that following the normal process would have delayed the approval of a World Bank project by six months or longer. This would have made continuity with the USAID project difficult as this was about to close. Conveniently, it also meant that the review[47] of our project design by colleagues in Rome, which could have resulted in further delays and/or changes, would be avoided.

We began our work by visiting a number of FFSs and seeing for ourselves how the training process worked. At first sight, it all looked straightforward. We had quite a task, which was to assess whether there was capacity in-country to train enough FFS trainers to expand the programme nationally under the World Bank project, what it would cost to train each trainer, what it would cost to hire staff once trained, how many farmers they could train, and what the savings to farmers and the country would be if it all worked as planned. We also had to give some thought to the organisational structures that would be needed and how these would fit in with existing farmer training programmes.

In our early meetings, the USAID team assured us they could provide the necessary information. As time went on, it became clear to us that, in fact, they were still at the early stages of their work. They were able to show that FFSs worked when carefully supervised, and that it was possible for farmers to practice IPM effectively – at least as far as BPHs was concerned. However, they had little idea how much it cost to train the trainers or train the farmers in using FFS, or what the saving would be. The economist on my team was near his wits' end by the completion of the mission, as he had had to work out most of these costs for himself, and we could only guestimate the benefits.

---

47. FAO/CP practice called for all projects to be carefully reviewed by non-team member experts before final release. A difficult review could delay a project or even result in a project being pulled.

Somewhat surprisingly, our project proposals were acceptable to the World Bank, and a project was duly financed and implemented. It was not a success. An impact report on the project (Feder *et al.*, 2004) indicates that the IPM programme did not have significant effects on the farmer graduates of FFS or their neighbours.

In many ways, this is an example of a project that contained three of the worst problems associated with aid. The first problem was an overconfident expert. The guy behind the project was the entomologist who had done the ground-breaking studies on IPM while working at the IRRI in the Philippines. Not content with recognition from his fellow scientists, he was determined to demonstrate his science on behalf of poor rice farmers in Asia. His enthusiasm was infectious, he had enormous energy and chutzpah, and he would never take no for an answer or admit he might be wrong. He was also behind a series of IPM failures in Bangladesh a few years later (see 3.13.). The second weakness was an agency (in this case, the World Bank) desperately looking for a project in the 'rural space'. Its people on the ground and in Washington should have done more due diligence before going ahead. The third was a government that had become so used to following the advice of the World Bank that it did not bother to do any homework itself as to whether a project proposal really made sense.

3.9.   Pakistan: *Peccavi* (I Have Sinned)

Adaptive Research

On my first visit to Pakistan in 1986, I joined a World Bank team that was undertaking an 'appraisal mission' for an 'adaptive research' project in the two largest provinces of the country: Punjab and Sindh. The proposed project's objectives were the final testing of new production technologies and the dissemination of those technologies to farmers. An appraisal is usually the last stage in the formulation of a development project before it is sent to the World Bank board for approval. Normally, a project – even a second-phase project, as this was – would have at least one preparation mission. We were, in effect, just a formality, although I was not aware of this at the time and duly did my best to check out the proposed investments. In this, I was massively helped by the fact that a colleague had just completed a project evaluation of the first phase of the project. He had found quite a number of worrying aspects, and I made it my job to try to ensure the same mistakes or abuse of funding would not happen again.

The training expert (Henk) and I spent the next week travelling around parts of Sindh and Punjab. It was not a tourist trip. I recall coming back to our shack of a hotel in Hyderabad one evening, starving and thirsty. We went straight into the dining room, where we waited for about 30 minutes before some grubby waiter

3. | Case Studies   149

turned up and informed us that there would be no cooked food that evening, as the cook had just died!

We visited a number of places where it was proposed to build some additional adaptive agricultural research stations (AARS), and we talked at length to the agricultural staff who had received support from the first project. None of the AARS built under the first project were functioning. One was in a swamp, another was in a saline area, and a third was on the edge of a town and would soon be swallowed up by it. The only one that was on good land was so far away from civilisation that it had no staff other than locally hired guards and field workers. I never did find out what the real purpose of an AARS was. Normally, field trials are carried out under close supervision by agricultural scientists on carefully managed research stations. Improved technologies are then field tested on farmers' fields to see how well they can be adopted by growers. The AARS concept simply seemed to add another unnecessary layer of bureaucracy, and it began to dawn on me that these AARSs were really not much more than an excuse to allocate some money for construction works, or what economic planners would probably call 'capital formation' – which was always popular in government circles.

I visited two sites that had been suggested for a new AARS, both of which were entirely unsuitable. I recall one was almost permanently under water. No doubt, some smart guy reckoned the project funds could be used to drain the piece of land and make it profitable. I discussed my concerns about the AARSs with Henk, and he agreed that it seemed strange to be funding more of the same. However, as a good consultant, he did not think it was in his interests to question in public the wisdom of the World Bank. The mission leader was a rather dreary Scandinavian who did not seem to appreciate meetings and discussion, so we reluctantly carried out our task of working out how many staff and facilities would be needed to extend the new research and extension approach to the whole of the Sindh and Punjab provinces. The mission leader, as the team's economist, then worked out how much it would all cost. In those days, no formal evaluation of benefits was considered necessary for such projects, on the grounds that it is simply too complicated to assess the benefits that can be attributed directly to research and extension. And anyway, surely no one doubted that research and extension were essential if agricultural production were to increase.[48]

So much for the field work; when I got back to my office in Rome, I sought out my boss. I told him that the proposed project was bound to fail, for the same

48. At the time, the World Bank was promoting the agricultural extension service using the so-called Training and Visit (T&V) approach. This was heavily based on the extension methods used in parts of Israel in the 1970s. It was a wonderful sponge for loan funds. The problem was that it was very difficult to quantify the financial and economic benefits from such investments. At that point, the senior economic adviser in the World Bank was a guy called Ernie Stern. He had the ear of the then World Bank president, who had accepted Ernie's advice that the benefits to agricultural extension were so obvious they did not need to be calculated.

reasons that the first phase had failed. Furthermore, I said that if there is ever an audit of our involvement, it might look like we had endorsed a dud project. He advised me to write a 'note to the file' outlining my technical concerns.

A few weeks later, I flew across the pond to Washington, DC, to present my report. It was my first visit to 1818 H Street, the headquarters of the World Bank, and after a little while, I found the office I had been told to report to. It was quite large – a director's office – and it was full of people who had clearly been waiting for me. Within minutes, I was being challenged over my note to the file. I had no idea it had also crossed the pond, albeit electronically. I thought it had just been written for the FAO files in Rome. Perhaps my boss thought it was a good way of alerting the World Bank to the weaknesses of the project, or maybe it was just that copies of all such things were automatically copied to the World Bank – after all, they paid two-thirds of our costs, so they had cause to see what we said officially. Anyway, the encounter felt a bit like a rerun of the Spanish Inquisition as the team leader's questions were so tough: 'What do you mean by challenging the feasibility of the project?' and 'Why did you not tell me of these doubts in the field?' I realised immediately that I was in trouble. We had a short debate about my concerns, and although no one would admit it, they all knew my concerns were valid. The problem was they had a World Bank board slot to approve the loan lined up, and the last thing they wanted was anyone drawing attention to problems.

After about an hour or so, when it was clear that I was going to have to reconsider my note in some way, they wheeled in an *éminence grise*: an older man who – if I am not mistaken – had been an expatriate farmer in Kenya. He had a pleasant, avuncular manner, and I sensed right away that he was looking for a compromise. He agreed with me that the first phase did not augur well for a second phase, but pointed out that this second phase was, in fact, part of a long-term (+/-15 year) investment that the World Bank was planning in Pakistan. Our project was known as a 'time slice'. Could I be sure that, after such a long time, things would still be so hopeless? I had to agree that I could not, and on the tacit assumption that the World Bank would honour its promise and provide support for 15 years, I agreed to write another note to the file (World Bank memo, 24 March 1986) in which I accepted the notion that a second-phase project would provide an opportunity to address the issues raised during the first phase. I was well aware that this was a convenient device to get the World Bank staff out of trouble, but equally, there was no way I could predict certain failure in the future with any confidence, so I amended my note. The whole sorry episode is a classic case of the overlap between aid, politics and corruption, albeit in special circumstances.

On the way back to Europe, I began to relax with some British Airways champagne (we travelled in business class in those days). As the champagne began to reach the parts other wines do not, I had a minor eureka moment that explained much about the sorry saga. The Soviet invasion of Afghanistan was in full swing, and as a front in the Cold War, the Western powers were also involved. They were not fighting with weapons on this occasion, but with financial resources. They were pumping money into Pakistan to help it cope with the influx of refugees from Afghanistan, and to help it provide weapons to the Mujahidin, which was mounting increasingly successful raids on the Soviet invaders. Our project was more about pumping money into Pakistan to help win this battle than helping Pakistani agriculture. This could not, however, be spelt out or explained to new boys like me. It was part of the Cold War realpolitik under which the West tried to appear as though it played by the rules: debate in the UN and sanctions, rather than hot lead.

If you like, the project was really as much a Central Intelligence Agency (CIA) initiative as it was a World Bank initiative. But some critics and cynics have pointed out that, in many ways, the World Bank was an unofficial branch of the CIA. In the case of Afghanistan, the Soviets pulled out in early 1989, not long after our visit, so perhaps my interrogation in 1818 H Street was nothing to be ashamed about after all.

Some 25 years later, in 2010, I had confirmation of my political suspicions while listening to an interview with Kamal Haider, the Al Jazeera correspondent in Pakistan at the time. He was being asked about a speech made by Hilary Clinton in Islamabad on 18 July 2010. He commented that, during the 1980s, when the Soviets were in Afghanistan, the US pumped billions into Pakistan in the effort to dislodge them. After the Soviets left, US interest in Pakistan evaporated and with it the aid flows. He felt that the authorities in Pakistan were reluctant to get too dependent on the Americans in 2010 in case the same thing happened again when the North Atlantic Treaty Organization (NATO) and the US pulled out of Afghanistan.

Oily Seeds

My next visit to Pakistan a few months later was a classic example of donor thinking not lining up with national thinking. I joined a rather good-natured Sri Lankan World Bank staffer, and we wandered around all four provinces of the country looking for agroindustry investments. Specifically, our terms of reference called for us to search for a project to stimulate the production of edible oil from sunflower and maize. On paper, it seemed to make sense. At the time, Pakistan imported a lot of palm oil to make vegetable ghee or *vanaspati*, the main oil used for cooking. *Vanaspati* is rather nasty: it has an unpleasant taste, and when it cools down after cooking, it congeals to leave a greasy, colourless smear on one's dinner plate. It is also associated with coronary artery disease, as it is thought to lead to fatty deposits in blood vessels.

Pakistan has a suitable climate for growing sunflower and maize, which both produce better quality cooking oil. It seemed to some smart guys in the World Bank that an oilseed project would have many potential benefits. It would provide a new crop for farmers, it would be good for the nation's health, and it would challenge the monopoly of the Ghee Corporation that produced most of the *vanaspati* used in the country. At the time, monetarism was the flavour of the month, and the World Bank had a policy of weakening or removing through privatisation the powers of state-owned monopolies that were seen as gouging consumers. Such a project would provide a good excuse for a slug of funding at a time when the government needed all the foreign exchange it could get. We got nowhere in any of our discussions.

It was obvious to us that the corporation had briefed the civil servants we were interviewing, and the idea of an oilseed project was a non-starter. If the World Bank had done a bit more due diligence, it would have realised this. But in those days, the World Bank had an arrogant tendency to think that others would follow where and when it advised. In fact, on reflection, it was probably the CIA or the US State Department that was putting pressure on the World Bank to find imaginative ways of pushing dollars into Pakistan, as had been the case with the adaptive research project outlined earlier.

Touch and Vanish

My next visit to Pakistan was a few years later in 1991, and it told much the same story of misguided donor ideas, but from a different perspective. This time, it was a six-monthly supervision mission looking at the implementation of an agricultural research and extension project in Baluchistan. 'Agricultural extension' is a fancy name for farmer training – knowledge being extended or transferred from scientists to farmers via a specially trained intermediary field force. To be honest, there is not much agriculture in Baluchistan, but I guess the province, which was always the last to get resources from central government, had put in and succeeded in a bid for the project. Punjab and Sindh provinces had received masses of World Bank lolly for such projects. (At this point, readers unfamiliar with arcane agricultural terminology might like to read section 3.18, which outlines the ins and outs of agricultural extension).

Once we started asking questions in Baluchistan, it did not take my team long to realise that the whole thing was a waste of money. The first thing we did was to ask to see some of the extension officer's field diaries. These were produced after a few days, and it was clear that all the entries had hastily been written following our request to see the diaries. Our field visits similarly indicated little or no farmer training, and we were unable to find a single contact farmer, subject-matter specialist or research scientist who could indicate a benefit from the project, other than shiny, new vehicles and office equipment. My report was carefully written to highlight these issues without rubbishing the concept. After all, we were only taking a one-off snapshot of what was happening. My report was quite well received by the World Bank staffer in charge at the time. Informally, he agreed that the project was a dud, but thanked me for not saying so too loudly.

Bovines

Some 30 years later, and somewhat to my amazement, the IFAD asked me to undertake a small desk assignment. They needed someone to review a livestock investment project proposal for the Pakistan Punjab. I started by reading the accompanying new-livestock-policy document. It was impressive and seemed to address the main weaknesses of the old livestock policy of the province. I then turned to the proposals. All of the projects were unconvincing. I did my best to look for their good points and identified three that, with a little extra work, might be worth financing. The others were hopeless.

Most noticeable, though, was the fact that none of the proposals had taken any notice of the new livestock policy, which had been prepared by a national consultant. Clearly, the left and right hands were moving in opposite directions. It was understandable, as the project proposals were essentially a call for more money to do what the livestock department had been doing for years. To adopt the new policy would have meant massive change: loss of power and influence, not to mention there would almost certainly be job losses. Someone had obviously thought the funding agency would be so keen to get their money out of the door that they would not look too closely at the proposals, but would simply give the go-ahead.

In some ways, the experience was encouraging, as it showed there is new thinking going on in some developing countries, and that at least some sections of some development agencies are sensitive to these developments. But overall, the impression I had is that bad habits are difficult to overcome and it will be some years before the aid agencies worry more about quality than quantity, as far as getting money out of the door is concerned.

3.10. India: Well, Well, Well

This little story concerns my first visit to India in early 1987, and although of minor importance to the World Bank, it was a major eye-opener for me. I was assigned as the agronomist on a team preparing a tube well project in Bihar. My basic responsibilities were to assess the 'with' and 'without' project cropping patterns and related crop budgets. The financial value of the incremental output was to provide the justification for the investment in the tube wells themselves. A tube well is basically a pump positioned at the bottom of a tube stuck into the ground to a depth of anything up to 25 metres. The tube well technology was innovative, but had proved to be very successful in the neighbouring state of Uttar Pradesh.

As far as work was concerned, I did what I had to do by way of investigating the returns to unirrigated cropping, and trying to decide what would be grown with irrigation and what yields might be achieved. It was not easy, as there was almost no published information available. Interviewing farmers through an interpreter also proved virtually impossible, as the interpreter himself and others who spoke a little English all wanted to give the answers to my questions. Somehow, I gathered enough basic data, and on my return to Rome, I wrote a report predicting what the incremental output would be. I sent my report over to the economist in Washington and waited. I did not have to wait too long before I got word by telex from the mission leader, who thanked me for my report, but said that his team thought my yield estimates were too low. He pointed out that this could jeopardise the whole project. In the circumstances, the economist had suggested they increase my yield estimates by some 25–50%, as this would ensure the project had an acceptable economic rate of return. He said he hoped I did not mind and asked if I would join them on the next mission to India.

I was a bit upset, as I had tried my best to get real answers when, in fact, all that was really needed were convenient answers, and these could just as easily have been conjured up in Washington. It was my first real insight into how project costs and benefits were fiddled to meet the lending programme's needs. Subsequently, on talking to other development practitioners, I realise it was really my naivety that was to blame – not just in trying to get realistic numbers, but in thinking that real answers were what the system wanted. What the system wanted was easy lending, and as professionals, we were employed to provide a gloss of integrity or respectability. Indeed, I soon came to learn that promotion was as much, if not more, a function of compliance with the system's needs than based on any technical merit.

3.11. China: Long Marches

Jiangxi

I had the good fortune to travel quite widely in China in the late 1980s and early 1990s. My first trip was to Jiangxi in the south-east in the spring of 1988; I went to help in the design of a wide-ranging rural development project. This tale is not overtly about the politics of aid lending, but the choice of Jiangxi for one of the World Bank's first projects was clearly significant. Almost certainly, it was due to the fact that the 1927 uprising in the capital city of Nanchang is famous for 'the firing of the first gunshot against the evil nationalists' by the CCP. It was also the place where the banner of the People's Liberation Army was first raised. The Long March also began in the village of Yudu in Jiangxi. This little bit of history almost certainly explains why the province was given an early bite of the World Bank cherry.

Travelling in China was not always comfortable in those days, but it was invariably interesting and memorable. One of the components was the expansion of a black-bone chicken wine factory. The black-bone chicken is a six-toed bird, unique to China, and the wine made using it is a delicacy – at least according to the Chinese. I recall having to swallow mouthfuls politely at official functions. The Thai economist on the project was, however, fascinated by the bird. According to him, black-bone chickens were worth a lot of money in Thailand, and he spent hours trying to work out how we could smuggle some fertilised eggs out of China. We never did.

The stay in Jiangxi had one or two memorable moments. One morning, as we were checking out of one of the hotels, there was quite a kerfuffle. We had an American woman who spoke Mandarin on our team, and she had discovered that our minder was double charging us for the hotel. We had been asked to pay in advance to book our rooms and now it seemed we were being asked to pay again. After a short but quite vocal exchange, things were sorted, and we were saved from a small rip-off. Our minder had clearly pocketed our upfront room deposits. However, it was useful to have learnt that folk will try to take advantage of visitors if they think they can get away with it. I had another similar experience a few years later. Somehow, it made things look more normal and human than the bland sameness of everything in those days.

This was one of my very early missions, and I did my best to put some numbers on the costs and benefits of the crop interventions that were to be supported by the project. I remember struggling to make sense of some of the interventions, but nobody seemed too worried. Looking back many years later, I see now that the mission was, in fact, little more than a Potemkin exercise.[49] The World Bank wanted to get a foot in the Chinese door, and the Chinese wanted some hard currency. Both parties were inclined to endorse almost anything that would have generated a project. The role of the FAO/CP was to give the whole exercise a veneer of technical respectability.

Potato Crisps

Four years later, I was back in China. This time, I was leading a small mission undertaking a post-project evaluation, known as a 'project completion report', for the second agricultural research project – a relatively small (US$59 million)

---

49. A 'Potemkin exercise' is where an asset is given a false appearance, often for the purposes of propaganda. It derives from an order given by Grigori Potemkin, a favourite of Catherine II of Russia, to build sham villages for her tour of Crimea in 1787.

project, partly funded by a World Bank loan. This was a fascinating, if tough, trip.

We first went to Hohhot in Inner Mongolia, where it was bitterly cold. The research station there had been sold some obsolete computers by an American firm – Hewlett Packard, if my memory serves me well. They were huge (about a metre cubed) and very slow, and there was no software that could be used on them by Chinese scientists. When asked why they had bought such lousy equipment, the embarrassed – if honest – reply was that they had no idea at the time of purchase what they were buying and had simply trusted the US supplier. Surely this was a case of *caveat emptor,* if ever there was one.

Our next stop was Wuhan in the centre of the Middle Kingdom, where we spent a night before a trip to the far west of the county. I had been dreading this part of the trip as it meant flying in a Soviet Antonov aircraft, infamous for its unreliability. We got up early and arrived at the airport in good time. When we got there, it was obvious that something was wrong. After a few minutes, our minder explained that one of the infamous Antonovs, transporting a group of French tourists, had landed early in a rice field the previous day. Fortunately, no one was killed in the accident, but Wuhan Air, the company flying the plane, had been grounded. I have to say I was more than a little relieved to have had such a near miss. I asked our minder if we could get there by road. He said we could, but that it would take over 18 hours, and he would have to make special travel arrangements. He asked whether it really was necessary to go to Enshi. I said it was important that we did, as no one from the World Bank had visited that research station during the five-year life of the project, and that I had been told to make sure I visited it. Our minder said we should go back to the hotel and wait while he tried to arrange a trip by road.

About an hour later, he called us to say all was arranged. We left Wuhan on a brand-new motorway, and I began to hope that his estimate of 18 hours was based on out-of-date information. But this new road came to an abrupt end after about 100 kilometres, and we joined a single-lane highway laden with cars, trucks, tractors, donkey carts, carts pushed and pulled by men and women, and lots and lots of bicycles. Every three hours, we stopped at some government guest house for a meal, which was waiting for us when we arrived. After about nine hours, we pulled into the grounds of a fancy hotel near the Three Gorges in Sichuan province and waited for a car that had been sent from Enshi to meet us there. It arrived after about half an hour, and we continued our trip, stopping every three hours or so.

The last leg of the journey was quite frightening, as we were travelling in hilly country by now, and on the downhill bits, the driver insisted on turning off the engine and coasting to save fuel. It was unnerving as it meant the driver had no way of using the engine to assist with slowing down when going round some really quite sharp bends in the road, which were quite slippery due to light rainfall. Needless to say, we made it to our destination in one piece by about 3am, and contrary to normal procedure, we were told to go straight to our rooms and sign the register in the morning. Looking back on the journey and how quickly it had been arranged, I had a small eureka moment as I realised that the Chinese did not really need management assistance from the West – they just wanted to bring the country up to date with our money, technology and science.

After a short night, we embarked on our visit to the national potato breeding station. It was up in the hills above the town of Enshi, high enough to be free from the aphid vectors that transmit potato viruses. The project had provided funds to purchase a number of growth chambers. These were basically rooms with controlled lighting and heating, which enabled seasonal plants to be grown throughout the year. It was in the days before genetic engineering had really taken off, and some plant breeders still used growth chambers to get two or more crops a year, thereby reducing the time to develop new varieties – potatoes in this case. At least, that was the theory.

In fact, the Chinese had been persuaded to buy the chambers from a Canadian company that no longer had a market for them in Canada, and the Chinese had not done enough due diligence before the purchase. The problem was that the research station was at the end of a power line with insufficient capacity to keep more than one of the chambers operational at any one time. When we were there, it was pretty clear that none of the chambers had been used as intended. As in the case of the computers in Inner Mongolia, in short, they had been sold a pup by their Western friends.

The story was a little more positive when it came to some of the other equipment purchased under the project; in particular, a potato-crisp frying machine that had been bought to help test the frying qualities of the new varieties of potato bred at the station. This machine was working at full blast when we were taken to see it. It was not only slicing and frying the potatoes but was sealing them in nice little packs ready for sale. I asked our hosts tactfully whether there was a good market for the packets of crisps. I was duly informed that the revenue received helped augment the meagre research funds received from government. Faces on both sides were duly saved.

After Enshi, we called in at a research station in Anhui province. The visit was pretty much a formality, and I remember nothing special occurred at the research station. I do, however, recall a conversation late one evening, while waiting for a train back to Beijing. It was a very cold night, and after we had been hopping around on the platform for about half an hour, someone asked if we would like to use a waiting room. The room was furnished with comfortable sofas, deep-pile carpets, TV sets and a stove. Without really thinking, I said to the young guide from the Ministry of Agriculture that I was surprised to see such luxury in China, as I thought everyone had the same facilities. He started to answer by suggesting that things were not quite so simple and that some people had special privileges. At this point, he suddenly stopped talking, and I realised he had been told to shut up by the older guide. Of course, the irony here is that the peremptory shutting up of the young guy made things a lot worse as it confirmed what we all believed to be the case – namely that, in the People's Republic of China, members of the elite (usually party members) have a much higher standard of living than your average Joe.

On the way back to Beijing from Anhui, I asked our minder about the graduate programme of the project, under which some US$1 million of the loan had been used to fund scholarships for Chinese scientists to study in the US. I asked whether this had been successful, only to learn that none of the Chinese scientists had returned to China. They had all secured green cards and had become American citizens. I asked rhetorically whether, in the circumstances, the Chinese should refuse to repay that portion of the loan. 'No way,' said the minder. 'That would upset America and the World Bank, and anyway, some of the scientists send money back and some have indicated they plan to come back to China eventually.'

I feel this answer reflects the wisdom of the Chinese. They were learning how to deal with the West and knew the learning curve would be expensive but would pay dividends in the end. They were right. Some 20 years later, I was involved in a review of biotechnology research in Asia, and it soon became clear that, by then, China had the best biotechnology scientists in the world after the US and Europe, and it is at the forefront of developing new varieties of genetically modified (GM) rice. They knew then that it would take time and cost money to get abreast of the necessary technologies, and that the investment would eventually pay handsome dividends.

Seeds

A year or so after the research project evaluation, I became involved in a large project to commercialise the seed sector in China. This was during what I call the 'period of monetarism in development aid thinking' (see *Chapter 1*). On the first project design mission, I had a small team that consisted of an Indian seed expert, who had his own successful seed company, and a young overseas Chinese horticulturalist who had spent some time in Taiwan. On reflection, the Chinese authorities must have had to swallow hard to give us visas, but once again, their recognition that the ends justify the means must have prevailed, and it would have been against the spirit of UN cooperation to make a fuss about our respective nationalities. Our little mission must have passed muster, and I was sent back with a much larger team a year later.

To be honest, I cannot recall much about the technical matters of the visit. There was one major issue, however, which caused quite a lot of angst. When we looked into the accounts of the local seed companies that we were trying to modernise, we found that staff employment was literally for life. By this, I mean all company staff stayed on the payroll, albeit as pensioners, until the grim reaper swung his blade. It was socially admirable at a time when there was no national pension scheme, but it made nonsense of making the companies commercially viable.

We tried to build redundancy money for pensioners into the project, and at one stage, it looked as though it had been agreed. Then some discussions further up the chain rejected the idea. I lost touch with the project around this time, so I do not know the details of the outcome, but I do know that a project was approved, and the final assessment by the World Bank's OED in 2004 considered it to be moderately satisfactory (a useful phrase, which covers everything from just about okay to quite good). In this case, the World Bank's evaluation department felt that 'not all the objectives were fully achieved and there were significant shortcomings'. I do recall a realisation, once again, that something that seemed a good idea in an office of the World Bank in Washington, DC, was not such a good idea in the real world.

3.12. Brazil: Tropical Christmas Trees

My involvement in Brazil was very short-lived, but nevertheless fascinating. In 1988, I had been transferred from Asia to work in West Africa, Latin America and the Caribbean. I had initially resisted the move, but I was persuaded when I was given the chance to learn Portuguese, with a view to working extensively in Brazil.

I duly set off in early 1998 to undergo some intensive language lessons before embarking on project completion reports for two large (US$160 million and US$184.6 million) rural development projects: one in the state of Ceará[50] and one in Minas Gerais. These were multipurpose rural development projects containing a bit of everything, so were often nicknamed 'Christmas trees'. The language lessons were fine. The problem was that the language school was run by an English couple, who entertained me with excellent caipirinha most evenings, so I did far too little language practice!

Undaunted, I was joined after a week or so by an English-speaking Peruvian economist, and we set off for Recife – the capital of Ceará. We spent the next week talking to government officials and looking at roads and clinics built under the project. Ceará is perhaps the poorest state in Brazil, and we certainly saw lots of poverty. I remember one remote farm household where they even made their own

---

50. In the case of Ceará, the loan from the World Bank was for US$56 million; for Minas Gerais, it was US$63 million.

soap from animal fat and ashes. What I could not really fathom from what we saw and heard was how the project had generated any economic activity that would have justified the loan in the first place. I looked at the project documentation to check the economic calculations that had been done at the time of project appraisal in early 1980. It read convincingly and stated 'the economic rate of return for the directly productive aspects [i.e. health and education excluded] has been estimated at about 19%'.

However, it was not clearly stated anywhere what the productive aspects actually were. There were bland references to the fact that the area was suitable for a wide range of crops and that some 60,000 farmers would benefit through increased agricultural production. Nowhere in the text was anything said explicitly about projected increases of any particular crops or, indeed, what would bring about these increases. I reread the whole document very carefully, including the tables in the annexes. Eventually, I found some numbers on which the projections had been based: over the five years of the project, the yield of the main crop grown in the area (perennial tree cotton, *Gossypium arboreum*) was expected to increase by 50–83% on average. These are very large increases for crop production, of the kind that might be expected if irrigation was being introduced. However, in this case, the increases were to come from the adoption of better rain-fed farming techniques, as a result of the substantial investments in extension services and better access to credit. There was no attempt to link the increases to specific technologies, such as better varieties, the use of more fertiliser or better fertiliser combinations. I could hardly believe my eyes, not least because Ceará is a known drought-prone zone. What was being projected was pure fantasy. I then checked to see the author of this falsehood, only to see the name of my old Israeli friend – the one who had cooked my numbers after our mission to India (see 3.10.). Needless to say, over the life of the project, the yields and output of moro cotton (a perennial crop) varied considerably, presumably reflecting the weather patterns, but continued to fall overall. Things were similar for annual or herbaceous cotton and, indeed, for most of the other rain-fed crops grown in the region. Despite frequent reminders by World Bank supervision missions, no monitoring of the output by project beneficiaries was undertaken. It was therefore not possible to calculate an ex-post-economic rate of return for the project, as insufficient data on cropping patterns and yields was available. From what information was available and from field observations, it was almost certain that the projected increases did not occur.

The situation in Minas Gerais was broadly similar, with all the evidence suggesting that the projected increase in crop outputs did not occur. Nevertheless, both projects did meet most of their targets in terms of the infrastructure created – schools, clinics and roads, in particular – all facilities that were badly needed in these resource-poor regions. There was also some indication of improvements in the manner that state institutions cooperated, which can be attributed to the project. However, the big questions that were never really answered remain: Were the projects really value for money? And were they worth borrowing such large sums for?

Also, what are we to conclude about World Bank procedures? One possibility is that the Brazilian authorities responsible for endorsing the projects were unable or unwilling to challenge the wisdom of the World Bank project preparation teams. After all, the World Bank is, or was, supposed to know everything there was to know about project preparation, and surely they could not make mistakes? In which case, the World Bank could be accused of deliberately deceiving the government of Brazil and should not expect full repayment of the loan.

However, it is difficult to believe that the Brazilian authorities were so naïve. It seems far more likely that they knowingly turned Nelson's eye to the dodgy numbers, as they saw the projects as a way of transferring resources from the richer parts of the country to the poorer ones, and they hoped that, when payback time arrived, the economy as a whole would be in better shape. It is also the case that the whole sorry episode took place during the height of the Cold War, when politics rather than economics was what mattered most, and the World Bank was really little more than a Trojan horse for Western support to a shaky Latin American regime.

Whatever the real reasons, and wherever the responsibility should lie, it is difficult not to come to the conclusion that the World Bank must take some of the responsibility for this misdirected borrowing by the use of dodgy economic-rate-of-return calculations. The big problem for the World Bank, however, is that it has no way of forgiving its loans to countries such as Brazil that do not qualify under the HIPC programme of the World Bank. I am not alone in my concerns. Far smarter folk, such as Teressa Hayter, long ago queried lending in Latin America.

3.13. Bangladesh: Basket Cases

Silk Road

In Bangladesh in the early 1990s, many of the large NGOs – such as BRAC, Grameen Bank and Proshika – were in the vanguard of much development effort in the rural space, where more than 70% of the population lived. One of the ideas being promoted was to increase the volume and quality of the silk yarn and fabric produced in the country. In previous centuries, Bengal (which then included what is Bangladesh today) was one of the leading producers of silk fabric in the world. Raising silk worms is very labour-intensive, but it can easily be fitted in among regular daily chores and, most importantly, it can provide a useful source of income for rural women, who have few income-earning opportunities.

For readers unfamiliar with silk production, it might help to know that silk yarn production is a multistage process. Mulberry trees have to be planted and looked after to provide the food (leaves) for the growing silkworms, or caterpillars. Someone – or some organisation – needs to produce silkworm 'eggs', which become the silkworms raised by trained rural households in a dedicated space. When mature, the worms spin a cocoon of silk fibre that then has to be carefully unwound or reeled using special facilities, and the resulting fibres are twisted to produce yarn.

At the time, quite a few pilot trials had been carried out by BRAC and Proshika, who had come to the conclusion that the main constraint holding back the development of rural silk production was the quality of available silkworm eggs (known in the business as 'disease free layings' [DFLs]). The Bangladesh Silk Board (BSB) – itself the product of an earlier generation of aid projects (in this case, the Colombo Plan) – had a monopoly, protected by law, on the supply of DFLs. Originally, this was intended to ensure that all batches of eggs were tested for pébrine, the devastating silkworm disease that was partly responsible for killing off the French silk industry in the 19th century. Unfortunately, the BSB had become more than a little run down, few of its microscopes were working and hardly any of its staff actually knew how to identify pébrine. Sure enough, in the late 1980s, there was a major outbreak of the disease, and the NGOs refused to source DFLs from BSB any longer. The problem was that there was no one else to buy them from, and the legislation prohibited anyone else from producing DFLs.

An imaginative Bangladeshi staff member, who was working in the World Bank office in Dhaka, became interested in the topic and realised that if the government could be persuaded to borrow money for a World Bank project to support silk production, such a project might provide an opportunity to revisit the DFL monopoly as part of a liberalisation drive. Persistent as well as imaginative, she was not easily deterred, and after a few false starts, a small project was initiated. The basic idea was to modernise and re-equip the facilities where eggs were produced, demonstrate improved rearing and reeling practices, and at the same time, establish a new agency to oversee and support the industry with representatives from all stakeholders (rearers, reelers, weavers and dyers). A condition of the credit was that the legislation protecting the industry was to be revised.

There was considerable resistance to the project from the BSB, the management of which could see their little empire collapsing before their eyes, and they mounted quite a fierce rearguard action. For years, the egg-producing operations of the BSB had actually been a sideline. Most of its annual budget subvention went to pay the salaries of workers at two nationalised silk mills in Rajshahi and Thakurgaon. These mills had been nationalised in the late 1980s when the workers claimed the previous owners were not paying them a decent wage. Things did not improve with nationalisation, however, and by the early 1990s, both mills were hardly producing any silk fabric and what they did produce was made using imported yarn. But they had a large and politically active workforce in a part of the country with few industries. No local politician could afford to even think of closing the mills unless he was prepared to literally risk life and limb. The mill workers had the BSB over a barrel, and they knew it.

The threat of trouble invariably brought promises from Dhaka that the BSB would not be closed down. At least, that had been the case until the silk project came along at a time when the government was beginning to take a tougher line with overmanned nationalised industries. In return for golden handshakes, a number of nationalised jute mills, such as Adamjee, had reduced staffing considerably, and similar arrangements were included for the silk mill workers under the silk project. Although there were some bureaucratic delays associated with determining eligibility for payoffs, a settlement was reached in the end, a project was initiated, and the BSB lost its main *raison d'être*.

During a visit to Bangladesh in 2001, on a mission to help supervise project implementation, I had an experience that caused me to reflect once again on the whole donor approach to aid. Early one morning, a group of about seven of us assembled outside one of the two international hotels in Dhaka and drove off in a rather old minibus to look at silkworm rearing in a district north of the city. After driving for a couple of hours, we had a most unfortunate accident. A group of young children were playing in a fountain of water sent up by a small irrigation pump set up by the side of the road. The driver slowed down as we approached the children, but the noise of the pump engine must have drowned out the sound of our vehicle, and at the very moment we passed the pump, a little girl jumped into the road. The driver managed to steer the vehicle around her, rather than run over her, but she still banged herself quite badly against the front of the bus. Fortunately, she seemed more shocked than harmed by the impact, although she was clearly very distressed. We spent a desperate few minutes trying to find a relative, and eventually, we found her father, who ran a small roadside stall. We put them both in the van and sped off to the nearest district hospital. When we got there, the father and daughter were taken straight into the emergency unit, where they saw a young female doctor. They came out after about half an hour to say that there were no broken bones, but that they wanted to keep the girl in overnight in case of delayed concussion. This meant, of course, that the father would also have to stay with her overnight. We had a whip round in the bus and raised about US$25 to pay for medicine, food and travel back home the next day.

As we drove home in a sombre mood, two things struck me: firstly, that there was a functioning hospital with a doctor in a remote part of the country, and secondly, that there were no gaudy signs up outside the hospital saying, 'a gift from the government of some European country'. I am aware that the facilities and medical care on offer was basic, probably very basic, but it was being provided by the government of Bangladesh. The lesson being that the things people really need and want are, as they should be, the priorities of the government. By implication, if nothing else, much of what the donor community provides is what they, the donors, consider to be priorities. Of course, the two priorities are not necessarily mutually exclusive, but it is important to realise that even some pretty lousy governments do have priorities, and the donor community owes it to everyone to respect and build on as many of those priorities as possible. In other words, donors should be a little more humble and should look and listen to find out what is going on before imposing their ideas and projects.

As it happens, I was associated with the silk project from beginning to end, as I had been on the design team in 1994, helped supervise the project and led the ex-post evaluation in 2003. This was an almost unheard of close association in the World Bank project process. This close association meant that I really did have a chance to follow the development of ideas into actions and also to understand why some aspects worked and others did not. Yet again, the experience brought home to me the dichotomy between donor priorities and those of the folk the donors are so often claiming to help. Not that it was a total disaster – far from it – but its achievements were much less than they could or should have been.

Quite successful and not to be underrated was the effect of the project on policy. Basically, the monopoly of the BSB was weakened, and all sections of the industry were liberalised. Less successful was the evolution of the replacement industry's apex agency: the Silk Foundation. The project called for the establishment of the Silk Foundation to replace the BSB, and for it to be headed by the private sector (mainly silk weavers). It was a classic case of a Western idea of an industry association designed to represent the interests of all stakeholders, and it was during the WC period (see *Chapter 2*). The Silk Foundation began life when there were project funds, but it was clear by the close that it had little or no chance of long-term survival. Indeed, if you go on the web today, there are plenty of references to the BSB, but none to the Silk Foundation!

The production side was also a bit of a flop, as despite access to good DFLs from new producers, demand for domestically produced silk remained flat, largely because of cheap imports of higher-quality silk from China. We knew about this competition at the start of the project, but we persuaded ourselves that the problem would either go away or be resolved within the lifetime of the project. Sadly, another trait of many donor initiatives is to turn a blind eye to awkward issues that might result in derailment of the mainline idea. It would not matter too much if the donors took the financial risks associated with the ideas they peddle, but this is not the case with loans, even soft loans.

Integrated Pest Management (IPM) and the Chemical Tree Huggers

Encouraged by the apparent success of IPM in Indonesia (see 3.8.) and supported by colleagues within the FAO, a major effort was made to spread IPM and related farmer training methods throughout the developing world, starting in Asia. Other donors (e.g. the FAO, DFID, Danida, the World Bank and the EU) were all persuaded to fund projects aimed at spreading the 'gospel' of IPM. All the projects had core similarities and were based on the use of FFSs. Typically, they were not called IPM projects, as such, but had rather suggestive titles and a more general overall objective of improving crop/agricultural production through the adoption of environmentally friendly techniques that were simultaneously selected to improve output or production.

In Bangladesh, for example, two famous projects supported by the EU were the New Options for Pest Management (NOPEST) and Locally Intensified Farm Enterprises (LIFE). It was never explained why the projects had such imaginative names. One probable reason is that they were located within a Ministry of Agriculture, and many staff had close links with the pesticide industry. They would not have been keen on IPM without a little subterfuge. An ex-post evaluation of NOPEST and LIFE that I was involved with in 2004 provided a rare opportunity to look at IPM and FFS in depth. The evaluation was very thorough, and it involved structured interviews with approximately 25% of the project beneficiaries, some four years after the project ended, and statistical analysis of the results of the survey. The results were amazingly consistent: the vast majority of farmers were still using pesticides, and the overall use of pesticides by rice growers had been increasing by about 5–10% a year for the past 10 years. I was not involved in the interview programme, but I was responsible for the field verification of the survey results.

I recall a classic Potemkin set-up one afternoon. Dr Hussein from the Bangladesh Agricultural University and I were directed by project staff to a site where we would meet a group of local farmers, who we were told were using the IPM technologies. We duly arrived on schedule and started to talk to the group. It was quite clear it was a set-up. There were a few farmers in the group, but also a couple of well-dressed and well-educated folk who tended to answer all our questions in English on behalf of the farmers. After about 20 minutes, Dr Hussein said he thought we were wasting our time. We thanked everyone and left. On leaving the site, we came across a small roadside stall. We stopped and started talking to the owner, who said he sold quite a lot of pesticides to farmers in the area and sales had increased in the past few years. On another field visit, I asked a farmer if he used pesticides. When he said, 'Of course,' I asked whether he used gloves when applying products. 'Oh no,' he replied, 'I do not apply the pesticides. I hire someone else to do that, and it is up to him to wear gloves.' These and other spot-check visits confirmed the results of the survey.

As for the FFSs, they existed while the project was operational, but ceased the moment the field agents from the implementing NGO stopped visiting. What makes the results so interesting is that the training provided to farmers during the project was of high quality. The trainers were all graduates who had themselves received season-long training in how to grow a healthy crop using IPM. They were also very regular in their visits to farmer groups. So, poor training in IPM was not the main reason why farmers had not, by and large, adopted IPM methods of pest control.

There are three reasons why farmers remain unconvinced about IPM in Bangladesh. The first and most significant is economics. Most rice growers in Bangladesh have tiny plots of land (typically less than half a hectare), and they have to sell their labour for as many days as possible, as well as tending their own fields. If they use a pesticide to control a pest attack or as insurance against an attack, it costs them about the same as they would earn from a day of labouring (US$2). This then gives them 30 or more days in which they can sell their own labour, without having to worry about their own rice field. On the other hand, if they practice IPM, they have to visit the field every other day and walk through it to check on the ratio of pests to predators. If things look bad, they have to either make up botanical pesticides or use physical methods like netting, hand-picking of insect eggs and light trapping to control attacks. Not only are such methods cumbersome but they are very time-consuming, and the time spent on IPM represents lost earnings. The second reason is the fact that IPM only works if all your neighbours also practice it, and this is almost impossible to achieve in a society like Bangladesh. Thirdly, unlike the situation with the BPH in Indonesia, the main rice pests in Bangladesh (stem borers, hispa and thrips) are not susceptible to predation by other insects, so only physical IPM methods such as hand-picking pest eggs off leaves are appropriate.

The real question in my mind, however, is not really why IPM did not work in Bangladesh, but why these points were not fully factored into the project objectives and design? The answer to this question, I believe, lies in what I can only call 'cultural imperialism'. That is to say, we in the FAO and the West know how bad pesticides are (*Silent Spring* and its disciples). You in the developing world need protection from the wicked pesticide companies, and we are going to show you how to protect yourselves. These are noble and not entirely incorrect motives. But – and it is a huge but – the poor little Bangladeshi farmer does not have the luxury of being able to worry about the environment tomorrow or even his own long-term health prospects; he has to feed himself and his family today. His values are based on survival, not environmental niceties. A similar naivety can also be levelled at the FFS concept in a country like Bangladesh, which does not have a developed cultural tradition of neighbours helping each other.

Had these economic and cultural considerations been fully factored in at the time of the project's formulation, the project design would have been different. However, that would not have fitted in with the IPM/FFS mantra, which basically says, 'Do what we tell you to, and all will be okay.' In my opinion, if the FAO and its fellow travellers in the aid community are really concerned about pesticide damage to health and the environment, they should be campaigning to get the government to improve the attitudes and behaviour of the pesticide companies. After all, not all insecticides are equally harmful – some break down quite rapidly in hot climates and are not very damaging to mammals, but do an adequate job of controlling insect pests. Surely, the overall aim should be to get better information to everyone about all products, and the use of some products should be encouraged while attention is focused on banning the really nasty products.

As a postscript to the evaluation, there was a presentation of the report in FAO headquarters. It was presented before a small audience, including the main promoter of IPM globally. He did not really seem interested in our findings, but he was keen to know whether the survey questionnaires had been kept. The mission leader reported that they were still in the FAO office in Dhaka. 'Good,' said the IPM expert, 'I will ask for them to be sent here to headquarters so we can confirm your findings.' In fact, he simply wanted them destroyed to hide the embarrassment of the whole exercise. It is perhaps important to stress that this was not a funded project but a grant, so the poor Bangladeshi citizens were not liable for a failed loan. In fact, the big loser is the West, which once again pushed a non-viable concept, and in the process, ended up with, at best, egg on its face and, at worst, a deteriorated reputation for technical knowledge – the very opposite of the kind of thing it is so anxious to present to the developing world.

Country Programme Evaluation (CPE)

The IFAD, one of the more political UN agencies,[51] invited me to join a CPE in 2005, while I was still working for the FAO. The purpose was basically to review the portfolio of projects that the IFAD had funded over the previous 10 years. It came at a somewhat embarrassing time for the IFAD in Bangladesh, as the country programme manager – who was pretty useless – had left under a bit of a cloud. It seems he had been taking a cut of the project funds from the local NGO that had

---

51. I have seen quite a few IFAD projects at close quarters, and they are among the worst aid initiatives I have come across. Why this is so is not entirely clear, but one reason is that, to compete with other donors, the IFAD tends not to worry too much about how its funds are actually spent. The priority seems to be to get the money out, rather than worrying about what it is used for.

been overseeing the projects for some years. The projects in question were mainly wholesale microfinance projects, with a national NGO with headquarters in Dhaka being responsible for passing on bulk funding to smaller NGOs to on-lend to women's groups in the regions. If a little went astray, the only people who would know this were the country programme manager and the head of the national NGO.

An IFAD staff officer from headquarters briefed us on our arrival in the country, telling us that the IFAD already knew the bad news about the programme and so our job was to find the good news. When I heard this, I immediately realised the whole exercise was going to be a cover-up, and sure enough, we soon came across what the team leader described as a 'classic Potemkin story'. Somewhere in the north-west region, we were taken to a village where the project had constructed a small textile compound consisting of about 20 small booths or shops where local women were supposed to be making and selling garments as part of a job-creation initiative. When we arrived at the village, we found a lot of empty booths, but one or two had some clothes for sale and several contained sewing machines with local women sitting beside them. At first glance, one might have thought things were as they should have been, but the large number of vacant booths was less than convincing, as was the fact that none of the machines were actually being used. We only had an hour or so to talk to the local folk before we had to rush off to the next appointment, so we did not resolve the matter on the spot.

Fortunately – or unfortunately, depending on your perspective – one of our team, a local economist, was left behind in the rush to move on. When he finally caught up, he told us that after we had left, all of a sudden, the sewing machines were taken from the booths in which we had seen them. As we had suspected, the whole thing had been set up for our benefit. Later, in discussion, we realised that the whole idea was doomed from the start. This is because, to operate as a seamstress, each woman would have needed to secure the permission of her husband, which was unlikely to be forthcoming in such a backward area. This was yet another classic case of a failed Western intention.

The IFAD was aware of the shortcomings of the project, of course, but was desperate for our team to focus on the tiny bits of good news, as they were keen to keep Bangladesh as a client. After all, the IFAD only existed if it had countries willing to 'borrow' its money. To this effect, for the final mission meeting with the Ministry of Finance, they flew out the chief of evaluations – a slippery Swiss economist. He did most of the talking during the meeting, which – if nothing else – prevented any of the team saying very much.

I realised that this was one of those situations where going too public with criticism ran the risk of having my views censored. So, I kept quiet at the meeting and wrote a fairly tame paper for the mission report, which did not highlight the project failures but was highly equivocal. A careful reader would, however, have had no doubt that the agricultural component had not achieved its targets. This was compatible with the overall mission report, which concluded that the project was only moderately satisfactory.

Agricultural Research

This is a slightly tedious tale about a failure to develop effective institutional systems; however, I think it is important because it highlights the difficulties – if not the impossibility – of transporting or transferring management systems from one culture to another. Over a period of about 20 years, from the mid-1970s to the late 1990s, Bangladesh received substantial donor support to develop and strengthen its NARS. Efforts started with a series of USAID projects in the 1970s, which involved the construction of a number of research stations/institutes and staff training. These were followed by five World Bank-supported projects,[52] with the research components having a total value of US$88 million. A considerable number of commodities (e.g. rice, wheat, jute and livestock) research stations and substations were constructed and equipped, and a considerable number of scientists received postgraduate training overseas. For quite a while, a job with the NARS was regarded as a highly attractive career prospect. Not only were there new labs to work in and a good chance of a visit to the US, Europe or Australia for a year or so, there was also money for the operational costs of research programmes.

I had the chance to follow quite a bit of the progress of these projects from the mid-1980s until 2000, during which time I had a chance to look at the evaluation reports of the projects as well as see for myself what was happening on the ground. My conclusions, which I shared publicly at a DFID-funded seminar in Dhaka in 2003, were that there was almost no new technology that could be attributed to this public sector investment. Perhaps more surprising is the fact that no one at the seminar tried to challenge my observations. Indeed, Mr Mintu, a leading local entrepreneur who was present at the seminar, said I had been too generous with my remarks.

I did not suggest in my presentation that much of the World Bank funding had been stolen, though I had my suspicions. At the time, there was a story going round that US$1 million of project funds had been spent on printing 10,000 extension manuals. At $100 each, they would have been pretty expensive manuals, but in fact, none were ever seen. It was the usual bogus invoicing system employed by a complicit printer and NARS staff. I did not mention my suspicions in public – there was an unwritten convention at the time not to talk openly about corruption, as it was simply too embarrassing for the World Bank and its client governments.

---

52. Extension & Research I and II, Agricultural Research I and II, and the Agricultural Research Management Project.

Why was the World Bank supporting agricultural research in Bangladesh? The main – albeit unofficial – reason was it provided a great opportunity to 'get money out of the door'. The World Bank has pumped billions into agricultural research and extension throughout the developing world. It was an almost bottomless pit for about 30 years from the time McNamara started lending to agriculture. The official rationale was more prosaic, in that investment in agricultural research in the developed world, especially after the Second World War, had been very effective in developing new technologies.

On my first visit in 1987, I looked at quite a number of research stations that had been supported by the first World Bank project. What I saw shocked me. Almost all the stations had been situated in remote parts of the country, and no research was being undertaken. The choice of site reflected the need to carry out trials in all the important agroecological zones of the country. While there is some truth in this, most of the country has a very similar agroecology, and the real reason for the locations was political – namely the opportunity to provide some construction opportunities in remote areas that were normally ignored or forgotten by the politicos in Dhaka, the capital. Being in remote areas, few staff wanted to work at the stations because there were no schools for the children in the area and medical services were minimal. Indeed, in many of the stations, the specially built research-staff accommodation was unoccupied, equipment was still in its packing cases, and the fields were mainly being used to grow crops for sale. Things were a bit better at the Bangladesh Rice Research Institute, just outside Dhaka. They had managed to develop some improved rice varieties from germplasm supplied originally by the IRRI in the Philippines.

The World Bank acknowledged these early failures and disappointments, attributing them to weak institutional structures and poor research administration and management. Bangladesh had a very disjointed NARS with some 12 research institutions that reported to six different ministries. Even within the Ministry of Agriculture (the ministry with the largest number of institutes), each institute operated entirely independently of the other ministerial institutes, even when farming systems called for an integrated approach. The result was – and probably still is – that all national research funds are spread thinly over a wide range of commodities, with very limited prioritisation on key crops and farming systems. There was also considerable duplication of research trials and a tendency to repeat the same experiment year in, year out, rather than looking into new problems.

In an attempt to improve research planning and prioritisation, the World Bank introduced a new institution – the Bangladesh Agricultural Research Council (BARC). This was to be the apex agency with overall national responsibility for research planning and funding. By keeping everything in one agency, it was hoped the whole system would be streamlined and the unnecessary waste and duplication reduced. A brand-new building was constructed in the middle of Dhaka with World Bank funds, and staff were appointed and paid for by the second World Bank project. A DG was appointed to head up BARC, with the same civil service grade as all the other institution directors.

In the event, BARC became a kind of general service provider for the NARS, undertaking strategic studies and preparing special reports. In the late 1990s, with no more donor funding in prospect, BARC staff were told that, when they retired, their posts would be abolished and effectively the agency would be killed off. Subsequently, some of them have experienced a stay of execution, as after a gap of several years, during which the history of the earlier project failures was conveniently forgotten, they had a lucky break. What should have amazed me, but does not in view of what I have seen elsewhere, is that the World Bank completely ignored the lessons from the first research projects.

In fact, the World Bank has continued to throw money at agricultural research in the country. In the early years of first decade of the 21st century, it lent for the First National Agricultural Technology Project (NATP I). The emphasis of NATP I was on providing operational funds to support scientists in the already apparently adequately equipped institutes. The operational funding was to follow competitive bidding procedures. That is to say, scientists were encouraged to prepare and submit proposals for research projects they considered to be priorities. A peer review mechanism would then select the lucky few.

A similar competitive contracting approach had been tried under an earlier project for agricultural extension. It failed totally, with all sorts of corrupt tricks being played. In 2009, NATP I was already being talked about as a problem project by the World Bank supervision mission, according to a consultant very familiar with the sector in Bangladesh. The Second National Agricultural Technology Project (NATP II), approved in 2015, had a total cost of US$215 million, with a World Bank contribution of US$176 million. Undeterred, it was followed by NATP IIA.

I think these agricultural research stories demonstrate three things. The first is the difficulty in transferring the management systems and methods associated with scientific research from one culture to another. To some considerable extent, this is a function of the fact that good science often takes a long time and dedication. In particular, it calls for regular funding and secure career prospects. Sadly, these are things that cannot be guaranteed by donor-funded projects that end all of a sudden, unless, of course, national governments can be persuaded to honour their earlier commitments and ensure adequate funding after the donor project has ended. The second – and equally serious – lesson is the blindness shown by the World Bank to fundamental weaknesses in their project designs. Rather than facing these head-on, they continue to come up with lame explanations that they claim can be fixed with yet more World Bank money. Finally, it shows how attempts to solve complex institutional issues with a single bullet approach (i.e. BARC) are often doomed to failure.

3.14. Zambia: Pestilence and Sweet Nothings

Poisonous Sips

This is a very sad story about a big confidence trick, arising from a series of little confidence tricks, and how they were covered up. In the late 1980s, a new idea swept through parts of the aid community. Instead of having lots of little projects funded by lots of donors, all trying to fly their own flags, there should be one big project in each main economic subsector, usually known as a SIP or a 'sector-wide approach'. Financing would be shared by a consortium of donors and the recipient government.

There had reportedly been some success with such an approach with a roads-and-transport SIP in Tanzania. The concept was being heavily promoted by the World Bank, and in particular, by an arrogant Swiss staffer, who had originally trained as an agricultural engineer and who had the ear of the then president, Jim Wolfensohn. For an international agency that prides itself on the promotion of pluralism and good governance, the World Bank had an amazing capacity for old-fashioned patronage, and few ever dared challenge those known to have a direct line to the boss.

The agricultural sector in Zambia had been identified as a prime candidate for a SIP. In 1992, a new government, which purported to support market liberalisation rather than state control, had just been elected. The new minister of agriculture was a leading player in the cabinet of Frederick Chiluba, the bus-conductor-turned-president. The price of copper – the country's main export – was down, and agriculture was seen as the new engine for economic growth. The larger-than-life Swiss national gave his approval. A series of missions from Washington went to Zambia to bring the government and the major donors together to agree on the investments and activities to be funded by the Agricultural Sector Investment Programme (ASIP). As part of the preparation process, a huge number of Zambian nationals were contracted to produce studies and proposals for projects to be included. Not surprisingly, all the national consultants wrote reports favourable to ASIP, so the World Bank was able to point to genuine national consultation and ownership. Confidence trick number one had satisfactorily been accomplished.

The second trick, getting all the donors into line, was much more difficult – but there are methods of persuasion. Full basket funding was never really achieved;

instead, the subsectors were parcelled out to the different donors with a bizarre and hopeless supervising system, which was meant to coordinate all programme activities. The more recalcitrant donors almost literally had their ears bashed.

During the period of project preparation, the first secretary of aid in the Netherlands embassy in Lusaka spoke up very loudly against ASIP. As a qualified veterinarian, he knew that some of the livestock proposals being made were very unwise, to say the least. He related how he got a call from The Hague one morning, from a senior diplomat in the Netherlands who told him – in no uncertain terms – to stop making trouble for the ASIP preparation. Not long after, he was transferred and then left the service. He told me this story over a mug of coffee in his office in the new consultancy partnership he had subsequently started in the capital, Lusaka, and I have no reason to doubt anything he told me. Confidence trick number two had been achieved by some high-level arm-twisting, no doubt following some off-the-record calls from Washington to The Hague.

The third trick came right at the end. It was a blatant manipulation of the findings of the evaluation team I led, which had been sent to prepare the evaluation or implementation completion report (ICR) in April 2002. For various reasons, not least of which was experience of south-eastern Africa and of ICR procedures, I was volunteered to lead the mission. I put together what I considered to be a strong team of experts with good knowledge of agriculture in southern Africa. We shared our findings quite openly while in Zambia, with both donor and government staff, and there was a general consensus that our assessment of the project's failures was correct.

One major project failure with international repercussions was the decision to privatise prophylactic veterinary care and make smallholders pay for the control of a serious tick-borne disease. Before the project, the government operated a number of strategically located dip tanks where cattle could be dipped for free. Dipping was the most effective way of removing the ticks that transmit the East Coast fever virus. Although free to cattle owners, the dipping system cost the government quite a lot of money. The World Bank, in its quest for privatising services, was persuaded that ticks could be satisfactorily removed by spraying cattle with a toxic chemical and, furthermore, that cattle owners would be willing to pay for the sprayers and the chemical. This aspect of privatisation failed totally, and today East Coast fever is rife in Zambia, threatening the livelihoods of stockholders there and in neighbouring countries, and eliminating any beef-export potential the country had.

The mission returned to Rome and wrote up the ICR, according to the structured guidelines called for by the World Bank. We had our ICR peer reviewed and approved in-house, and according to protocol, sent it over as a draft to the World Bank project task team leader. Normally, we would then get back some suggestions for changes or corrections of factual errors, and we would submit a final corrected version. Instead, I just got a one-line email saying he thought our criticism had been a bit too hard.

Some six months later, I received a copy of the final version of the ICR. All our assessments had been upgraded, much of the text had been changed, and yet my name had been left on the front page as the primary author![53] I protested quietly to my managers, but almost to a man their response was, 'What are you making such a fuss about? Surely you are not surprised?' Well, of course I was not surprised – I had expected something like this to happen. But I have prepared more than 10 ICRs in my time, and never before had the World Bank tried to rewrite the story quite so blatantly; I thought my management ought to give me some support and not be totally supine. I learnt later that the World Bank was reviewing its funding of our unit in the FAO at the time, and it was not a good time for our management to stand on principle.

Unlike many of these stories, however, this one actually had a happy ending. Some two years after I received the printed version of the ICR 'attributed' to me, I learnt to my delight that the internal quality control unit within the World Bank – the OED – had undertaken a subsequent assessment of their own ICR, and this had led to the project ratings being downgraded from those published by the task team leader back to what I had recommended. This was doubly rewarding to me, as the author of the revised evaluation had previously appraised another of my ICRs (for a project in Bangladesh) that he had fully endorsed. In other words, here, at last, was someone who was saying things as they really are or were, rather than opting for a quiet life and to keep the system running. The lesson for me from the experience was like the lesson from Sudan in 1985: what matters ultimately is the truth, and even in the aid business (as in most others), it is best to be straight and not try to gild the lily too much. The truth is likely to come out eventually, and the winners will be those with integrity rather than interests.

I cannot resist another short postscript to this story. Some five years after my first encounter with the task team leader of the Zambia SIP, I ended up working with him again, this time in Pakistan on an avian influenza project. As before, he tried to tell me what to do, but this time, he did not try very hard, and I managed the mission on my own terms. I think he knew that I would not have been asked to lead the mission in Pakistan if the World Bank did not respect my technical judgement and competence. We were – I hasten to add – perfectly civil to one another, but as expected, there was no real empathy between us. Perhaps this is a good place to remind the reader of the suggestion made in the introduction to this book that development aid can be a good business to be in and those unsure

---

53. We had scored the overall outcome as 'highly unlikely'; the task manger had changed that to 'unsatisfactory'. We had scored the institutional development impact as 'negligible'; the task manager had changed this to 'modest'. I could go on, but you get the drift.

of their own ability, understandably, do their best to tell the bosses what they think they want to hear – at least in the short run – in order to keep their jobs. I was lucky I told it as I saw it and still kept my job. Not all was rotten in the State of Denmark.

Honey Trees

In late 2005, I led a team undertaking a mid-term review of a forestry project funded by the IFAD in the north of the country. A key thrust of the project was to try to create livelihoods for forest dwellers by intensifying the collection of wild honey and other forest products, such as edible fungi. This was to be achieved largely by introducing better hives and providing marketing services for the honey gathered. Our job was to see whether things had progressed well in the early years of the project and whether any modifications were needed for the final years.

It was not easy to get hold of any hard data, but we soon realised that this was another unmitigated disaster. One evening about halfway through the mission when the team was up country in Ndola, we got together after supper, and I asked everyone to provide an assessment of the project from what they had seen so far. I suggested they write a number from one to ten on a piece of paper. A score of one was to indicate a very poor performance and ten indicated a very good performance. I then collected the bits of paper from the six of us. Not one had given a score higher than three, and there were several ones. So what had gone wrong? Well, the main problem, as so often, was the project design. Apart from the honey gathering, there were no really viable commercial activities to promote, and the honey gathering had been hijacked by the international NGO responsible for processing and marketing the honey.

To help with the honey production, a couple of German beekeepers had been persuaded to work alongside the project. They were backed by German aid funds and worked in an advisory capacity. They asked to meet us in the German embassy and said they were not at all happy with much of what they had seen. They explained they were sure that the NGO responsible for marketing the wild honey was only passing on a small percentage of sales revenue to the gatherers and was pocketing the rest. Our findings supported this claim, and the Germans pulled out, not wanting to get involved in any sticky business if they were found out to be the whistle-blowers.

The other big revelation came a bit later when we discovered that, at the halfway stage, the national management team funded by the project had already spent their entire budget for the whole lifetime (five years) of the project. In addition, they wanted us to endorse a massive increase in their budget. If the project had been going well, we might have been sympathetic, but given the mess we found, this was out of the question. All we could do was pass the request on to the donor. If the IFAD felt an increase was in order, it would be up to them.

The overall lesson learnt was not really a new one as much as a confirmation of Peter Bauer's observation that aid is often a tax on poor people in rich countries and a gift to rich people in poor countries, and affirmation that the IFAD is one of the worst offenders of this inverted taxation.

3.15. Bhutan: Bird Flew

One of the most popular destinations for 'development tourists' is the Buddhist Kingdom of Bhutan. The country is very small and difficult to get into. Even *bona fide* aid workers need to go through an elaborate ritual to get a visa. The airport at Paro is not for the faint-hearted traveller. The flight in has the plane flying down a valley with hilltops on either side, way above the wings of the plane, followed by a tight right turn at the end of the valley for the final approach. This is followed by a dreadful journey to Thimphu, the capital, up a winding road that clings to hillsides before darting suddenly across narrow bridges over fast-flowing streams. The whole journey seems designed to keep casual visitors at bay.

Bhutan is superficially – and, indeed, philosophically – very different from almost anywhere else I have visited. Nowhere else can one expect to see large images of an erect penis painted on the walls of both public buildings and private houses. It is also, as far as I know, the only country where visitors are forbidden to bring in cigarettes. This is reported to be to discourage the locals from smoking, although judging by the fact that many of the young people I saw were smoking, the ruling does not seem to have much effect! All male government employees wear the rather garrulous and colourful traditional robes, and the national sport is archery. Both are features that give the place a quaint look, as far as the visitor is concerned.

Scenically, Bhutan is spectacular, but travelling around is not easy as the roads are very narrow and winding. It took me eight hours to drive from the capital Thimphu to Phuentsholing in the south of the country – a distance of 175 kilometres. When I was there, the hotels and hostels were basic, to say the least. It is very cold in winter, and the food is dominated by a ghastly kind of chilli pepper and a cheese dish known as *ema datshi* – an acquired taste if ever there was one.

My visits in 2007 were associated with the global avian influenza (aka H5N1 bird flu) scares in the early years of the 21st century. The World Bank had made available a large amount of money (US$500 million) to help affected countries prepare for an outbreak by strengthening their quarantine and veterinary services. It was all a bit surreal, as with less than 50,000 intensively reared chickens in a couple of farms, Bhutan was very low risk as far as bird flu was concerned. Almost all poultry meat consumed in the country was, in fact, imported frozen. Being good Buddhists, the citizens of Bhutan never deliberately kill animals themselves.

The conclusion of our mission was that Bhutan was not a priority for bird flu funds, and this was fully supported by veterinary colleagues in the regional FAO office in Bangkok. The World Bank, however, was less inclined to look at the science than to see another chance to get involved in Bhutan. It was also the case that there was grant money available from the World Bank for bird flu initiatives, and Bhutan was determined to have its share. The World Bank was also keen to keep a foot in the door of Bhutan – it is next door to China, after all, and it has financed a number of very successful hydropower projects in Bhutan. For all intents and purposes, it was a political visit.

So, despite our report that the country did not really need a bird flu project, I duly went back a few months later as the leader of a team preparing a project for the World Bank, or more strictly, support from the IDA. By this time, the big players in the region had already dipped into the trough, and there was only about $1.5 million left for little Bhutan. I was nevertheless advised that perhaps I had misunderstood the geography of the country, and that I had better visit the area of the border with India to see for myself how the disease might cross over from India and how better quarantine facilities at Phuentsholing were needed.

I had to agree that, in theory, it would be quite possible for an unscrupulous trader to bring diseased fowl or eggs into Bhutan from India. However, no amount of official security would be able to dissuade a determined trader who could easily slip across an unmanned section of the border, and no amount of equipment at the official crossing would stop such an event, just as no one had stopped me from slipping into India from Bhutan for a short while.[54]

Back in Thimphu, we continued our discussions with the staff of the Ministry of Agriculture. Well, that is what we tried to do. The problem was that, for reasons not spelt out to us, the ministry had split into two the section responsible for animal disease control. The old bit was left with the veterinary diagnostic laboratory, just outside Thimphu. This was where we felt any investment should be focused. These projects were designed to be preventative. That is to say, to help countries identify an outbreak as soon as possible and take measures to stop its spread. To this effect, diagnosis at the veterinary laboratory was the project priority. Unfortunately, the new section for disease control thought they should get the lion's share of any goodies going.

I had one of my two moments of real discomfort while carrying out my official duties during this second visit to the country. I am not, by training, a veterinarian, but most of what we were proposing in our projects was preordained by either

---

54. When we got to Phuentsholing, my guides asked me if I would like to slip across the border into India. I was not sure this was a good idea, but I was assured it would be okay, and it was.

standard veterinary or medical procedure, plus a dose of common sense. Bhutan, with less than 50,000 chickens in the country and no wet markets, was a very low risk for an outbreak of H5N1.

During the course of our work there, I upset the young graduate in charge of the new disease control unit, who wanted to install an X-ray machine at the airport to check whether people coming in from India were importing frozen chicken in their luggage. During disease outbreaks, it is standard practice to forbid imports from affected countries, and India had suffered a few outbreaks. I felt this was a ridiculous idea, as only live birds carry the virus, and the limited resources available for the project in Bhutan were better spent on other things. I advised the young graduate how much of the project I felt we could allocate to him, and I asked him to get back to me to confirm that this was acceptable.

Sadly, he decided to play dirty and did not get back to me. Instead, at the public mission wrap-up meeting, he said I had not listened to him and that I had unilaterally reduced the allocation for his section, the disease control unit. I explained my reasoning at the meeting, but clearly, I was dealing with someone who was used to getting his own way. The older guys from the old disease control unit, who I thought had agreed with me and who were to benefit most, stayed ominously quiet.

At the meeting, the young Bhutanese virologist spoke in favour of developing his newly formed disease control section, and as part of this, he repeated his plan, saying he wanted the project to pay for, *inter alia*, X-ray equipment at the airport. Given that any freezing would have killed off any virus material, this was simply stupid. However, although very junior, he was obviously much higher up the social scale than the guys we had been working with; he wore the official dress of senior members of the ruling caste. I made the mistake of challenging him publicly, saying this was neither what had been agreed nor what was needed. It may have been that he was acting on orders and the X-ray machines were really intended to pick up cigarette smugglers. Whatever the real reason, the Bhutanese wanted the X-ray machines – though they were not going to be of any use as far as bird flu was concerned. I said as much during the final wrap-up meeting, and quite a heated discussion arose. To calm things down, the World Bank staff present said all would be resolved during the next and final mission, and the wrap-up meeting came to an end.

Afterwards, the World Bank staff on the mission let it be known that they were certainly upset with me, and I got a quite severe dressing down. I tried to explain where I was coming from, and although they could see my technical logic, the leader of the World Bank team let it slip that it was very important not to upset 'the client'. At this point, I realised that, as so often, technology had got in the way of politics and process, and as the awkward messenger, I was the one likely to get shot.

Shortly after this, when back in my office in Rome, I received a call to say I would not be needed on the final project preparation team. I was neither surprised nor disappointed. There is, after all, a price to pay for integrity.

Of course, there is no new moral here; it is simply another case of the powerful making a grab for easy money, and the World Bank being its usual helpful self – all the more so if it can get the money out as simply as possible. It might also have had quite a lot to do with existing World Bank investments in Bhutan. The national economy is quite healthy, largely due to the export of electric power to India. India has constructed at least three large hydropower plants in Bhutan, and the income from these exports keeps the country afloat. Just before my trip, the national airline had purchased two A319 aircraft from Airbus Industries for cash. They had chosen the A319 as it is very manoeuvrable and can make the tight turn around the mountains during the approach to the airport at Paro.

3.16. Grenada 2004: Nuts in November and February

In the autumn of 2004, Grenada was badly hit by Hurricane Ivan, a category three storm that caused an immense amount of damage. I was sent on a short mission to see how bad things were from an agricultural perspective. The island lies in the equatorial belt, just north of the equator, and the main crop of economic significance in Grenada is nutmeg. The Indonesian island of Flores, which is the other main global source of nutmeg, lies in the same belt but just south of the equator. It is clearly an ecologically fussy tree. It is also a rather delicate tree with weak timber that cannot stand strong winds – almost every tree on the island had been blown over. My job was to see what, if anything, the international community could do to resurrect the nutmeg industry. The island was still in shock when I arrived, and it was not easy to get into the field, but I managed to visit at least one area of production near the capital, St George's. On my return to Rome, I advised that the situation was serious and suggested a follow-up mission.

A few months later, in early 2005, three of us – a horticulturalist, an economist and I – set off for the island to see if it made any sense to rehabilitate the nurseries for nutmeg and cocoa (the other important tree crop on the island). Soon after we arrived, we went out to revisit the site I had briefly visited on my first visit. It was one of the most useful field visits I made in more than 40 years of tramping round farmer's fields. There, beneath the remains of the fallen nutmeg tree I had seen on my first visit, were half a dozen healthy seedlings, each about 25 centimetres tall.

The next thing we discovered was that the cocoa nursey had survived the storm, but there was no nutmeg nursery anywhere on the island. A few further questions to staff from the Grenada Co-operative Nutmeg Association (GCNA) confirmed that most of the trees that had been blown over were some 50 years old, and they could trace their origin back to Hurricane Janet in 1958. In other words, nutmeg trees effectively self-seed, and there was no need for a nutmeg tree nursery. Furthermore, our economist had established that the GCNA had some 7,000 tonnes of nutmeg in store, equal to more than twice the annual global demand, and that the shortage arising from Hurricane Ivan was the best thing since sliced bread as far as they were concerned, as it meant a price rise was inevitable.

Our visit was not entirely a waste of time. We had ruled out the need for a special nutmeg rehabilitation project, but we had alerted donors and nationals to the need to be careful when clearing up the remains of the fallen nutmeg trees. In particular, Oxfam had swamped the island with power strimmers to help clear vegetation around homesteads. We managed to arrange a workshop to discuss what we had found, and advised all (including the sensible Oxfam staffer) that great care should be taken when clearing land around fallen nutmeg trees, so as not to cut down and kill young nutmeg seedlings.

Nutmeg aside, there was perhaps another side to the interest of the West in Grenada at the time, and the opportunity to show the nice side of the capitalist face was almost certainly in the shadows behind the genuine concerns about the damage caused by the hurricane. This is not really the place to examine in detail the short history of Marxist rule in Grenada (1979–83). However, as with quite a number of the Caribbean islands, Grenada was home to Cuban-inspired and supported leftists at that time. In fact, the communist reign was staunched fairly swiftly by a US invasion in 1983. However, ever since the invasion, the West has kept its eyes on the island, ready to prevent any revival of communism, and Hurricane Ivan was a golden opportunity to fly the Western flag. I am pretty certain of this political dimension for two reasons: the first was the ease with which I secured the okay and funding for a second mission; and the second was that, while I was on the island, the then president of the World Bank, Jim Wolfensohn, paid a flying visit to see for himself what needed to be done to shore up Western/US interests. I had hoped to meet him and prepared myself in discussions with some of his staff, but in the end, he cut his visit short. I suspect he was adequately reassured that a communist revival was not likely and that his big cheque was not needed.

3.17. Botswana: False Promises

Nickel and a Dime

In the spring of 2009, having retired from the FAO, I was persuaded by another retiree to join a mission to Botswana, funded by the European Commission (EC).

I must admit to having certain doubts about the whole exercise after reading the proposed mission's terms of reference, but I accepted the offer and duly arrived in Gaborone, the capital city, on 15 April 2009.

The mission was not without its moments, and it was nice to be back in southern Africa. However, this is not a travelogue tale but yet another exposure of the darker side of development. The purpose of the mission was ostensibly to look at economic diversification activities for the mine workers of Selebi-Phikwe, in the event that the nickel mine and related smelter closed within the next five years or so.[55] Aware of this possibility, a 'diversification unit', funded by the EU and headed by an expatriate consultant, had been set up in the town of Selebi-Phikwe. Some previous consultants from Ireland had suggested that there might be good prospects for agriculture – in particular, for intensive horticulture – as a diversification intervention. In turn, they had based their suggestions on some earlier consultants' reports, which seemed to indicate that there might be enough water from two large dams in the area to irrigate about 1,750 hectares.

The first thing we discovered when we met with officials of the Ministry of Agriculture was that no one had any idea of this proposed development, and furthermore, that most of the land in the area was unsuitable for irrigation. Our next discovery was that there was no water available for irrigation from either of the two dams. Indeed, it is declared government policy that all reservoir-stored water is for domestic and industrial use only.

At this point, I began to smell a bit of a rat and looked again at my terms of reference. They clearly referred to the two dams and the area of 1,750 hectares. However, when I showed this to the mission leader, he said something must be wrong as the mission's terms of reference did not refer to the dams or the areas specifically. I did not press the matter, but obviously, between the time of my terms of reference being prepared and the final approval by the EU authorities in Gaborone, someone had woken up to the possibility that the water and areas were more mythical than real. So, the final terms of reference was a fudge.

So what was the back story? The situation was – as it so often is in development – convoluted. Under the eighth European Development Fund (EDF) disbursements, Botswana had been allocated €30 million for the economic diversification of the mining sector. The funds were granted to the government of Botswana (GOB), which on-lent them to two state-owned mines. The interest and capital repayments of the two loans were then deposited in a redeployment account to be used to finance activities aimed at diversifying the economy of Selebi-Phikwe. Although, strictly speaking, these were GOB funds, during the period of the eighth EDF

---

55. The mine was owned at the time by a Russian company, and it is more than possible that our mission was partly a way of keeping an eye on what the company was up to.

(which ended in December 2009), the EC could – with GOB agreement – use some of the redeployment funds for studies related to diversification. The idea being that the studies would, *inter alia*, provide details of the subsequent cost of interventions to diversify the economy of the town. The most important point was the date. After December 2009, the EC lost access to the funds, and so was open to pressure from European consultancy companies to agree to pay for as many studies and related inputs as possible before that date.

Our study was simply one of the diversification studies that had been very broadly identified by the Irish consultants: a little money-spinner for a European consultancy, providing they could convince the EC delegation in Gaborone of the need for a study. If it had been clear at the start that there were really very limited prospects for agriculture in the area, then there would have been no point in the study. I know from discussions with the staff of the delegation that they had entertained their doubts about the viability of the whole idea. However, they did not have the time or resources to check things out for themselves. The consultancy company that had hired the two of us, aware of the problem, had the original terms of reference massaged by the diversification unit in Selebi-Phikwe to exclude any direct references to the two sites. It worked – the EU delegation in Gaborone gave the go-ahead and funds were committed.

We held various meetings and discussions with folk in and around the mine and in the capital. We wrote up our findings, and I like to think that by telling the real story – that there is no available water in the region for large-scale irrigation – we at least prevented any further waste of resources. It is also the case that the GOB could have stopped the whole nonsense if they had spoken out against the study, and one cannot really blame the German consultancy company we were hired by for picking off the low-hanging fruit. It is just a bit sad to think that the €100,000 spent on the study – which was to all intents and purposes wasted – could have been used more effectively. There is no moral to the story, just another observation that development processes and systems can be and are constantly abused by both donors and recipients.

Diamonds Are Not Forever

During the course of the work I did in Botswana in 2009, I came across one of the worst examples of agricultural consultancy advice I have ever seen. It was so bad that I think the story has to be recorded. In the late 1990s, an Israeli firm was commissioned to undertake a major study of the agricultural potential of the country. Their report, which was based on an exhaustive technical review of existing data and some new investigations, came up with a handful of technical recommendations that seemed to take little account of the social and cultural features of the country. One of the main findings of the study was to confirm the shortage of water for agriculture in much of the country and that all possible sources should be used. It recommended that, close to the main towns, treated sewage water should be used for intensive horticulture. This is not intrinsically a bad idea, but to make maximum use of the water, the consultants recommended using high-tech glasshouses in which temperature and humidity could be controlled, liquid fertiliser could be injected into the drip-irrigation systems, and plants would be grown on coconut coir rather than soil. Initially, the idea was that a couple of these sophisticated units would be operated as demonstrations, after which a cluster of farmers would take over the running of the facilities.

In the event, the two pilot demonstrations became little more than a sad joke. Nearly 10 years later, they were being run by a unit of the Ministry of Agriculture and were rapidly falling into a state of disrepair. So much so that a tender was issued in the first half of 2009 for a new glasshouse to replace one that was giving up. As if this were not enough, farmers complained that the government production was undercutting their efforts to make a living!

At one of the sites, there was an even sorrier story. Some 17 hectares of land had been planted with olive trees. It is clear that 17 hectares would never produce enough to justify an oil mill, so any olives would have to be sent to South Africa for processing – and as most of the value-addition takes place as a result of processing, there is not much in the concept for Botswana.

Then there was the dairy scheme. Botswana imports most of its fresh milk, but with it having a large cattle herd, no doubt someone thought some of the females could be used for milk production. The trouble is that almost all the cattle in Botswana are for beef, and beef breeds are rarely good milkers, so expensive dairy cattle needed to be brought in. Such animals require reliable sources of high-quality feed if they are to yield well. Such feed is not available in Botswana and has to be imported from South Africa.

Not surprisingly, this was yet another scheme that failed. The backstory to this sorry saga will, I am sure, never be revealed, but I suspect there is a connection somewhere between the South African company responsible for Botswana's diamond industry and the recruitment of the Israeli consultants. After all, Israel is one of the most well-known diamond-cutting centres. Sadly, the diamond industry in Botswana has currently lost its sparkle, and so it would seem has one of its offspring.

I find it sad at best, and dishonest at worst, that reputable technical advisers can be so short-sighted and not focus their advice on technologies appropriate to the technical competence of the intended beneficiaries. While I was there, I learnt that the government had woken up to the issue, and the Israeli technical advisers were having difficulty in getting their contracts renewed.

So what are the lessons, if any, that can be drawn from this experience? My first thought is that things might have been different if the Ministry of Agriculture had enough competent senior staff able to challenge, or at least guide, the external advisers. The trouble is that, in such a hierarchical society, I doubt that this would be sufficient. There was almost certainly some vested interests within the higher echelons of the government in the selection of the advisers, and they would not relish having to explain why such a mess has been made.

3.18. Farmer Training: Touch and Vanish

After the Second World War when the colonial influence was still apparent, agricultural extension or farmer training was largely self-financing in many countries in South Asia. The village-level worker (VLW) was an agricultural graduate paid a small stipend by the state. Much of his income, however, came from commissions he made on selling inputs and veterinary medicines. The system kept the costs to the government low and encouraged the VLW to be active. If he slept on the job, his commission earnings would be negligible. The system had its flaws, but on the whole, it seemed to work quite well. However, it is true that the emphasis was on training farmers to improve export-crop output, rather than to improve food-crop production.

Things began to change following the green revolution in the 1970s, which called for more intensive farming methods and, in particular, for the training of farmers in how best to use the new technologies demanded by the new dwarf wheat and rice varieties.[56] The World Bank, which was heavily involved in promoting the green revolution, became frustrated by the old extension systems in India and Pakistan. They wanted something that would get more farmers to adopt new technologies as soon as they were available.

In the early 1970s, long before I joined the FAO, the World Bank started promoting a new form of agricultural extension called Training and Visit (T&V) (Van den Ban and Samanta, 2006). As so often with novel World Bank approaches, it looked good on paper as a cost-effective way of getting farmers to use better production techniques. The basic idea was to get a leading or progressive farmer to train a nearby cohort of similar producers. The leading or contact farmer would be taught by a specially trained government officer, known as an 'extension officer'. Each

56. The famous wheat breeder Norman Borlaug would only allow seed of his new dwarf wheat varieties to be sold in India if the farmers were also provided with access to fertiliser, pesticides and training on how best to use these production inputs.

extension officer would receive special training in crop or livestock production, which they would then impart to their leading farmers. It was all a bit militaristic, with each extension officer supposed to visit bi-weekly a given number of contact farmers, and receive regular training himself from subject-matter specialists. There was also a built-in link between research scientists and extension officers through subject-matter specialists. Each extension officer would keep a diary to record the names of the contact farmers visited and knowledge imparted, together with any special features. Pilots of the approach had seemed to work for irrigation projects in Turkey (Ceyhan) and in India (Madhya Pradesh and Rajasthan), and the clever guys in Washington thought this sufficient evidence to launch the idea globally.

The T&V system of extension, colloquially known as 'Touch and Vanish' in India, was the brain child of the big-brained president of the World Bank, Robert McNamara – he of Ford Motor Company and Vietnam War fame, who once said, 'Brains, like hearts, go where they are appreciated.' Sometime after he became president of the World Bank (1968–81), he visited Israel and was particularly impressed with the fruit farms he visited in and around Beersheba in the Negev Desert. He noticed that all the farms seemed to be using similar production technologies and getting high yields. He asked how this had come about and was subsequently introduced to the senior agricultural extension officer in the region, Daniel Benor. Benor explained his system of T&V was based on a few highly trained extension officers passing on information to a wide range of farmers through visiting contact farmers.

McNamara, who knew next to nothing about agriculture in the developing world, was captivated and offered Benor a job on the spot. Benor was nothing if not crafty, and turned down the offer initially, saying he would rather stay in Israel. McNamara persisted and is alleged to have asked Benor, 'What would make you change your mind and come to work for me?' The answer he got was 'An office next to yours and an agreement that I never have to write reports.' Robert agreed, and so T&V became part of the World Bank's mantra, and it started pushing out T&V projects as fast as it could. In total, I estimate that at least US$4 billion was spent on such projects globally – most of it in the form of World Bank or IDA loans. Anyone challenging the system was sent to sit on the naughty step.

To make things even worse, the World Bank's chief economist at the time, Ernie Stern – the ex-Peace Corps manager who virtually ran the World Bank until Lewis Preston took over as president – was on record as saying to his staff that there was no point in doing economic rate-of-return calculations for extension projects. He considered that conventional cost–benefit analyses were not relevant or needed for T&V projects. This was because of the problem of attributing the impact. According to him, it was not possible to assess the impact of extension because of the difficulty of knowing what the before-project baseline situation was. In most agricultural situations, this background information was not known, and in such situations, cost–benefit analyses were simply guesses, so it was better not to waste time doing academic calculations. Furthermore, any benefits might come from things beyond the control of the extension staff, such as good weather, changes in prices or better varieties. Instead, it was simply assumed that such projects would pay for themselves in the long run through the increased output of food.

To make things even less speculative, there was no way of capturing any income from the increased output to pay for the loan, as few – if any – poor farmers paid taxes on their crop sales. The only tax that might have been raised in much of South Asia was octroi – an arcane tax levied on goods transported on public roads. However, macro-economists in the World Bank had long wanted to abolish octroi, which they saw as distorting and inhibiting trade, as well as providing an opportunity for corruption. Road tolls on bridges built with World Bank money support were fine, but not the old-fashioned vestiges of colonial administrative rule – they had to be expunged. In fact, T&V was a total scam, and a cynic might be tempted to say that the ideas of Ernie Stern were, in the main, designed to please McNamara, who saw agriculture as a key sector for support in developing countries for strategic reasons.

After the Second World War, some Western political strategists who had observed the success of Mao in China, the emergencies in Malaysia and the political background of the Vietcong in Vietnam believed that any communist insurrection would start in the rural space. It was therefore important not to ignore the rural space. Historical analyses since the 1960s have challenged the idea that revolution starts in the rural space. It is true that the rural population was involved in these revolutions, but that was under duress and through control by clever communist manipulators. The rural folk were not the instigators of trouble. Indeed, life was so precarious for most rural families in Asia that there was no spare time, money or energy for insurrection.

When I joined the FAO/CP in 1984, it was a capital offence to even think about criticising T&V. Such projects were being implemented or were about to start almost everywhere. The World Bank had operations in dozens of countries in Africa and Asia, and large sums of money – and promotion prospects – were at stake. So overwhelming was the push for T&V that the FAO's own extension service, which had not formally endorsed T&V, was effectively wiped out.

Of course, all would have been alright if T&V had done the job and led to production increases that more than covered its own costs in some way. This might have been the case from savings on food imports that were avoided as a result of increased production. The trouble is that it did not work for three main reasons. Firstly, few NARSs were able to keep up the production of new useful technologies and so the system soon ran out of messages to deliver. Secondly, partly because of a shortage of messages and partly because they never got paid their travel money, few extension workers kept up their regular routine visits to their contact farmers. I well recall finding this out for myself during a trip to Baluchistan to review a T&V programme in late 1986. Thirdly, there was the problem of contact farmers: few, if any, farmers really wanted this honour, and even those who did want it had no means of getting round the patch to visit their neighbours– unlike their Israeli forerunners.

Furthermore, the idea of sharing good ideas is often anathema in a competitive world, especially where markets are inefficient. Why should farmer A tell farmer B how to produce more wheat if the net result is a price fall that hurts both growers? In Israel, with its efficient cooperative marketing systems, it was in all the farmers' interests to produce as much good-quality produce as possible to encourage cooperative activity and growth. These criticisms were well known from the start, but few had the courage to voice them out loud when faced by the 'wisdom' of the 'wise' men in Washington.

The whole nonsense might still be going on now if the cost side of the equation had not come into the open. These projects were not cheap. There were substantial capital investments in buildings (housing and staff offices), transport (cars and motorbikes), staff training (at home and abroad) and expensive international TA, and there were substantial annual running costs (staff salaries and operational costs). Indeed, it was just these shopping lists that made the World Bank's managers purr with approval. In the first years of the project, all incremental annual operating costs, including the salaries of the newly appointed staff, were paid for by the project. With no initial demands on the Ministry of Agriculture budget, it was quite easy to persuade the incumbent minister that he or she needed a T&V project. It was, for them, a golden opportunity for patronage, and they would almost certainly have moved to another ministry by the time the problems began to appear.

Things were less rosy in the eyes of the people in the treasury and finance. They could see the longer-term cost implications when the projects no longer covered the annual salary and operating costs, and of course, they wanted to see the benefit stream from the investment. This, however, was not easy to show. The basic facts are that in no country did any T&V project generate any meaningful or taxable revenue, and it did not take too long before T&V lost favour in the ministries of finance and elsewhere in government. I well recall a meeting with the senior officer of the Indian Administrative Service in Rajasthan in the early 1990s, during which she poured considerable scorn on agricultural aid initiatives. Her most telling comments were about the dreadful drain on her treasury by the lapsed T&V project in the state. This had increased the state's public sector pension burden significantly. At the start, no one had thought about the long-term cost implications. She was simply describing chickens that had finally come home to roost.

By the mid-1990s, the show was almost over. T&V projects were almost nowhere to be found, and where they did exist, they were always referred to as 'modified T&V'. This was little more than a convenient euphemism for *sui generis* initiatives. The last T&V project was approved for Cameroon in 1998, bringing to an end nearly 25 years of the donors' promotion of an ineffective approach to farmer training. The evaluation report for the Cameroon project says its achievements were satisfactory. This is classic World Bank speak for not a disaster.

Not everyone in the World Bank was so blind. Three World Bank staffers – Jock Anderson, Gershon Feder and Sushma Ganguly, two of whom I had worked with – wrote a paper entitled 'The Rise and Fall of Training & Visit (T&V) extension: An Asian Mini-Drama with an African Epilogue' (Van den Ban and Samanta, 2006). Their analysis of T&V was that it was pretty much a failure, due in the main to limited benefits and the immense cost. The responsibility for the fiasco lies firmly at the feet of Robert McNamara, whom you may remember as the guy who thought the US could win the war in Vietnam by spilling more and more blood. As Lord Acton once said, 'Power corrupts and absolute power corrupts absolutely.' No president of the World Bank – or any UN agency, for that matter – should go unchallenged, especially when dealing with matters (such as agriculture) that they know nothing about.

The subject of agricultural extension has come full circle. Although the debate continues as to how much public money should go into extension services and how independent of input suppliers they should be, the fact of the matter is that no one believes in an exclusively government-funded extension service any longer. In the late 1990s, in Neuchatel, Switzerland, experts from all over the world shared their experiences of agricultural extension. They concluded that a plurality of extension providers – including neighbouring farmers, NGOs, government services and input suppliers – all have a role to play. And as if on cue to confirm this observation, a major farmer study in Bangladesh, financed by the UK DFID in 2000, found that farmers only got 12.5% of their advice from the government extension service; they got the rest from other sources, notably from input suppliers or, in other words, the private sector.

3.19. Horn of Africa: Real and Political Drought

In early 2000, the countries of the Horn of Africa suffered yet another bad drought, and the lives of millions of people and livestock were put at risk. As is so often the case in such circumstances, the governments concerned sent out SOS messages for emergency assistance and post-emergency rehabilitation assistance. It all happened at a time when UN reform was a big issue in the development community, a major thrust of which was getting UN agencies to work together. Those in the business may recall the United Nations Development Advisory Framework (UNDAF) programmes that were supposed to link all UN activity in a country/region under a common umbrella. An exercise that can be likened to herding cats or, in the case of the FAO, locusts.

Anyway, the drought in the Horn of Africa seemed a golden opportunity to put UN coordination ideas into practice. The Secretary-General of the UN at the time, Kofi Annan, called Jacques Diouf, the DG of the FAO, and asked him to take overall responsibility for analysing the situation and developing an early warning system that would alert the global village to future droughts in the region and provide a reserve of resources to address any such emergency. Other members of the UN family were called into action, with the World Bank picking up a large part of the cost of sending teams of 'experts' into the affected countries, and with other agencies such as the WFP, WMO, IFAD and UNDP all contributing their wisdom and limited resources here and there. The choice of the FAO probably had something to do with the threat to food production, but was also because the FAO was able to come up with the funds for the study fairly quickly, and as it was an African problem, it would look good if the African head of the FAO could deliver a solution.

A planning unit was established at the FAO headquarters in Rome, and after a number of seminars and smaller gatherings, two teams were established and sent off to some of the worst-affected countries. Their task was to ask senior government officials and donor representatives what they thought should and could be done. I had the dubious honour of leading the team that, at the end of July 2000, went on the first fact-finding mission to Sudan and then Uganda, before attending a series of wrap-up meetings in Addis Ababa, Ethiopia. At the time, Sudan was virtually closed to itinerant travellers, and we were carefully chaperoned from arrival to departure.

We spent a pleasant few days in Khartoum, talking to donor representatives and Sudanese government officials, explaining what we were trying to do and trying to get them to tell us what should be done in future to prepare for the next drought or natural disaster. I have to say that, although we were politely received, we were given few serious suggestions as to how to prepare for such emergencies in future.

From Khartoum, we went on to Uganda via Nairobi, Kenya. We had a small diplomatic incident on arrival in Entebbe, as the immigration people were not keen on allowing our Sudanese forester to enter the country. Unlike the rest of us, as a consultant, he did not have a UN passport and had not bothered to get a proper visa. Despite being neighbours and good members of the African Union, there was not much love lost between the two countries at the time. After they had harassed him for a couple of hours, I managed to persuade the immigration officials to let him in. We drove up to Kampala, where we were booked in to the Imperial Hotel, which was infamous for being where Idi Amin had got the swimming pool filled up with the corpses of his enemies. Our discussions with government and aid officials there were basically as unproductive as those in Khartoum.

The more geographically minded may wonder why we went to Uganda at all, as it was not really suffering the same level of drought as the other countries and is not really in the Horn of Africa. The answer lies very much in the fact that the White Nile starts in Uganda (the Blue Nile starts in Ethiopia), and anything Uganda does or plans to do with the waters of the Nile is of immense concern to the countries downstream. If any proof of this concern were needed, all one has to do is count the number of Egyptian hydrologists stationed in Uganda or read the reports of the Nile River Basin Initiative.

From Uganda, we flew to Addis Ababa, where we holed up in the Hilton Hotel for a few days of fairly inconclusive discussions with the Ethiopian authorities and among ourselves. About the only thing we could agree on was the need to do more work in the region and to arrange a massive final workshop in Nairobi.

The second fact-finding mission took place over a year later in September 2001. The emergency was not entirely over by then, but it takes quite a long time to set things up in the UN, particularly among countries that – although neighbours – do not really like meeting each other face to face. Despite the delay, the second trip was more interesting in many ways, if equally unproductive. For me, things started with a few days in Kenya, followed by a solo visit to Eritrea. That is not an easy country to get to, as there were no longer any direct flights from Ethiopia. I had to take a British Airways regional flight that went to Asmara via Khartoum.

The visit to Asmara itself was surreal. In one of the poorest countries in Africa, I was staying in a brand-new luxury hotel, which I shared with what seemed to be half the Italian army, who were there on UN peacekeeping duties. Asmara itself was also a pleasant surprise; perched on top of a high escarpment, it was much cooler than I had expected. I had difficulty in getting to see the authorities concerned, which was very frustrating as the main purpose of my visit was to convince them to send someone to the big jamboree planned for Nairobi. I soon realised that the main problem was not me, but that the Eritreans did not want to agree to be seen at the same meeting as their bitter enemies from Ethiopia, even to discuss such an uncontroversial topic as drought in the region. Eventually, I was seen by a senior official who, although very polite, refused to confirm whether they would attend the meeting in Nairobi.

I flew back to Nairobi and then on to Djibouti with two colleagues for discussions with staff of the Intergovernmental Authority on Development (IGAD).[57] Djibouti is not yet, and probably never will be, on the tourist trail, for obvious reasons: being on the coast of the Red Sea and 12 degrees north of the equator line, it suffers from constant high temperatures and humidity – quite the worst of climatic combinations. There is nothing to see, unless you want to spy on the French – or, indeed, other military bases – and the hotels are ridiculously expensive.

Our discussions were pretty fruitless. The IGAD people were only interested in telling us that they, not the FAO, should have been in charge of the whole exercise, as drought was – or at any rate, had been – part of their mandate. Our mission leader was not the most diplomatic of guys, and instead of looking for common ground, he seemed to enjoy the verbal spat. In the end, they agreed to attend the meeting in Nairobi as observers, once we had agreed to pay for their travel costs. The fact that this meant the IGAD was, in essence, a guest at the workshop, and therefore had no real influence or authority, did not seem to bother them. As is so often the case in the development business, it boils down to who pays and which individuals benefit, and this was no exception. A factor encouraging the decision to attend, at our expense, may have been the fact that the senior IGAD officer was a Kenyan, and this would have meant a paid-for ride home!

The workshop in Nairobi was, I have to say, well organised and quite well attended. In true management-consultant fashion, we broke up into little groups to discuss topics – the main conclusions of which we were then supposed to present in the plenary session. In fact, as so often happens, the plenary was dominated by the heavyweight attendees, and as usual, wild promises were made about possible financial support if clear projects and programmes from the involved countries were developed.

Back in Rome, the study team leader struggled to come up with a report full of innovative and practical recommendations. For reasons that I never really understood, he steered right away from any attempt to rehabilitate and reconstitute the early warning systems (such as better meteorological stations and river gauges), even though the fieldwork had shown that these were effectively moribund in most countries. Instead, he proposed the establishment of a large fund (US$100/500 million) that could be drawn down in a hurry the next time there was a drought to provide immediate emergency assistance. I recall a somewhat awkward moment during an internal meeting to discuss the fund idea when I asked who would control the fund. The answer, as I suspected it would be, was 'the donors'. When I suggested that this might appear somewhat patronising, if not imperial, I was given the coldest of stares.

---

57. Previously known as the Intergovernmental Authority on Drought & Development (IGADD).

Needless to say, the specific fund was not established, although the UN has now created an emergency assistance fund – the Central Emergency Response Fund (CERF) – which was established in 2005 under the then UN Secretary-General, Kofi Annan. The CERF has a rapid response window and one for underfunded emergencies. It is replenished annually by member-country governments, the private sector, foundations and individuals. Since its establishment, its 126 member countries and other organisations have disbursed US$5.5 billion in lifesaving assistance in more than 100 countries. It has an annual funding target of US$1 billion.

So, in hindsight, what had been achieved by this massive exercise? Some estimates suggest it cost well over US$1.0 million, all told. Well, the rich world – in the form of the UN – had been seen to take the drought seriously and had tried to come up with suggestions to minimise the effects of future droughts. Rather like an insurance policy, a small amount of money had been spent to buy calm in the affected countries, if not political favours. As far as the countries themselves were concerned, they were not too keen to have all their weaknesses exposed, so they too were quite happy that the whole thing withered slowly on the vine. And anyway, they all knew that the most cost-effective way for them to provide for the next crisis was to spend nothing in advance, but simply to invite the global media in to take pictures of starving babies when the crisis happened. This had always worked in the past, and they saw no reason to think it would not work in the future.

In many ways, what I witnessed first-hand by being part of the exercise was a golden example on the same theme as a large part of development assistance – namely the proffering of false promises or Trojan horses. False because they always come with conditions that the donors know cannot or will not be met. Other examples include the much-heralded MDGs, the SDGs and, I suspect, the Paris Declaration.

What makes the whole thing very sad is that drought stuck the region yet again 10 years later. Thousands of people suffered tremendous hunger and many of their animals – on which their livelihoods depended – perished. The humanitarian agencies did what they could, but with the global financial crisis soaking up massive amounts of government resources, there were insufficient funds to buy and supply all the food that was needed. In September 2009, the WFP appealed for an additional US$1 billion to meet needs in the Horn of Africa, but it did not meet this target. Of course, global financial crises and drought rarely occur simultaneously, and maybe next time there is a severe drought, there will be plenty of aid money available to bail out the afflicted countries. But maybe, just maybe, 'Wolf!' has been cried too often?

I think it is significant that, at the World Summit on Food Security held in Rome in mid-November 2009, the donors refused to come up with yet more money to help poor countries address the problems of food security and food production. Instead, the conference declaration made it clear that it is national governments that have the primary responsibility for food security. This was a new departure for the aid business. In the past, national governments were rarely held accountable for natural disasters – the rich rallied round and dug in their pockets. But while this helped bring immediate relief, it did nothing to prevent such humanitarian tragedies happening in the future. Perhaps the tune is beginning to change, and the donors have remembered the old proverbs of 'physician heal thyself' and a 'stitch in time saves nine'. In other words, we will help, but only when we can see that you have done everything possible to prepare for – and mitigate – the effects of disasters for yourselves. This includes things such as reliable early warning systems, adequate and well-maintained grain reserves, trained personnel, and adequate logistical supplies.

3.20. Codex Alimentarius (CA): Something to Beef About

The CA is run by a commission consisting of member nations (188 in 2019). Its basic function is to provide global food-safety standards. The commission is staffed by experts from the FAO and WHO, with the FAO providing a permanent secretariat in Rome. The secretariat does not have the facilities or staff to do product testing itself. Instead, it relies on subject-matter specialists and establishes commodity committees, made up of world experts, to undertake and report on tests. It is these committees that draft the standards and make recommendations to the commission. Different countries host the various committees, with the US hosting the subject committee dealing with residues of veterinary drugs in food. Great care is taken in appointing the scientists to the product committees that test and approve products.

Towards the end of the last century, the CA was asked to approve the use of a patented hormone treatment for beef production. US scientists had developed hormones that, when injected into young beef animals, increased their rate of weight gain. Farmers in the US wanted to be able to use these hormones to compete against lower-cost producers elsewhere in the world. The problem was that residual traces of the hormones in beef carcasses were known to be carcinogenic. The job of the CA was to approve dosage rates for the hormones that would not result in any residual carcinogenic traces at the time of slaughter.

Sadly, there is clear evidence of manipulation of the testing and approval process for these hormones. The head of the nutrition section of the FAO, who was in charge of selecting committee scientists at the time, was an American national who had previously worked in the food industry in the US and was about to retire. This meant he had to act fast and would not be around to pick up the pieces if things went belly-up and there was anything to beef about.

The committee of scientists duly met after the testing process and agreed a level or dosage rate for the hormone that they considered to be 'safe', according to the trials they had undertaken. They did what they had been contracted to do, which was to comment on and approve a specific dosage rate; i.e. a given volume of hormone at a specific concentration for an animal of a certain weight at a certain age. They did this by testing different levels of hormone at different growth stages to determine the level that did not result in potentially harmful residues in slaughtered animals. The problem was – and for that matter, still is – that while it is easy to ensure that the correct dose of hormone is injected under laboratory or trial conditions, it is almost impossible to ensure that an accurately measured and correct dose will be injected into each animal under normal farming conditions. To do so would mean that all animals had to be weighed accurately and the dosage adjusted for each animal; this is possible, but very time-consuming and not likely to happen in practice.

When the committee's report was published, a number of European countries, led by the French, were very critical of it. In turn, this led the EU to establish a European Food Standards Agency in Parma, Italy, and the findings of this agency have precedence over CA tests. The sad end to the tale is that the CA itself now seems likely to end up as a residue because the WHO announced in 2005 that it would be reducing its financial support of the CA in the future.

3.21. Avian Influenza: *Cura Te Upsum* or Physician, Heal Thyself

Bird flu or avian influenza – more accurately, highly pathogenic avian influenza – was a major preoccupation of a number of governments and aid agencies for a couple of years (2005–07). It is difficult to be sure whether there was too much or too little concern and/or donor intervention – virus behaviour is not something that even the finest epidemiologists fully understand. Nevertheless, this is an interesting story as it is an example of how international donor assistance can work with sovereign governments to strengthen key national human and animal health services to the benefit of everyone, both in the countries concerned and elsewhere. It also demonstrates rather nicely how such crises are seen by some aid agencies as opportunities to rattle their begging bowl for funds. While the results of the agencies' involvement are difficult to assess, I have no doubt that the publicity provided by the global campaign was helpful in making governments more aware of the problem and the best ways to manage an outbreak. My own involvement was largely as an observer, as the leader of teams preparing World Bank projects for avian influenza in much of South Asia.

The bird flu in question is caused by a subtype of influenza A virus (H5N1) that is lethal to poultry (mortality rates are over 85%) and can infect many other species of birds and some mammals (cats and humans). Since the strain reappeared in 2003, it has been confirmed in over 50 countries and has caused serious economic loss in some 10 countries, where huge numbers of birds have died or been culled to prevent the spread of the disease.

Culling to prevent the spread of a virus is standard veterinary practice, along with selective vaccination – providing supplies of high-quality vaccine are available (they were not at the start of the 2005–07 outbreak). Apart from the economic effects on the poultry industry in the affected countries, there were a number of human cases of illness from the poultry virus (258 by January 2007), and more than half of those cases were fatal.

I was asked by the World Bank to lead a joint FAO/WHO mission to Pakistan in early 2006. At our first and last meeting in Islamabad, the guys from the WHO said they were unhappy with the mission's terms of reference and they would prefer to produce their own mission report rather than doing a joint report. This was simple code for non-cooperation and the hope that they would bag most of the goodies on offer. It was all a bit tricky, as I had a human disease epidemiologist appointed by the World Bank on my team, and without him, the WHO guys had little to offer. As it turns out, the split worked in our favour as the Pakistani veterinary guys were up to speed and very keen on a project, while the public sector medical folk were in a mess and were not sure whether they wanted a World Bank project. When we saw the permanent secretary in the Ministry of Health, she basically showed us the door.

In Bangladesh, where the disease was endemic, the government refused to accept the World Bank project. This is reported to have been because no agreement could be reached on whether any international experts involved in project implementation would have to pay local income tax. It seems unlikely that such a reason would have held up a project the government saw as essential. Project or no project, the poultry industry in Bangladesh was considerably knocked back by the outbreak, and it took about five years for production to recover.

India managed to contain the disease without World Bank support. In Nepal and Bhutan, the World Bank money was used to strengthen veterinary services, but there is no certainty that this had, in fact, contained the spread of the disease.

58. Bangladesh, Bhutan, Pakistan and Sri Lanka in 2006/07.

In Sri Lanka, UNICEF, which had secured early funding from Japan for awareness campaigns, was somehow under the impression that it would implement a large section of the project, and we had great difficulty extracting them from a close relationship with the Ministry of Health.

An unpleasant side effect of the whole event was the naked grab for resources and publicity by agencies such as the WHO, FAO and UNICEF. The UN agencies were quite open about how they hoped to get large slices of the World Bank project credits to fund their TA efforts, and as events in the field showed, they competed with one another for resources.

In many ways, the whole exercise demonstrated yet again the dreadful hypocrisy of much of the aid world, which is more interested in its own immediate future than the longer-term benefits of well-thought-out and well-financed support. The UN agencies and the bilateral agencies involved were shameless in their attempts to secure funding and kudos. As far as the World Bank was concerned, it made little secret of the fact that it saw the disease as a golden opportunity to get back into the veterinary world.

That said, there is no counterfactual. We have no idea if things might have been a real global disaster if no action had been taken by the aid community, and on balance, I think the aid initiatives, together with the general awareness of the risks of the disease reported by the media at the time, were what spurred governments to take essential action and get on top of the problem. As to the efficacy of the World Bank-supported projects to contain the disease, it is difficult to draw any firm conclusions, but sadly, the indications are that nothing very substantial has been achieved in terms of strengthening either veterinary or medical services. Fortunately, the disease itself came to the rescue by mutating and burning itself out.

4.

Small Case Studies and Technologies That Do Not Work

The stories in this chapter mainly concern individuals rather than aid agencies or countries. I think they are important, however, as they provide a window on to an aspect of the aid business – namely self-serving benefit – that is rarely talked about. Of course, such things go on in all walks of life, but the aid industry somehow aspires to the moral high ground, and these stories challenge that aspiration. The stories in the UK press in 2017 and 2018 of sexual predation by aid workers hardly came as a surprise to those of us who have worked in the sector. After all, part of the attraction of working in far-flung places is the chance to do things you would not necessarily do at home. The last section of this chapter reviews some of the low-cost technologies that have been tried, but largely failed, in developing countries.

4.1.   A Lucky Consultant

A common feature of donor-assisted projects and programmes was – and to some extent, still is – the inclusion of TA experts to help with training, and the introduction of new skills and approaches. According to theory, a top-notch expert hired for a short period of a month or so (or for up to three years in extreme cases) will help in training national staff and/or introducing new skills and approaches. A good example is the introduction of IPM techniques (see 3.8. and 3.13.).

In the early days of aid, almost all such experts were from developed countries, and although there were a number of rogues, on the whole, most had something to offer and usually fitted in well to an overseas lifestyle. As time went by, things began to change. In the first place, there was an increasing shortage of Western (especially specialist) expertise in such fields as rice breeding and oil palm cultivation. At the same time, a number of developing-country nationals began selling their services, often at a markedly lower cost. While many of these experts were, and are, as good as their Western counterparts, there was and probably still is a sizeable minority who survive on patronage rather than prowess.

I well recall meeting one such gentleman in Bangladesh sometime in the late 1980s. He was the chief technical adviser (CTA) on a USAID agricultural project that was about to come to an end. We were preparing a similar project for World

Bank funding, which also had a large TA input. I'll call him Mr Lucky. He was quick to offer us hospitality and find out what we were proposing, and sure enough, he ended up as one of the TA experts hired under our project when it became operational. Over the next 15 years, I ran across Mr Lucky quite a few times in Bangladesh as he moved from one donor project to another: the USAID, the World Bank, the ADB and, finally, the IFAD. It intrigued me how he managed to move effortlessly from being one kind of technical expert, such as an agricultural extension expert, under one project to becoming another type of expert, such as a horticultural expert, on the next.

As might be expected, he became quite well known in Bangladesh's agricultural circles, and on one occasion, I asked a Bangladeshi colleague how he managed to get so many contracts, one after the next, especially as everyone knew he was only moderately competent as both an agriculturalist and a manager. The answer from my colleague was simple: 'He promises and then pays a month's salary for every year's contract to the government officers responsible for recruiting project consultants.' I was not really surprised as a 10% cut is often the going rate for a job in the Indian subcontinent. What did concern me was the attitude of the IFAD headquarters staff when I asked them why they had allowed the guy to be hired on their projects. They simply said it was the government's decision as to what they used the IFAD's money for, and that they, the IFAD, did not get involved in selecting consultants.

In fact, this is only partly true; I know from other countries that the IFAD can and does get involved in the selection of consultants. What I was really being told was that it is too much trouble to try to get involved as it simply means interminable delays, and our main job is to get the money out, not watch what it is used for. There is also a considerable risk that they – the IFAD headquarters staff – would be branded as imperialists who did not trust Bangladeshi officials.

The IFAD, I hasten to add, is by no means alone in this use of Nelson's eye. In fact, it has become so common in some countries that donor-funded TA is seen as the easiest way of making a quick buck. It is sad that it really is a case of killing the goose, as increasingly, less and less use of TA is being made, and fewer and fewer new technologies are being transferred – at least in the public sector. Graft goes on everywhere, but in the private sector, if there are no results, things rapidly come to an end.

4.2.   A Lucky Non-Governmental Organisation (NGO)

On the same visit to Bangladesh, I was similarly intrigued to learn that, over a period of about 10 years, the IFAD had used only one NGO to implement all its projects. What is more, this was a little-known NGO with no real status and, perhaps more significantly, no track record. When I asked about this, I got a similar answer to my question about Mr Lucky: the government chooses the project NGO, and this NGO was known to pay the best 'speed'[59] money. In fact, this NGO had done extremely well out of a string of IFAD projects as the result of a convenient oversight.

At the time, most IFAD projects in Bangladesh had a line of credit as a major component. This was in the form of a lump sum of money made available to the implementing NGO for it to on-lend to the rural poor as microcredit for income-generating activities. The idea was that each microcredit loan would be returned to the NGO at the end of a specified period and then re-lent to another borrower, and so on, until the end of the project. All outstanding loans should have been repaid by then, and the original lump sum lent to the NGO would then be repaid to the IFAD or the government, as specified in the project agreement. However, in the case of this string of IFAD projects, no mechanism for the repayment of the lump sum had ever been worked out, and no one seemed to have noticed. When we raised questions about this, all we got was silence and dirty looks from both the NGO and IFAD staff. As always, the name of the game was to get the money out and ask no awkward questions. And anyway, by the time someone found out what had happened, most of the *dramatis personae* would have moved on and the managers would be left to sort things out.

4.3.   Another Lucky Non-Governmental Organisation (NGO)

On a later visit to Bangladesh, I had come across another nice little TA scam. This time, it was EC money being wasted on the staff of a famous international NGO; one that started life in the US after the Second World War. A considerable amount of money – about US$100,000, if I recall correctly – was to have been used for local consultants to provide regular monitoring of the project. No monitoring was done, and the funds were kept until almost the end of the project, when some of the NGO staff were sent on training courses in Europe for some quite lengthy periods.

One lucky guy, I seem to recall, managed to get a master's studentship out of the funds. On this occasion, I am sure the expatriate staff of the NGO were to blame as they were responsible for ensuring that the project implementation guidelines were followed. Why they allowed it to happen, we will never know. It could have been

59. 'Speed' is a colloquial expression used in much of South Asia to mean a bribe.

incompetence or too many changes of project managers, or it could also have been a way of retaining good staff throughout the project. Competition for good local staff is fierce in Bangladesh, and pay scales tend to be fixed, so a good incentive is to offer overseas training. By saving things up to nearly the end of the project, the staff would have been retained, and yet all the money would have been spent – another cardinal rule of donor-assisted projects. Money left over is an embarrassment all round, as there is usually no way it can be recycled.

4.4.   Helicopters and Rice

The Marcos years in the Philippines were infamous for 'crony capitalism'. I came across a small example when I visited the country for the first time in 1975. At the time, the minister of agriculture (a renowned *bon vivant*, known by everyone as Tanco) was among President Marcos's closest friends. Among his many luxuries was a helicopter to ferry him between his office in traffic-snarled Quezon City and his rural island homes. He needed some spare parts for his helicopter, but did not have access to sufficient ready cash.

Fortunately for him, a World Bank agriculture project designed to increase rice production was under preparation. He suggested they include a helicopter engine as part of the project.

The first reaction of the World Bank staff working on the project was rejection, saying it was not a transport project. Tanco's response was equally blunt: 'No engine, no project.' The problem was now the World Bank's, and its management reconsidered their position and realised the proposed project design had overlooked the need for some means of monitoring rice production, which could best be done by aerial survey by – yes, you've guessed it – a working helicopter, and so an engine was duly included after all.

4.5.   Spinning

This little story and the two that follow are classic examples of how aid funds can be used for political gain. Soon after he took over as the DG of the FAO in 1994, Dr Jacques Diouf, a successful Senegalese agricultural scientist, introduced a major new programme to improve food security in poor member countries, which was called the Special Programme for Food Security (SPFS).[60] It was predicated on

---

60. At the time, this was the then DG's flagship programme; it was a TA package designed to demonstrate how, by using better technology, food production/security can be improved in low-income, food-deficit countries.

large-scale pilot demonstrations of on-the-shelf technologies. These technologies were to be demonstrated to farmers and government officials.

The idea was to scale up the successful demonstrations nationally and – hey presto! – solve the food-shortage problems. One or two doubting Thomases raised questions about why the technologies had lain unused. They were informed that the programme would provide a unique chance to find out the technical, financial and social constraints that had led to non-adoption earlier, and the programme would identify ways of removing any such constraints.

Nepal was one of the first 15 countries selected for a pilot (most were in Africa), and I put up little resistance when asked to join the team sent there to prepare a project. I knew the country quite well by then and always liked visiting, even if I had some doubts about whether the Special Programme in Nepal (SPIN) would achieve very much or simply spin out of control.

The FAO representative at the time, Mr Wooster, was a very friendly American, and he and his wife joined us for a working safari as we visited various parts of the country to see what technologies might be demonstrated. It became clear early on that if the SPIN were to be politically acceptable in Nepal and make a real mark, the benefits would (a) have to be applicable in both the hills and the Terai plains, and (b) would have to lead to yield increases and/or cost savings in the order of 25–30%. The only technology that seemed to fit the bill was to improve 'on-farm water management' through a combination of intensive training and better access to inputs.

In the hill areas, this meant realigning field canals to ensure an equal and even distribution of irrigation water flows to fields. In the flat land of the Terai plains, it meant demonstrating the value of lining the channels used to distribute the pumped ground water. The basic idea we planned to demonstrate was that, with a reliable water supply, farmers would invest in better seeds, more fertiliser and use better crop-protection measures. The project would make these inputs available to participating farmers at the right time.

During the mission visit, we selected a number of demonstration sites and worked out the cost of the three-year programme. At the time, each country's programme was generously funded to the value of US$250,000 a year, and in Nepal, such an amount of money goes quite a long way. We sold our ideas to all and sundry, with almost no resistance, and hired an excellent local team consisting of an agronomist, an irrigation engineer and an economist, who doubled as the project manager.

As always, the first year had a few teething problems, but the initial results were encouraging. In the second year, things really began to look up, with substantial yield improvements and farmers queuing up to buy inputs for the next crop season. Two things soon became apparent as the programme got under way: (1) farmers responded well to a programme of intensive training, but they only needed to be told how to do things once; and (2) the programme showed that a major constraint to raising farm output in the selected areas had been a shortage of inputs at the right time.

By the simple expedient of providing these inputs at planting time, the project had removed a major constraint. If it achieved nothing else, the SPIN demonstrated beyond any doubt that, with a little encouragement and advice, farmers were keen to intensify their production, and furthermore, they would find the money to buy input, if they were available on time. The project did not have a credit component.

Having had such initial success, the national team was looking forward to a third year, during which the aim was to demonstrate on a larger scale a modified extension/training system based on an intensive one-shot approach linked to proactive access to information and inputs, as needed. If successful, it might have shown how a nationally cost-effective extension system could have been run. It was therefore a major shock to learn that the FAO was cutting off any further funding on the grounds that the SPIN had already been sufficiently successful and it was now up to the government to support it.

At least, that was the official story. The real reason for the cut-off was more political: it was due to unanticipated funding shortages. Initially, 15 countries were selected for the SPFS, and the monies approved were divided up accordingly in quite generous aliquots. Globally, the programme was overseen by an aptly named 'oversight panel' of wise men – including one ex-World Bank vice president.

I had the fortune to attend the oversight meeting to present the SPIN findings in late 1998, when it was agreed to increase the number of countries eligible for SPFS projects. An FAO colleague, who had obviously been well briefed, also attended the meeting. He made an emotional plea for the programme to be expanded to any country that wanted to participate. He based his argument on the grounds that it was unfair that only some countries were able to have such a wonderful and successful programme, and that many food-insecure African countries felt excluded. It was a powerful argument, and it carried the day. The only problem was that the oversight panel had no access to additional funds, so all they could do was authorise the thinner spreading of what funds remained.

It was, of course, pure politics. Jacques Diouf, mindful of his upcoming re-election campaign, needed to have every African vote in the bag to ensure success. Indeed, a colleague who accompanied Diouf on a trip to Africa at this time, in relation to the SPFS, was told by Diouf that he was not concerned about the technical aspects of the SPFS; the most important thing for him was that it gave him access to senior government officials and politicians.

The 54 votes from Africa, plus those of the Caribbean, are usually enough to secure a majority of votes for anyone standing for DG of the FAO. Anything and everything Diouf did from that point onwards was geared towards doing the right things in Africa. Nepal, after all, was quite likely to vote for an Asian candidate, whatever the FAO did on the ground, and so there was little need for the organisation to go out of its way to continue to court favour in Kathmandu.

I had suspected for some time that the whole programme would spin out of control sooner or later, at least as far as the truth was concerned. And so it did.

4.6.   Special Programme for Food Production in Little Lesotho (SPILL)

SPILL was a project that started, as usual, with a design phase. An advance allocation of some US$30,000 was made to cover the cost of project design by a local team of consultants. The money was spent on a vehicle that was rolled within six months, and US$8,000 was spent on a report that was never written. Undaunted, the FAO started all over again.

This time, an irrigation expert from Zimbabwe was sent to prepare the project. She prepared some neat engineering proposals and identified five possible sites. The final choice of sites was left to local experts. However, they were reluctant to accept the proposals as they felt the project would not work in Lesotho. This was because they called for the realignment of field boundaries into neat squares that could be irrigated accurately by a tidy grid of overhead sprinklers. Such a layout may be appropriate in Zimbabwe, where the pressure on land is not too great. In Lesotho, however, the pressure on land is enormous, and most fields are divided into many small, irregular pieces farmed by a number of farmers.

Two years passed, but no decision was forthcoming on the sites for the demonstrations, and the project came to an abrupt end, having achieved absolutely nothing. So what did the FAO do? It financed a follow-up project. Why? Probably because the FAO bureaucrats had been told by the DG that there had to be an SPFS project in every country (in Africa) that was eligible, and all SPFS projects had to involve irrigation. Just coincidently, his second re-election campaign was in full swing by then, and the proposed project in Lesotho ticked both boxes.

The sad thing about this little story is that there is a long history of failed irrigation projects in Lesotho, going back to the 1960s. The potential irrigable area in the mountainous country is less than 12,000 hectares. Indeed, Lesotho has such limited agricultural potential, with poor soils and limited rainfall, that it is essentially a pastoral country. It would have made much more sense to look at ways of improving livestock husbandry, rather than focusing blindly on irrigation.

4.7.   Mr Brouhaha

This is a nice little story about how an individual can benefit from public interest. In December 2000, at rather short notice, I was asked to go to India for two weeks on a mission to look at the possibilities of expanding the FAO SPFS project in India. From the start, I had some serious misgivings about the purpose of the trip, which seemed a bit convoluted. A few months earlier, during the biennial FAO council, the secretary of state for agriculture in India – I call him Mr Brouhaha (Mr B) – had made personal representation to Jacques Diouf, the then DG of the FAO, regarding the delays in getting a number of Indian TA experts into the field in a couple of countries in southern Africa.

Earlier in the year, it had been decided that technical advisers were needed to ensure that the SPFS demonstrations in various countries were done correctly; to minimise costs, these advisers would be recruited from more-advanced developing countries under what is known as South South Cooperation (SSC). India, with its armies of experts desperate for a chance to earn some hard currency, leapt at the opportunity and offered opportunities for Indian experts in Eritrea, Lesotho and Mozambique. All had been agreed between the three cost-sharing parties – India, the FAO and the recipient countries – except for one small matter, namely where the money would come from to cover each recipient country's share of the costs. This was causing a delay in getting the Indian experts into the field. There had been some suggestion of accessing special funds made available to the AfDB by the government of India to meet the recipient country's cost, hence Mr B's visit to Diouf.

His visit set in motion a series of internal meetings, and memos were sent to and fro between the FAO and the Indian authorities. The basic message conveyed by the FAO was that it was delighted at India's support for the SPFS and SSC, and it looked forward to being able to confirm the availability of funds for the recipient countries' contributions, although no indication was provided as to how or when they would be available. In the meantime, it was suggested that India should receive an inward mission to look at ways in which the recently completed SPFS activities in India could be expanded. The FAO would, of course, bear the US$30,000 cost of this little mission.

I set off with a colleague, who had been brought back from retirement, and we dutifully reported to Mr B's grand office in New Delhi before setting off to visit four states in 12 days. The first piece of information that came our way was that India had just experienced a record harvest, and the country had 40 million tonnes of cereals that were surplus to requirements. Clearly, Indian agricultural technology had been very successful in raising output, and in the circumstances, it seemed that the SPFS in the country had been a case of teaching grandmothers how to suck eggs.

I recall discussing this with the mission leader over a beer one evening in the delightful Imperial Hotel in Delhi, asking him, 'Why did India need an SPFS project if it already had enough food?' He replied, 'Ah. There may be enough food, but not everyone can afford to buy it, and we need to find ways to help the poor raise their incomes. The country might have an overall surplus, but there are still food-deficit areas, and we should focus on these.' I was not really convinced, and I ventured to suggest that perhaps Mr B had accepted our mission to please Diouf and he hoped to get a job out of it for himself. 'No, no, no,' said my mission leader, 'That cannot be possible. The FAO does not work like that.'

Undeterred, we travelled to the four states where rain-fed agriculture predominates and where there are food shortages in most years. We spoke to a few farmers, some extension agents and some researchers, and we were told all about the national water-management programme that aims to encourage communities to build water storage and harvesting structures. It was clear that Indian scientists and administrators were already addressing the problem in a very pragmatic way and there was really very little scope for expanding the SPFS project in India.

We finished our field trips and prepared an aide-memoire for discussion with Mr B and his staff at a wrap-up meeting. It was a memorable occasion. The aide-memoire was as dry as toast, and no one – least of all Mr B – was interested in what we had to say. At the earliest convenient moment, he cut the meeting short, and we left to do some Christmas shopping, pack and catch a plane home.

Back in Rome in the New Year, we prepared a short report containing the recommendation that there were some possibilities for SPFS support within the states visited, but that it was now up to the states themselves to put together project proposals, perhaps with some assistance from the FAO office in Delhi. To my knowledge, the report was received by the government of India, but six months later, no action had been taken, and I suspect it simply joined hundreds of similar reports under a pile of Delhi dust.

So, what was it all about? Well, the simple answer is, of course, politics – in this case, both personal and national politics. The SPFS was one of the DG's main interests. He hoped that it would lead to dramatic improvements in food production in a large number of low-income, food-deficit countries, and that both the organisation and he would reap the kudos for solving the problem of hunger. But he was having a problem convincing the main donors that the SPFS was a good idea. Most of the major donor countries (G7), and many beneficiary countries and other donor agencies were not convinced that the SPFS was effective. Securing India's public support and commitment to the SPFS would have been quite a publicity coup.

There was also a political angle, as far as India was concerned. Public endorsement of the SPFS was neither here nor there; even if the programme had withered eventually, no one in India would have been held responsible. However, India did have an active interest in the SSC aspect of the SPFS, especially as the FAO paid a large share of the cost of the SSC programme. Indian bureaucrats saw this as a low-cost way of giving Indian technicians a chance to get overseas experience, and hence launch themselves into the international consultancy market – a market largely dominated by developed-country nationals. There was also the possibility that trade and business opportunities for Indian companies might follow. So, by accepting an inward mission to look at SPFS opportunities in India, the Indian government was really putting pressure on the FAO to implement the outstanding SSC commitments.

In addition, as I discovered quite by chance, there was a more personal political interest. Early in the May after our visit to India, I bumped into Mr B in a lift in the FAO headquarters. I buttonholed him politely and said, 'You probably do not remember me, but I was on the SPFS mission to India last December. Are you here in Rome for the annual meeting of the Committee on Food and Agriculture?' He replied, 'Oh no, I reached 60 years of age and retired from government service in January. I am here for briefing before I set off on an assignment for the FAO.' This assignment was followed by eight months of full-time employment as an FAO representative in Myanmar, which ended when he turned 62 – the mandatory retirement age for FAO staff. Needless to say, he managed to find himself quite a few little FAO consultancies after this second retirement.

4.8.   Fear of Real Science

The Tropical Agriculture Association is a loose grouping of largely British agriculturalists with an interest in tropical agriculture. The association holds meetings on topical tropical-agriculture subjects a few times a year. I was fortunate enough to be able to attend one such meeting, held in the Linnean Society rooms off Piccadilly in the autumn of 2001. One of the speakers was a remarkable scientist (a Fellow of the Royal Society) and communicator who presented a paper on some fascinating work he had done in Kenya to control striga weed and the stem borer moths, two major pests of the maize crop. Both pests can be controlled by intercropping maize with a legume (silverleaf desmodium [*Desmodium uncinatum*]) and planting Napier grass (*Pennisetum purpureum*) around the crop. The silverleaf desmodium repels or pushes the moths away, while the Napier grass attracts or pulls the moths towards it. The overall process being known as 'push–pull' IPM. In addition to controlling the moths, the silverleaf desmodium also exudes chemicals that suppress striga (Hassanali *et al.*, 2008).

I was impressed with what I heard and thought how useful it would be to have the lecture repeated to my FAO colleagues in Rome, many of whom were promoting IPM as a low-cost and environmentally friendly way of managing pests. Without too much trouble, I persuaded my managers to pay for the speaker to visit Rome for a day and present his paper. Before the great day, I circulated a note around the building inviting people to attend. I was devastated when only six people turned up, and only one of these – a Latin American soil scientist – seemed to really understand what was being discussed. Later, over a beer in the Lancelot (a favourite hotel for visitors to the FAO), I apologised to the speaker for bringing him all the way from London for what appeared to be almost nothing. He was more philosophical, saying he would rather speak to a handful or even one really interested person than a bunch of uninterested also-rans. Fine words, but they butter no parsnips.

My assessment was less charitable. To me, the poor turnout was yet more evidence of something I had been worried about for a number of years, namely the fact that real science terrified most of my FAO colleagues, and they did not want to be exposed. The organisation had become staffed almost entirely by social scientists of one complexion or another, and even the technical heavyweights, such as the micro-biologist veterinarians, seemed more concerned about the political ramifications of what they said rather than its technical correctness.

I have no idea what the speaker said to his colleagues at Rothamsted Research Station (the oldest and probably still one of the leading agricultural research institutes in the world) when he got back to England about his day out in the Eternal City with the FAO. I doubt he would have minced his words – he has a reputation for straight speaking – and it is more likely than not that he would have told his colleagues and the scientists he knows in the UK DFID not to waste their time and money on the FAO in future.

4.9.   Green Power

For many years, the FAO housed a fertiliser liaison unit, funded by a consortium of fertiliser manufacturers, at its headquarters in Rome. Working closely with the soil scientists of the FAO, the unit helped with a series of simple fertiliser trials undertaken in almost all developing countries. The results of some of these trials were previously available on the FAO website. Hard copies might be available in some national libraries such as the one I have for Lesotho (Doyle and Van Den Berghe, 1973).[61] I suspect most of the results would still be valid, at least as a first approximation. Sadly, the programme came to an abrupt end in the mid-1990s, so there has been no updating of fertiliser-response information by the FAO as new varieties and technologies have been introduced. Intrigued as to why the programme had stopped so suddenly, in late 2000 I asked the one remaining officer who had been involved in the programme to tell me what had happened. It was an example of how outside interests can – and do – sidestep official protocols for their own selfish interests.

For a number of years, the then DG of the FAO used to enjoy the odd weekend hunting wild boar in the forests of Germany as a guest of Helmut Kohl, the then chancellor. On one occasion, Kohl apparently complained about the FAO fertiliser programme or, more precisely, the links with the fertiliser industry that the Green Party in Germany were most unhappy about. They saw the unit as little more than a marketing device – one aimed at encouraging the use of chemical or mineral fertiliser by poor farmers in the developing world. The Greens wanted the unit closed, and Kohl needed their support for some political reasons. On his return to Rome, the DG told the director of the liaison unit to close it down.

While there probably was some validity in the concerns of the Greens (at least in so far as the fertiliser industry was not keen on the FAO promoting organic fertilisers), there is no hard evidence that the FAO was promoting harmful practices in its mineral fertiliser recommendations. What is perhaps more interesting is that one member country – in this case, Germany – could get what it wanted without having to go through a complicated procedure of tabling a resolution at the next FAO member conference!

In some ways, the Greens probably achieved more than they could have hoped for as far as the FAO is concerned, as by 2018, the agency was playing down the need for mineral fertiliser and was promoting organic fertiliser instead. The cynical part of me says the Greens have indirectly contributed to Europe's immigration problems by discouraging increased food productivity in Africa, thereby encouraging folk to leave the continent in large numbers. This is, of course, an entirely speculative statement, but there is no doubt that there are usually serious consequences from major policy changes, and these consequences should be fully understood before any changes are made.

---

61. I know this is the work of the liaison unit that was carried out in Lesotho, Botswana and Swaziland, as it was being done by Jim Doyle, an FAO soil scientist, when I was in Lesotho in the early 1970s.

4.10. Banned Aids

In the early 1990s, when the world became aware of and concerned about HIV/ AIDS, a plant virologist in the FAO, who had worked in Malawi early in his career, realised the disease was likely to have serious implications for African agriculture. In particular, he felt that it would lead to tremendous labour shortages, which would, in turn, lead to more hunger as folk were unable to produce enough food. He convinced the organisation to train all its staff in the basic facts of the disease, how it was likely to affect rural livelihoods in Africa, what might be done to mitigate the effects of the disease and how staff should be careful when having sexual relations in countries where the disease was rife. The training programme was centred around a series of interactive seminars, and all staff were expected to participate. Interest was surprisingly high, not least because four members of staff had recently died of the disease, and everyone wanted to learn how best to protect themselves, if nothing else.

I do not have the precise numbers, but about half the staff had been trained before the whole programme was stopped. On making some discreet enquiries, I discovered that a number of African governments had objected to the seminars, which they felt presented an unfair and biased account of the disease in their countries. In order not to offend these governments, which had recently just elected him DG and which he hoped would re-elect him in due course, Jacques Diouf cancelled the programme. With hindsight, it is sad to reflect on the fact that, had more people within the organisation known more about the disease all those years ago, they might have been able – through the provision of simple advice, such as using a condom – been able to prevent a considerable loss of life. It also shows once again a fear of real science within the organisation. A weird irony really, given that the FAO was always seen as one of the key scientific organisations of the UN.

4.11. Boys' Jobs

These stories are about recruitment within the FAO and serve to confirm the old adage: 'It is not what you know but who you know that matters.' They also help to illustrate that, among other things, too much merit is not necessarily a good thing. Like all good institutions, the FAO has an annual appraisal system to assess staff competence, performance and training needs. It is a bit of a joke really; everyone is assessed as having 'above average performance', as no manager dares to tell the truth about their staff for fear of retribution or accusations of their own incompetence in having such poor staff.

One of the consequences is that, when it comes to selecting managers from the pool of aspirants, there is really no merit card to consult or refer to. In practice, however, this is really rather convenient, as it means some other selection procedure has to be used – namely good old-fashioned patronage. The trouble is that it often means giving jobs to folk who cannot do the work, and while all organisations have their share of dead wood, once the rotten branches reach a certain height, the effect is to hollow out the institution itself.

M&Ms

This little story is about a sweet set of deals for the sons of one of the FAO's ex-employees; let's call him Mr Magnificent (Mr M for short). He was, after all, a brilliant forester, athlete, linguist, talker, politician and administrator, who once stood for election to be head of an important UN agency. Mr M had three sons, all of whom were educated in the West, rather than their native South Asian country. This meant that, on graduation, they had aspirations of employment alongside their peers in the West. The only problem was that they had neither residence status in Europe or the US, nor were they sufficiently like Mr M himself and clever enough to find a private sector employer who would help them get residence status.

The solution to the job problem was simple: get them a job in one of the three UN agencies based in Rome, as that would give automatic residence rights. And so it was that one got a job at the IFAD, one in the WFP and, finally, in 2005, one was employed by the FAO. Now, of course, it may well be that they were the best candidates for their respective posts, but corridor gossip (which is usually not a million miles from the truth) suggests that, at least in the case of the FAO, Mr M made full use of his contact with the assistant DG in the finance and administration department – who, coincidently, was originally from the same part of the world – to secure the job, much to the chagrin of a number of existing employees who had applied for the post in hope of promotion.

Postscript: It is true that, like all UN agencies, the FAO tries to prevent nepotism by specifically ruling out the employment of dependents. However, at the time all three offspring were employed, their daddy was not an employee, as he was on a pension! To be fair, this case is exceptional, but it is by no means unique. The UN payroll is currently awash with children of ex-staff.

Mr Good

Mr Good was an agronomist from a Latin American country who had worked for many years on an FAO TA project in Southeast Asia. Eventually, the project came to an end, and things were not looking too bright for Mr Good. The FAO TA programme globally was winding down, and there were no projects that he could have transferred to. Luckily, however, he got on well with his boss (the CTA) who, in turn, was a good friend of the US national who was the director of a large division at the FAO headquarters in Rome. Gossip at the time was that the director used to be entertained in bacchanalian style on board the CTA's yacht on his visits to the country where the TA project was operational.

No one will ever know what the actual deal was, but Mr Good had clearly been promised something. I know this because my boss called me into his office one day and said, 'Here is a pile of applications for a vacancy that we want to give to Mr Good. As a fellow agronomist, I would appreciate it if you would screen the applications and do the needful.' He said nothing more and handed me the file of applications.

I started to look through the applications, and it soon became apparent that no good was going to come out of the exercise. Mr Good had applied for a post that he was basically not qualified for. The job called for proven experience in leading agricultural investment project design missions. Mr Good might well have been a good agronomist, but he had never done any investment project preparation work. True, he was about to complete a short-term posting in our unit, but his performance during the posting was distinguished by being undistinguished. In other words, not only did he not have the paper qualifications but also he had not really demonstrated any aptitude for the work involved.

At the time, it soon occurred to me that I was being used to whitewash or make good a bad job. As a respected technical person myself, if I had given my blessing to Mr Good's application, it would have given it more credibility than if a non-technical person had done the screening. Feeling somewhat compromised, I refused to be 'good' and said it would be better to get someone else to do the screening. By chance, I later saw a memo from the officer responsible for the screening saying how unhelpful I had been in the matter. Needless to say, Mr Good did get the job eventually and, as I predicted, he was not much good at it. He did it for about five years and then, with enough annual pension contributions, he scuttled back home to Latin America.

Ali and Ali

Around the year 2000, a vacancy arose for the post of service chief in a part of the FAO that deals with preparing agricultural investment projects in Asia. Of course, the retirement of the incumbent had been known about for quite some time (everyone had to retire at 62) and there had been masses of speculation in the corridors as to who would get the job. In the bad old days, it would probably have gone to one of two Brits, who had both been in the service for more than 10 years and each was well regarded, both as mission leaders and technicians.

In the past, massive underrepresentation from countries such as the US, Japan and Germany had allowed a number of other (mainly European) nations to be over-represented. Jacques Diouf, the DG at the time, considered this to be unfair and stated that it was his job to share any spare quotas among candidates from the developing world. Furthermore, he saw much merit in a policy of appointing nationals from the various regions of the world to posts with a regional bias. For example, the FAO had a policy of appointing Asians to FAO representation positions in Asian countries, and Africans to countries in Africa. The vacancy referred to was a case in point.

Being well aware of this, two Asian colleagues – I'll call then Ali and Ali – expressed interest in the post. Both were economists, ambitious, Westernised and quite well connected to their own diplomatic establishments. As soon as the starting whistle blew, they moved into action, lobbying their case. Dinner parties were set up, at which the director of the division and the respective country ambassadors to the FAO were the main guests. Every effort was made to please the director, especially in public venues, such as attending the annual staff Christmas lunch, which most people boycotted by then.

For a while, it was not at all clear who had the edge, but the mist lifted eventually. Management – i.e. the director, a somewhat overconfident and clever but lazy American who had spent almost all his working life in the FAO – had decided that he wanted the younger Ali (I'll call him Ali 2). In many ways it was an understandable choice as Ali 1 was considerably older than Ali 2, was wise to the ways of the FAO, was more than a bit laid back and – most important of all – had a mind of his own. In contrast, Ali 2 was the perfect stooge who would do the director's bidding without batting an eyelid.

There was just one little difficulty. Ali 2 was really too young and inexperienced to be parachuted into such a senior position. So, the director and his merry men hatched up a neat little solution, which they sent to the DG in the form of an internal memo. The idea was to put Ali 2's name forward as the preferred candidate, but to suggest that the post be filled *ad interim* by a very senior member of staff who was about to retire. During the interregnum, Ali 2 would be groomed for the job. It was a win-win solution for the director, as he would get the man he wanted, whatever the DG decided; it was just a matter of now or a little later. The DG apparently liked the interim idea and scribbled his agreement and signature to this effect in the margins of the memo one morning. He then had lunch with various ambassadors from a number of Asian countries and, in the afternoon, he crossed out his earlier agreement, appointed Ali 2 forthwith instead, and sent the doubly marked memo back to the director.

The director, probably to cover himself by showing that the decision to appoint Ali 2 immediately was not really his idea, informally circulated copies of the marked memo. Subsequently, he had good reason to be pleased with his choice, as Ali 2 showed himself to be most cooperative when it came to staff recruitment within the service, going out of his way to keep slots vacant for the director's men. (The aforementioned Mr Good is a case in point.)

The Asian ambassadors were also pleased because they were able to look forward to affirmative action as far as the recruitment of nationals from Asia – as both full-time staff and consultants – was concerned. And this is what it is all about at the end of the day: jobs for the boys, rather than any disquiet about the quality of the work they might do. The irony is, of course, that as the quality of staff drops, so does the demand for their services; eventually, the unit shrinks or closes down, and there are jobs for nobody – but that is tomorrow's problem, not today's.

The risks of such patronage and sycophancy soon became apparent. Some four years after Ali 2's appointment, the director who appointed him retired, and no sooner had he retired than a huge hole in the division's budget appeared. Although not directly responsible for the hole, Ali 2 had contributed to it in some way and his fortunes began to change. Over coffee one day, he explained to me that he had recently been carpeted by the assistant DG for the department and advised to look for another job within the organisation. I must admit that I was amazed by his frankness, but I soon realised it was part of his natural chutzpah or bravura that refused to believe that he could ever do anything wrong. He was really telling me he had been wronged and was seeking my sympathy.

Despite the little problem with the budget, Ali 2 continued to carry out his agenda of hiring and promoting Asian candidates. To be fair, some of them deserved their appointments on merit, but others were a little lucky. Around the year 2000, I remember being asked to help screen applicants for an economist post. We used a simple scoring system that awarded marks for qualifications and experience. Using the system, it was clear that the best-qualified candidate was a Canadian national. This upset Ali 2 considerably as he had as good as promised the job to an old friend from his postgraduate days at Oxford, even though this guy had no relevant investment project experience, having spent many years as a university economics lecturer. In the end, he got lucky as another post came up, and having been number two for the earlier post, it was easy to get him in.

As for Ali 2, after a while, he decided to get out of the kitchen. About six months after Mr Good took himself off, Ali 2 announced to his staff that he too was leaving the service. He had secured a transfer within the FAO to a post that he claimed offered a greater challenge. What he really meant was better promotion prospects as he would be substantially closer to the seat of power. It also meant he could escape from the service before it collapsed around his ears. On his watch, the number of staff in his service had fallen from 15 to 8. I had told him when he got the job that, as the incumbent, he would probably be the one to turn off the lights, as it was quite clear that the World Bank was phasing out lending for agriculture. He did not like what I said at the time, but I suspect he knew I was probably right. His departure had been suspected for quite a while, so it was not really a surprise in itself.

What was a surprise, at least to me, was his blatant abuse of influence to secure jobs and/or promotion for some of his 'mates' before he left. It would be wrong to go into details, but at least one candidate was encouraged to put down erroneous facts on his application form for a promotion, and another was appointed to a technical post for which he knew full well that there was little or no demand. Internal promotions in the UN are notoriously opaque, and almost invariably, they go to someone from the service or division, rather than from elsewhere within the organisation. In many ways, this is not really a problem. After all, if someone has worked well for 10 years or so, they can reasonably expect a promotion in situ – as they would in any organisation. Nevertheless, there has to be a series of interviews at which candidates are asked the same questions by an 'independent' panel. I have it on good authority that, on at least one occasion, Ali 2 showed his preferred candidates the questions they were going to be asked!

When I commented on this lack of integrity to a European colleague, I was advised to reflect on the fact that Asian and European values are not necessarily the same, nor indeed should one be considered as better than the other. While possibly true in a metaphysical sense, to me, there is only one standard that technical merit should be assessed by, and my colleague's explanation sounded very much like an apology for the hollowing out of the UN. Another colleague was even more illuminating. When I discussed the strange pattern of promotions, he said that, a few years earlier when the time came for his annual performance appraisal, Ali 2 let it be known that to secure a good appraisal report he would appreciate some reciprocation. 'You mean money?' I asked in horror. 'No, not necessarily,' came the reply. 'There are other ways of paying back dues; for example, convincing one's national representative to the FAO that Ali 2 was an excellent fellow, and implying that a good word would be appreciated when applying for a very senior post!'

These sad stories confirm that merit is largely of secondary consideration by now as far as many jobs in parts of the UN are concerned, and that – perhaps even more worrying – there seems to be no attempt to put a bit of rigour back into the recruitment and promotion system.

4.12. United Nations (UN) Management Weakness

One of the best opportunities for patronage and the biggest causes of weakness in the UN system is the appointment of country representatives. Following the general UN structure, the senior representative in a country is the UN resident coordinator as appointed by the Secretary-General. Beneath him/her in the pecking order are representatives from all the other agencies; in particular, the larger specialist agencies such as the FAO and the WHO, which consider themselves important enough to have a person on the spot in most member countries. These country representatives are appointed by the DG of the agency concerned and report directly to him or her. The smaller agencies tend to rely on the office of the UN coordinator.

Of course, the job is very attractive to nationals from developing countries, as it comes with a US dollar salary and generous expatriate perks. A classic entry route is to switch from being a national country ambassador at a UN agency's headquarters to being a UN representative in a developing country. Diplomats by profession, they are often very good at representing the personal interests of the DG who appoints them. Whatever the route taken, the result is that UN representatives in many countries today are better at attending official events in their flag-waving cars and pressing the flesh than they are at promoting their agency's technical interests and skills. In my time, I came across at least half a dozen FAO representatives who were unable to even write a memo in English, French or Spanish (the agency's main working languages in those days) or display any technical knowledge about agriculture.

In early 2007, the FAO representative in Nepal was a Chinese ex-translator (not exactly a nationality or profession one associates with expertise in agriculture). The new head of the FAO sub-regional office in Harare was also Chinese; this time from the external affairs section of the Ministry of Agriculture. No doubt, he was a useful asset or go-between for Robert Mugabe and Hu Jintao. Whatever the route taken, the point is that such people are frankly a very expensive waste of limited resources – a conservative estimate puts the cost of a UN representative at US$400,000 a year – often more than the TA programme they are supposed to be overseeing!

UN reform calls for, *inter alia*, a rationalisation of UN representation, with one senior person representing all agencies, supported as appropriate by a number of technicians for the different agencies. If housed in one complex, substantial savings could also result from the sharing of office overheads. The trouble here is that few within the UN system are willing to endorse and support such reform publicly for fear of being labelled a traitor to their specific agency's cause. Those outside the system – who sit on agency boards or councils, or who vote at annual membership conferences – are equally reluctant to vote for reform for fear that they be seen as closing off attractive job opportunities for their fellow countrymen and women. Turkeys, as they say, do not normally vote for Christmas. There is really no obvious way to bring about any such meaningful change.

It is tempting to think that trimming the budgets of the agencies would force them to trim their sails and follow reform recommendations. The problem with this approach is that it opens the door for someone else to walk through. The Covid-19 outbreak is a classic case in point. At the time of the outbreak, the US was severely behind with its assessments (or regular biennial payments) to the WHO. This shortfall was made good by extra voluntary payments from China, and when the outbreak occurred, the WHO was very careful in its comments about the role of the Chinese government in its handling of the matter. Conveniently for China, the previous DG of the WHO had been a Chinese national from Hong Kong and had been able to appoint sympathisers to important posts within the organisation.

Probably the only way to reform the UN agencies is from the inside – ensuring that a sufficient number of senior posts are filled by Western nationals of real competence. This will not be easy, but it could be done by secondments from national civil services or universities, with a guarantee of a good job back home after the UN service has been completed. Similarly, ambassadorial postings to UN agencies should be given to up-and-coming diplomats, not those about to go on pension. In this way, better information would be transferred to Western capitals in good time to prevent or minimise the unhelpful constitutional changes so loved by DGs from the developing world.

Apart from patronage, another weakness – albeit perhaps not a major issue nor peculiar to the UN system – is nepotism. The risk of this was recognised at the birth of the UN, and provisions were introduced from the start to prevent it. All vacancies require applicants to declare whether any family members are employed by any UN agency, and some agencies have 'no spouse' employment regulations (unless people working in an agency meet there and then decide to get married). The applicant declaration goes some way towards reducing abuse, if folk are honest. However, it does not take much imagination to realise that the use of a maiden name enables a spouse to declare no UN-employed relatives, and in my experience, agencies rarely check to see if a spouse is employed in another agency in the same duty station. In Rome, where there are three large UN agencies (the FAO, WFP and IFAD), as a rough estimate, they probably have no less than 5% of staff with a spouse working in one of the sister agencies.

Spouse employment is not necessarily a bad thing, providing selection is based on merit. After all, in a number of situations, a spouse cannot get work in a given duty station because of nationality considerations. US nationals cannot officially work in the EU without their own work permit, and vice versa. In such situations, it seems unfair for a spouse to be denied employment with a UN agency, providing they have the necessary skills and experience. Of possibly greater significance is second-generation employment.

4.13. Technologies That Did Not Work (Water Does Not Flow Uphill)

One of the biggest shibboleths of development is that low-cost, intermediate technologies and systems are best for poor rural people. Quite a number have been promoted – often in the face of obvious resistance by the 'beneficiaries' – because some aid worker somewhere thought it was a good idea. I summarise in the following sections some of the classics that I know about, but I am sure there are many others. Like much in development, there is a bitter irony associated with such initiatives, which are often promoted on behalf of the poor by folk with well-paid jobs in aid.

Azolla

This is a tiny aquatic fern that that lives symbiotically with a blue-green algae (*Anabaena azolla*) in the cavities of its leaves. Its potential value is that the algae fix nitrogen from the atmosphere. In theory, when azolla is encouraged to grow in rice fields, it can supply up to half the nitrogen needs of a crop. The technique was once widely used in China and Vietnam, and it was promoted heavily in the Philippines in the 1980s as a cheap source of nitrogen.

However, it has not taken off in a big way, and to my knowledge, one rarely hears anyone talk about azolla technology these days. That said, there was a report about azolla (*The Economist*, 2014A) that hinted at the possibility of improving the efficiency of the current species of azolla by genetic manipulation.

On the whole, the use of azolla largely remains a research topic with potential, which remains on the shelf in practice as it has too many drawbacks. It is very labour-intensive, as special beds have to be constructed to generate enough algae, which must be done 20–40 days before transfer to the rice field. The azolla then has to be incorporated into the soil two or three times using a rotary cultivator to get full benefit. As if this were not enough, azolla will only grow well in soils with at least 20ppm of available phosphorus, and it requires an initial source of inoculum. As with vetiver grass (see section 'Vetiver Grass' on page 222), the source is usually a government agency as the technology is of little interest to the private sector.

Biogas and Biofuels

A great hope of technophiles in some parts of Asia was biogas digesters. These are simple sealed pits into which organic waste (ideally cow dung) is placed to decompose. One of the products of such decomposition is methane, which if captured, can be piped into a house and used as a cooking fuel.

The technology works and, on paper, looks quite attractive; however, as we know, looks can be deceiving. The whole facility is expensive to construct and is complicated to install, requiring plumbing beyond the skills of most village communities. Therefore, they are invariably only found as and when a special project – usually aid- or NGO-funded – has been set up, with subsidies to cover the full costs. This constraint, although serious, need not be limiting as there are plenty of cash-chasing good ideas to help the rural poor.

The real problems arise from utilisation issues:

1. The pit requires quite a large area of land, which is often more than the poorest can easily provide.
2. The dung from five or six animals is needed to keep a plant going, and few farmers have as many cows or oxen.
3. The collection of dung may not be a problem for stall-fed animals, but even these are usually let out to graze whenever possible and, unfortunately, tend to leave their dung whenever and wherever it suits them. It is also the case that many farmers know the value of dung as a plant food and prefer to apply what they have to their fields, and in much of India, they already use it as fuel, but dried on sticks. The premixing before feeding the digester is unpleasant work and very unpopular with housewives.
4. The fact that the gas in a household facility is produced under very low pressure, usually only producing enough gas to boil a kettle or pot very slowly is ultimately the killer.
5. Finally, methane is a notoriously bad greenhouse gas, and its use is now generally discouraged.

Improved Wood-Burning Stoves

Wood-burning stoves are ubiquitous in the rural villages of the developing world. Their design varies from simple troughs made of two stones or a line of bricks to much more sophisticated moulded units made of fired clay. The latter typically have four sides or are bowl-shaped, with a small side opening to feed in the wood and a wider opening at the top, on which the cooking vessel sits and through which the fire's flames and hot gases evacuate.

Well-meaning technophiles from the West have measured the efficiencies of these stoves; they consider that much energy (heat) is lost by most traditional stoves and that more sophisticated designs with a different exhaust opening can save energy, thereby consuming less valuable wood. The main 'improvement' is to minimise the gaps between the cooking vessel and the sides of the stove. Basically, the cooking vessel now sits snugly onto the whole of the upper opening, and there are three or four special side vents to allow heat and gases to escape. The effect is to create three or four tongues of hot gas that heat the pot. The main aim is to minimise energy loss by directing most of the fire's heat onto the cooking pot.

It all sounds too good to be true, and it is. The traditional stove will allow wood to burn whichever way the wind is blowing, as the cooking pot imposes no constriction on the exit gas flows. However, the improved version is much more sensitive to wind direction, and the fire tends to burn best nearest the vent that is closest to the prevailing wind. If there is not much wind cooking takes much longer. So, even if it saves wood, it takes up more of the women's valuable time. This is another example of a focus on technology rather than on people, as it fails to appreciate the value of time and labour to rural people.

Rice-Fish

This technology was highly popular with some development agencies and NGOs in the last two decades of the 20th century. I must admit, in theory, it has a lot going for it. In much of Asia, rice fields are kept under water for much of the growing season, and although there is not much depth of water, there is often enough to keep fish alive. The basic idea is to put some fish fingerlings into the rice field after the rice has been transplanted and the field flooded.

The main problem is that rice fields have to be dried out or drained during the season for weeding and fertiliser application, so the fish have to be captured in some way during these operations. To do this, part of a field is dug out as a small pond in the hope that as the field dries out, the fish will have the sense to migrate to the pond. To some extent it does work, but many fish do not make it to the pond. Most farmers are also reluctant to construct a big enough pond as they need every square inch for rice production.

In nearly 40 years of wandering around the rice paddies of Asia, I have yet to see the system in regular use when unsupervised by some enthusiastic expert from Europe or the US. There are undoubtedly some rice–fish producers in countries such as Bangladesh and Thailand, but in general, the technology has not caught on.

System of Rice Intensification (SRI)

The original SRI was developed in Madagascar in the 1980s. It was claimed to increase yields of rice substantially at almost no additional cost, as it relied extensively on low-external-input use (organic matter for fertiliser and manual weeding). However, it did require very good crop husbandry, especially the accurate control of water levels in paddy fields, so as to facilitate the careful control of irrigation depth, and to allow alternate wetting and drying cycles. It also called for the transplanting of single young (10–15 day old) seedlings. The scientific basis of SRI has been extensively studied, and the underlying principles conform to those of standard good management practices for rice production, such as the use of young seedlings, wide spacing, and alternate wetting and drying.

As with many 'better' technologies and production practices, there are hidden disadvantages to SRI that tend to be overlooked or even ignored by its promoters. In particular, it requires substantially more labour than traditional rice farming. Young seedlings require much more care in transplanting than older seedlings, and they are more vulnerable to pests, but most difficult of all, SRI requires careful water control, which very few small farmers can achieve.

The system also requires much more weeding. In SRI trials undertaken in India (Andhra Pradesh) over a period of six years (2002–08), yields of rice were significantly improved (by 12–42%) and water use was significantly decreased (by 21–48%). However, the farmers were not convinced by these benefits as the SRI plots required much more weeding (thrice at 10-day intervals after planting) and better water management (i.e. keeping the fields saturated until panicle initiation) was too difficult.

Despite these difficulties, some wild claims have been made for SRI (up to 20 tonnes/hectare beyond the theoretical yield levels possible for a non-C4 crop[62]). The system (or simplified versions of the system) attracted support among some less-technical development experts around the last turn of the century. This was perhaps understandable, given the low costs and claimed benefits of SRI. However, it is important to realise that most assessments of the published studies of SRI and modified versions have failed to show any significant benefits (Dobermann and Dawe, 2008). In fact, the majority of reliable studies show SRI to produce lower yields and returns than the best local management practices. This was certainly the case for Bangladesh, where SRI was tried quite extensively in the early 1990s, and where both on-research-station and on-farm studies showed lower yields and profitability for SRI (Latif et al., 2005).

Since then, there appears to have been little interest in SRI in Bangladesh. In fact, farmers have been far more interested in and have recently adopted a range of other technologies, few of which are naturally aligned with SRI. It is also the case that the increase in the area of irrigated Boro rice in Bangladesh (some 6 million hectares annually) underlines the difficulties in promoting SRI for four reasons:

1. Most of the irrigation is by shallow tube wells, each with a small command area of two to three hectares. While each individual farmer attempts to

---

62. Plants can be broadly defined as being either C4 or non C4, depending on their photosynthetic pathways. C4 plants are more efficient converters of carbon dioxide into plant matter. Most crop plants grown at lower latitudes, with the notable exception of rice, are C4 plants.

level their fields and control water application depths as best as they can, in general, they have little or no control over either their neighbour's surplus irrigation water or rainfall running off the watershed as a whole.

2. Most farmers tend (despite all the research evidence to the contrary) to keep up to 10 centimetres of water in their paddy fields during most of the growing season to suppress weeds.

3. The cost of irrigation water represents only about 10–15% of production costs. Any savings in water use through the use of SRI would therefore only represent an estimated saving of 1–2% in overall production costs. This is not sufficient to persuade farmers that accurate land-preparation costs are worthwhile.

4. The alternative drying and wetting cycles of SRI can lead to the soil cracking deeply and subsequently leaching of valuable irrigation water.

Treadle Pumps

These are fairly simple pieces of engineering that enable small quantities of water to be raised manually up to 7 metres. They consist of two long arms attached to a simple double-action suction pump, similar to the two interconnected barrels of a bicycle pump. By alternatively raising and lowering the arms, water can be lifted from a shallow well or ditch. The main attraction is that they do not need any fuel; all the work is done manually by an operator endlessly moving the treadle arms up and down. They are also fairly cheap and easy to make in remote places.

That is about it as far as the good news goes. They are fiendishly difficult to keep working, as they depend on a simple valve mechanism that frequently leaks after a few hours' pumping. However, the main problem is that operating them is very hard work, and I have rarely seen one being used by farmers, except to demonstrate it to unsuspecting visitors. Really, the point is that treadle pump protagonists have tended to look at only one side of the equation, namely it being a low-cost device for lifting water. They have failed to consider the value of time to the farmers, and perhaps even more significantly, the energy required for pumping.

It is not just farmers who question the value of treadle pumps, which only have a possible role to play in situations where a farmer has a small plot of land. Volker Branscheid (1984), an FAO irrigation engineer, calculated how much of the calorific value of a crop of rice is needed to provide the energy required for working a treadle pump. Branscheid's calculations (based on field studies in India in the 1980s) indicate that the equivalent of 15% of the calorific energy of an anticipated crop of 400 kilogrammes of paddy rice would be consumed in raising or lifting enough water 5 metres to irrigate such a crop, and the equivalent of 20% of the calorific energy would be needed to lift water 7 metres. If – as would very likely be the case – the farmer does not operate the treadle pump himself but hires someone to do the work, Branscheid calculated that the total cost in terms of calorific energy consumption (energy for pumping and labour cost in terms of the value of rice produced) would rise to 40% for a 5-metre lift and 60% for a 7-metre lift. This, he estimated, is some 15–20 times the cost of the electricity needed to power an electric pump to lift the water 5 or 7 metres. So, it is not really surprising that even very small farmers prefer to use powered pumps. (It should be said that these calculations do not fully allow for the value of the benefit an Indian farmer secures from subsidised energy costs, but even without subsidies, it would be cheaper to use electric rather than human power.)

Vetiver Grass

For about 10 years from the mid-1980s onwards, the World Bank furiously promoted the use of vetiver grass (*Vetiveria zizanioides*) as a multipurpose technology for small farmers – they even got the last king of Thailand to give it his blessing. Vetiver is a very tough grass that grows in a clump and is ideal for securing the bunds or edges of fields, particularly terraced fields, to prevent soil erosion. Vetiver, or *khus* as it is known in India, has four key features that make it suitable for creating such bunds:

1. It has to be established by vegetative means, not seeds, and so it will not spread from where it has been planted and become a weed.
2. It is unpalatable to ruminants, so it will not be eaten away.
3. It is drought tolerant, with roots that can go to a depth of 1 metre to get to water in dry spells.
4. It is very long lived: in parts of Zambia, there are rows of vetiver still growing that were reportedly planted in the 1920s.

There is no doubt that planting vetiver on field contours can help reduce or even stop soil loss from erosion, even on land with a slope of 12% and in regions where rainfall exceeds 2,000 millimetres a year. In parts of Fiji, the sugar cane industry was 'saved' from extinction due to soil loss by planting vetiver on contours.

The problem with vetiver is that, while it is very suitable for farms with large fields, it is not really suited for small-scale subsistence farming. If you only have a quarter of a hectare of land, you do not want to give any of it up for non-productive purposes, and the chances are that if the land is steep, it will already be terraced, so there is rarely a need for more protection.

Establishing vetiver in medium-sized fields, where it might limit soil loss, is not as easy as it sounds. This is largely because there has to be a good source of planting material (slips) available at the right time. This may not sound like too much of a problem until you look at the economics. There is little – if any – money to be made from establishing a vetiver nursery and selling slips, so the responsibility for supplying slips invariably ends up with the national agricultural extension or research service. As with so many bright ideas imported by foreign experts, this works while there is an externally funded project. The problems start when the money runs out, as few national extension or research officers seem to be convinced that they should spend time and money on vetiver.

It is also the case that the grass has other competing commercial uses. The leaves are good for thatching; the fine rootlets contain vetiver oil, which is used in the perfume and cosmetics industry; and the coarser roots can be made into mats and screens. Thus, farmers may be tempted to sell their vetiver plants rather than leave them in the fields as bunds.

I am sure there are places in the world where vetiver has been introduced and is helping to stabilise small-farm fields, but I am equally sure that it was oversold by the World Bank in the late 1980s, and that this overselling has done little good to the World Bank's reputation as an impartial adviser.

Low-External-Input Technology (LEIT)

Modern farming in the developed and middle-income countries is heavily dependent on the use of external inputs – water for irrigation, quality seed, fertilisers, pesticides and machinery – in order to achieve high and, hopefully, profitable yields. All of these inputs cost money and usually require access to reliable and regular sources of credit. They also call for good transport, markets and distribution facilities to ensure that the necessary inputs are available in the right quantities at the right time.

In Asia, many countries that were food insecure are now able to feed their populations most of the time as a result of a tremendous increase in the use of external inputs. In the mid-1980s, Bangladesh produced about 10 million tonnes of paddy rice a year, and planners were very worried that many would go hungry unless they could increase production substantially. By 2015, the country was producing more than 35 million tonnes annually through an increase in the use of all external inputs. It is interesting that, in the case of Bangladesh, this has been done largely through savings and sharecropping arrangements as farmers generally have little access to seasonal or crop credit.

In India, the home of the first green revolution, Norman Borlaug (the Norwegian Nobel Prize winner who bred the first dwarf wheat varieties) would only allow seed of his famous dwarf wheat varieties, which were the basis of the revolution, to go to India if the government guaranteed to increase the availability of external inputs. By 2000, India was a net exporter of cereal grains. Since then, the supply and demand situation has changed somewhat, but India will never be able to return to simple low- or no-input farming.

Similar stories can be found across most of Asia and much of Latin America. In Africa and a handful of very poor countries in other regions of the world, modern farming methods have yet to arrive or, at least, to arrive on a substantial and regular scale. There are various reasons for this state of affairs:

- Irrigation systems are very expensive to build and maintain.
- The road system in many poor countries is largely limited to main trunk roads, leaving millions of farmers very far from good transport and communications.
- There are few dealers able to supply inputs or buy surplus produce.
- Credit systems have been tried, but they rarely work (microcredit is not appropriate for seasonal-crop credit).
- Rain-fed farming is a risky business that discourages investments, as they may well be lost if a crop fails.
- There is also the issue of land tenure – or rather lack of land title. Some observers say this is the Achilles heel of African agriculture, as without a land title to use as collateral, few farmers can access credit or consider it worth investing substantially in their land.

There is no doubt that these obstacles are real and severe. Indeed, quite a number of development experts consider them to be too severe and have convinced themselves that there is an alternative, namely LEIT. The intellectual starting point for this school of thought is that resource-poor farmers cannot afford to buy inputs, and LEIT can be the basis for human and social capital formation. In essence, it calls for the use of minimum or no purchased inputs, but relies on the maximum use of good crop husbandry (i.e. the selection of good seed, timely planting and weeding, the good cultivation of soil, the use of compost and manure, and mechanical methods of pest control).

There is little doubt that such technologies can and do result in higher yields. However, they are generally very labour-intensive, and furthermore, there is clear evidence that the main beneficiaries are not the most resource poor but the better-resourced poor with access to markets (Tripp, 2006). These concerns were echoed forcefully by Sir David King (chief scientific adviser to the British government) in an address to the British Science Association in 2008. He accused the NGOs that promote green/organic farming methods of turning farmers against the use of sophisticated farming methods, which are needed if Africa is to raise its agricultural output (King, 2008).

The ex-World Bank agriculturalist Stephen Carr, who has spent his long working life in Africa, was at one time an enthusiast for LEIT (Carr, 1989). He identified a number of technologies that can result in improved yields; these are things such as timely planting, use of good seed, spacing and weeding. But he also recognised the importance of providing adequate plant nutrition. This, he planned to demonstrate when he moved to Zomba in central Malawi in 1989. When I was on a visit to his homestead there in 2000, he showed me the four large compost pits he had had constructed, into which he had religiously put all the vegetable matter he could find. He had the pits turned regularly to aerate and hasten the formation of compost. His initial hope was that this compost would enable him to fertilise and produce maize on a decent scale, and that he would then convince the community where he lived to follow his example.

When I met Stephen, he was singing from a different song sheet entirely. He had come to realise, from his own experience, that compost alone was not going to supply the necessary nutrients to grow even a modest crop of maize (2 tonnes/hectare). Instead, he was now supporting a national programme to give farmers vouchers to access seed and mineral fertiliser. He had worked out that it was much cheaper and simpler to give farmers fertiliser than to give everyone imported maize, at a time when the typical local producer rarely grew more than 600 kilogrammes/hectare. The programme of 'starter packs' that he helped introduce in Malawi was a regular national programme for some years, jointly funded by donors and the government, which raised average yield substantially.

In some ways, Malawi is a quintessential agrarian African country, and what works there to increase food production should work elsewhere. It is also living proof that the 'romantic supporters of LEIT', as Professor Paul Collier (2008B) calls them, do not have the answers to food insecurity. If you need further evidence of the paucity of the LEIT message, just compare the average yields of crops in India with those in Africa, and then look at the amount of fertiliser used. When I last did this comparison, the average annual fertiliser usage in India was over 100 kilogrammes/hectare; in Africa, it was less than 10 kilogrammes/hectare!

I should perhaps say at this point that I fully recognise the harm that intensive farming can do to the environment. However, if there is a choice between feeding people or allowing them to grow hungry or become dependent on imported food, I think modest intensification is the only sensible option. In the UK, we did this out of necessity during the Second World War. By the end of the 20th century, we no longer needed to plough up every possible acre of land and could allow some to return to less-intensive land farming or, indeed, alternative land use. This is because we could afford to import food we cannot produce efficiently ourselves. This is not a luxury open to many developing countries in Africa, where much farmland is very infertile.

At this point, a bit of scientific explanation may be helpful. Much of sub-Saharan Africa and quite a few countries in Asia lie in the tropics, where the natural climax vegetation is rainforest, and the soils are typically acidic and not very fertile. The traditional form of land use was 'slash and burn': the forest was cut down and burnt, and when cleared, the land was quite fertile for a few years and was good for cropping. The trees' roots had brought mineral nutrients up from the deep layers of the soil. When the trees are cut and burnt, some of these nutrients are retained in the surface layers. After a few years, when all the accumulated fertility has been used, the land was abandoned, and forest slowly recolonised the area. Today, with population growth, this extensive land use is no longer possible, and crops can only be grown if nutrients are added. LEIT does not include the replacement of these nutrients, and this is the main reason why it does not work. The transmigration project in Indonesia (see 3.8.) was based on challenging this traditional form of land use.

5.

What Works and Why

This chapter provides a summary of some of the key aid investments, technologies, policies and institutions that have significantly helped to address rural poverty and improve lives in developing countries. With the exception of disease control, this chapter does not cover emergency humanitarian aid, such as food aid, as this is not aimed to address the issues of economic growth directly and sustainably; neither does it cover remittances.

5.1.   Infrastructure

The design and construction of infrastructure – be it airports, bridges, dams, ports, railways, roads, telecommunications or other essential public sector buildings (schools, hospitals, universities, etc.) – has consumed the largest share of aid finance by far. Most but not all of this in the 20th century was through concessionary loans from Western organisations such as the World Bank. Since the turn of the century, China has also extended loans for dozens of infrastructure projects in many developing countries, although few of these are believed to be similarly concessionary.

In many ways, such projects financed by Western agencies or China are win-win stories. The borrowing country gets much-needed new infrastructure, such as the bridge over the Brahmaputra River in Bangladesh or the Aswan High Dam in Egypt. The donors award juicy contracts to some of their national civil engineering companies, and they also get back a good percentage of the loan money for onward lending.

The bridge over the Brahmaputra River is a classic development story in its own right. After independence in 1971, Bangladesh was one of the poorest countries in Asia, if not the poorest country. The Western powers (mainly the US) were reluctant to finance the project as they did not believe it was economically viable. However, Japan and Korea were keen. In the end, the bridge was built at a cost of US$700 million, financed by the IDA, the ADB, OECD special funds and the government of Bangladesh. The project took 10 years from the initial studies to its opening in 1998. It has been a great success economically, although some engineering problems have recently been discovered. The bridge has brought about a small commercial revolution for the north-west province of the country.

When I first went to Bangladesh in 1991, getting to the north-west by road from Dhaka, the capital, was a hit-and-miss affair. There were ferries, but getting a place on a ferry was a bit of a lottery as there was no guarantee that it had enough diesel to travel or that the crossing had been adequately dredged. I recall one occasion when we almost came to a halt midway, and it was only the momentum of the moving vessel that enabled us to slide off the sandy bottom of the river. As a foreigner, I was usually able to get a place on the ferry for my vehicle; the trucks full of fresh produce waiting to cross from the north-west sometimes had to wait days for a crossing and then only managed it by handing over massive bribes. Today, the trucks cross over on the bridge in minutes and deliver their produce to the hungry millions in Dhaka. They have to pay a fee to cross the bridge, but the fees paid have more than covered the cost of the loan to build the bridge and the cost of collecting toll monies. Clearly, it is an example of a very good aid-supported project and has undoubtedly played its part in the economic growth of Bangladesh, which has achieved average annual GDP growth rates of 5% since the turn of the century.

Many, but not all, of the big projects have proven to be economically successful and have enabled the loans to be serviced. Bhutan has borrowed extensively for hydropower plants, which generate the electricity that it sells to India. India has also borrowed extensively for dams for power generation and irrigation supply. In Africa too, there have been some good hydropower projects, such as the Kainji Dam in Nigeria, built in 1968; the Kariba Dam between Zambia and Zimbabwe, built in 1958; and the Muela Dam on the Senqu River (or Orange River) in Lesotho, built in 2004.

Whether Chinese-supported infrastructure (see *Appendix D*) will have the same positive outcome is by no means certain. There are signs that Chinese loans are often provided as much for political reasons as economic ones, and quite a number of projects are already unable to service the loans taken out for construction. Some well-known problems are the railway projects in Ethiopia and Kenya, and the port in Djibouti. Given past practice, once China realises the importance of rigorous cost–benefit analyses, I suspect it will be more circumspect about which loans it approves. There was also a reduction of such Chinese lending towards the end of the second decade of the 21st century, and problems with servicing earlier loans.

Large dams are not without their critics, many of whom's concerns are not without cause. In the first place, there are maintenance issues arising from unexpected wear and tear. This is a big problem with Kariba Dam. It is also an issue with the Coca Codo Sinclair Dam in Ecuador (see *Appendix D*). In Asia, the big worry is what is happening to the Mekong. This river rises in China, and China has already constructed 11 dams in the upper reaches of the river and has plans for another eight. Flows in Thailand, Laos, Cambodia and Vietnam are already severely reduced for much of the year. In 2019, flows in Cambodia were the lowest since records began more than 60 years ago. Furthermore, big dams do not always do everything they were designed to do. The huge Three Gorges Dam on the Yangtze River failed to prevent massive flooding downstream in mid-2020.

Finally, recent financial analyses suggest that it is now much more cost-effective to build renewable systems of electricity generation or small hydropower schemes than costly large ones. The era of big-dam building may be coming to an end.

5.2.   Social Services, Industrialisation and Governance

During the peak years of the Cold War, the development banks started lending for almost all aspects of modern economies, ostensibly to address the problems of poverty globally but also for political reasons. There were loans for education, health, research (mainly agricultural), industrialisation and governance. There were also complex projects combining some or all these things. These were probably the least effective projects, as they invariably involved a range of ministries, and cooperation and coordination was not usually forthcoming or effective. I had the privilege of seeing such projects up close in Nigeria (4.7.) and Brazil (4.12.).

Freestanding projects for education and health were among the better social-sector investments. At least essential hardware was constructed in the form of schools or hospitals, and teaching and medical supplies were provided. There was also some considerable benefit from the overseas training provided; some of the recent achievements of Chinese scientists can be attributed to the training many received in the US in the last years of the 20th century, funded by aid projects.

The real problem with this type of loan is often the recurrent costs involved, rather than the capital costs. Thus, almost invariably, a health project involved an increase in the number of doctors and nurses, and education projects encouraged more teachers. Typically, during the life of the project, these salaries were met partially or entirely by project funds; the idea was that, as national taxation revenue increased during the life of the project (in part attributed to the project), the borrowing country would then be able to pay for more doctors, nurses or teachers from its own resources. Sadly, this was overoptimistic in many cases (see 3.18.). Few people involved in aid challenge the importance and value of providing basic education and healthcare, and there is no doubt that, where communities have been provided with basic education and healthcare, the economy as a whole benefitted, but rarely enough to service the associated loan.

My experience of agricultural research projects supported by the development banks was, without exception, disappointing (see 3.7 and 3.13.). Much as with education and health projects, buildings were constructed and equipped, and salaries were paid for a number of years. But to my knowledge, there is little evidence that any significant new technologies were produced, with the possible exception of China. Despite this, the World Bank continues to lend for agricultural research.

I have little first-hand knowledge or experience of industrialisation, finance or governance projects. Industrialisation accounts for a very small share of development bank lending, as this is really the preserve of the private sector. Finance and governance lending was not prominent in my day, other than for budget support, and those few that existed certainly achieved little. Judging from the annual reports, it looks as though these two sectors each now account for some 7% of World Bank lending, similar to the amount spent on agriculture, fisheries and forestry. The latter were sectors that accounted for some 30% of World Bank lending during the Cold War. Clearly, priorities have changed.

5.3.   New Agricultural Technologies

There have been major changes in agricultural production in many countries over the past 50 years or so. Basically, farming has intensified in many countries, as populations have increased and there are more mouths to feed. The movement of people from rural areas to jobs in towns has also encouraged this intensification and greater dependence on machinery and inputs. Some of these changes have come about directly or indirectly as a result of aid. I summarise some of these changes in the following sections.

Dwarf Cereal Varieties

The introduction of dwarf rice and wheat varieties is probably the biggest single agricultural initiative since the demonstrations of the benefits of adding nitrogen fertiliser to crops by Sir J.B. Lawes in 1891. In the 1960s, India was facing famine as it could not produce enough wheat and rice to feed its growing population. The big advantage of these dwarf varieties is that they do not lodge or fall over when they are heavily fertilised. Average yields increased from two tonnes/hectare to over six tonnes/hectare within a decade. Today, India is more than self-sufficient in normal rainfall years.

The green revolution in India owes a great deal to aid, including the financing of two research centres: the International Maize and Wheat Improvement Centre in Mexico, where the new wheats were developed, and the IRRI in the Philippines, where the new dwarf rice varieties were bred. Rice production in Bangladesh has similarly benefitted from dwarf cereal varieties, and the introduction of other production technologies, as shown in Table 3:

Table 3 The Increase in Paddy and Rice Production, Fertiliser Usage, and Population in Bangladesh Since Independence, 1971–2018

Year	Paddy Production (million tonnes)	Rice Production (million tonnes)	Fertiliser Usage (kilogrammes / hectare)	Population (millions)
1971	15	9.9	130	70
2013	51	34	254	150
2018	54	36	280	165

Source: Original data taken from internal World Bank documents that cannot be referenced. However, please see Bangladesh Rice Research Knowledge Bank (2014) and United States Department of Agriculture Foreign Agricultural Service (2018)

It was the successful breeding of dwarf cereals that encouraged the creation of the internationally funded research stations around the world – the CGIAR (see 2.20.) – to develop new varieties of the other key crops grown in developing countries. Although there has been some success in crops such as cassava and beans, at the time of writing, there has been nothing like the success associated with dwarf cereals.

Hybrid Rice

Conventionally, rice is grown using open or self-pollinated seed. Farmers can keep some of the rice crop for sowing the next season. Hybrid seed is formed when two or more varieties are crossed to produce a hybrid. Producing such seed has to be done by special seed-producing companies, and new seed has to be purchased every season. Hybrid seed is quite a bit more expensive, but it is higher yielding and less seed is needed as only one seed needs to be planted per hill. So, overall, the higher cost is not a serious deterrent. Yield improvements over conventional varieties of 20–30% are being reported in some countries.

A number of rice-growing countries in Asia are using hybrid rice. In China, some 50% of the rice area is sown with hybrid varieties. Hybrid rice responds to high levels of fertiliser application and is particularly popular in the irrigated Boro season in Bangladesh. In India, less than 10% of the area is sown with hybrids, although the government has much higher targets.

Other Production Policies and New Technologies

Table 3 shows the substantial increases in paddy and rice production in Bangladesh in recent years, which have come about through the adoption of good policies by the government and the use of better technology by small farmers. In the first place, the government and the aid community began promoting family planning soon after the country gained its independence, and the national birth rate has dropped dramatically from a high of over six children per family to below three.

In the second place, the government listened to technical advice from international experts and got its rice pricing policy right. Rice or paddy prices in Bangladesh are fixed at around the landed price of rice on the world market, meaning there is little incentive for local dealers to import or export rice, or to hoard rice waiting for price rises.

In the third place, the aid community played a role in introducing better production technologies, which the government has endorsed. In particular, hydrology studies by the Canadians in the 1980s showed that there is little danger of overexploiting groundwater reserves, as the amount of annual rainfall is sufficient to recharge by irrigation any groundwater extracted in a given year. In fact, the awareness of this alone and the expansion of the Boro season irrigation area has probably done more than anything else to raise output in the country. Of the paddy rice produced in 2013, more than half (29 million tonnes) came from the irrigated dry season or Boro crop.

Mechanical Cultivation

One of the biggest changes in farming in much of the developing world has been the gradual introduction of mechanical cultivation. Farmers with larger farms have bought or hired tractors (both large four-wheel machines and two-wheeled cultivators) from other farmers. In much of Asia, at planting time, one no longer sees a couple of tired-looking bullocks slowly pulling a shallow plough. Instead, two-wheeled mechanical tractors from China dominate. Not only do they do a better job (and at three or four times the speed) but their use means there is no need to keep and feed the bullocks for 365 days a year. As far as greenhouse gases are concerned, this change is probably a zero-sum game, as the reduction in the use of oxen means less methane production, but the consumption of diesel in the tractors results in more carbon dioxide production. Such machinery is also useful in the adoption of conservation agriculture (see section 'Conservation Agriculture' on page 233).

Fertilisers and Agrochemicals

There is no question that there has been a dramatic increase in the use of these inputs in farming globally, except perhaps in much of Africa. Riots over fertiliser availability in Bangladesh in the early 1980s brought down a government, and since then, no government there has risked a fertiliser shortage at rice planting times. The use of mineral or artificial fertiliser is heavily criticised by those in favour of organic fertiliser (compost and manure), and there are problems with its use, especially micronutrient imbalances and damage to the natural soil flora and fauna. However, without the use of mineral fertiliser, the world would not be able to feed itself with the currently available agricultural technologies.

Chemical products used for pest control (mainly insects), for fungal disease control, as a growth regulator and as a weedkiller have revolutionised global crop production. Not only have they prevented crop losses – sometimes total crop failure – but they have also saved hundreds of man hours of labour. Many of the early agrochemicals – products such as the chlorinated hydrocarbons (e.g. dieldrin, aldrin and endrin) and the organophosphorus insecticides (e.g. malathion and parathion) – were incredibly toxic to mammals, fish and birds, and have been withdrawn from use in most of the world. However, this was not before Rachel Carson's famous book *Silent Spring* (Carson, 1962), which was one of the first publications of the green movement that shared concerns about the use of these chemicals with the general population. Since then, less-toxic agrochemicals have been developed (e.g. synthetic pyrethroids for insect control), and although there are always some risks if products are not used according to manufacturer's instructions, the use of such products is now standard practice in most of the world.

Conservation Agriculture

'Conservation agriculture' is the term used to describe farming systems that are designed around the concept of minimum tillage, or the planting of crops into soil that has not been ploughed. It is characterised by three principles:

1. Minimum soil disturbance
2. Permanent soil cover or mulch
3. Rotation of crops rather than mono-cropping (continuously growing the same crop)

For centuries, if not millennia, farmers have ploughed their fields before sowing the next crop. The main reasons for ploughing are to bury crop residues and weed seeds, to create a surface that encourages rain to penetrate the soil rather than run off and to create a fine tilth (crumbly surface) that helps newly planted crop seeds to grow. However, ploughing is very energy and labour dependent, and recent research has shown it may not to be essential everywhere. Thus, if crop seeds are sown into a small slit or furrow made in the soil's surface, germination is just as good as when seeds are sown into a ploughed field, providing vegetative cover is maintained.

Machinery to do this has been available for some time; the main constraint to its use has been how to control weed growth, which can smother young plants. This problem can be solved with the use of herbicides; notably, through the agrochemical glyphosate, commonly known as Roundup®, which kills almost all plants but is itself a virtually harmless chemical to all other forms of life.[63] However, while still patented, glyphosate was expensive and was not universally available. Today, glyphosate is off-patent, the price has dropped dramatically and it is widely available.

In the 1970s in Brazil and other parts of Latin America, farmers growing soya were quick to see the possibilities of using glyphosate to kill weeds, but the uptake of the technology was fairly slow. By 2009, some 70% of farmers were using conservation agriculture in Brazil. There is also some evidence that organic matter levels in soil are conserved as a result of its use, with fertility and carbon sequestration benefits.

Brazilian farmers are, on the whole, highly capitalised and were able to buy new direct drilling or minimum-tillage equipment suitable for large-scale farming. The breakthrough for smaller farmers in Latin America and elsewhere, notably in India and China, came with the development of seeding machines for use with small two-wheeled tractors. By 2009, it was estimated that some 110 million hectares globally were cropped using conservation agriculture. This had risen to nearly 180 million hectares or some 12% of the global arable area by 2015 (Kassam et al., 2018).

Aid agencies, particularly the FAO, have done much to promote conservation agriculture globally, which is now found in much of Asia and Africa, promoted by NGOs and Ministries of Agriculture.

Livestock

Livestock plays an important role in most developing countries, providing both a good source of income and valuable food for farmers and their families. Small ruminants such as sheep and goats are important as a source of meat in locations where there is some grazing and where pigs are not acceptable, but they are far less important than poultry and cattle. Typically, in the developing world, poultry production is by small private entrepreneurs supported by national veterinary

63. There was a legal case in California in 2019 where a man successfully claimed his cancer was caused by exposure to glyphosate, and he was awarded massive damages against Monsanto, the company that developed the product. The case is bizarre to say the least, and it is probably linked to some fetish group that hates big pharmaceutical companies and paid for the trial. Blaming Monsanto alone is nonsense as the product is off-patent and is now made by many chemical companies. It is also the case that the product has a very low LD50 (which is the measure of the lethal dose of a toxin); indeed, it is a modified sugar molecule, and in all the years it has been used, there has never been any suggestion that it causes cancer or any other disease in humans. Bayer, the company that now owns Monsanto, has said it will appeal the verdict, and it will very likely win. The only people who will benefit will be a few ambulance-chasing lawyers.

services. Aid has a limited role in poultry production in normal times, but it can and does step up to the plate when there are emergency disease outbreaks.

Attempts to introduce high-yielding milk or beef breeds from Europe and the US to the developing world have almost invariably failed, largely because of problems with heat tolerance, disease and inadequate feed. However, there have been some successes, notably Operation Flood in India, which is one of the most successful aid projects in many ways. It transformed India from a position of having a serious milk shortage into becoming the world's largest producer.

It all began with the happy coincidence of a remarkable man, a simple good idea, political support and appropriate aid. The man was Verghese Kurien, who ran a large, successful dairy cooperative in Gujarat State. The basic idea was to cut out the middlemen and link milk producers directly with consumers through a network of dairy cooperatives. The political support came from the then prime minister of India, Lal Bahadur Shastri. The aid came largely in the form of skimmed milk powder and butter oil, provided as a grant from the European Economic Community that was on-sold in India to raise funds for the project. There was also the involvement of the WFP, and additional funding from the World Bank.

In the first phase (1970–79), 18 large dairies were established near major urban centres. During the second phase, the number of dairies was increased to 118, which were supplied with milk from 43,000 small producers. In the third phase, more-intensive production systems were introduced, based on artificially inseminating native breeds of cow with semen from exotic breeds such as Holsteins, Friesians, Brown Swiss and Jerseys; providing veterinary medication; training producers; and adding a further 30,000 producers to the project.

Mobile Phones

Mobile phones have revolutionised rural communities that are dependent on agriculture and fisheries, mainly by providing up-to-date information about market prices and demand, but also by providing banking services in some countries, notably Kenya and Bangladesh.

5.4.   Disease Control, Elimination and Eradication

The global control of disease is not, by any means, exclusively within the remit of aid, although it is increasingly one of the more successful aid initiatives and well-supported by the rich world. In fact, most disease control started in the richer countries of the world where vaccination systems were developed and the costs could be met by national taxation. It then became apparent that if a disease were to be eradicated globally, action would be needed in poorer countries where a disease was or still is endemic.

Diseases do not respect borders. The 2019 case of polio in Australia occurred in a young man who had just returned from visiting his family in Pakistan. The 2020 Covid-19 pandemic has confirmed in spades just how little respect viruses have for national borders. Global eradication campaigns involve aid to provide adequate funding and the initial operational mechanisms for control programmes. Developing-country governments that are members of agencies – such as the WHO, FAO or the Joint United Nations Programme on HIV/AIDS (UNAIDS) – can hardly refuse to participate in an eradication campaign, especially when the campaign is funded by aid money. These agencies open the door to other public and private sector providers, such as the Bill & Melinda Gates Foundation, Gavi and the Global Fund.

Smallpox in Humans and Rinderpest in Cattle

A disease is considered to have been eradicated when its prevalence in the global host population is zero. As of 2020, only smallpox in humans and rinderpest in cattle have been eradicated. The first to be eliminated was smallpox, which is caused by the variola viruses. In 1980, the WHO certified the global eradication of the disease, following an intense vaccination campaign in those countries where the disease had still been endemic. A disease can be considered as controlled when treatment substantially reduces the number of new cases.

After the Second World War, rinderpest was a serious problem in much of Asia and Africa. It is a highly contagious viral disease of cattle, with a high mortality rate. Like smallpox, it is caused by a single serotype, and an efficacious vaccine was developed. Monitoring of rinderpest on a global basis led to the recognition in the 1990s of six long-standing endemic reservoirs.[64]

In 1999, the FAO, along with other agencies (notably the Office International des Epizooties [the World Organisation for Animal Health]), embarked on the intensification of an eradication programme that focused on the following:

- The containment of the virus in reservoir areas.
- The intensive monitoring of outbreaks and, where necessary, vaccination programmes.
- The sero-surveillance of reservoir areas to ensure the verification of freedom from rinderpest.

---

64. The borders of South Sudan with Uganda and Kenya, southern Somalia, the southern tip of the Arabian peninsula, parts of Turkey and Iraq, Pakistan and Afghanistan, and Asiatic Russia and northern China.

In turn, this was linked to the cessation of mass vaccination campaigns in affected states in order to be sure that there were no residual endemic reservoirs. The work was done almost entirely using the FAO's Technical Cooperation Programme staff and resources, with some help from EC-funded livestock-health development projects. It also depended heavily on the cooperation of the veterinarians in the countries with endemic reservoirs. That this was achieved in parts of the world wracked by conflict at the time is a tribute to all involved and is perhaps one of the most successful recent aid stories.

Yellow Fever and Polio

Two other viruses are on track to be eradicated. Yellow fever is a nasty virus transmitted by mosquitoes. In 2017, the WHO launched a programme involving 50 partners to eliminate the disease. It is endemic in a number of tropical countries in Africa, Central America and Latin America. A single vaccination provides lifelong protection. The WHO aims to vaccinate some 1 billion people by 2026, when the disease will have hopefully been eradicated.

However, a big worry about yellow fever eradication is the presence of the disease in Angola, and the growing business contacts between Angola and China. By 2016, there were already a number of yellow fever cases in China among Chinese nationals returning from Angola. Some medical experts think it could spread in China and a number of other Asian nations where the mosquito that carries the disease (*Aedes aegypti*) is commonly found.

The other virus targeted for eradication is polio, which is transmitted in dirty water or food. It is a disease that is often fatal, but even survivors are usually severely crippled following the paralysis and wasting of leg muscles. Polio can be contained by the use of vaccines, but it is a complicated process. There are three types of polio virus, and each type needs its own vaccine. Vaccination campaigns have to start by identifying which virus strain is prevalent in an area. Despite these complications, since the Global Polio Eradication Initiative was started in 1988, there has been a dramatic 99% reduction in the number of cases globally.

Most of the world is now considered free of polio, but pockets of infection remain in Afghanistan and Pakistan, and there have also been outbreaks in northern Nigeria since the turn of the century. In all three countries, control has been hampered by religious leaders who have spread the rumour that the vaccine sterilises women. However, there is another problem with polio eradication, which is vaccine-induced polio. There are two basic kinds of polio vaccine. The first is injectable and is based on dead virus tissue. The other is an oral vaccine that is based on weakened live virus tissue. Oral vaccines have a big advantage in that someone treated with such a vaccine will excrete the weakened virus for some weeks, and this can result in herd immunity among other people in a community and provide them with protection. In places where sanitation is poor, this is a big advantage. Oral vaccines are also easier to manage in control campaigns. However, oral vaccine virus tissue can mutate and regain strength. In 2017, type 2 polio viruses derived from the oral vaccine caused cases in Syria and the DRC, and in 2018, similar cases occurred in Nigeria, Niger, Somalia and the DRC. This means that eradication will only be achieved when only injectable vaccines are used, and this is expected to substantially prolong the eradication campaign. Nigeria was reported to have eradicated polio in August 2020.

Human Immunodeficiency Virus (HIV) / Acquired Immune Deficiency Syndrome (AIDS)

The other big virus in the headlights of the controllers is, of course, HIV/AIDS. The UNAIDS and WHO control programme (90-90-90) originally aimed to ensure that, by 2020, a target of 90% of those infected will have been diagnosed, that 90% of those diagnosed will be receiving anti-retroviral medication and 90% will have the disease supressed. This is perhaps a little optimistic, as the latest (2019) statistics suggest that some 38 million people are infected globally, and to reduce this to less than 30 million in 2020 is a tall order.

Unlike polio, there is no vaccine to control HIV, despite the best endeavours of the pharmaceutical industry for more than 30 years. The only way to eliminate the disease is to treat all infected for as long as it takes for the disease to burn itself out, which will happen when the last infected person dies. This is no mean task and costs some US$8 billion a year, which is effectively a transfer of resources from the rich to poor countries. But unlike much traditional aid, this humanitarian aid works and is a win-win situation, as it benefits both givers and recipients.

According to the UN SDGs, the next target is 95-95-95 by 2030. At current rates, that would be equal to a total cost of $80 billion – the equivalent of four times the total annual UK aid budget (pre-2020) of £14.0 billion a year – unless a vaccine is developed. This is quite a lot of money for a relatively small population.

Measles, Mumps and Rubella

These three viruses are easily contained by vaccines. However, false medical information linking the vaccines with autism has been a real problem. It has discouraged some mothers, mainly but not exclusively in the developed world, from having their children vaccinated. This has led to recurring outbreaks in countries where it was thought the disease was under control; the most notable being a severe outbreak of measles in Samoa in late 2019, which killed more than 100 people. All of which goes to show that constant vigilance is needed if diseases are to be eliminated or eradicated.

Neglected Tropical Diseases (NTGs)

A number of parasitic diseases that affect millions of people in tropical countries could be controlled, eliminated and even eradicated. Not only would this improve lives but it would have considerable economic benefit as it would enable treated people to still do a full day's work. The seven diseases discussed in this section are considered prime targets for control campaigns, as with one exception, they affect millions of people, but good control measures exist. There are some 18 tropical diseases that are not usually life-threatening but can kill and that usually cause a great deal of discomfort.

Yaws

This is caused by a spirochaete bacterium, *Treponema pallidum*, which is related to the bacterium that causes syphilis. It causes skin ulcers that, if left untreated, can lead to painful joints and limbs. It is spread by contact with fluid from an infected ulcer.

Yaws is relatively easy to treat and cure using antibiotics, and an eradication campaign in the 1950s and 1960s led to a 95% reduction in its incidence globally. More recently, yaws has made a comeback in nearly a dozen tropical countries. The worst-affected countries are Ghana, Papua New Guinea and the Solomon Islands, and the WHO has a renewed eradication programme. Given the ease of treatment and the fact that it is a disease of minor significance (with less than 60,000 cases globally in 2016), it should be possible to eradicate yaws. But the yaws experience shows how important it is to continue eradication programmes for many years.

Guinea Worm

Guinea worm (or Dracunculiasis) is an exception in that it has almost been eradicated. In the mid-1980s it afflicted more than 3.5 million people in Africa (where 90% of cases occurred) and Asia. Like many parasitic diseases, its lifecycle involves fresh water. People catch guinea worm by ingesting infected copepods, which are small crustaceans or water fleas that live in stagnant water. Once inside a human or a dog, the adult water fleas are killed by stomach juices and the released larvae develop into male and female nematode worms. After mating, the male worms die, but the females migrate to the lower limbs, and after about a year, they emerge through a blister on the skin. If an infected person then goes into water, the female releases larvae that end up in water fleas, and the cycle is repeated. It is not a killing disease, but it is very debilitating and painful. As the worm emerges it is usually slowly and painfully wound onto a stick. This can take several days as worms can be over a metre long.

Control is relatively easy, and can be done by training a dedicated field force that provides people in infected areas with special cloth filters, the use of a larvicide to kill copepods, training people how not to reinfect water courses and helping those infected to wind out worms. The filters provided strain out the copepods and make the water safe to drink. The global eradication campaign owes much to the Jimmy Carter Foundation, which identified guinea worm as a target for eradication in 1986. These measures and careful surveillance have almost eradicated the disease.

In 2019, the WHO estimated that there were fewer than 60 cases of guinea worm in the world. The trouble is that these 60 cases are in inaccessible parts of a handful of countries, notably Chad, Ethiopia, Mali and South Sudan. While it should be possible to control the parasite in most of these countries, a real problem has arisen in Chad. In this country, the larvae of the worm have been found in people and dogs that have eaten raw fish from Lake Chad.

Onchocerciasis

By 2016, more than a billion people globally, many in Africa, had received effective drugs to treat onchocerciasis (or river blindness). The disease has already been eliminated in Colombia, Ecuador, Guatemala and Mexico. It was taken to the Americas, along with most of the other NTGs, by slaves in the early 19th century. The disease is caused by a nematode worm that is transmitted to humans following a bite from a black fly that lives near tropical rivers. The nematode lives in the human body for years, but when they die, the body's immune system reacts fiercely by destroying tissue, especially vulnerable eye tissue.

The eradication of onchocerciasis in Latin America was achieved by the distribution of the wonder drug, ivermectin. This was made available for free by the pharmaceutical company Merck Sharp & Dohme (MSD) and was distributed by aid foundations in Latin America, according to the book *Under the Big Tree* (Agler, 2019).

Schistosomiasis

Something similar is possible with schistosomiasis (or bilharzia). This is a nasty parasite that lives part of its lifecycle in water-loving snails and part in humans. Inside humans, the creature produces hundreds of eggs, each with a sharp spine that enables them to travel through the body to the bladder or the large intestine, from where they are discharged back into the water from whence their parents came.

In China, under Chairman Mao, the disease was eventually controlled by a massive campaign to kill the snails physically. Efforts to control snails elsewhere and/or discourage people from coming into contact with infected water have largely failed. However, all is not lost. The drug praziquantel damages the outer skin of the worm and allows the human body's natural defence mechanism to attack the worm, effectively preventing infection from developing. In Egypt in the last half of the 20th century, an intensive campaign using praziquantel has almost eliminated the disease.

Shin Poong, a Korean pharmaceutical company, has made praziquantel available at low cost, and the WHO has a programme of delivering millions of tablets a year to people in the infected areas of Africa. But the parasite is difficult to eradicate, and long-term supplies of praziquantel, better distribution mechanisms and improved information programmes about hygiene will almost certainly be needed in much of Africa for the foreseeable future.

Lymphatic Filariasis

Like malaria, lymphatic filariasis (or elephantiasis) is transmitted by mosquitoes. An infected mosquito injects filariae (small, hair-like worms) that live in the lymphatic system's vessels. Some of these develop into adults, which then release thousands more filariae into the blood stream and can be picked up for transmission by another mosquito bite. The large worms cause blockages in the lymphatic system, eventually leading to massive swelling. In 2017, there were estimated to be more than 100 million people infected, of whom at least a third were incapacitated by very swollen legs or scrotums.

China eliminated the disease by the use of the drug diethylcarbamazine in the 1980s, and since then, another eight countries – mainly island nations in the Eastern hemisphere – have eliminated filariasis. India is on schedule to eliminate this dreadfully disfiguring disease by 2030. I still have memories of the first case I ever saw on a field trip in Bihar. The poor man's legs were so swollen he could not walk.

The disease is quite easily controlled by a combination of drugs (ivermectin and diethylcarbamazine/albendazole). The drugs kill the small filariae and last for a year. The use of bed nets to prevent mosquito bites is also recommended. Funds are needed to buy the drugs, train health workers in how to convince people to take the medication, administer the drugs and ensure they are distributed to villages where the parasite is prevalent.

Trachoma

This is a most unpleasant affliction that often ends up blinding the sufferer. According to the WHO, there were some 1.9 million cases in 44 countries in 2020, a slight reduction from the 2.0 million reported in 2016. The majority of cases were in Africa, but there were also cases in Asia, Australia, South America and the Pacific

Islands. The disease is caused by a bacterium, *Chlamydia trachomatis*, which makes the eyelids turn inwards. This causes the eyelashes to scratch the cornea every time a person blinks, and eventually, the scaring of the cornea results in blindness. The bacterium is spread by the eye and nose discharges from infected people, very often children. Trachoma is preventable through cleanliness, good sanitation and regular face washing. It is treatable by using a single dose of the antibiotic azithromycin (Zithromax) and simple surgery to remove the eyelashes.

In 1996, the WHO launched the Alliance for the Global Elimination of Blinding Trachoma by 2020 (Mariotti *et al.*, 2003). This target was not met, but there has been good progress. By 2020, 13 countries[65] had reported that they have eliminated trachoma as a 'public health problem'; that is to say, there is a very low prevalence of the affliction: less than one person affected for every 1,000 of the population. This is no mean achievement and demonstrates that it should be possible to eliminate or even eradicate the disease globally. The elimination campaigns depend on trained public health workers able to visit people in remote areas. Often referred to as 'SAFE' campaigns, they are based on four lines of attack:

- **S**urgery to remove eyelashes from badly affected people
- **A**ntibiotic treatment
- **F**ace washing
- **E**nvironmental improvement, especially sanitation and the provision of latrines

All of the aforementioned require resources and funding. Fortunately, the disease has attracted quite a lot of international support.

Intestinal Worms

Intestinal worms (or helminthiases) – such as hookworm, roundworm and whipworm – are soil-transmitted helminths that cause a great deal of discomfort and debilitation, and they have an economic cost in terms of reducing a person's ability to work. There are two main types of hookworm: *Ancylostoma duodenale* and *Necator americanus*. Both are indigenous to West Africa but were transported to the New World by slavery. They have similar lifecycles, which start with soil-inhabiting filariform (thin or hair-like) larvae that enter the human (or other mammal species) by penetrating the surface of the skin, usually a bare foot in humans. The mouths of the larvae have two pairs of teeth to enable penetration. Once inside the body, the larvae migrate to the lungs, and from there, they are coughed up to the mouth and then swallowed. They then travel to the small intestine where they moult to

65. Cambodia, China, Gambia, Ghana, Iran, Iraq, Laos, Mexico, Morocco, Myanmar, Nepal, Oman and Togo.

the adult stage. Male and female worms mate, and the female produces massive amounts of eggs that are passed out with faeces. In moist, warm soil, the eggs hatch into larvae, and the cycle starts all over again. Hookworms feed on blood, and infected people are severely weakened by them.

Roundworms (*Ascaris lumbricoides*) are parasitic worms (nematodes) that infect the small intestine. They are common in the tropical and subtropical parts of the developing world where there is no modern sanitation. The infection usually causes no symptoms, but severe infections can affect the lungs or intestines. Infection occurs by ingesting the roundworm eggs, which are found in soil contaminated by human faeces or contaminated uncooked food. Children typically become infected when they put their hands in their mouths after playing in infected soil. Once ingested, the eggs hatch in the intestines, and the larvae migrate to the lungs, where they mature. From the lungs the mature worms move to the throat, making infected people cough, and are then swallowed. Once back in the intestine, the worms mate, and the female produces eggs that are then excreted to enable the cycle to continue.

The simplest way of preventing infection is through better hygiene, especially by only using clean water and by not defecating in the fields, but using pit latrines. Severe infections can lead to blockages of the intestine or other body ducts and to nutritional deficiencies. Treatment is through the use of drugs such as albendazole, ivermectin or mebendazole.

The last of the triad, whipworms (*Trichuris trichiura*) – so called because one end is thick like a whip handle, and the other end is thin like a whip – is one of the most common of the helminths. At least 1 billion people living in hot, humid climates are believed to be infected. The majority of cases are in Africa, but it is also common in parts of Asia and Latin America. One of the reasons for its prevalence is that dogs and other mammals are also carriers.

Whipworms have a fairly basic lifecycle. Infection starts when eggs are ingested. Once in the small intestine, the eggs hatch into larvae, which mature into worms that move to the large intestine. Male and female worms mate, and each female then releases from 3,000 to 20,000 eggs a day. Many of these are passed out with faeces, and they remain viable in moist soil until picked up to repeat the cycle. The eggs are typically picked up by people working the soil with their hands who then rub their dirty hands on their face and inadvertently swallow the eggs. Eggs can also be found on unwashed fruit and vegetables.

Malaria

Malaria is not by any stretch of the imagination a neglected tropical disease, and it is not easy to control. However, evidence from Europe suggests it can be eliminated.

It was endemic in Italy until as recently as 1970, when a campaign of spraying insecticide (dichloro-diphenyl-trichloroethane [DDT]) on mosquito breeding sites and distributing free quinine led to its elimination. Nevertheless, the disease was still endemic in other parts of Europe until 2015.

Globally, and particularly in Africa, malaria remains a very serious disease. It is caused by one of five *Plasmodium* parasites. In Africa, 99% of cases are caused by *Plasmodium falciparum*. The parasite is carried by Anopheles mosquitoes and injected into humans by mosquito bites, typically while people are sleeping. Once inside the human bloodstream, the parasites travel to the liver, where they multiply before invading individual blood cells and multiplying further. The main symptoms are headaches and alternating fever and chills. Many adults build up a degree of immunity to the parasite, but children are very susceptible and many die.

Currently, there are four basic ways to control malaria:

1. Destroying mosquito breeding sites (stagnant water pools) by draining them or spraying them with insecticide
2. Sleeping under bed nets, ideally treated with insecticide
3. Taking prophylactic medication regularly
4. Taking curative medication such as artemisinin, either alone or in combination with other drugs, to reduce the chance of drug resistance developing

If these measures are followed, the disease can be held at bay. The vast majority of people in Africa do not have access to these facilities, and for years, scientists have been looking for simpler control measures, such as a vaccine or a way of sterilising male mosquitoes.

To date, campaigns to eliminate malaria have needed to resort to using treated bed nets, spraying house walls with insecticides and treating it with cocktails of antimalarial medication. A major campaign directed by the WHO and, since 2002, by the Global Fund (see *Chapter 2*) has achieved some success.

The most recent WHO annual report on malaria suggests that efforts to control the disease, based largely on the use of treated bed nets and a combination of drug therapies, have stalled (World Health Organization [WHO], 2018). This same report identifies that there were more than 220 million cases worldwide in 2018, leading to 405,000 deaths, which is down from more than 700,000 in 2010. Some 90% of cases and deaths occur in Africa. This is far more than anticipated if the control measures were working fully, and it will almost certainly mean the target of eliminating the disease by 2030 will not be achieved. The main reasons for the slowdown are a combination of mosquito resistance to the main insecticide (pyrethrins) used to treat nets and spray walls, resistance to the main drug used (artemisinin) and, perhaps above all, badly managed control programmes. In well-managed programmes, such as those in Uganda and India, there has continued to be a fall in cases.

On a more optimistic note, there was some good news reported by the BBC about malaria on 4 May 2020 (Gallagher, 2020). Scientists from the International Centre of Insect Physiology and Ecology, while working on the shores of Lake Victoria in Kenya, have made what could be a ground-breaking discovery. They have found that mosquitoes infected with the fungus *Microsporidia MB* do not carry malarial parasites. How this works is not yet clear, but the scientists are very excited about the potential of this finding to lead to an effective way of controlling the disease and perhaps even eradication. And in 2021, the University of Oxford vaccine team announced successful results of a new vaccine against malaria that was very effective against the disease in children.

5.5. Microfinance/Microcredit

The terms 'microfinance' and 'microcredit' are usually associated with small-scale loans to poor rural women, administered by NGOs. They are also often associated with the Grameen Bank in Bangladesh and Muhammad Yunus, both of whom shared the Nobel Peace Prize in 2006.

The main distinguishing feature of microcredit, when compared to a conventional bank loan, is the replacement of traditional forms of collateral or security with peer pressure. The whole concept is essentially a way of lending to poor people with few, if any, resources, but who can and do repay loans used to finance small income-generating enterprises. The details of such programmes vary tremendously from country to country, and even within countries when between different agencies. On the whole, the more successful schemes are those that lend to groups of women in rural areas. A typical microcredit group is outlined as follows.

In Bangladesh, a microcredit group starts when a number of women in a village agree to form a small savings group. Such a group has some 15 members who subscribe small savings (US$1–5) into a group account as a membership fee. The savings are administered for them by an NGO official who issues a savings passbook to record the amount saved. Borrowers have to be members for a set period (usually 12 weeks) and must have attended group meetings regularly before they can borrow. When a sufficient amount (e.g. US$100–200) has been accumulated by the group, borrowing can begin. Loans are usually quite small (US$75–150) and have to be repaid on a regular basis – weekly or monthly. Repayments are recorded in passbooks. If anyone defaults, the other members of the group are obliged to make good the loan – this is the peer pressure element.

Microcredit loans are not cheap, but they have the great advantage in that the money is made available in the village with the minimum of paperwork and administration. What is more, unlike the case with many bank loans, borrowers are unlikely to have to pay an under-the-table bribe to the NGO loan officer. The repayments include an element of interest that covers the transaction costs of administering the loan, and any interest payable by the NGO on the capital it has borrowed for on-lending. The annual interest on microcredit loans was 29% in Bangladesh in 2012. Globally, in 2014, microcredit interest rates were 30–35% (*The Economist,* 2014B). This is more than the official interest charged on a bank loan, but is considerably less than the 100–150% charged by money lenders.

Some economists consider that there is relatively little evidence that microcredit actually reduces poverty. However, there is plenty of evidence that it is a dynamic and fast-changing subsector of the financial world. The microfinance barometer of the sector, kept by BNP Paribas, shows that, globally, there were 124 million microcredit borrowers in 2016, with a loan portfolio of $104 billion. India had the largest number of borrowers, followed by Vietnam, Bangladesh, Peru and Mexico. In 2018, there were 140 million borrowers with a loan portfolio of $124 billion. The annual growth rate of borrowing has been increasing at some 7% a year.

Most microcredit is used for small enterprises, some is used for consumption in lean times and before wages are paid, and some is used for agriculture. Repayments vary from village to village and from NGO to NGO. But the better NGOs regularly recover 98% of the amount lent. While the success of microcredit has perhaps been hyped by some development experts, there is little doubt that it has made a tremendous difference to the lives of millions of poor people in Bangladesh and elsewhere. The main requirement for success is, however, competent and well-trained NGO staff. What distinguishes microcredit from almost all other aid initiatives is that it originated in an emerging economy and was not yet another Western development idea. Maybe that is why it has been so successful. The success of microcredit would seem to confirm Thomas Bauer's contention that, if the circumstances are right, credit will materialise (see *Introduction* 'Putting Aid into Perspective' on page 13).

5.6. Large-Scale Farming in Developing Countries

During the first 15 years of the 21st century, there was a growing interest in investment in large-scale agricultural projects funded by the private sector, with contributions from national governments and development agencies. The overall concept was not really new – during the 1970s, 1980s and 1990s there had been a massive expansion of oil palm estates in Southeast Asia, and even earlier, during the colonial period, a number of large-scale schemes had been developed. Perhaps the most famous are the Gezira scheme in Sudan, started by the British in 1919, and the irrigation scheme based on the barrage at Sukkur in today's Pakistan. There were many others managed by the UK's Commonwealth Development Corporation (now known as CDC Group) during the colonial years, and similar organisations belonging to other European colonial countries. I recall visiting in 1973 the sugar scheme run by the CDC Group in the Lowveld of Eswatini (Swaziland), and in 1988 I visited the oil palm and cocoa projects in Popondetta, Papua New Guinea, managed by the CDC Group. One of the better-known CDC Group schemes is the Mumias Sugar Company in the western province of Kenya, which now supports several thousand smallholder growers.

An extensive review of large-scale investments in agriculture by the CDC Group in 2013 (Tyler and Dixie, 2013) looked at the results of 160 CDC Group schemes implemented between 1948 and 2000 in sub-Saharan Africa, Southeast Asia and the Pacific. One-fifth of projects were total failures, one-third generated acceptable rates of return on investments and over half (55%) were financially viable. Overall, the majority of projects survived and achieved their targets in terms of jobs created and the level of turnover anticipated. Although clearly risky, this review confirms that large-scale agriculture can be profitable in developing countries and helps an economy to grow.

Exports of flowers, vegetables and avocados from small and large commercial growers in Kenya have also made a major contribution to that nation's economy. (In 2018, Kenya exported 70,000 tons of avocados, making it the largest exporter of the fruit in Africa.) So, investment in large-scale farming in developing countries seems to make sense, if done properly.

The main source of data about large-scale agricultural investment is the Land Matrix – an independent global land-monitoring initiative that collates data from a variety of sources, including the media. It produces up-to-date data on its website (Land Matrix, 2021). As of late 2019, some 1,700 schemes had been planned, covering 80 million hectares globally. Of these, 14% had failed, 23% had yet to start and 62%, covering 50 million hectares, were in operation. The geographical location of the deals is shown in Table 4.

Table 4 Global Location of Schemes in 2019

Region	Africa	Southeast Asia	Eastern Europe	Latin America	Far East	Pacific	India
Number of Schemes	561	356	335	288	58	43	23

Source: Land Matrix (2021)

The size of deals ranges from a few hundred hectares to more than 500,000 hectares. Typically, each is around 10,000 hectares, such as the Addax/Sunbird scheme in Sierra Leone. This 10,000-hectare scheme, located near the town of Makeni in central Sierra Leone and started in around 2010, was to produce ethanol from sugar cane. This scheme differs from older schemes, which were usually nucleus estates (a consortium of small growers around a central processing facility and nursery), in that it is managed as a large-scale farm. The older schemes were essentially designed to provide a living for smallholders, while the newer large-scale investments are principally for commercial profit, with some job creation for locals and outgrowers. In both types of scheme, land holdings have to be consolidated, and appropriate leases and rents have to be agreed with usufruct owners.

The Addax scheme appears to be typical of many schemes planned in the early years of the 21st century, in that it was planned at a time when commodity prices – in this case, ethanol – were high. The investment was made by a private Swiss company (Addax & Oryx Group [AOG]) with some financial support from European agencies, notably the Emerging Africa Infrastructure Fund (EAIF)[66] and the IFC of the World Bank. Although rigorous soil and social surveys were carried out to determine the potential of the land and to secure the cooperation of local land users, the project was not a success, and AOG sold a majority shareholding to Chinese company Sunbird Bioenergy in 2016.

Basically, Addax failed for technical reasons. The sugar cane yields were much lower than anticipated, and the centre-pivot irrigation systems proved very difficult to operate in the terrain. To a considerable extent, this can be attributed to the failure of Addax to investigate fully the agricultural potential of the area. A number of grow-out trials took place, and the plants seemed to grow well. In fact, they grew quickly, but they grew too tall, and the canes were thin and tended to lodge or fall. Before making the investment, it should have carried out trials for at least three years to determine if good yields could be achieved by better fertiliser regimes and in different weather patterns. The project also suffered from a global collapse in ethanol prices. Sunbird Bioenergy has the benefit of sunk costs met by AOG that include a new processing plant and available land with long leases. It is already experimenting with other crops, such as cassava, that seem to do quite well in the area. Unlike sugar cane, cassava is a popular food crop in the area, and its production may end up being more profitable than ethanol.

A much larger failure is the ProSAVANA project in northern Mozambique. This massive scheme, planned in 2009 by a joint Brazilian and Japanese venture, aimed to use technology developed in the Brazilian Cerrado to produce soya

---

66. The EAIF is part of the Private Infrastructure Development Group that is supported by the private sector and donor agencies such as DFID, KfW (Germany), SIDA (Sweden), ADB and other development banks.

beans on an area of more than 1 million hectares, near the town of Ribaue. To date, there is almost nothing to see other than a research station and a few model farms growing onions; not a single soya bean plant has been grown. The jury is still out on the reasons for the project's failure so far, but it almost certainly hinges on cultural misunderstandings. The Brazilian farmers promoting the project were encouraged to believe the land was largely unpopulated. In fact, it is populated, if only lightly, as the soils are poor and only support shifting cultivation; the land is farmed for a few seasons and then left fallow to recuperate. The Brazilian farmers thought they could make the land productive using modern farming methods and, egged on by civil servants, expected local farmers to cooperate when shown new, more productive ways of using their land. The local population was not properly consulted and considered the project to be little more than a land grab. In this, they were aided and abetted by various national and international organisations. The Brazilian farmers have now returned to Brazil to open up new lands there. The Japanese maintain an interest, but whatever happens will be much more modest than originally planned.

In the early years of the 21st century, there were fears that China was making a grab for land in Africa to grow food for its own people. In her book *Will Africa Feed China* , political scientist Deborah Brautigam (2015), suggests that China has, in fact, only leased some 250,000 hectares of land on the continent. While some observers question some of her data, it is clear that China has not been 'grabbing' land in Africa. My guess is that China has looked carefully at the experience of other investors and has only become involved where the returns look good and there are no problems with existing land users – such as the Sunbird Bioenergy investment in Sierra Leone.

5.7.   Cash Transfers

One of the most important new approaches to poverty reduction being explored by rich and poor countries is cash transfers. There are three basic types of transfer, as follows.

Conditional Cash Transfers (CCTs)

CCTs are well-established. In their book *Good Economics for Hard Times*, Abhijit Banerjee and Esther Duflo (2019) report that CCTs existed in more than 100 developing countries by 2014, and 52 of these schemes were specifically for poor households. Most schemes were in Latin America, but there were quite a number in Africa. In total, they estimate that 1 billion people globally have benefitted from such schemes.

The basic idea is that, in return for their children being vaccinated or going to school regularly, the parents receive a small cash payment. Evaluations of such schemes, based on RCTs, suggest that they can play a role in improving human capital (better health and learning). In particular, there is some evidence that children whose families have received such payments do better at school and end up with better jobs, and that their cohorts who were not so lucky or did not use the money wisely do not do so well. Such studies also indicate that, contrary to popular opinion, relatively little of such money is wasted on alcohol and tobacco, and most is used for food and clothing as intended. Furthermore, there is no evidence that such schemes discourage people from working.

In 2007, the government of Indonesia introduced a large CCT across the country in 438 subdistricts and involving 700,000 households. An assessment of the programme after nearly 10 years of operation indicates that it led to improvements in the health of children and their school attendance. However, households were not measurably richer, and some observers think that the sums of money involved were too small to make a real difference to incomes. This experience tends to support the contention that CCTs do make a contribution to welfare, but there is no substantial evidence yet that they make a quantitative and sustained contribution to economic growth. It is also the case that they are not universally popular. Some poor parents do not sign up to CCTs linked to children's schooling as they are not sure they can meet the requirement that their children attend school every day.

There are quite heavy costs associated with CCTs. Surveys have to be carried out to establish who is eligible in a location, and then monitoring checks have to be made that the commitments entered into are undertaken, and that the money is going to the right people. In Mexico, screening consumed 34% of the Prospera scheme's costs and monitoring a further 25%. Schemes are also only effective if they last for a number of years, and only governments with reliable revenue can realistically embark on such schemes.

Unconditional Cash Transfers (UCTs)

Under these schemes, small amounts of cash are distributed, usually to the poorest of the poor. Like CCTs they have a role in countries without a functioning welfare state. They also have set-up and distribution costs, even if they do not need monitoring to check on obligations being met, and the money to fund them has to come from somewhere.

In the early years of the 21st century, the UCT concept was quite widely promoted by a number of development economists. The Mchinji Social Cash Transfer Pilot in Malawi, started in 2006, is quite a good case study. It was funded by aid agencies to see if the approach could be scaled up nationally. It was implemented and funded by UNICEF and the national branch of the Global Fund at a total cost of US$600,000. The project provided selected households with US$4.0 on average every month for two years. The objective was reducing poverty and hunger, and increasing school enrolment in one of the poorest parts of the country. If successful, it was planned to scale it up to a national programme that would have cost US$41 million annually.

An evaluation of the project by an international team in 2011 was somewhat equivocal (Miller *et al.*, 2008). It reported that participating households had told them that they had benefitted, and there was some evidence of less illness and disease. However, there was very little quantitative evidence of improved livelihoods in terms of sustained increases in household expenditure or asset accumulation. Part of the problem was the way the project was implemented. It is clear that the results were not sufficiently positive for the rollout of a national programme. Nevertheless, there was an expansion to eight districts and 100,000 households in 2009, and a further increase in 2015 to 18 districts and 170,000 households, each of which received US$3.5 a month on average.

An in-depth evaluation reported in the *World Bank Economic Review* in 2012 (Kohler and Thompson, 2012) was marginally more positive than the earlier evaluation. It states that participating households increased their productive investments, especially farming, and that there was a measurable increase in school attendance. However, there was a caveat in that, to a considerable extent, it appears the increases in investment were achieved using more child labour in the fields and in doing household chores.

GiveDirectly, an organisation based in Cambridge, Massachusetts, was founded to take advantage of modern money-transfer technologies using mobile phones and some evidence that UCTs work. GiveDirectly started operations in Kenya, but in subsequent years, expanded considerably in East Africa. The co-founder of Facebook (Dustin Moskovitz) has provided GiveDirectly with over US$40 million. An evaluation of GiveDirectly's cash-transfer programme shows a lack of clear, positive long-term benefits and no evidence of increased spending on health and education.

While there are still experts in favour of CCTs and UCTs, the experiences of the first years of the 21st century have not been as positive as some had hoped. In particular, the lack of clear economic benefits and the high costs associated with such schemes have led to a reconsideration of their place in aid aimed at improving economic welfare. To some extent, the discussion has moved on to universal basic income (UBI) programmes.

Universal Basic Income (UBI)

In both rich and poor countries, economists and social scientists have been developing, trialling and, in some places, introducing UBI schemes. In the rich world, the attraction is the simplicity of such schemes, which do away with the means testing associated with traditional welfare schemes. On such a scheme, everyone, regardless of income, would get a basic sum of money from the government. The amount given being just enough to keep the unemployed or those who cannot work for whatever reason from starvation, but too small to stop most people from seeking regular paid jobs. In fact, a lot of the interest in UBI schemes concerns whether they encourage or discourage people from looking for employment. Funding for a UBI has to come from national taxation, as do other welfare payments, but there would be substantial costs savings from not having to identify and monitor welfare needs. Some calculations suggest that up to half the cost of such schemes could be met from the savings associated with not having to identify and monitor the beneficiaries.

There are one or two small-scale schemes in the US. One in Alaska – the Alaska Permanent Fund – has distributed US$2,000 a year to all residents since 1982, based on recycling some oil wealth. This is not really enough money to be considered a UBI and is perhaps more of a bonus for not emigrating. Another well-known scheme in the US is the US$4,000 a year paid to Cherokees from casino profits. Although not a king's ransom, this makes a substantial contribution to average reservation earnings. Both these schemes are virtually self-financing and are independently funded from local resources, rather than coming from the national treasury. Perhaps more significantly, they do not seem to discourage people from looking for work.

In Europe, there has been some interest in UBI. In Finland, 2,000 unemployed people were paid £500 a month over a two-year period that ended in 2018. The objective was to see if a low income that would continue whether or not they found work would encourage them to take up low-paid employment. The basic idea was to see if a low-cost UBI scheme would be a cheaper and more effective way of addressing problems of unemployment than traditional welfare systems. Although it is believed that the scheme encouraged some of the 2,000 to find additional work, it was not heralded as a great success. In Switzerland, a petition in favour of a UBI led to a referendum that was roundly defeated.

In India, the government does not have any UBI scheme as such, but it has a self-targeting welfare-for-work programme that provides poor rural families with 100 days of work at the minimum day rate. This is very popular, but it is not a panacea as there are considerable financial costs and administrative burdens associated with finding construction work for the rural poor.

Although attractive – in theory – as a way of addressing issues of inequality, on balance, there would seem to be less scope for UBIs in the developing world than in the rich world.

6.
Factors Likely To Affect Future Aid Policy and Practice

The famous New York Yankees baseball player Yogi Berra is alleged to have said, 'Never make predictions, especially about the future.' I am inclined to think that anyone who makes predictions about development aid should follow that advice; there are so many variables at play that any predictions are really only guesswork.

So, you have been warned – my predictions are little more than just informed or thought-through guesses. It is also the case that aid, being largely a political initiative, is a second-order chaotic system. That is to say, it is one that, by definition, cannot be predicted with any accuracy, as the chaos changes with any predictions made about it. Just think about how the price of shares is often as much about sentiment as hard fact. Any attempt to predict the main focus and direction of Western aid policy could affect the way both donors and recipients react, and it could, in turn, affect any outcomes. For example, if recipient governments think donors are going to provide more or less medical aid, will that affect their own spending on health? Perhaps if recipient governments really believe they can no longer rely on budget support from donors, they will improve their tax-raising measures, and vice versa.

That said, as indicated in *Chapter 1*, the experiences of aid since the end of the Second World War have resulted in a much better understanding of the economics of development and the key preconditions for economic growth. The first section of this chapter is an attempt to summarise the now generally accepted tenets of economic growth and to review how these might influence Western aid policy. The subsequent sections look at the big questions facing aid in the future.

The provision of aid is likely to continue to be a political matter. However, this is likely to be less another Cold War-type ideological competition and more of a straightforward competition on how best to use aid to secure commercial interest, political influence and security. Good evidence for this is the increasing interest many countries have in Africa. This is manifested most obviously in the number of new embassies and military bases in Africa that have been established by countries such as China, India and Turkey. The bottom line is that 54 seats – more than a quarter of the total – in the UN General Assembly are held by African countries. If a little aid helps an African country vote the right way in the UN, it would seem to be money well spent.

From a more broad-based perspective and looking back over the period since the end of the Second World War, it is increasingly clear that much of the free world's liberal order 'was in fact controlled by the US, largely in its interests' (Thompson, 2019). It had paid in blood and treasure to end that war, and its prize was subsequent global economic and political domination. During the Cold War, the US offered military guarantees to Western Europe in exchange for subordination. It was all done quite cunningly, with Western European powers being given seats at the high table (e.g. the head of the IMF was always to be a European), but ultimate control lay with Washington and the dollar.

According to Helen Thompson (2019), Trump differed from his predecessors in that he no longer tried to or saw the need to hide the power of the US. Biden has yet to show his cards fully, but on foreign policy, he has retained quite a few of Trump's positions. Thompson's analysis, when expanded to include aid policy, suggests that this, too, has essentially been driven by US policy since 1946. It is interesting to speculate whether things on this front will now change with the apparent retraction of the US from its global domination and the emergence of China as a competitor to the US. By mid-2019, there were clear signs that, under President Trump, the US planned to scale back its responsibilities as the world's main policeman. It seems he felt that the costs to the US outweighed the benefits. In the short term, withdrawing or threatening to withdraw American forces may save some money.

In the longer run, however, it could prove very costly. Few doubt that the 'Long Peace' (Pinker, 2018) since the end of the Second World War, husbanded by the US and its allies, allowed 'a rising tide to lift all boats'. And the US has benefitted economically as much, if not more, than any other country as a result of the peace it helped secure. The scaling back of American power and influence in the second decade of the 21st century has allowed serious conflicts to re-emerge in places such as Kashmir, Iraq, Syria and Yemen. If such a trend continues and spreads, it will put up the cost of trade and slow down global economic growth. All countries will be losers.

6.1. Economic Growth, Poverty Reduction, Governance and Culture

As far as economic growth and poverty alleviation are concerned, there is a growing body of evidence that the two are closely linked. In his book *The Great Escape*, Angus Deaton (2013) convincingly argues that if the basic institutions are in place, a rising tide does lift all boats. His work was preceded by some interesting supportive studies. Perhaps the most well-known is 'Growth is Good for the Poor' (Dollar and Kraay, 2000), which looks at data on economic growth and incomes from 80 countries over a period of four decades. Their findings show convincingly that, on average, the incomes of the poor rise one-for-one with all incomes. In other words, growth really does help the poor as it raises their incomes by about as much in percentage terms as it raises everyone else's income.

The work of Deaton, Dollar and Kraay, and many other development economists has, in many ways, done little more than confirm the importance of economic growth as the route out of poverty. And it was this belief in the importance of economic growth that formed the underlying policy basis for much early Western aid. However, it was not so much that the fundamental economic thinking was wrong, but that the prerequisites for economic growth were not fully understood or were conveniently ignored for political reasons. The big difference in economic thinking post 2000 is that sustainable economic growth will only happen if the right supporting institutions exist, together with effective governance. The somewhat pious hope that liberal democracy alone was a necessary precondition has been well and truly challenged.

These newly understood preconditions could create a problem for the West as they might result in poor countries being tempted to follow the Chinese autocratic governance model, which seems to have produced faster economic growth for more people in a shorter period of time than Western democracy has achieved in recent years. According to the IMF, by 2030, the liberal democracies of the West (including Japan) will account for less than a third of global GDP compared to more than half in the second half of the 20th century. According to Yascha Mounk (2018), as the economic power of the West declines, it is likely that the ideals of liberal democracy as a precursor to economic growth will lose favour in emerging nations.

Another important development that is likely to affect aid, arising from recent political and economic thinking, is the challenge to liberal democracy in the Western world itself. Political scientists studying the rise of populist politics in Europe and the US have come to the conclusion that the reason voters are disillusioned with liberal democracy is that, for some 30 years, it has failed to produce any real increase in wealth for most voters and has, in fact, led to a great increase in inequality, with a small minority getting much richer while the majority see no improvement in their living standards.

The people most affected by this stagnation are worried about the future and tend to put their faith in politicians who promise to bring back the old way of doing things: 'Make America Great Again'. The statistics are not in question and are the result of much slower economic growth rates in the Western world in recent years on the one hand, and a decrease in the share of taxes paid by the better off on the other. While the tax issue ought to be relatively easy to solve, the problem of poor growth rates is much more complicated. To some extent, it is due to globalisation, and in particular, manufacturing jobs moving from the richer West to countries in Asia.

The problem is that there is no easy way of reversing the trends identified by Mounk (2018) in his book *The People vs. Democracy*. As far as aid is concerned, a loss of confidence in liberal democracy is likely to have two effects. The first is that it will give a boost to autocratic leaders, who will scorn the need for democracy and will have little compunction about taking aid from China. The second effect is likely to be a decrease in aid funds from the West. If folk in the West are getting poorer, they may be less supportive of the generous aid programmes supported by their governments. Indeed, in 2020, when the UK government slashed its aid budget, its main supporters raised no objections.

That said, it is probably a bit too soon to dismiss liberal democracy entirely. It may recover its mojo and lead to higher economic growth rates and better equality in the next few decades, and there is equally no certainty that the economic progress made by autocratic regimes will continue unabated (see 6.6.). However, the recognition of the importance of institutions and competent governance means that, in future, aid will no longer be provided to all emerging countries in need, regardless of their institutions. Instead, development aid other than emergency aid will increasingly go to those that have the necessary institutions and can use the aid effectively.

At this point, I think it is helpful to say a little about governance, starting with a brief reflection on the observations of Alexis de Tocqueville in his famous book *Democracy in America*, first published in English in 1835. You may wonder why this book is relevant, given that it was written nearly 200 years ago. During a visit to New England in 1831, he was fascinated to find that the settlers from Europe – the Pilgrim Fathers – had developed a new egalitarian system of governance. A system that recognised all were equal before the law; there was no small, rich, powerful aristocracy or elite that ruled a poor majority. Although based largely on protestant Christian values, it was in many ways the origin of what we now call 'representative liberal democracy'. Its key features were the separation of the powers of the executive, legislature and judiciary. At the time, Europe was ruled largely by aristocratic elites, but gradually, they too were forced by circumstance to copy the basic American model. De Tocqueville recognised that the Pilgrim Fathers had a blank slate upon which to draw up their plans for governance. The Pilgrim Fathers arrived in the New World of their own volition; many were from the educated middle classes and could have made a reasonable living back in England, but they wanted their own kind of freedom, in particular, a freedom from the corrupt and unfair governance back in England.[67]

The echoes and relevance to aid today is the lack of a blank slate in many

---

67. Of course, not everything the Pilgrim Fathers did in the new land, especially to the native population, was beneficial or has stood the test of time, but from the perspective of systems of governance, their ideas have proved remarkably effective.

developing countries, as far as governance is concerned. Or to put it another way, if liberal democracy is to replace existing governance structures in such countries, it has to challenge and supersede traditional power bases and attitudes. To make matters worse, many of these traditional power bases are buttressed by religious beliefs, which are controlled in turn by religious clerics who are often in league with the governing elite. At the time de Tocqueville visited the US, the Enlightenment, which began some 150 years earlier, was in full swing in Europe, and one of the big changes it brought about was a challenge to the power of religion. In particular, people began to understand and believe that natural – not supernatural – forces explained how things worked.

From my years working in development, I am convinced that there is a strong link between governance, culture, discipline and economic development. This is not meant to discredit or dismiss the intrinsic values and importance of traditional systems of governance and cultures, but to underline the difficulties of marrying or grafting economic development on to traditional governance systems and related cultures. As I see it, there are two basic difficulties or problems with such marriages. Almost all traditional societies have long-established power bases. Typically, they consist of a hereditary ruler and are often linked to religious beliefs.

A good case study is outlined in the book *Government in Old Oyo Empire* (Balogun, 1985). Under the old Oyo system, the Alaafin of Oyo was seen as an omnipotent leader of the Yoruba, the largest ethnic group in the western region of Nigeria. His power was checked by various councils, but in essence, he was a 'divine monarch' who got his powers from a god (Olodumare). The colonial period weakened the powers of the Alaafin and other traditional leaders, but their power and influence remains. The Yoruba are just one of hundreds of African ethnic groups with their own traditional governance and leadership structures. These leaders are, understandably, reluctant to surrender power, and many of their followers also cling to such traditional leadership systems, as they often offer greater security than that tendered by weak, Western-type political structures based on economic ideology (socialism or capitalism), which have yet to deliver an effective welfare state.

The age of realism (see 1.8.) has allowed some serious reconsideration of the values and importance of understanding traditional cultures. There is a growing recognition that the difficulties of grafting Western ideas of how to run a nation on to the institutions and structures of pre-industrialised countries are severe – and in some cases, insurmountable. In his book *The Places In Between,* Stewart (2004) makes the point that, in a country like Afghanistan, the international community has totally underestimated how conservative villagers are and how resistant they are to foreigners and their ideas.

In this context, it is interesting to reflect on the fact that, in the early days, the World Bank often employed anthropologists in the design of country programmes.

In the case of transmigration in Indonesia (see 3.8.), the consultant anthropologist hired by the World Bank very nearly succeeded in stopping the programme. To buy her off, the World Bank gave her a job on the understanding that working from the inside would give her more chance of influencing things. Sadly, she fell for the trap and was effectively silenced – staff members do not challenge the president!

I doubt that we will suddenly see a resumption of social and anthropological inputs into all development project proposals. However, it would be a lot cheaper to design projects and programmes that have a good chance of success, rather than wasting more money on grandiose schemes doomed to fail. It would also be a lot cheaper than the cost of sending 30,000 Western troops to a country like Afghanistan, only to have to pull them out after 20 years or so of abject failure to effect any meaningful social and economic change.

The problem with the growing awareness of the importance of culture is that it raises more questions than it provides answers to. The most basic and related questions are these: (1) whether we should we try to modernise traditional societies and (2) whether we know how to bring about the necessary cultural changes to help traditional societies modernise. One answer to the first question would seem to be to resist trying to change the most traditional societies. The trouble with this approach is that it means knowingly condemning a lot of people to long-term poverty, and possibly increasing the global problems of security and disease. As far as the second question is concerned, I fear the answer is that we do not know how to bring about such changes, other than very gradually over time. There is some evidence (*The Economist*, 2020B) that education is the key, and that those countries that have invested in schools, such as Kenya, are doing better than those that have paid less attention to education.

One of the most intractable aspects of culture concerns the link between culture and faith in external powers, especially fundamentalist religious beliefs. As far as culture and economic development are concerned, to paraphrase Spinoza,[68] it is important to part with the crutches of superstition. Or to put it less poetically, there will only be significant change when people take responsibility for what happens, rather than blaming external powers. A classic real case study of what I think this means and its implications is the failure of some 350 people to leave their homes when advised to do so, just before Mount Merapi (the infamous volcano on Java, Indonesia) blew its top in October 2010. Citizens disbelieved the official warnings to leave, preferring to rely on attempts to placate, with gifts and prayers, the spirits that they believed controlled the mountain. They were all destroyed by the volcano. History is full of stories of religious sects that believe Armageddon is approaching

68. The 17th-century Dutch philosopher Spinoza is considered by many to be one of the fathers of the Enlightenment. He believed that God was the sum of the natural and physical laws of the universe.

and commit mass suicide.[69] If economic growth requires people to do things that challenge their beliefs and cultures, this is much more of a difficulty than a shortage of capital for investment or technical knowledge.

Such traditional beliefs can be challenged successfully, but to succeed, the motive for change must be home-grown and not imposed. A good example comes from rural Bangladesh where many women now use contraception. This is frowned upon in the Quran, which calls for women to bring forth as many children as possible. On several occasions in the 1990s, I interviewed microcredit groups of women in Bangladesh, and after discussing their credit stories, I asked them how many children they had. Most had no more than three, and with few exceptions, they all used the contraceptive pills provided by a 'barefoot' health worker who visited the village regularly. These women had realised that, with only small plots of land to farm, there was no way they could support a large family, so they had chosen to ignore the cultural mores of their holy book for economic reasons.

Such a pragmatic change is easy for all to understand and for the community to accept. No fundamental belief was challenged; the rules associated with the belief system were just reinterpreted intelligently in that God is in control of people's lives, and that if they challenge religious and political leaders, they do so at their peril. At its most brutal interpretation, such faith condemns the poor to poverty or charity and gives riches to the rich, because that is what God wishes.

The other big cultural change required by many traditional societies is the importance of discipline. If your culture encourages you to do what you like, when you like, most economic activity will be largely by and for the individual, rather than a team. Think small-scale peasant farming, simple trading, or craft industries such as blacksmithing or weaving on handlooms. The individual can work as hard as they wish when they want to. The big advantage is that an individual does not have to take instructions from a factory or estate manager. However, in economic – if not social – terms, it is an inefficient use of time.[70] If someone comes along with the idea of a factory to make things on a larger scale and more efficiently, a big cultural change is needed by individuals. You do not need to be a student of economics to understand the benefits of the 'division of labour' described by Adam Smith (1776) as one of the keys to the success of the industrial revolution. He

---

69. In March 2000, 235 members of the Restoration of the Ten Commandments of God sect locked themselves in a church in the small town of Kanungu in Uganda and set fire to the building. All died for a weird belief. Perhaps more famous is the mass suicide or murder of 900 members of the Temple cult led by Jim Jones in Jonestown, Guyana in 1978. They died from poisoning by cyanide, having fallen out with the leadership of the cult.

70. A rather uncharitable tale from colonial times concerns a headman in a village who was sitting under a big tree relaxing one day when a colonial official turned up. The official asked why he was not working in his fields. 'With the right technology,' the official said, 'you could make a fortune from this land. A fortune that would enable you to pay someone to work for you, so you could sit and rest at your leisure.' To which the village head replied, 'What do you think I am doing now, and without all the hard work?' In fact, it was, of course, the labour of the other villagers that enabled him to relax, but the point is that economic growth means more work and benefits for all, including the head person.

showed convincingly that it makes much more sense for the workers in a factory to specialise in one task rather than trying to do all the tasks, as single operatives have to do. But such use of labour requires training and, above all, discipline.

On a visit to Maseru in Lesotho in 2019, I came across a case where just such a lack of discipline threatened an emerging garment industry. A number of Chinese entrepreneurs have opened up factories making garments for export to the US. These factories require quite large numbers of employees to work regular shifts. The employment is quite popular with local people, but they do not like the discipline associated with having fixed hours of work, and many come to work late, leave early or help themselves to finished garments. To get over this problem, the owners now lock the doors of the factories once the labour for a shift has arrived, and only open them at the end of the shift. In other parts of Africa, garment manufacture has been abandoned because of problems with the supply of regular workers. The ability of Africans to do the skilled work is not in doubt; it is a problem of culture and discipline. In much of the developing world, traditional aid has been unable to change this kind of cultural attitude to regular work.

In addition to such practical matters, a key aspect of culture is the institutions it creates and maintains. These are things such as a constitution, the separation of the powers of government, property rights, the rule of law, press freedom, a central bank, tax-raising measures and knowledge-based educational systems. In many African countries, these vital institutions are in their early stages of development, and more traditional institutions such as the 'tragedy of the commons' still predominate (see *Appendix E*).

The economists Rodrik, Subramanian and Trebbi (2004) looked in detail at the influence of institutions, geography and trade on economic development. They found that, once institutions are controlled for geography and trade, the quality of institutions trumps everything else, as far as economic development is concerned. Their analysis shows that, in those countries that were settled or colonised for long periods by Europeans or the Japanese – places such as North America, Australia, Canada, Korea, India, New Zealand and the larger countries of Latin America – it is the institutions these settlers and colonisers brought with them and developed that account for much of the subsequent successful economic growth of these nations.

One of the key missing institutions that is holding back economic progress in much of the developing world is a lack of property title (i.e. a document that proves ownership of a piece of land or a building). This vital legal document does not in itself create wealth, but it enables the owner to access capital by selling the land or by using the title as collateral for a loan. The Peruvian economist Hernando de Soto (2000) wrote eloquently and convincingly about this in his book *The Mystery of Capital*. Since then, studies have shown that the introduction of titling has increased agricultural output in parts of Asia and Latin America, as owners have been able to secure credit to buy inputs using a title as collateral. In much of the rich world, almost all land – except publicly designated and owned land – is owned privately. Such ownership is rare in much of the developing world. In Africa, less than 10% of the people currently have formal title to the land they farm or use.

Measuring out land is relatively easy; using aerial photography, Rwanda has titled all its territory, but the titles remain largely unused. In Rwanda and in many other African countries, this is because of a lack of the necessary additional legal institutions (laws, lawyers and courts) to support property rights and a culture that still prefers customary ownership rules. The importance of formal title has been recognised by economists and development experts for many years, but establishing a system of secure, workable property rights is extremely difficult. The colonial rulers of the 19th and 20th centuries relied largely on customary systems. To a large extent, this was because the pressure of land was not as great in those times as it is today, and also because they knew how politically risky any threat to customary systems would be. But if poverty is to be sustainably addressed in much of the developing world, the introduction and acceptance of individual property rights and supporting institutions would seem to be among the highest priorities for change in the future.

There is also a small but growing body of evidence suggesting that the importance of good institutions applies in developing countries. In May 2019, there was a general election in Malawi that was clearly flawed. Boxes of ballot papers were found with the original crosses Tippexed out. People demonstrated, and the opposition parties went to the Constitutional Court. To everyone's surprise and delight, the judges ruled in favour of a rerun of the election. This was held on June 2020 and was won by the leader of the main opposition party. What this shows convincingly is that, when a country has working institutions of integrity, bad government can be challenged and overturned without bloodshed. It is, of course, too soon to know if this will lead to better economic performance, but it will certainly encourage businesses and donors to consider investing in Malawi – once again, providing that the new leader practices the plurality of power sharing that helped him get elected.

It is notable in this context that China has a long history of quality institutions. In the mid-18th century, China's key institutions[71] were different from but not inferior to those of Europe (Mokyr, 2016). Almost certainly, this institutional tradition enabled China to take off economically at speed once the nonsense of Maoism was rejected in the last years of the 20th century. In contrast, many of the nations of Africa, Asia and Latin America that were not settled or colonised, never fully developed these essential institutions.

---

71. China had a central administration based on a meritocratic civil service, and a functioning legal system of law and order.

This review of the fundamentals required for economic growth to succeed suggests that governments in countries considered to be badly governed will find it much harder to access aid funds from Western powers in future. Aid funds will still be provided for selected activities – including global public goods (such as climate change and disease control) and for humanitarian purposes – but not as often to replenish government coffers as has happened in the past. In those few countries where serious attempts are being made to develop the necessary institutions and improve governance, Western aid will – I am sure – have a role to play, and there may well be countries where, for strategic reasons, a blind eye is turned towards the rulers of an autocratic regime. Given the decline in confidence in liberal democracy, it is possible that efforts to encourage liberal democracy will play a smaller role in Western aid policy in the middle decades of the 21st century. This does not rule out the provision of some aid for strategic reasons and perhaps to compete with China for influence.

That said, there are reasons to be optimistic, provided Western aid policy continues to evolve into a listening rather than an imposing mode of operation. One of the most important ways the Western world was able to 'modernise' its systems of governance and economy was through education. As more and more people became able to read and learn about the world around them for themselves, they began to demand – and in many cases, fight for – more equality and the sharing of resources. In the UK, the signing of the Magna Carta in 1215 clipped King John's wings for a while. But it was not really until more than 400 years later, during the Civil Wars in England in the 1640s, that the power of the monarchy (divine right) was seriously challenged, following the execution of King Charles I in 1641. However, it was not until the Glorious Revolution of 1688 that the power of the monarch was effectively subjugated to the people via Parliament.

What is interesting – and is of relevance to many developing countries today – is the massive use of propaganda in the form of petitions and pamphlets by both sides in the English Civil Wars. These were methods that could only work because an increasing number of working people could read and write, and so they felt able to think for themselves rather than follow what the king, the lords of the land and the bishops told them to believe. Yet again, an obvious priority for aid is education.

6.2.   Is There a Global Need for Aid?

One way to answer this question is to look at the profiles of countries that are eligible for aid. The DAC of the OECD classifies poor countries into three types according to their annual per capita income levels. This is an economic assessment based on the annual GNI divided by the population. Although not described as such, it is really a measure of poverty and, by implication, a need for aid. If a country has great wealth from hydrocarbons, diamonds or other natural resources, but a small population, it is classified as upper-middle income, even if most of the population is poor. This is because most of the wealth is captured by a small elite, like in Gabon. Given the difficulty in getting accurate statistics on GNI and population, the scoring is somewhat arbitrary, but it does provide for making comparisons and monitoring change over time. The estimated classification results for the three years to 2020 are as follows:

Table 5 Classification of Countries by Annual Per Capita Income

Classification	Per Capita GNI (US$)	Number of Countries Globally	Countries in Africa
Low Income	<1,005	47	34
Middle Income	1006–3,955	37	11
Upper Income	3,955–12,235	57	8
Other (Seychelles)			1
Total		141	54

Source: DAC list of ODA recipients (OECD, n.d.A); development finance data (OECD, n.d.B)

This table is quite an eye-opener as it indicates that, of the world's 195 countries,[72] some 141 (or 70%) are classified as being eligible for aid. The full list is shown in Appendix A. Perhaps even more startling is that it shows, with the exception of the Seychelles, all the states in Africa are eligible. The table also reveals that, of the 54 African countries listed, only eight (or 15%) are in the upper income group. Furthermore, these countries – with the exception of Mauritius and South Africa – owe their wealth to hydrocarbon or minerals (gold and gems), not balanced economies. The table indicates that, according to the DAC classification, most of the continent will be eligible for aid for the foreseeable future. It is also notable, from the full table in *Appendix A*, that almost all countries in Latin America are also eligible for aid. The same is true in much of Asia. However, it is important to note that many of the larger countries in Latin America and Asia are already in the upper income group (group 3).

Countries that exceed the upper-middle income classification for a period of three years are considered to have 'graduated' and are promoted to the list of developed countries. They are no longer on the list of those eligible for ODA. Before the Covid-19 pandemic, the DAC estimated that the following countries

---

72. The 195 is made up of the 193 members of the UN, plus the Holy See (the Vatican) and Palestine.

were expected to graduate by 2023: Angola, Vanuatu, Antigua and Barbuda, and the Cook Islands. Large countries in group 3 that were expected to graduate by 2030 include Argentina, Algeria, Botswana, Brazil, Colombia, Cuba, China, Iran, Iraq, Lebanon, Malaysia, Mauritius, Mexico, Namibia, Peru, South Africa, Thailand, Turkey and Venezuela. China is really an outlier in group 3. The country is only there because of the size of its population, and it almost certainly has internal access to the technical knowledge and financial resources to grow its economy. It does not need aid any longer.

Many of the countries in group 3, although technically eligible, received little or no government-to-government aid as of 2018. Most have diversified economies, although some are heavily dependent on oil or gas exports, the price of which can fluctuate wildly. Taken together, they account for nearly 2.3 billion people or just under one-third of the global population. Most of the other countries in this group are relatively small countries with fragile economies; many are island nations in the Caribbean or the South Pacific that will almost certainly need financial assistance for a number of years to come, but the actual amount of aid needed to help these countries will probably be modest.

Group 2 countries include Egypt, India, Indonesia, Pakistan, the Philippines, Nigeria, Ukraine and Vietnam. These are countries with reasonably diversified and solid economies (except perhaps Nigeria, which is very dependent on oil), but they have large populations and massive underemployment. Some of them – notably India, the Philippines and Ukraine – should move up to group 3 within a few years, but all will remain eligible for aid for the foreseeable future, according to the DAC. In total, their population is also close to 2 billion. Group 1 countries are predominantly small, with fragile economies. Their total population in 2020 was estimated at around 0.5 billion, but it is growing rapidly. Over half are in Africa.

This breakdown shows that, as far as the future is concerned, there will almost certainly be a need for aid, according to the DAC classification. Furthermore, history suggests that the rate of graduation of the poorest countries is slow, so the need will be there for many years to come.

The table does not indicate whether the countries in most need are also those that can use aid effectively. Many of the difficulties, problems and paradoxes arise when trying to assess aid needs on a broader basis than per capita income levels. This is because, by and large, aid is most effectively used in and by countries with effective governments and diversified economies, and where there is some recognition of the importance and respect for the 'rule of law'. Most of the countries that the DAC expects to graduate over the next few years meet these criteria to some greater or lesser extent. So, if you want aid money to achieve economic improvement for a population, the focus should be on these upper-income countries. However, this highlights one of the great paradoxes of aid, namely that many of the countries that can use aid effectively can and do attract private finance, and are therefore less dependent on aid funds.

Closer analysis of the group 1 and 2 countries in the table suggests that there are broadly four types. The first are countries with valuable natural-resource wealth, which is almost invariably in the hands of the elite. It is tempting to call them kleptocracies. It includes countries such as Algeria, Angola and Gabon, which have considerable foreign exchange earnings from hydrocarbons and do not really qualify for aid. However, much of the wealth remains in the hands of a small elite, and until the political systems in these countries becomes more pluralistic, they will continue to have large poor populations. Sadly, there is not much that traditional aid can do to bring about meaningful change in such countries. Attempts in the past have never been successful, so there really is no precedent to build on. This type of country is probably best left alone, except perhaps for specialist interventions such as disease control (see 5.4.) or climate change mitigation (see 6.9.).

The second type have more robust economies with the potential for growth and are democracies of a kind.[73] They can conveniently be described as emerging economies that would seem to be potential beneficiaries of aid. They probably need better traditional aid: things such as better infrastructure; access to markets – notably, tariff-free access; education; skills training; and help in establishing effective legal, tax-raising and administrative institutions. As a rough estimate, this type of country probably accounts for some 2 billion people globally. In general, they need better traditional aid that is linked to modest political and financial reforms.

In many cases, the third type are failed states, either because of war / civil war (e.g. Lebanon, Libya, Somalia, South Sudan, Syria and Yemen) or internal strife (e.g. Afghanistan, Bolivia, Cameroon, Guatemala, Iraq and much of the Sahel region of West Africa). These countries can really only expect to receive humanitarian aid in the foreseeable future, perhaps with some military intervention in some situations. Until the fighting is over, there is really nothing that aid – other than humanitarian aid – can do to help economic growth and poverty reduction.

The fourth type are mainly group 1 countries that have very weak political systems and economies that may never become entirely self-supporting. These countries are often called 'fragile states', and the population in many of these states is increasing faster than anywhere else. It also includes a number of countries that have better potential but have never managed to get off the starting blocks; these are countries such as Cambodia, Eswatini, Lesotho, Myanmar, Nepal, Tanzania and Zambia (see footnote 85). Some of these may, in fact, never really graduate and will

73. Countries such as Bangladesh, Benin, Ghana, Ethiopia, India, Kenya, Nigeria, Pakistan and Senegal.

probably need aid for budgetary support (albeit for security as much as economic reasons) for the foreseeable future (see 6.8.).

The preceding analysis suggests that, based on the DAC financial analysis, there is considerable need or scope for the West to provide aid in the future. However, based on the development aid experiences of the past 70 years, current policies in the West and things happening on the ground, there are a number of pointers to consider other than the DAC ratings. In particular, the large number of countries that are eligible according to the DAC classification but are ineligible for other reasons. This considerably reduces the number of countries that are likely to receive aid. This could mean either more aid for those countries that meet all eligibility criteria or a need for less aid overall. The subsequent sections of this chapter review the prospects for aid on a regional basis.

6.3.   Africa

The previous section of this chapter has identified Africa as the region of the world with the greatest number of countries eligible for aid. And if further evidence is needed, some other statistics from the last decade of the 20th century confirm this. According to the World Bank, in that decade, the number of people living in poverty in sub-Saharan Africa increased from 242 million to 291 million (Devarajan *et al.*, 2001), and unless the economies of these countries grew substantially, the World Bank projected that the number living in poverty would increase considerably. Indeed, by 2015, some 413 million Africans were living in poverty. Post Covid-19, the number of poor could well increase even more.

As of 2020, while writing this book, it was difficult not to see the continent of Africa once again as it was previously nicknamed: the Dark Continent. Not only are many of its economies in a hopeless mess but much is wracked by political crisis, from the top of the continent to the bottom. In Algeria, there was a political stalemate between the 'people' and those who claim to be their government. In neighbouring Libya, a civil war has been raging on and off for 10 years. In the centre of the continent, Sudan has just survived (albeit temporarily) a massive economic and political crisis brought about by a desperate military regime, supported by a dreadful consortium of international interests. Further south, in South Sudan, a civil war has been ongoing since 2015; in Burundi and the DRC, there was no effective governance; and Zimbabwe has remained in economic and political crisis. Next door, in Mozambique, Liberation Front of Mozambique (Frente de Libertação de Moçambique [FRELIMO]) and Mozambican National Resistance (Resistência Nacional Moçambicana [RENAMO]) were preparing to reignite the country's civil war of the 1980s, and Islamist groups were also on the rampage in the north-east of the country.

In the far south, South Africa was struggling for survival after an amazing period of corruption and theft by the political classes. Neighbouring Eswatini (formerly Swaziland) was ruled by an eccentric, egomaniacal monarch with 15 wives, and even Botswana (which had been one of Africa's success stories) appeared to be heading for political trouble. In Lesotho, the prime minister and his current partner have been accused of allegedly arranging the killing of the prime minister's wife.

In the West, things were not much better, with chaos in Liberia, civil war beckoning in Cameroon and an Islamic insurgency in the Sahel region – and that is before mentioning the long-standing dispute over who owns Western Sahara. In the spring of 2021, the leader of Chad was shot dead while inspecting troops, and further instability seemed certain.

Perhaps the most significant thing about this continent-wide chaos was the apparent lack of interest or concern from the countries of the Western world, and a slowing down in the amount of aid provided. It is interesting to try to understand why there was so little concern in the West about the turmoil in much of Africa towards the end of the second decade of the 21st century. After all, in the early years of aid, after the Second World War, Africa was a major player in the Cold War and a recipient of massive amounts of Western aid.

In the first place, I think the West no longer has any serious fears of a leftist/communist takeover of any country in Africa, along the lines of what happened in Angola in 1975 and quite a few other countries, such as Benin and Ethiopia. The Angolan story was perhaps the most prolonged surrogate conflict of the Cold War. At one point, there were more than 25,000 Cuban troops in the country – basically, a militia supported by Moscow – facing the Western-supported Angolan military leader, Jonas Savimbi.

While there was no leftist threat immediately after the collapse of the USSR in 1989, China's interests in Africa could offer a similar but different threat in the years to come, and it needs to be carefully watched; this is similar insofar as the Chinese one-party system of government is close to the communism espoused by the USSR.

Unlike the USSR, however, China has the big advantage that it has lots of money to lend or provide grants to countries in Africa, and this has already enabled it to establish a substantial foothold on the continent, without a shot being fired on its behalf. By 2020, China had massive trade with almost all the countries in Africa, with reports that there were over 10,000 Chinese businesses on the continent. Therefore, there is already evidence that influence, if not real power, is shifting from the Western hemisphere to the Eastern hemisphere. That said, I do not think China offers the same degree of threat that the USSR did during the Cold War, as there is no evidence that it threatens to impose its kind of socialism wherever it can. China's interests are predominantly commercial: access to resources and markets, and returns on investments. It also wants its power to be recognised, but it shows little interest in any form of colonisation.

In the second place, there is the failure of democratic governance to gain a secure foothold in most of the countries of Africa, and the domination of autocratic leaders. In the majority of African countries, absolute power rests with a single individual, his family and close consorts. To some extent, this reflects the need for strong control to contain a large number of disparate interests and tribal groupings, and on the whole, this has reluctantly been accepted by country nationals. It also reflects the fact that, in quite a number of countries, power has been in the hands of military leaders who have held on to it down the barrel of a gun. Sadly, it is also the case that such situations have been tolerated if not supported by the international community, on the grounds that *some* government is better than *no* government.

I have looked at the statistics, and more than one-third of African countries have had leaders who have held power for more than 30 years. A handful of these are traditional kings who have actually ruled rather than being ceremonial monarchs. Furthermore, nearly two-thirds of the countries in Africa have each had its own same leader for a period of 20 years or more. This kind of leadership presents the West with a big problem: to support such leaders endorses their autocracy. During the Cold War, this was conveniently overlooked by the West, and after the Cold War, it has proved difficult – if not impossible – to remove the strong men. If only to placate its own citizens, the West has resorted to calling for democracy, knowing very well that its cries would fall on deaf ears, and that it could conveniently throttle back the aid taps. This is another example of the hypocrisy associated with much aid.

An important third factor is corruption and the failure of the rule of law to prevent or limit it in almost all 54 countries. Somewhat ironically, the problem of corruption is as bad, if not worse, in those countries that have something like representative democracy.[74] The corruption ranges from simple bribes being paid by individuals to secure services from government employees and politicians to the massive theft of tax revenues and aid funds. A recent survey suggests that some 75 million people in Africa paid bribes to secure basic services in 2018. Typical examples of massive theft include the loans the World Bank pumped into the Nigerian Electricity Power Authority in the 1970s and 1980s – loans that all knew would not end up providing a better service. For more details, read *The World Bank and the Gods of Lending* (Berkman, 2008).

74. Botswana, Ethiopia, Ghana, Kenya, Lesotho, Mauritius, Namibia, Nigeria, South Africa, Tanzania, Tunisia and Zambia.

In South Africa, one of the continent's democracies, there has been massive theft from Eskom, the power authority, which largely contributed to its debts of R420 billion (US$30 billion) in early 2019. These debts were incurred during the time when Zuma was president. In addition, there was also theft from many SOEs, such as South African Airways, as well as dubious arms deals (submarines that are holed up in port because there are no sailors trained to operate them). It was almost as if the politicians felt they had a right to plunder the wealth of the nation. I say *almost*, as one of the additional ironies is that – at least in South Africa – the theft was done in such a way as to make it look like the correct tender procedures for contracts had been followed. Closer examination of the situation in South Africa (Myburgh, 2019) shows that there was considerable sleight of hand or the use of Nelson's eye in following tender rules – abuses that senior politicians clearly knew of but were not concerned about. The relevance to aid is that it is difficult for Western politicians to authorise giving aid to countries when knowing much of it will be stolen. This provides yet another reason for throttling down the flow of aid funds and the related potential influence.

One of the consequences of this lack of concern has led to many African countries to being designated as fragile states. In Africa, 17 (or nearly one-third) of the continent's countries were classified as fragile states by the AfDB in 2019.[75] These countries are in such poor shape that there is little that aid can do, other than provide humanitarian assistance for things such as the containment of the Ebola virus or assistance to civilians caught up in the crossfire.

Then there is the debt problem. In 2018, the IMF was concerned about debt distress in 20 African countries, and by mid-2020, another debt crisis loomed. There is some overlap between fragile states and debt distress, but overall, the countries with debt problems are the larger, potentially better-off countries, not the fragile states that no one would want to lend to anyway. Debt is distressed when the cost of servicing the debt exceeds a country's ability to service it.

The Covid-19 pandemic has made things much worse, as tax revenues have fallen and government expenditure has risen. Being aware of the problem, the G20 countries and China have agreed to suspend bilateral debt service for the rest of 2020 (at time of writing) for 73 countries globally. However, there is a catch. If a country requests this relief, it runs the risk of putting up the cost of servicing bonds sold abroad to raise foreign currency, as the bond holders will see this a sign of increased risk, and indeed, Moody's has said it could result in a downgrade. This worry is particularly acute right now, as some 30% of African government debt is

---

75. Burundi, Central African Republic, Comoros, Republic of Congo, DRC, Djibouti, Guinea, Guinea Bissau, Côte d'Ivoire, Liberia, São Tomé, Sierra Leone, Somalia, Sudan, South Sudan, Togo and Zimbabwe.

owed to private investors. Debt restructuring looks inevitable, but this will simply kick the problem down the road, as will the private sector's suggestion of a debt holiday. Unless a solution can be found soon, a wave of defaults is expected in 2022 when a huge number of bond payments fall due.

What does all this mean for development aid in Africa? The short answer is that it may not even be worth trying to help many countries on the continent develop economically using traditional aid. As far as kleptocracies are concerned, there would seem to be little reason – either economic or political – for such countries to receive Western aid, other than perhaps to assist with addressing public goods (things such as disease control, climate change adaptation and mitigation measures).

The same is largely true for failed and fragile states, perhaps with the exception of humanitarian aid, given the inability of national governments to help their own citizens, and possibly military intervention for global security reasons in some cases. This leaves only the emerging economies as the states likely to receive the bulk of aid in the future. Ironically, the few African countries that have done the best economically are those that are democracies, and they probably do not need much aid as they have been able to secure finance from the private sector in the recent past. However, it not clear whether they will be able to access private funds post Covid-19.

If this analysis is realistic, it means overall that Western intervention in Africa will in future – as indeed it was for much of the past 50 years – be essentially for political and strategic reasons rather than for economic development. The big difference with the past is that it will be closely tied to watching what China is up to on the continent, rather than what the now defunct USSR was doing.

The debt crisis will probably have to be solved by debt forgiveness. There is a clear precedent for this as far as the West is concerned, but it is not at all clear whether China will follow suit. With respect to the West, debt forgiveness will almost certainly result in less money for other forms of aid and will almost certainly come with conditions similar if not identical to IMF loans (i.e. sort out your government's finances). It is understood that many Chinese loans have clauses in them that give China long leases on infrastructure built with Chinese loans in the event that the borrower can no longer service the debt. The question here is if an asset built with a Chinese loan is not financially viable, what value is such an asset to China? The worry is that China will take over ownership of the asset on a long lease to solve an individual loan problem, but it will demand access to commodities produced by the borrower at preferential rates in compensation, as it has done in Ecuador (see *Appendix D*).

Until the essential political and institutional change is realised and consolidated, especially in the fragile states of the continent, the West should – where possible –

concentrate on providing security and politically neutral, technical aid programmes, largely supported by NGOs. These include the provision of prophylactic medical care and disease elimination, agricultural research and the introduction of improved food-production technology, climate change adaptation and mitigation measures, education and training, and humanitarian assistance. This might also incorporate the provision of technical expertise in key ministries to provide advice on how best to assess infrastructure investment proposals, so as to avoid dud investments like the Coca Codo Sinclair Dam in Ecuador (see *Appendix D*).

More traditional Western aid should be focused on the dozen or so sub-Saharan African countries that have good economic potential and some semblance of good governance. These are countries such as Botswana, Ghana, Ethiopia, Kenya, Namibia, Senegal and South Africa, and possibly also Benin. This list might be expanded to include Malawi, Sudan, Uganda and Tanzania. There will also be cases where military interventions cannot be avoided, such as in the Sahel and possibly Mozambique. Overall, I suspect the amount of Western aid money available to Africa will fall rather than increase, as a result of the number of countries unable to use aid effectively and an overall reduction in Western aid budgets.

6.4. The Islamic World

The Islamic world in 2020 consisted of a wide range of countries centred on the Middle East but stretching as far west as Morocco, as far east as Indonesia, and including the 'Stans' in Central Asia and a number of countries in West Africa. The Organisation of Islamic States (OIC) is made up of 57 countries that are Muslim or where the Muslims are numerically significant (e.g. Russia, where 10% of the population is Muslim). Together with Muslims in other non-OIC states, it is estimated that the Islamic world accounts for some 1.8 billion people (or a quarter of the global population) and more than a quarter of the countries of the UN. So, improving the well-being of the people of the Islamic world would contribute significantly to reducing global poverty and meeting the UN SDGs. Given the number of people living in the Islamic world, it is important that their needs for aid are assessed realistically. Almost all the poor Islamic-world countries are eligible for ODA, according to the DAC.

There is thus no doubt about the need for aid in the Islamic world, although recent history suggests that there is limited scope for Western aid to help address this poverty, as Islamic polity does not welcome the cultural attributes associated with much Western aid (see 6.8.). In apparent recognition of this, the unpublished position of Western aid donors appears to be that the provision of aid for the poor in the Islamic world should be a priority for rich Arab countries, not the West. The financial help (US$30 billion) received by Egypt from Kuwait, Saudi Arabia and the United Arab Emirates (UAE) in 2013, following the overthrow of Mohammed Morsi by Abdel Fatteh el-Sisi being a good example of this in practice.

Of course, there are exceptions to this, notably when there are security and/or strategic considerations. I well recall my time in Egypt in the late 1970s when Anwar Sadat kicked out the Soviets, and the West jumped in to provide development assistance. The World Bank lost no time building up its lending programme for Egypt, starting with the West Nubariya irrigation scheme (see 3.5.). Unquestionably, from a global strategic perspective, Egypt is very important as it controls the Suez Canal, which accounts for a massive amount of merchant shipping from Asia to Europe.

Aid to the Islamic world does highlight a number of paradoxes, however, starting with the wide range in wealth within the Islamic world. The richest Islamic countries are Saudi Arabia and those located in the Gulf of Arabia. In these lucky countries with small populations, incomes based on hydrocarbon resources are very respectable. In Qatar and Kuwait in 2018, the annual per capita GDPs were US$69,000 and US$34,000, respectively. In lower–middle income countries with large populations, incomes were much smaller. The annual per capita GDPs of Algeria, Indonesia, Iran and Turkey in 2018 were US$4,100, US$3,900, US$5,400 and US$9,400, respectively. At the other extreme are very poor countries with large populations; these are countries such as Egypt, the Yemen and Pakistan, where in 2018 the annual per capita GDPs were US$2,550, US$944 and US$1,500, respectively. Most of the Islamic countries in Africa are also very poor.

Apart from a shared faith, the other common factors in the Islamic world include much of their history, the predominance of autocratic governments, and poor economic growth in recent years, with or without aid. To some extent, the recent weak economic growth can be attributed to economic activity that is largely based on the exploitation of natural resources (such as hydrocarbons), agriculture, plantation crops, textiles or tourism. Relatively few of the countries – with the exceptions of Turkey, Egypt, Indonesia and Malaysia – have any significant manufacturing industry or service sectors. It is difficult not to see a link between autocratic governance and poor economic growth in the Islamic world. This is partly because – with the exception of China – autocracy and economic growth are not good bedfellows, but it is also partly because of history. A brief understanding of Islamic history helps to appreciate the link between governance and economic underdevelopment in the Islamic world.

The founder of Islam, the Prophet Muhammed, was also the head of state. He governed a place (Medina), dispensed justice, collected taxes, commanded an army, and made war and peace. In the universal Islamic polity, as conceived by

Muhammed, there was no need for a secular leader or government structures; there was only God, the sole sovereign and source of law. After his death in 632 CE, a successor to the Prophet, known as the caliph, was appointed. According to the book *The Crisis of Islam* (Lewis, 2004), under a succession of caliphs, the community of Medina grew into a vast empire that covered much of what we call the Middle East today, and that stretched as far west as Morocco. It also developed a most successful civilisation based on universally accepted rules and principles that lasted for more than 1,000 years. Many in today's Islamic world still see the Prophet's rules and principles as the bedrock of their governance.

Therefore, Islam is not just a religion, it is also a political community. A distinguishing feature of the old Muslim empire was the lack of nations as we know them today. It was more like a religious community divided into nations, rather than a community of nations. There were geographical distinctions, but governments as we know them today were generally mistrusted and discouraged, as they might challenge the leadership of the caliph and God's sovereignty. For the Islamic world, problems began to arise at around the time of the Enlightenment or the Age of Reason, which occurred in Europe in the early 18th century. The importance of this period was the thinking of intellectuals, which challenged the powers of divine monarchs and the Church. There is a direct connection between the Age of Reason and the economic development of the Western world; it is from this time that the relative power and influence of the Islamic world began to decline.

A key feature of this decline – which explains quite a lot about the slow economic progress in much of the Islamic world today – is a continued aversion to modern political and institutional systems, such as those derived in the Western world after the Enlightenment. As explained in the first section of this chapter, economic growth depends substantially on systems that have been designed by people on the basis of rationale, measurement and understanding (e.g. vaccines) rather than on beliefs, and above all, on voters being able to change a government – ideally, a representative liberal democracy. This presents a real problem for the Islamic polity, which does not easily countenance anything that might challenge the teachings of the Prophet. In practical terms, this means that, while a democratic government in a Muslim country might allow voters to vote in an Islamic government, an autocratic Islamic government would not allow voters to vote in a democratic government. This is the Muslim electoral paradox, which is often referred to as 'one man, one vote, once'.

This is not just rhetoric; it happened in Algeria in 1989 and in Egypt in 2012 when Mohamed Morsi, a pious Muslim, was elected as president. After his election, with support from Islamist colleagues, he tried to change the constitution, guaranteeing the president unlimited powers that would preclude any subsequent elections. In both Algeria and Egypt, the military stepped in, and the government returned to autocracy. Most if not all of the governments of today's Muslim nations are genuinely fearful of free elections. Instead, these nations end up with autocrats who tend to either fully endorse Islamic teaching (Iran and Saudi Arabia) or endorse basic Islamic laws and teaching (Egypt, Indonesia and Pakistan).

Of course, it is very difficult to run a modern state as if it were still part of a caliphate, so most Muslim countries have governments with a nominal separation of the powers of the legislature, executive and judiciary that resembles that of more modern states. And quite a few (mainly ex-European) colonies have fledging democratic governments. However, this really presents yet another paradox in that these governments do not have a totally free hand in what they do, as they have to secure the approval of unelected religious leaders and their followers for any new legislation or social development to be accepted. This is particularly important as far as education is concerned, but it also affects preventative medicine in some cases.

Basic literacy for boys and girls is understood to be a cornerstone of any modern economic society. In many Islamic countries, religious leaders discourage such education, which they believe might enable people to think for themselves rather than follow religious tradition. In this context, it is a bit scary that, during the Covid-19 lockdown in 2020, the 'Protectors of Islam' or religious leaders in many Asian Islamic countries have challenged government authorities and have kept many mosques open.

Yet another paradox arises from the tendency of the Western powers to tolerate autocratic Muslim leaders such as Assad in Syria, Mubarak in Egypt, the Saudi royal family, and Sukarno and Suharto in Indonesia. They have done and continue to do this to develop and maintain political and business relations. In the process of doing so, however, they run the risk of alienating nationals seeking reform and modernisation, and they are seen as hypocrites who promote liberal democracy as the best form of government but support autocrats in Muslim countries.

In the past, much Western aid funding in the Islamic world has been in the form of military initiatives to secure peace in the Middle East. Billions of dollars have been spent on campaigns in places such as Afghanistan, Iraq and Kuwait. With few exceptions, these campaigns have achieved very little, and in some cases, they have made things worse. In future, it seems likely that the West will avoid such major campaigns, though there may well be smaller campaigns to arrest terrorist groups, such as those active in the Sahel region of West Africa. Any such future interventions are likely to be with the support of the host country and only rarely at the initiative of the Western powers.

The West has also tried to play kingmaker in the past by supporting Islamic leaders it saw as sympathetic or removing those it saw as unsympathetic. Probably the most famous example is support for the Shah of Iran in the 1970s, which ended ignominiously in his removal from power in Iran and his subsequent death from cancer in Egypt. Other important examples include the removal of Saddam Hussein from Iraq in 2003 and the removal of Colonel Gaddafi from Libya in 2011. All three cases ended with security in the concerned country and regions taking a turn for the worse. What is more, this interference in the affairs of state of Islamic countries has fuelled anti-Western sentiment and encouraged organisations such as the Muslim Brotherhood. These organisations, in turn, have supported fundamentalist groups calling for *jihad* or war against the non-believers or most people in the West.

If military initiatives have largely failed in the Islamic world, more traditional Western aid has experienced mixed success. Some useful infrastructure has been developed with aid loans, but not all of these have been serviced. Sudan may be an outlier, but it is one of the few countries that could not secure funding from Western financial sources for many years while it was in arrears with its loans from the World Bank (see 2.13.). It is also the case that a considerable number of countries in the Islamic world are wracked by chaos and conflict.[76] I see no reason to think these problems will be resolved satisfactorily any time soon, as one of the key features of these wars has been the determination of extremists on both sides to avoid meaningful peace negotiations. War has a devastating effect on a nation's economy, making its people much poorer, but until peace is secured, there is little aid can do other than provide some humanitarian aid, as the WFP has been doing in Yemen since 2019.

Mindful of the problems outlined previously, Western aid has been focused in the past on those poor Islamic countries with some form of stable democratic government, which were under the suzerainty of European colonisers at some stage; these are countries such as Bangladesh, Egypt, Indonesia, Jordan, Nigeria, Pakistan, The Gambia and Senegal. It seems probable that this policy will continue, with an emphasis on improving education, health and other basic services. Overall, Western aid is likely to remain limited to relatively few countries in the Islamic world.

The collapse in global oil prices in 2020 will present major problems for the Islamic world, which will almost certainly lead to much more poverty and increase the need for aid. The Algerian government announced a 50% cut in the budget in 2020, and many of the rich Gulf states were having to dip into their sovereign wealth funds to maintain government expenditure. Things look bleak for the non-oil-producing Islamic countries.

---

76. In 2020, the list of such countries included Afghanistan, Algeria, Chad, Iraq, Lebanon, Libya, Somalia, Sudan and Yemen.

6.5.   Latin America

With the exception of Chile, all of Latin America is eligible for aid, according to the DAC. Broadly speaking, this region of the world can be divided into three groups. The first is made up of the larger countries of South America, most of which were close to graduating in 2020. Countries like these with fairly diverse economies can access finance for investment from the private sector and are not strong candidates for concessional aid. However, the economies of these countries are heavily dependent on the export of primary commodities such as beef, copper or soya beans, and when the prices of such commodities fall, these countries often experience economic difficulties. When this difficulty is added to the problems associated with servicing private and public sector loans and with populist redistributive policies, it can and does lead to the need for help from the IMF. Since 2017, Argentina, Brazil and Colombia have all accessed lines of credit or loans from the IMF, and much of the continent is expected to remain dependent on Bretton Woods' support for the foreseeable future, if not on World Bank project lending as in the not-so-distant past. While this might be seen as bad news from an economic perspective, it actually plays into the hands of the West quite nicely as it means these large countries remain bound to the Western alliance.

The second group of countries includes Mexico and the medium-sized poorer countries of South America. These countries are still eligible for and are receiving concessional project loans from development banks, such as the World Bank, for essential infrastructure and public services, typically in the health and education sectors. There are also a number of projects to help governments improve tax revenue.

The third group includes most of the countries of Central America, the small coastal countries of South America that face the Atlantic Ocean, the Caribbean Islands of Cuba and Haiti, and Venezuela. Most of these countries, with the notable exception of Costa Rica, are politically unstable, and many are associated with drug and people trafficking. In an attempt to secure political stability and address poverty, some have relatively small World Bank or IDA projects similar to those in the second group.

Given the difficulties of providing aid in many of these countries, it is tough not to conclude that much of the aid is provided for political and security reasons. Although no firm evidence for this assumption exists, there is no doubt that if the West were not providing any aid, it would open the door to other countries such as China and Russia, allowing them to step in. Indeed, China has already provided a massive amount of aid to Argentina, Brazil, Ecuador and Venezuela. China does not provide reliable statistics on its loans, but it is estimated that China has lent over

US$130 billion to these four countries since 2008. Cuba and Venezuela are essentially blackballed by the US due to their internal politics and support from Russia.

Overall, although there are many poor and disadvantaged people in Latin America and there is clearly a need for aid, the opportunities for dispensing aid effectively are fewer than might be expected, largely due to political instability and/ or weak governance. I do not expect to see any significant increase in Western aid for Latin America over the next few decades.

6.6.   China

According to the DAC, China is still eligible for aid on the grounds that per capita annual incomes are still low overall. However, given the recent success of the Chinese economy – which is expected to continue to grow, albeit at a slower rate than previously – China should be able to graduate without further donor aid. Indeed, most Western countries have stopped providing aid to China, and the World Bank has reduced its lending to China considerably. This section is therefore not about the country's need for aid but is an attempt to put Chinese aid into the context of China's approach to international relations.

China offers two basic challenges to the West's aid policies and actions, and to understand them fully, a more detailed analysis and review is needed for China than for any other aspect of the future of aid. The first challenge is political, namely the economic success (at least in the early decades of the 21st century) of an autocratic regime, and the second is the size of the Chinese wallet. After the fall of the Berlin Wall in 1989, much Western aid was directed towards supporting democratic initiatives. China's economic success challenges this basic policy, and Xi Jinping – the current president of China – makes no attempt to hide his ambition of advancing its statist model on the global stage.

Despite past failures with social autocracy in countries such as Benin and Ethiopia,[77] a number of developing countries are wondering whether they too would do better to follow the Chinese – rather than the Western – liberal democratic model of governance in their quest for economic growth and poverty reduction. An article about Angola (*The Economist*, 2018C) confirms that some African leaders see Deng Xiaoping as their role model. An added bonus of such

---

77. After the fall of the Derg (a Marxist junta) in Ethiopia in 1991, the country's still authoritarian government tried to introduce business-friendly policies along Chinese lines. For some years, it seemed to work, with economic growth rates approaching 10% per annum and a measurable increase in per capita incomes for millions of Ethiopians. However, much of the growth was dependent on credit and massive public borrowing. By 2018, the country was effectively broke and in need of major economic reforms, particularly of the inefficient SOEs.

an approach to economics would, of course, effectively legitimise the autocratic regimes found in many African countries.

A closer analysis of what actually happened in China after Mao suggests that it is not single-party rule per se that has led to its amazing economic development but the way in which it has allowed, encouraged and, indeed, supported a remarkable amount of free enterprise. This state-sponsored free enterprise is sometimes called 'neoliberalism' or 'illiberal democracy'. That is to say, you are free to make as much money as you can from commerce and trade, providing you accept that ultimate political power rests with a handful of unelected communist party members.

This is a very hard (if not impossible) model to repeat elsewhere. The CCP, which grew out of Mao Zedong's barrel of a gun, had realised by the time Deng Xiaoping took over that it stood a better chance of surviving if it shared the benefits of increasing economic wealth. In his book *Enlightenment Now*, Pinker (2018) attributes the economic success of China to Deng Xiaoping's embrace of a form of capitalism and the reversal of Chairman Mao's mad socialist policies. The 'household responsibility system' introduced by Deng allowed farmers to profit from the sale of a surplus. It was introduced in 1971 and had been adopted by most farmers by 1983. His industrial policies were similar in that if manufacturers met their official production targets, they could sell any surplus at a profit.

There is little evidence for such imaginative, pluralist economic thinking in Africa, the Middle East or Latin America. Instead, in many of these countries, it is really only the dictators and their cronies who get their hands on any wealth. The Chinese have tried, through intensive training courses, to persuade civil servants and politicians from developing countries to follow their socio-political model, but there is no evidence to show that they have yet convinced any countries to adopt the model. In many ways, I suspect this is because the Chinese model ultimately depends on Chinese culture and, in particular, the need for, recognition of and acceptance of discipline, order and leadership.

I was fortunate to visit China several times in my career. The first visit was to Jiangxi province in 1988, when almost everyone was still wearing Mao dungarees rather than Western clothing, drank gallons of green tea and chain-smoked. During this and other visits over a period of more than five years, it became clear to me that most people in China do what they are told to do, most of the time. Not all do; there are plenty of small and not so small characters who challenge the status quo when given a chance. But fear of the CCP keeps most in line.[78] Perhaps equally important

---

78. It is easy and perhaps a bit risky to make generalisations about a people. But my own experience and those of my missionary great-grandfather (George Henry Bondfield), recorded in letters he wrote from China to my grandfather in the late 19th century, suggest that China needs very strong leadership in order to keep a wily bunch of individuals from self-centred opportunism, be it gambling, financial sleight of hand (see 3.11.) or exploitation of the weak by the strong (slavery!).

is the fact that the CCP has delivered a rising standard of living for most Chinese people in recent years, resulting in a considerable degree of trust in the government as well as fear of retribution.

Political theory suggests that most autocracies collapse in the end, as was the case with the USSR. That said, the leadership in China in the early years of the 21st century does not appear to be under any serious threat, although the abolition of term limits for the supreme leader during the 19th National Party Congress in October 2017 suggests that Xi Jinping is putting more of his faith in the constitution than his political popularity within the CCP – a clear sign that he feels threatened by something. This apparent weakness of the strong man will not go unnoticed at home, and before long, he will almost certainly have domestic rivals.

However, it would be unwise to even begin to guess when the CCP will lose power, especially post Covid-19. No one knows for sure, but by mid-2020, it seemed that the country was on top of the virus and its economy was beginning to recover. The rest of the world may not be entirely enamoured by the West and its values, especially the US when led by Donald Trump, but few would argue that China is going to find it easy to make friends and influence others, given its recent poor handling of important political issues. I am sure that this, in turn, will hinder its attempts to secure allies with its aid programmes, which are largely in the form of loans for large infrastructure projects. Overall, I do not think the Chinese domestic political model may be too serious a challenge for the West, and attempts by the West to foster democracy should be continued.

The promotion of an autocratic system of governance is only one aspect of China's global political ambitions, however. More important than encouraging other countries to adopt its domestic political system is China's overwhelming interest in being recognised as the emerging global superpower. It would seem to have a twin-track approach to achieving this goal. The first is to spread its wings in global arenas, such as the UN, and the second is through a massive programme of investment in and lending to developed and developing nations.

As far as global influence is concerned, since the turn of the century, China has begun to flex its muscles in the global corridors of power. Following the end of the Cold War in 1989, there is a growing body of evidence (albeit some is admittedly apocryphal) that the West has begun to lose interest in quite large aspects of the UN. Of particular significance is the fact that the West no longer seems too bothered about who heads up the UN specialist agencies – the World Bank and IMF excluded. Thus, as of March 2021, four of the 14 UN specialist agencies (the FAO, ICAO, ITU and UNIDO) are headed up by Chinese nationals. And the WHO was headed by a Chinese from Hong Kong until 2017.

China clearly sees value in being in control of UN agencies. After all, the head of an agency oversees the recruitment and promotion for all senior positions in an agency and can thereby influence things for many years. For example, a previous head of the WHO, Margaret Chan, is a Chinese/Canadian national who – although born and brought up in Hong Kong – was delegated by the People's Republic of China. China has achieved these positions by the simple expedient of securing the necessary number of votes from member countries at election time.

For those who are not familiar with the UN system, it is important to point out that, until the end of the 20th century, the UN was by and large part of the West's soft-power apparatus, so China is simply now doing what the West used to do. It is too early to say whether this will pay China dividends. Its influence at and over the WHO at around the time of the Covid-19 pandemic was highly questionable, notably its refusal to allow Taiwan to participate in the 73rd World Health Assembly in May 2020, what looked like deliberate delays in providing the WHO with vital important information about the virus, and putting pressure on the WHO to delay announcing Covid-19 to be a pandemic. In 2021, China clearly tried to influence the findings of an international team looking into the cause of the outbreak, which has raised eyebrows in many countries.

The use of soft power in international fora is a subtle art that depends more on being able to convince others than simply telling them what you want them to hear or buying loyalty. China may have secured overwhelming influence over the WHO, but were the US to withdraw its funding for the agency permanently, it would be irreparably damaged, and China would be held responsible for its demise.[79]

However, China's interest in the FAO is not simply political opportunism. In recent years, it has increased its imports of food tremendously. Estimates suggest that it imported foodstuffs worth US$14 billion in 2003. By 2017, this had increased sevenfold to more than US$100 billion. It has also invested in large-scale farms in Africa (see 5.6.) and the China–Pakistan Economic Corridor (see details on the BRI later in this section on page 283) has a subcomponent for seeds, pesticides and a large fertiliser factory. No doubt this is to help Pakistan produce more grains, which China would be able to purchase at a discount or as debt service. Obviously, China has an eye on producing food in other countries to meet its own needs. This would not matter too much if it followed best environmental practices and paid the real price for the food, but there is no evidence of any transparency associated with such deals, and if it controls the FAO, it will more than influence the global agricultural standards others have to follow. In 2021, it was reported that the US and China were sharing ideas that might allow the FAO to promote GM seed

---

79. The election of Joe Biden in November 2020 appears to have removed this threat.

technology. Up until this point, the FAO has been neutral in its support for GM seed (Hruska, 2021).

China has also increased its strategic military influence considerably, most noticeably with the new Chinese-built ports in the Indian Ocean. The so-called String of Pearls – which includes the new ports in the Indian Ocean at Gwardar, Djibouti, Hambantota and Colombo – built under the BRI (see page 349). These ports provide a neat way of allowing China's merchant ships and navy vessels to conveniently control the sea lanes around India, China's biggest Asian rival. China also has a controlling interest in a number of large European ports, including Piraeus in Greece. There is also talk of a Chinese warm-water port off the coast of West Africa. Students of history will not need reminding that *Pax Britannica* and *Pax Americana* were closely linked to economic and military (especially naval) supremacy, so it is hardly surprising that China seeks a new maritime global order, or *Pax Sina*. China denies this and says the ports are only for commercial use, not military use. However, it is difficult to see how warships could be prevented from using these ports. Maybe the West will have to build more warships using aid funds to patrol the seas around these ports, on the grounds of ensuring they are only used for trade.

As far as the second key challenge to the West – China's financial influence – is concerned, its actions in some ways reflect the commercial motives behind the European expansion in the 18th and 19th centuries that led to the European colonial empires. China emphatically rejects all accusations of colonialism, and it is the case that it has not planted its flag on any territory in recent years. However, there is a fine line between control though direct administration and indirect control though financial influence, and Chinese money certainly has influence. Up-to-date and accurate statistics are not easy to come by, but there is hardly a country in Africa that has not received substantial aid and investment from China. According to Sebastian Horn and Christoph Trebesch's[80] (2019) study, China has provided loans totalling more than US$1.5 trillion to developing countries since 2000. This makes China the biggest global source of credit. Understanding this lending is so difficult because nearly half of these loans are 'hidden'. That is, neither the World Bank nor the IMF have any information on the details of these loans. A list of some of the largest projects is given in *Appendix D*, together with a review of some of the problems associated with related loans. However, it is important to recognise that, since a peak in 2016, China has scaled back its lending considerably. This appears to be in response to problems with loan servicing and a reappraisal of lending policies (see *Appendix D*).

---

80. Of the Kiel Institute for the World Economy.

We also know that China has invested massive amounts of money in a number of African countries for infrastructure, trade and manufacturing. In September 2018, at the Forum on China–Africa Cooperation, 51 out of a total of 54 African heads of state were promised a further US$60 billion in aid over the next three years by Xi Jinping himself (*The Economist*, 2019C). China also has massive trade with that continent; it buys raw materials (notably oil and metal ore, and especially rare earth minerals), it sells a wide range of goods and it has established a considerable number of manufacturing facilities. The total value of annual exports from and imports to Africa has increased massively, from US$10 billion in 2000 to some US$200 billion annually by 2018 (Chen, 2018).

There is also evidence that China uses the loans to secure business advantages in the form of licences to invest in a country. In 2017/18, Ethiopia awarded some 1,300 investment licences to Chinese investors. It is too soon to know how this will work out in Ethiopia and whether it will be a model used elsewhere, but if nothing else, it suggests a small army of Chinese experts will be based in the borrowing country to oversee the projects in question for many years. The question that then arises is whether the Chinese will want more political influence as well as financial control over its investments. This is one area where the competition with the West will be greatest.

At this point, it is appropriate and important to say a little about the BRI or, to give it its full title, the Silk Road Economic Belt and 21st Century Maritime Silk Road. This is a massive programme that is ostensibly to create infrastructure – notably new roads, railways, pipelines, ports, telecommunications facilities and anything else that can be seen in the broadest sense as 'international industrial capacity cooperation'[81]– linking the countries of Eurasia, Asia, Africa and the Pacific to China. The proposed land-based investments consist of a series of trunk routes across Eurasia from China, along with a number of side corridors containing industrial parks. The big idea being that the increased transport facilities will stimulate the establishment of factories in parts of the world with low labour costs. The maritime investment is essentially a series of ports at convenient points in the Indian and Pacific Oceans.

The BRI was announced by Xi Jinping in 2013, during visits to Kazakhstan and Indonesia, and is a key element of his foreign policy; so much so that it is now incorporated into the CCP's constitution and cannot easily be ignored by the CCP, whatever happens to Xi Jinping. It is seen by China as a way of improving the economies of the involved countries through better infrastructure, stimulating improved trade links and manufacturing facilities that would be paid for by

---

81. A suitably vague term that appears to emphasise economics but does not preclude political priorities.

Chinese loans and, conveniently, executed largely by Chinese companies and workers. The Chinese are promoting the BRI as a win-win situation, under which countries get essential infrastructure and access to markets for their goods and services, and China gets access and influence. Most observers agree that much new infrastructure is needed, and the World Bank has calculated that BRI transport projects in Asia could raise the GDPs of participating countries by some 3%.

Critics, however, see it more as a foreign policy initiative designed by the CCP to reshape the world order more to its liking (*The Economist*, 2020A). They see it as pushback against the US 'Pivot to Asia' policy announced in 2013 – an attempt to reassert US influence in the region, or the so-called Blue Dot Network set up by the US, Japan and Australia to fund infrastructure projects in the developing world. China does not overtly deny that it is more than a big spend on infrastructure. It is being promoted as the way to develop economies fast, following the Chinese model, and as such, it is about helping countries develop through cooperation. However, there is little evidence that infrastructure alone will stimulate economic growth.

If every project identified by China was to be completed, the estimated total cost could be as high as US$5 trillion – by far the largest aid initiative ever conceived. That said, early indications are that the full programme will never be realised, not least because of poor overall direction. Projects are implemented and financed by a plethora of Chinese banks and agencies – including SOEs, local governments, ministries and special infrastructure-funding organisations – with little or no interagency coordination.

No reliable information is available on the number of active projects and/or the investment made to date. Various sources quote different statistics. In the book *Red Flags: Why Xi's China Is in Jeopardy* (Magnus, 2019), it is suggested that some 115 countries were actively involved in BRI projects by April 2019, although most of the estimated investment of US$600 billion was in only 10 countries[82] by that date, all of which have special economic and political ties to China. In contrast, some observers, such as Chatzky and McBride (2020), consider that only 60 countries have signed contracts for BRI projects, valued at US$200 billion.

There is a general agreement that the largest single project so far is the US$68 billion China–Pakistan Economic Corridor, which includes road and rail links though Pakistan connecting China to a new port at Gwadar on the Arabian Sea. This could enable China to move troops effortlessly from Xinjian in the far west of China to the Indian Ocean to the east of India without having to travel all the way around India. The other large initiative is the dry port of Khorgos in Kazakhstan,

82. Bangladesh, Egypt, Indonesia, Iran, Laos, Malaysia, Nigeria, Pakistan, Russia and the UAE.

where a rail head and large free-trade industrial zone has been under development since 2015.

By mid-2020, some countries were having second thoughts about their BRI projects. India has given it the thumbs down. Egypt and Bangladesh have cancelled plans for new coal-fired power stations, Pakistan has sought easier payment terms for US$30 billion worth of power projects, Nigeria is reviewing its Chinese loans, and the Khorgos project is basically an economic failure. This is because the rail link to Europe is only possible if Chinese exporters are subsidised to use the route. Rail transport is far more expensive for container transport than sea transport.

Experts consider that a wave of defaults is inevitable, and the big questions are how China will respond and what the reaction to its response will be. As far as loan financing and rescheduling are concerned, there are worries that contract clauses may result in up to 60% of the value of assets being claimed by China as collateral for loans that fail. This would go down like a lead balloon in countries that understood the BRI loans to be an initiative to help them, not a backdoor way of taking over assets. In contrast, Western (Paris Club)[83] loans do not require this kind of collateral. Can China afford the diplomatic risks associated with enforcing these collateral clauses or will it simply have to forgive some of the loans? The whole sad story highlights the trouble with the BRI as a foreign policy initiative, in that it is a typically Chinese single-component initiative based on money. It does not have the all-important soft-power initiative needed to generate willing followers, nor does it address the significant need for sustainable, effective institutions.

No one – probably not even the Chinese – knows quite how big their international credit programme really is and/or how much is economically and financially viable. Little is known about the terms of many of the loans, but they are either for strategic infrastructure (notably the BRI), for trade (to secure access to mineral or hydrocarbon resources), for building manufacturing facilities or, in some cases (notably Central Asia), for political reasons. We do know that the cost–benefit analyses used to justify many of these initiatives have shown themselves to be seriously faulty, and many initiatives are not generating sufficient revenue to service the associated loans. Similar things have happened with Western loans in the past, resulting in considerable debt forgiveness by Western lenders. It is not yet clear how much debt China is ready to forgive, and unlike the West, it has no formal mechanism for assessing which loans to forgive.

In this context, I was intrigued to read an article in the UK press that reported China had asked the UK DFID for help in improving the way in which Beijing lends to poor countries. China has also established the Multilateral Cooperation

---

83. The Paris Club of nations has agreed to provide debt relief to developing countries on a case-by-case basis in the event that loans extended by club members run into difficulties.

Centre for Development Finance, based in Beijing, and has signed memorandums of understanding with eight development banks – including the World Bank – in order to improve its lending to poor countries. China is clearly aware that it needs to assess prospective project loans more rigorously in future. China has also asked for other countries to help finance the BRI (*The Economist*, 2019B), suggesting that it may have bitten off more than it can chew alone on this initiative.

On the subject of creditor imperialism or 'debt-trap diplomacy', I was intrigued by a two-page advertisement by China Focus (2018). This sought to justify Chinese investment in the BRI. It refers to accusations of 'creditor imperialism'; that is to say, concerns in the West that China will lend vast amounts of cheap credit to countries where the roads and ports are being built, which will effectively create a 'debt trap' for the borrowing governments, forcing them to cede natural assets and sovereignty. The advert was obviously designed to challenge this accusation, but in fact, it only served to share the concern with a wider audience. If nothing else, the advert's text hints at China's worries about how other countries perceive its aid initiatives and its ambiguous ambitions to influence the countries it lends to.

At this point, it might be helpful to take stock of the Chinese economic miracle and where it might be heading in relation to aid. At the start of 2019, according to analysts at the Morgan Stanley bank, there were signs that China's current account surplus (the margin between savings and investment) was heading for a deficit. In other words, on an annualised basis, the nation was going to invest more than it saved. China is not going to run out of cash anytime soon, as it has massive foreign exchange reserves (US$3 trillion), and the change may be largely due to short-term effects, such as the trade dispute with the US. However, at least some of the change is due to Chinese tourists spending money on overseas travel. Some estimates suggest that Chinese tourists spend US$250 billion a year on foreign travel (*The Economist*, 2020A).

In late 2018 and 2019, China had to pay higher prices for essential imports (such as food and oil), and it has rising costs from the healthcare and retirement of an ageing population. If these trends continue, China will have to dip into its reserves or reduce investment, and it may have to adjust its fiscal policy to facilitate borrowing from abroad. This probably would not matter too much if the Chinese economy were still growing at incredibly high rates, but in late 2019, Chinese growth had dropped below 6% per annum, the lowest in many years.

George Magnus (2019), in his fascinating book *Red Flags: Why Xi's China Is in Jeopardy*, posits the opinion that – contrary to the views of many China-watchers – the Chinese economy may well not exceed that of the US anytime soon. His analysis is quite simple. In 2018, the Chinese GDP was estimated at US$12 trillion, compared to the US GDP of US$20.5 trillion. If the Chinese economy continued to grow at the then rate of 8% per annum and the US economy continued to grow at 2% per annum (as predicted at the time by the IMF), by 2028 the Chinese GDP would be US$26 billion – very close to that of the US, which would be U$28 billion. However, if the Chinese economy only grew at 5%, the Chinese GDP by 2028 would only be US$20 trillion – considerably smaller than that of the US. If, as also seems quite likely, the yuan/renminbi is devalued from seven to the dollar to eight to the dollar, the value of the Chinese GDP would be US$16 trillion in 2028, which is much smaller than that of the US. Since these sums were first done, both the Chinese and US economies have been hit by the Covid-19 virus, which – although predicted to reduce the growth rates of both countries – has in fact led to an increase in growth rates that will almost certainly still leave the US as the largest economy for some time to come.

George Magnus (2019) considers that a slowdown in China's economic growth rate is more than likely over the medium term. He has identified four traps that he believes China may have difficulty overcoming. The first of these is the debt trap. There is quite a lot of evidence that this is a problem. On 25 November 2019, China National Radio launched a mini-series aimed at lauding President Xi Jinping's stewardship of the economy, and in particular, the need to address the problems associated with companies that are experiencing financial difficulties (*The Economist*, 2019D). According to those who follow and understand China, this seems to mean that the country is at last facing up to a debt problem it has been trying to deny.

The second, and in many ways related to the debt trap, is the overvaluation of the currency against the US dollar, which makes exports too expensive. There is now general agreement that, during the first decade of the present century, China deliberately devalued its currency to secure export markets.[84] Since then, the value of the yuan has recovered a bit, reducing the profits of exporters who now receive fewer yuan for each dollar of sales.

Then there is the trade war with the US. Contrary to what is often taught in economics courses, trade is not always beneficial, especially in a huge economy like the US. If the trade war between the US and China continues for any length of time, China will be the big loser. This is because the US does not really need to import anything to survive and prosper. It produces more than enough essential items, such as food and energy, domestically. It also has a wide range of manufactured goods and services. Most of its imports are speciality products it can do without, such as French wine and Scottish whisky. China is not so lucky – it has to import much of its food and energy supplies, for which it needs dollars earned from exports.

The third – and perhaps the most difficult trap to avoid – is the ageing Chinese population. Soon, there will be far too few workers to pay the taxes needed to

---

84. In 1993, US$1 = 5.78 yuan; in 2000, US$1 = 8.28 yuan; and in 2019, US$1 = 7.00 yuan.

provide for the long-term welfare (healthcare and pensions) of the ageing Chinese population. The results of the national 10-year census reported in May 2021 indicate that China's population was no longer increasing by then. By 2019, the national pension system was paying out more than it received in contributions, and it is estimated that the national pension fund will have run out of money by 2035. This is because there are too few young people joining the workforce as a result of the earlier one-child policy. At present, employers pay 20% and staff pay 8% of salaries into the fund – these rates are high by world standards, and it is difficult to see how they can be increased sufficiently to cover the predicted shortfalls. Conversely, the pension ages of 55 for women and 60 for men are low by world standards. Raising the pensionable age will cause the CCP massive problems.

The fourth and last trap is the middle-income trap. In the early years of economic growth at the end of the 20th century, much productivity improvement came from the supply of cheap rural labour moving to industrial jobs and building infrastructure. Now, China appears to be trapped in a lower-productivity mode with fewer jobs for such unskilled labour, but it shows no sign of knowing how to get out of the trap.

The party could address some or all of these traps, but to do so, it would have to surrender more decision-making power to businesses and entrepreneurs, otherwise known as 'the market' – something that it refuses to do. Instead, the CCP is taking more and more control of the economy. Political theory[85] and experience elsewhere in the world (Algeria, Cuba, the USSR and, more recently, Venezuela) tell us that governments are not good at making the right decisions for economic growth and business in the medium to longer term. This means that China will probably not be able to colonise the developing world financially with 'aid' loans, as it might have hoped to, as its own growth may stall. It will not stop lending to poor countries, but its rate of lending will very likely slow down from its recent peaks, and in future, it will undertake more rigorous cost–benefit analyses before writing cheques. The message for African and other developing-country leaders is that they should read the small print in any Chinese loan agreements very carefully and make sure they only sign contracts with legal clauses that will, if necessary, stand up in an international court. They also need to be sure that they are not signing away valuable assets and/or committing to uncontrolled Chinese immigration.

---

85. Popper (1945) has shown the link between the higher living standards and the free institutions of liberal democracies. This is because many decisions affecting an economy are essentially predictions, some of which will fail. In a democracy, the market will usually compensate for such failures by making alternative decisions. Autocracies find it much more difficult to effect such compensations. A good example is steel making. All countries need steel for making things and construction. Democracies and autocracies can both set up steel-making plants. However, while democracies can close steel works when they become unprofitable, autocracies find it very difficult to close such factories as there are no other jobs for the workers to go to. In other words, state planning of an economy tends to be much less efficient than allowing the market to plan the economy.

For the West, any slowdown gives a bit more time to develop a strategy to observe China's aid programmes and to provide some cautionary strategic advice to the leaders of developing countries. I think the West needs to continue to monitor Chinese activity in the developing world very carefully. The Chinese have learnt much about Western ways in recent years by close observation. The West now needs to return the compliment and gain a deeper understanding of the reasons for and practices of Chinese lending. If done properly, it should be possible, sooner rather than later, to identify Chinese-supported projects and programmes that have or will go wrong that can be used to persuade developing countries that China may not be the unquestioning magic money tree it pretends to be. The Coca Codo Sinclair Dam in Ecuador is a good example of bad borrowing (see *Appendix D*).

The West also needs to review its own relations with China in relation to Chinese aid and how China is using its aid to compete. I do not expect the competition to develop into a second Cold War for a number of reasons. Firstly, China has historically refrained from global power struggles. During the Cold War, when it was close to the USSR ideologically, it preferred to remain neutral rather than support Moscow, and furthermore, it has few powerful allies willing to support its side in any such competition. Secondly, it is aware of the cost of such an ideological competition. What is more, it is very dependent on its links to the US dollar, as its own currency is not fully convertible, and it cannot really afford a major challenge with the West. Finally, it is terrified of what might happen internally and with its neighbours if it needed to devote a massive amount of political capital, time and resources to such a conflict.

This means that, while the West cannot sit back and do nothing, the best thing it can do is to increase its available concessional loans to meet the infrastructure needs of the developing world. To some considerable extent, the West would seem to have got this message already. The UK's *Sunday Times* (Glancy, 2018) had an article in which there was a brief reference to the US national security adviser John Bolton and his announcement regarding a new policy towards Africa, aimed at countering massive Chinese investments in the continent. No details were provided, but the message was almost certainly this: if you need investment funds, we are also able to help; in 2021 (at time of writing), President Biden appears to support such lending.

The West also needs to ascertain whether it has become too dependent on China for certain products and for Chinese investment, and whether it needs to pay much closer attention to Chinese strategic initiatives on the waves and in the airwaves. This will almost certainly involve building and maintaining strong relations with India and the Pacific countries. China's spectacular economic growth has looked like a win-win situation for all, as cheaper Chinese goods filled the shopping baskets of the world, and Chinese money kept stock markets buoyant. However, no one factored in what would happen when China started to demand recognition of and obeisance to the power of its financial strength.

6.7. India

India presents one of the biggest challenges to aid in the future. On the one hand, it is a country with significant potential, having the resources and talent to grow economically. It is a democracy with considerable proven technological skills. It has its own nuclear deterrent and almost succeeded in landing a module on the moon in 2019. And until 2018, it had a robust and apparently growing economy. Taken at face value, it would not seem to be a strong candidate for aid.

As if in sensible response to these factors, the UK announced in 2018 that it would provide only a modest amount of aid – £98 million over two years – which would not go to the government, but would instead be invested in Indian enterprises to create jobs and provide technical expertise. This policy reflects a number of factors:

- It seems counterintuitive to provide aid to a government that prioritises space exploration rather than domestic issues of poverty and pollution.
- In some years of the second decade of the 21st century, the Indian economy was reported to be the fastest growing globally (10% per annum), and this was expected to help take millions out of poverty, eliminating the need for aid.
- India's non-aligned position with either the West, China or Russia is important, and modest amounts of aid help to maintain access to India's leaders.

It is also the case that India has deep-seated structural problems and is probably home to nearly half of the world's poorest people; many are trapped in a rural economy that is heavily dependent on unsustainable agricultural subsidies. In 2019, India had a grain surplus of 70 million tonnes and a sugar mountain of 15 million tonnes. The impressive growth rates prior to 2018 now seems to have been a chimera or the result of statistical manipulation. In the quarter to June 2019, growth slipped to 5% – the lowest in six years. This is well below the rate needed to raise millions out of poverty, and the government seems unable or unwilling to make the necessary labour and tax reforms to get the economy going again and build up a modern industrial – rather than agricultural – economy.

Added to the economic problems, India has the world's worst air and water pollution. Some estimates suggested that some 800 million people in the Gangetic Plain suffer from life-threatening air pollution for much of the year, and that greenhouse gas emissions from coal-powered generators have doubled since 2005. Most of India's major rivers are biologically dead, overloaded with sewage and chemical waste. Added to that is a political system that is nominally or superficially a representative democracy but that often looks more like the elite dominated 'anarchy' that was exploited by the East India Company in the 17th century.

Against such a background, it seems irresponsible as well as naïve to expect the government alone to solve its problems, and it is notable that the World Bank had continued to lend considerable sums to India under its previous president. It will be interesting to see if the new World Bank president, David Malpass, cuts back lending to India as part of the Trumpian ideology of reducing support for multilateral agencies. I suspect this will not happen, as this would encourage India to look towards its old friend Russia. It might also encourage the country to stretch out an arm to China. However, I think the latter is unlikely, given the tensions on their shared northern borders, which have rumbled on for decades with no sign of rapprochement and which flared up again in 2020. It is also the case that India has a good record of servicing its World Bank loans, so there would be no reasons not to continue to lend based on financial performance.

While it is reasonable to expect the world's third-largest economy to be primarily responsible for addressing poverty itself, it clearly is struggling, and there is a strong case for continued multilateral and bilateral aid to address specific problems. I would suggest this can best be done by addressing things such as climate change and air/water pollution with technologies developed elsewhere, and by shining a light on some of the stupidity of current Indian policies, such as the over-subsidised agricultural sector.

6.8.   Small and Fragile States

Many of the world's poorest live in small or fragile states that have limited prospects for sustainable economic development. A handful of small-island states have developed specialist economies based on tourism or tax avoidance, and these countries will only really need emergency aid to help recover after natural disasters, such as hurricanes or disease epidemics. For the other small and fragile states, there would seem to be three main issues:

1. Security or military support
2. The most effective kind of financial support to provide
3. How to encourage better governance

The first of these will almost certainly involve Western powers for some years to come, and it concerns efforts to prevent them from providing a springboard for terrorist activity or the kind of destabilising insurrection in Afghanistan that has been ongoing for decades. In this regard, it was somewhat alarming to hear a BBC report on the crisis in the Sahel region of West Africa in June 2018 (BBC, 2018). This vast, sparsely populated part of the world appears to have been taken over by two Islamic fundamentalist groups, which are using it as a base for smuggling people from Africa into Europe and to force the local population to embrace extreme Islamist practices. The situation is potentially very serious. Unless the fundamentalists can be contained, there is every reason to think that West Africa could become a springboard for terrorist activity in Europe and elsewhere. To counter this activity, some Western countries – including the US, France and the UK – are providing military advice and personnel to help contain the actions of the Islamists.

However, policymakers in the West are divided in their thinking on how to address the problem. On the one hand are those who believe the important thing is to root out the Islamic fundamentalists by force through increasing military intervention as soon as possible. On the other hand are those who think that the reason the fundamentalists have been so successful is because there has been so little development in this part of the world and that more effort is needed to stimulate economic activity in these areas. This group think that simply helping to supress the fundamentalists will not improve things and could make matters worse.

The problem with this kind of thinking is that there is no precedent for stimulating sustainable economic growth in war-torn areas – just take a look at South Sudan. Like it or not, I see no realistic alternative to military interventions, at least in the short to medium term. However, this needs to be done very carefully, as there is mounting evidence that, unless military force is used wisely, it will achieve little. It is certainly the case, for example, that the scorched-earth policy used by the Nigerian authorities in the northern states in recent years has not helped and is not the model to follow.

The West cannot sit back and do nothing. Some countries – parts of West Africa (Nigeria included) – are already getting military aid, ostensibly to train local soldiers to counter the threat of Islamic extremists, but it is probably also to help directly in these conflicts through the provision of strategic advice and possibly logistical support. Four US troopers were killed in Niger in early 2018, and some French soldiers were killed in the region after this. I am fairly sure this kind of localised military assistance will become more common, and furthermore, that it will appeal to politicians in many Western countries as it will justify moving tax revenue from traditional aid ministries to the defence sector, thereby providing good jobs for the nationals of the rich countries. It would also, of course, be a good way of keeping ears and eyes to the ground to find out what is really going on in these countries. Such surreptitious military support seems likely to continue for long periods. I think this would be acceptable in the West if the number of casualties was low and if the military presence helped keep the governments of the affected countries aligned with the West.

The real problem for the Western policy makers is not so much whether to assist in the use of military force, but how to do so and for how long? The Maiduguri kind of 'containment', under which folk were herded into safe garrisons but divorced from their fields and livelihoods, could last for many years and could be quite bloody, as was the attempt to sort things out in Afghanistan. I do not foresee any substantial Western investment in military force of this kind. The voters in the West no longer want to see their young men and women sacrificed for causes they do not really understand, nor for military action that does not seem to bring about meaningful solutions. In this regard, it is salient that the West has steered clear of becoming involved in the civil war in Syria, knowing that there was little it could achieve by getting its armed forces involved. It is also fairly obvious that Russia's involvement has not achieved much for the Kremlin. China, very wisely, continues its old policy of steering clear of such conflicts. And the US decision to pull out of Afghanistan in 2021, supported by both Republicans and Democrats, would seem to confirm the West's intentions to follow China's lead and steer clear of insoluble civil insurrections or wars.

As far as financial aid is concerned, the idea of taxpayers in rich countries providing continuous budgetary support to fragile states no longer makes good financial sense. But if they are not helped in some way, they may sooner or later become – if they are not already – a source of illegal migrants or a drug-running centre.

It is notable that many of these countries are in Africa, where according to UN demographers, the population is expected to increase from 1.2 billion in 2018 to 2.5 billion by 2050. This is in contrast to most of the rest of the world, where populations are static or even declining. Demographers have a good record in projecting population growth rates, so one has no reason to challenge these figures. That said, some demographers think the population growth rate in Africa will be much slower than the UN estimates (Bricker and Ibbitson, 2019).

Whoever is right, the figures are startling. They suggest that, on the continent of Africa as a whole, there will have to be a massive increase in the amount of food produced or imported and in the number of jobs needed in just over 30 years. Given the economic achievements in most African countries over the past 60 years, it is difficult to see how these challenges will be met, and the pressure on young Africans to emigrate will almost certainly increase. The European countries of the Mediterranean will not be alone in wanting to stop a potentially massive increase in economic refugees in the next few decades. The questions then become these:

- Can aid prevent such massive emigration?
- Does the developed world have deep enough pockets to meet this challenge?
- How much aid is needed on a per capita basis?

In their fascinating book *Good Economics for Hard Times*, Banerjee and Duflo (2019) provide some answers to all these questions. As far as emigration is concerned, they suggest that even the poorest people are reluctant to move from their villages, let alone emigrate. If they are right, emigration may not be such a big issue, and it is usually the better educated and resourceful who emigrate and probably add value to the countries into which they immigrate. Banerjee and Duflo (2019) consider that the rich world in general is affluent enough to share some of its wealth with the poorest, and it would be immoral not to do so. As far as per capita needs are concerned, they suggest that CCT has proven to be a low-cost way of alleviating poverty and a case can be made for UBI programmes. I am not quite so optimistic and have looked at their ideas in more detail in *Chapter 5*.

The problem I have with such schemes is not the basic economics but both the risk of obviating the responsibilities of sovereign governments to fund their own welfare programmes and how to end such programmes. If effective ways of delivering such aid directly to its beneficiaries (rather than through corrupt and incompetent governments) can be found, they should be tried. An interesting UBI trial of this type is the 12-year trial at Magawa in western Kenya, sponsored by the US charity Give Directly. If this initiative provides answers to the aforementioned key questions raised, then it might prove to be a model worth replicating. I also think such schemes might provide ways of improving basic education and healthcare, including helping women to have fewer children.

The issue of governance failure is not limited to fragile states, but it is certainly a feature of a fragile state, and until governance and leadership really improves, many countries will remain poor. This was first brought home to me during an official visit to Nigeria in 1988. My national counterpart, a very thoughtful and decent young man, gave me a copy of the book *The Trouble with Nigeria* (Achebe, 1985). Chinua Achebe is a fine writer and has a gift for distilling important issues into simple sentences. His basic analysis of Nigeria's problems of governance indicates that it stems from poor leadership that has done nothing to curb problems arising from tribalism, indiscipline, corruption and false pride. Achebe's hope was that, by the turn of the century, a decent leader of integrity would have emerged and things would have improved. Sadly, some 30 years since I read the book, things have – if anything – got worse and show no sign of getting better. Potentially rich in resources (notably oil and skilled manpower), Nigeria should, in theory, no longer be classified as a developing country – in fact, if anything, it is slipping back into being a fragile state.[86]

---

86. In her book *Ladder of Bones*, Ellen Thorp (1956) paints a picture of the warfare and chaos in the kingdoms of Nigeria in the early 19th century, when the most important trade was slavery. She describes societies where only the fittest and most ruthless survived. Some 90 years of British rule (1853–1960) did much to improve things for the average person, but perhaps the hand-holding period was too short. Western democracy is a fragile flower that needs careful nurturing for hundreds of years and survives best when supported by a vibrant, broad-based economy.

Unfortunately, Nigeria is not alone. It is one of more than 50 emerging nations that threw off the cloak of imperialism in the second half of the 20th century. The hope was that, with the wicked colonial masters out of the way and no longer exploiting national resources, everyone in the newly independent countries would see their living standards improve. With hindsight, this now looks like a pious hope as far as many countries are concerned. Indeed, I would go as far as saying it was a deception and one that suited the colonial masters, who were desperate to hand over responsibility for governance, and a handful of national politicians, who saw great opportunities to enrich themselves.

But it is important to recognise that it is not all bad news. Quite a number of countries in Asia that were colonies of Western powers have made progress in improving governance. Overall, however, the main lesson of independence is that it takes years for reliable systems of self-governance to evolve, and that inappropriate aid can actually make things worse.[87] In particular, bad technical advice (see 3.14.) and poorly designed loans, which have enabled a few politicians and civil servants to get rich, have not contributed anything to long-term development. The lesson here is that if aid is to really work, it has to be very carefully tailored to the country's needs, more so in the countries where governance is weak.

At the end of the Cold War, there was a rethink among aid experts. They convinced many aid-giving Western governments to link aid with (or to) democratic governance, and in particular, to fair elections. In this way, it was hoped that leaders and politicians of integrity would be elected, and aid funds would be more fairly distributed. The rationale for such thinking, which has been discussed earlier, is based on the fact that most developed countries have representative governments, and overall, folk are better off in such countries compared to developing countries without such governance.

An opportunity to see whether this new approach would work came at the time of the so-called Arab Spring at the end of the first decade of the 21st century. I happened to be on a short mission to Egypt in 2011. We were working with the government that was still in office, but it was not possible to be unaware that a major political uprising calling for a change was going on all around us. I did not venture into Tahrir[88] Square myself, but one of my mission members did. He reported a relaxed crowd, many of whom had brought their children with them, who were clearly demonstrating peacefully for change. In a way, they were successful. The government listened, and in 2012, elections were held for a new president, who would be elected by the people rather than appointed by the military, as had been the practice in Egypt for decades.

---

87. For details, see Gill (2010) or Moyo (2009).
88. *Tahrir* in Arabic means liberation.

After two rounds of voting, in June 2012, Mohammed Morsi – supported largely by fellow Muslims – won by a narrow margin.

At first, political observers in Egypt and outside the country took a deep breath and said quietly to themselves, 'We hope this works.' The early signs were quite encouraging, but it soon became clear that Morsi was in the pocket of Islamists (see 6.4.), and before long, the military struck back. In July 2013, General Sisi took over the reins of power. This was soon followed, somewhat surprisingly, by substantial loans/grants (US$30 billion) from rich Arab states. The message being sent by these funds was clear. We, the richest states in the Middle East, do not want our traditional autocratic regimes threatened by democracy, even if the democrats are also Muslims.

Since then, the West has effectively backed off from promoting democratic initiatives in the Middle East, but there are signs that Western governments are returning to the cause, at least as far as some countries in Africa are concerned. In early 2019, the Danish government and the EU withheld aid funds to Tanzania in response to the president's moves to muzzle the press and silence opposition politicians by locking them up.

Other likely developments are a greater emphasis on helping countries that have shown clear signs of taking responsibility for their own destinies, linked wherever possible to supporting nascent liberal democratic regimes rather than autocratic ones. There is no recipe book for this, but evidence suggests that, where national politicians have realised they are responsible for their nation's economic development, they can be helped by well-crafted aid. This includes placing much more emphasis on supporting the private sector to create jobs. The recent success of the garment industry in Lesotho suggests that preferential market access to the US for its ready-made garments has been very important. In a handful of countries that are considered to have significant but dormant economic potential, efforts could be made to help unlock this dormancy through advice on strengthening a country's basic institutions, such as a free press and legal system, together with basic national building requirements – things such as effective tax-raising systems, and both constitutional and electoral reform.

Improving basic education is probably the most sure-fire way of helping a country to move forwards. Perhaps bilateral Western aid should focus on providing help directly to schools through NGOs rather than via loans from development banks, which provides opportunities for corruption and inefficiency. After all, this is effectively what Saudi Arabia does with its help to madrassas in countries such as Pakistan and Bangladesh.

I do not expect to see any major regime-change initiatives such as those that were common during the Cold War. The Western world has learnt from bitter experience that interfering in a nation's politics rarely brings about the hoped-for benefits – think of Afghanistan, Angola, Iran, Libya, Syria and Venezuela, to name just a few. In Venezuela, the West kept its distance from the crisis in late 2018 and early 2019, based on earlier lessons. Regime change is not really aid, of course, but it was seen in the past as a precursor to the provision of aid, which would have largely gone to the regime's opponents once they took over the reins of power.

6.9.   Climate Change

There is little doubt that climate change is one of the most important issues facing all countries at the start of the third decade of the 21st century. It affects everyone in the world to some greater or lesser extent through changes in weather patterns, and it will almost certainly have devastating effects in the future as the sea levels rise and parts of the world can no longer support agriculture, and more extreme weather patterns become common almost everywhere. The 2018 report of the UN Intergovernmental Panel on Climate Change (IPCC) (Masson-Delmotte *et al.*, 2018) shows that the consequences of the 1°C increase in global warming to date has already resulted in rising sea levels and more extreme weather. Unless appropriate action is taken soon, it expects that between 2030 and 2050 there will be an overall rise of 1.5°C. If the rise reaches 2°C by 2100, there will be a further 10-centimetre increase in sea levels and virtually all coral reefs will disappear.

Opinions differ as to the causes of climate change, with some people convinced it is part of a natural process. The majority, however, recognise the link between climate change and mankind's dependence on carbon-based fossil fuel sources of energy (coal, oil and natural gas). This link is clearly demonstrated by the measured annual increases in the levels of carbon dioxide in the atmosphere over the past 150 years since mankind began using coal, oil and natural gas in a big way. Weaning mankind off carbon-based sources of energy is the obvious solution to the problem. How to achieve this is not so obvious, even though the experts assure us that the technologies exist to wean us off most fossil fuels. Things such as hydro, wind, solar, hydrogen and tidal power are not only effective but they are also rapidly becoming economically viable, at least as far as new investments are concerned. In 2020, at least one renewable-energy company in the US had a higher value than any traditional oil company. What is more, renewable-energy sources are also often cheaper to run – there is no charge for sunlight or wind power!

In the UK, by 2020, some 25% of electricity was produced by renewables, and these sources are substantially cheaper to install than nuclear power. Some observers point out that electricity produced by hydro, wind and solar power is dependent on the weather, and that a more reliable generation source is needed to stabilise the overall supply. However, with improvements in batteries, the use of tidal power and power-swapping arrangements,[89] it is possible to envisage a situation in which electricity generation could be met in most countries in a relatively short period of time, largely by renewable or non-carbon-based sources. Most mitigation[90] measures (e.g. electric vehicles), however, call for a massive increase in electricity generation, and it is difficult to see no role for nuclear power generation in many countries in the medium term.

These measures still leave a need for hydrocarbon fuels for some transport. Air travel presents the biggest difficulty as there is not yet a substitute for jet fuel, although a small electric-powered light aircraft flew for the first time in December 2019. Buses, trucks and cars can be and are already powered by rechargeable batteries. As far as rail is concerned, electrification is the basic solution, and where that is not possible, recent tests show that hydrogen power can replace diesel power.[91] Heating – and for that matter, cooking using natural gas – presents a problem of cost, rather than technology. Many homes have heating systems that depend on gas boilers and gas-powered stoves. These can be replaced by electric appliances, and ideally, as far as heating is concerned, using air-sourced or ground-sourced heat pumps, but the cost of any such change is considerable, and systems of subsidy will almost certainly have to be introduced or augmented.

Tests are underway in the UK to see if it is technically possible to use the existing gas-pipe networks to supply hydrogen to domestic houses, and at least one manufacturer has developed a water boiler that runs on hydrogen. Initial results are encouraging, but hydrogen is very explosive, and it may not be possible to use it for cooking, even if it can be used for heating boilers. However, not all such technologies are universally applicable, and care is needed in selecting the right technology for each situation. There are also considerable cost implications; in particular, how to persuade individuals and the private sector to invest in low-carbon technologies.

The point is that technologies already exist to enable us largely to phase out carbon-based fuels and replace them with electricity for most purposes in the richer countries of the world. In these countries (with the possible exception of some states in the US), the climate change issue is no longer *what* to do but *when* and *how* to do it. In 2008, the UK government passed the Climate Change Act,

89. The UK has cable links to Norway (hydro) and France (nuclear) from where it receives spare supply as and when needed.
90. The term 'mitigation' is used to describe the measures taken to address the effects of climate change, such as replacing or compensating for the use of carbon-based fuels. It also covers change of land use, afforestation and other forms of carbon dioxide sequestration. The other term frequently used in discussion of climate change is 'adaptation'. This means learning to live with a new climate by, say, growing different crops that tolerate hotter temperatures.
91. Hydrogen is easily produced by the electrolysis of water, and when burnt, it produces water, so it is carbon neutral.

calling for the levels of greenhouse gases (carbon dioxide and methane) to be 80% lower in 2050 than they were in 1990. Since then, pressure has been building to reduce these emissions to zero by 2050, if not earlier, as this is now UK government policy, along with the aim of phasing out the sale of non-electric vehicles by 2035 or even sooner. Other European countries are setting similar targets, as are quite a few other countries.

It is less clear how to transfer appropriate technologies to many of the poorer countries of the world. The biggest challenge is how to phase out the large number of coal- and gas-fired power plants around the developing world and in China and Japan. This is where aid could play a big role, as the two things that these poorer countries will need are funds and technical advice. It could be a win-win situation if aid funds are used to support developing countries through investment in carbon-neutral technologies that were developed in richer countries. The poorer countries would get the technologies at competitive prices, while the manufacturers of carbon-neutral energy facilities, such as wind turbines, will benefit from increased sales. Overall, everyone will benefit from a slowing down if not cessation regarding rising global temperatures. There are already quite a number of adaptation and mitigation projects supported by European developed-country aid budgets, and if nothing else, these provide an entry point or pathway to future help.

The UN General Assembly in September 2019 was focused on climate change, spearheaded by the young Swedish activist Greta Thunberg,[92] which has brought about a massive change in the locus of the climate change debate, if nothing else. It is no longer the preserve of academia, but is at the top of the political agenda and looks as though it will remain there. The good news on this front is that, under the BRI, China has begun to scale back its support for coal-fired power stations; one of which in Bangladesh was cancelled in mid-2020. It is not clear why, but this almost certainly follows global campaigns such as those started by Greta Thunberg.

It also seems likely that politicians in democracies will have to introduce much tougher laws about gas emissions if they want to be elected in the future. As if aware of this, at the UN General Assembly Meeting in September 2019, Boris Johnson announced that the UK would double its contribution to the International Climate Finance fund that provides aid to the poorest countries to deal with the causes of climate change; this would bring the UK's contribution to £11.6 billion over a period of five years. At the end of September 2019, the German government announced a large increase (€440 million) in funding for afforestation in Germany to replace dead and dying trees. There is little doubt that we will see a large increase in funds for climate change adaptation and mitigation measures in both donor

---

92. Greta Thunberg is a phenomenon that may or may not stand the test of time.

countries and aid budgets. There are also signs of a growing moral awareness in rich countries that they have to take a lead in climate change, partly because they started the problem at the time of the Industrial Revolution, but also because they have benefitted the most from using hydrocarbon sources of energy, and they now have the technical and financial means to help others.

It is early days as far as aid and climate change is concerned, but there are already quite a number of aid-supported mitigation and adaptation projects in Africa, Asia and Latin America funded by Western aid budgets. One of the best-known adaptation measures is the cyclone shelters in Bangladesh. Some 30 million people in Bangladesh live in low-lying coastal areas that are subject to cyclones. Since the devastating Cyclone Bhola in 1970, which led to 500,000 deaths, some 2,500 shelters have been built, largely funded by donor agencies such as the World Bank. In May 2020, when Cyclone Amphan struck, fewer than two dozen people lost their lives, as they were able to use the shelters during the storm. Although not originally designed as a climate change adaptation measure, this is effectively what they are, given the increasing frequency of cyclones due to the changing weather patterns caused by climate change.

Another important combined adaptation and mitigation measure with tremendous potential is the small-scale off-grid electricity generation system (wind, hydro and/or solar power) of the kind promoted by the Acumen foundation, which has been quite successful with its solar scheme in Africa. The UK aid budget is already supporting a number of alternative energy projects globally in a range of countries from Burundi to Colombia.

One major thrust, as far as mitigation is concerned, will be to encourage afforestation, (this has an important role to play as trees absorb a large amount of the carbon dioxide produced by using hydrocarbon fuels), wherever there are good prospects. I can imagine links between aid programmes and tree planting, for example. In small and fragile states that have limited prospects for economic growth, budget support from the rich world could be connected to tree-planting programmes linked to CCT programmes. These would require extensive and detailed feasibility and planning programmes to identify appropriate locations and tree species, the establishment of management institutions, the training of operatives, and supervision by donors. This supervision would be essential to ensure targets are met and to minimise corruption and wastage.

6.10. Traditional Aid Policy and Institutional Change

Security

To put this section of the chapter in context, I think it might be helpful to remind the reader that aid policy since the Second World War has been a major component of the strategic global security policies of the US and other Western allies. The term 'security' is used here to describe not only military security but also security for commerce, trade and the movement of people. The allies of the US paid for their share of the cost of this security, largely by allegiance and support for the Bretton Woods Institutions and NATO. The bulk of the funding, however, came from the US. These allies have developed their own aid priorities and funding systems, especially the ex-colonial powers, but aid policy overall has been directed from Washington: 'He who pays the piper calls the tune.' By and large, the system worked quite well and was the foundation of the Long Peace, during which trade and commerce flourished, and economic growth was phenomenal, with almost everyone on the planet benefitting.

Towards the end of the second decade of the 21st century, things looked as though they are about to change and possibly go into reverse. President Trump indicated that he was not happy with global policing responsibility. In 2019, he was on record as saying he sees no reason why the US should spill blood and treasure keeping the peace in foreign countries. To some extent, Trump's attitude to intervention is understandable. The wars in the Middle East, for example, seemed to have no end and have cost the US a great deal. In some ways, it is not so much *what* he did but *how* he did it that has caused alarm. He announced plans to withdraw US troops from Afghanistan before settling any effective peace agreement there; in October 2019, he summarily pulled US forces out of Syria; and in June 2020, he suggested the US was going to withdraw nearly half the troops it has based in Germany. The message to all is clear: 'You can do what you like, where and when you like, as long as you do not cause us any direct problems.'[93]

Even before these developments, it was becoming obvious to all that the US was not going to interfere in regional disputes any longer or take any serious action as and where human rights were being abused. In the western region of China,

---

93. President Joe Biden has reversed Trump's position on climate change and the UN as part of his policy of re-establishing the position of the US as the world's most important superpower. However, at time of writing, he has not reversed the Trumpian policy on Afghanistan and all US active forces have been scheduled to leave the country by September 2021, if not before. This decision was questioned by some of the allies of the US, as they considered that the exit was too swift and done at a time when the Afghan army was unprepared. Nevertheless, none of these allies was prepared to take over and do the heavy lifting. Biden's decision on Afghanistan should not be seen as general withdrawal from global policing so much as a recognition that Afghanistan is a special case and one that has been at odds with Western thinking for decades, if not centuries.

Muslims are being badly mistreated by the authorities, and although Washington condemns the practice, it takes little concrete action. In South Asia, India has torn up a long-standing agreement with Pakistan over the governance of Kashmir. Again, Washington has said nothing, even though it has been a long-time supporter of Pakistan. Similarly, it has allowed a dreadful war to rage in Yemen. Europe, sadly, as so often, looked on with tears in its eyes but did very little to counter Trump.

One possible benefit from the new US attitude to global policing might be a reduction in the share of US aid that goes towards military support. However, it will probably not mean a drop in overall military spending – far from it. With the spectre of China building up all sections of its military capability, I do not see the US and its Western allies reducing overall military expenditure. It is too early to know whether any of the savings on military aid will be used for other forms of aid. There are some signs that they might be used to augment some traditional soft-power-type aid investments in infrastructure.

Other forms of traditional aid, such as budget support to poor countries, will almost certainly be scaled back. It is now generally accepted that Gunnar Myrdal was wrong in that inflows of capital are not the key solution to underdevelopment, unless the right supporting institutions are in place. Simply providing emerging-nation governments with funds often does more harm than good. The recognition of this fact has led to a virtual cessation of budget support for developing countries, throwing on to them the responsibility of raising taxes to pay for essential services.

Furthermore, most economists now agree that, although economic growth is the key to poverty alleviation, governments are not very good at stimulating this growth. In fact, most economists consider that the private sector is far better at this than the public sector. From a review of Western-country aid policies discussed earlier, three key themes emerge:

1. There is a growing focus on the private sector.
2. In future, Western economic aid will be directed predominantly towards countries making progress with establishing liberal democratic governments, linked to the development of the associated essential institutions of a modern state.
3. There will be a gradual phasing out of government-to-government aid, except in certain strategic circumstances. There is also a growing realisation that change will take time.

These themes are echoed in the report of the Commission on State Fragility, Growth and Development (2018). Chaired by David Cameron, the former UK prime minister, the report begins with the somewhat frightening statistic that it is estimated half the world's poor (some 1 billion people) will live in fragile states by 2030. The report states that much of what has been done in the name of aid by the rich world has failed in the past and has arguably made things worse. It goes on to say that these fragile states potentially pose a threat to the rest of the world, and if only for reasons of international security, new approaches are needed to help these countries alleviate poverty. Above all, aid agencies must start to work with governments rather than around them. This is a tactful way of saying that these agencies should no longer come along with the promises of money on the condition that a government follows the advice of the agency. Instead, the agencies need to listen to and work closely with the governments.

This commission makes 12 realistic recommendations:

1. Put less emphasis on OECD models of governance, based on political parties and elections. Instead, the commission calls for a gradual process of state development, involving the introduction of effective checks and balances on power, developing the rule of law, the protection of minorities, and power sharing.
2. Put a greater emphasis on international and regional security, and have less dependence on temporary measures reliant on UN peacekeepers. (This would seem to reflect the views of Paul Collier [2008A], see *Chapter 1*).
3. Identify and use pivotal moments when transformative change is possible (e.g. Ethiopia following the elections that brought Abiy Ahmed to power).
4. Establish limited but purposeful long-term goals.
5. Build legitimacy and confidence through small steps.
6. Focus on economic governance (this echoes the aims of the MCC).
7. Support private sector job creation.
8. The IMF and World Bank need to develop new strategies for fragile states.
9. International financial institutions need to build resistance to economic shocks, develop more effective use of humanitarian assistance, and provide support for domestically generated government initiatives.
10. Build institutions, legal capacity, taxation systems, public administration and management.
11. Invest in urban infrastructure (roads, sanitation, water and electricity supply).
12. Develop domestic means of building resistance to economic shocks.

It is difficult to argue against these recommendations. As is so often the case in development, few dispute the analyses of the problems or well-intentioned recommendations. It is how to turn them into practical action that is the problem, and sadly, this is where the commission's report (like so many others) is weakest. Its main premise is that it is ultimately up to national governments to do the right thing for their citizens, hopefully with coordinated support from the international community.

I was surprised to see no reference to education and health in the report. Perhaps it is assumed that these services are already adequately supported, both nationally and internationally. I suspect that these might have been deliberately left out to avoid provoking a negative reaction from Muslim states, where Western education is not popular. What the commission's report does – and in fact, this may be its main objective – is to underline current thinking. Namely, it is not only the rich world that has the responsibility for poverty reduction, but poor and fragile states must also step up to the plate and do what they can.

As part of overall support for the private sector, I would not be surprised to see a small increase in aid used for CCTs (see 5.7.) to encourage people to participate in disease-eradication programmes or climate change measures. There will also continue to be support for humanitarian aid, especially in response to natural disasters, but also in areas of conflict. In 2020, the UK had a programme of supporting the destitute in war-torn South Sudan, and the WFP had a massive programme of supplying food to hungry people in Yemen. This kind of aid will continue and will possibly be increased.

More controversial perhaps, but very much within the overall security umbrella, is that there will almost certainly be an increase in aid funding used to address extremist terrorist movements, such as those causing havoc in the Sahel region of West Africa. Most of the jihadists in Africa are fighting their own (often incompetent) governments, but they attack Western targets too. There will also be a continuing need for UN Blue Berets in the DRC and possibly in northern Mozambique. It is the view of security experts that, if the West cannot control the extremists in Africa, they will end up having to fight them on the streets of Europe. This is because, once they have established a stronghold in Africa, they will use this as a springboard to promote their idealism elsewhere. Thus, when the Islamic State (IS or Isis) caliphate was pushed out of Syria and Iraq, it moved its operations to Africa.

The current (at time of writing) UN emergency relief coordinator and the president of the International Committee of the Red Cross both say that the Sahel region is their biggest worry, as the violence there is spreading rapidly and tearing poor communities apart. The task is proving very difficult for the Western military, not least because of a lack of real support from the governments of the region. Some protesters, presumably with government support and notably in Mali and Niger, have asked France to withdraw its forces, claiming that the Western military is threatening recolonisation. Western nations are reluctant to put more soldiers on the ground unless they can be sure of support from national governments, but unless the security strategists change their minds and decide to allow anarchy to flourish, there is really no alternative to an increase in military support if the extremists are to be contained.

The Bretton Woods Institutions

Another almost certain change – possibly the most important, I suspect – will be the slow demise of some of the Bretton Woods and UN systems set up after the Second World War. These were very effective during the Cold War but have begun to show signs of approaching their sell-by dates. However, even ramping down is very difficult, as far as the Bretton Woods agencies are concerned. For example, according to its charter, the IMF is to be headquartered in the country with the largest economy. While this has been the US since the end of the Second World War, no one seems to have figured out what to do if China becomes the biggest global economy. Either the IMF will have to move from Washington, DC, to Beijing or the charter will have to be changed. Whatever happens, it will mean less influence for the US in global monetary affairs. As of 2020, leading China-watchers do not see the Chinese economy overtaking that of the US much before 2030 at the earliest, if at all, but it is still a possibility.

The World Bank does not have this charter problem, but it has major problems of its own. In particular, it is running out of large, important clients. No longer can it influence things in Brasilia, Beijing, Delhi, Jakarta or Lagos simply with a big cheque. These countries can get finance from the private sector or from China. This leaves the World Bank with lots of little poor countries that take most of their credit from the IDA, the soft and unprofitable window of the World Bank. As discussed earlier, numerous well-known economists have suggested that the World Bank may have reached (or is close to) its sell-by date. There have been a number of reviews of the World Bank, most notably by the Meltzer Commission at the end of the last century, and more recently, the report of Senator Richard Lugar in 2010. None of the reviews have led to major reforms; indeed, the recommendations have largely been ignored by the World Bank because, as Lugar points out, the World Bank is an international bureaucracy answerable to no single government – even the largest one of all, the US.

In essence, the World Bank and the other development banks are independent little kingdoms, which are very difficult for their owners to reform, let alone close down. There are several reasons for this inertia. Firstly, as Lugar has stated, is the ownership structure and the associated complexity of getting all member countries to agree on reform or closure. Secondly, closure of the World Bank is not a priority as far as US political issues are concerned. Thirdly, although some question its efficacy as an aid agency, it does not cost the taxpayer in the West very much; as apart from modest contributions to the IDA, it makes a small surplus on its lending. Fourthly, it has been a convenient and helpful friend of the CIA at times.

Finally, and perhaps most importantly, its closure would require some means of recalling the outstanding loans (some of which are for 50 years) or forgiving them. Both are approaches that would cost the owners of the World Bank – and, indeed, the other development banks if they followed the same path – a large amount of money. Instead, it seems the policy is to let the organisations wither on the vine by focusing increasingly on small loans to small countries by the IDA. Call it the 'Hotel California', solution if you like.

Clear evidence of the slow erosion of the relevance and importance of the World Bank came on 7 January 2019, when the then president, Jim Yong Kim, announced he was leaving three years before the end of his contract. No reasons for his departure were given, other than that he had found employment in the private financial sector.[94] This is a post that has attracted some big names in the past, such as Robert McNamara, Jim Wolfensohn and Paul Wolfowitz. All were men who relished the power, influence and profile the job provided, and who were able to effect changes in the organisation's way of doing business. Although Kim gave no reasons for his departure, World Bank-watchers say he had achieved his main tasks – namely an increase in the World Bank's paid-in capital, together with a difficult reorganisation that was loathed by staff. It is also suggested that he was at odds with Donald Trump's decision to pull the US out of the Paris Accord on climate change, and his support of China's BRI was not popular in the US Treasury Department. My guess is that Kim had realised the organisation is no longer very important, further significant reform is impossible, he can do more for climate change in the private sector, and he wanted to leave before he was accredited with the agency's demise.

The choice of his successor was in the pocket of Donald Trump, and in April 2019, David Malpass was confirmed as the new president of the World Bank (*The Economist*, 2019A). His appointment was not widely welcomed by many of the World Bank's 185 member countries. At the time of his appointment, he was a Republican who supported Trump's bid to become president, and was the US Treasury Department's undersecretary for international affairs. He is known as a critic of international agencies such as the World Bank and the IMF, which he considers have tied the US's hands. There is no doubt that he will try to bring about further reforms (including more transparency and the better evaluation of lending operations) to improve the operations of the World Bank. He will almost certainly reduce or phase out lending to China, which he believes no longer needs World Bank support. He considers that the World Bank has implicitly supported China's BRI, which he sees as being driven as much by politics (chequebook diplomacy) as economics. He will also focus the World Bank's lending on poorer countries and

---

94. Global Infrastructure Partners.

the private sector, and overall, he will reduce the influence of the World Bank on global public goods, such as climate change.

Although Malpass is an economist, he graduated in physics first. This suggests his economics is quantitative, rather than qualitative or socio-economic, and he will almost certainly have a hard job managing the institution. The World Bank is definitely not staffed with leftists, but most of the staff are smart and have a well-developed social conscience; they will not roll over without a fight. His appointment will, if nothing else, mark the beginning of the end of the World Bank as we have known it. I say this as the World Bank is essentially a US institution, and if the US has lost interest, other countries will soon follow.

Of course, it is possible that concerns about China's possible dominance in the provision of loans for infrastructure in the developing world could breathe new life into the World Bank and regional development banks. There is definitely a need for investment in infrastructure. However, there is a bit of a catch here. Such investments only really make sense if they contribute to economic growth rates over and above the population growth rates. In many of the countries that might take such loans, the prospects for such economic growth rates do not look too rosy. In stark contrast, those countries with good growth prospects can almost certainly raise funds on the markets or by issuing bonds, and they do not need traditional development bank concessional loans that invariably involve masses of bureaucracy and policy promises. Ultimately, much will depend on China and whether it will continue to lend on the same scale in the next 10 years as in the past 20 years, since the turn of the century.

The ex-foreign minister of Portugal, Bruno Maçães, who has extensive knowledge of China, writes in his book *Belt and Road: A Chinese World Order* (Maçães, 2018) that the BRI is more about politics than money or economics, and China may well continue to finance the initiative, even in loss-making situations. That said, by 2020 (since he wrote the book), there have been some signs that China will scale back its lending for such infrastructure. This is partly because it does not want to end up owning (albeit on a long lease) lots of railways, toll roads and bridges that lose money, and partly because there is limited evidence that the BRI is convincing participating nations to endorse China's global hegemony. China will probably be less worried about owning loss-making ports around the world for strategic reasons. If – as seems quite likely – Chinese lending for infrastructure in the developing world decreases over the next decade, I suspect funding from the World Bank and regional banks will also slow rather than increasing, given the need for such loans (even concessional ones) to generate incremental tax revenue to service the loan.

The United Nations (UN)

The UN also faces pressure to reform. Quite a bit of the UN system is approaching or has reached its sell-by date. Strong evidence for this came home to me in mid-2018, during a conversation with an old university friend who also spent his life working for development agencies. He had recently spoken to a well-known BBC world affairs editor while on holiday in St Petersburg. The famous editor was not sure of the name of the current Secretary-General of the UN (ex-Portuguese prime minister, António Guterres), who was appointed in 2016. As my friend remarked to me, for a man of his standing in foreign affairs not to be aware of the name of the head of the UN suggests that the organisation has lost much of its influence and relevance, at least as far as the West is concerned. Previous heads of the UN, such as Dag Hammarskjöld, Javier Pérez de Cuéllar and Kofi Annan, were household names in many Western countries.

Further evidence of the declining importance of the UN comes from the replacement of Nikki Haley, the competent US ambassador to the UN, with a woman with no relevant experience. This showed that the Trump administration did not consider the UN to be important. In her speech to the UN General Assembly in September 2017, Theresa May, the then UK prime minister, threatened to withhold 30% of UK contributions of £90 million to the UN, unless there were significant efficiency reforms. She did not name it, but she singled out at least one of the UN specialist agencies that the UK was reluctant to finance.

In a recent book, Wickstead (2015) writes that there is a global discussion about the focus of the UN and its associated agencies. These were institutions that were developed in the interests of, and were largely paid for by, the Western powers. Since the start of the 21st century, other countries and cultures now feel it is time that their values and morals should be better catered for by the UN. This can be disputed from an academic perspective, as it hardly makes sense to replace or water down the egalitarian liberal spirit of these Western ideals with those of more traditional cultures and autocratic regimes. However, one cannot deny that there is a big, growing gulf between the governing aspirations and methods of the Western democracies and many of the more powerful emerging nations. In fact, this gulf in aspiration is, in many ways, turning the UN inside out.

There was an unwritten code under which support by newly independent emerging nations for Western interests in the UN would result in aid and other forms of support.[95] By the end of the second decade of the 21st century, it was the non-Western nations – notably China and Russia – that were using the emerging

95. The best example of this I know is the UN vote to establish the State of Israel in 1948 by a majority of votes. I rather doubt that such a majority would be achieved in a UN vote in the third decade of the 21st century.

countries to vote for their own interests in the UN arenas. If nothing else, this change of sponsor has contributed to a loss of Western influence in both the Bretton Woods and UN systems, and it looks as though this decline will continue. An acid test for the UN is how the WHO reforms following the Covid-19 pandemic of 2020–21 (and still ongoing at time of writing). If the agency can demonstrate genuine independence from any single country or group of countries, it may grow in strength and value to the world. If not, I suspect it will start to lose influence.

Concern about the declining importance of Western values has been growing since the end of the Cold War in 1989. In a classic book on global civilisations (Huntingdon, 1996), there is a prediction that Confucian and Islamic societies would attempt to expand their economic and military power to balance that of the West. This is a prediction that has come true to a considerable extent – at least as far as the UN is concerned and with respect to China. The effects of this will be with us for many years to come and will almost certainly have a major influence on Western aid policy.

As any realistic analysis sadly shows, it is also the case that the UN is increasingly ineffectual in conflict resolution. In the early days, the Blue Berets (the UN's peacekeeping force) were able to help resolve quite a number of conflicts – perhaps most famously, the cessation of civil war in what was the Congo in the 1960s. With hindsight, it is quite likely that the presence of Blue Helmets on the ground in the Congo hinted at more powerful support from Western powers waiting in the wings. Today, the Western powers no longer seem to have much confidence in the UN peacekeeping initiatives, and they are no longer the iron fist in a velvet glove. In 2018, a brave attempt by the UN to resolve a dreadful civil war in the Yemen failed, largely because the Islamic powers sponsoring the war felt they could ignore the wishes of the West with impunity.

That said, the UN's Blue Berets would still seem to have a role to play in containing localised conflicts, rather than civil wars, in badly run countries. In many ways, the failure of António Guterres to have any influence on things in Libya in April 2019 once again underlines the impotence of the UN to resolve such crises. The West pays lip service to the UN and its initiatives, but is not prepared to put steel into its gloves of friendship. To a considerable extent, this reflects the failure of Western and UN-backed initiatives to resolve political crises since the end of the Cold War, notably but not exclusively in the Arabic-speaking world, and the UN having an undeclared policy of no direct involvement in insurrection and civil wars. Yemen, at the start of the third decade of the 21st century, is perhaps the clearest case of such standing back.

Of perhaps greater significance than the failure to send in the Blue Berets to help sort things out in the Yemen is the possibility that it was a strategic decision of the West not to send them and to try not to get too involved at all. Huntingdon's (1996) argument is that confrontation with Islamic states almost always backfires because, with the exception of Saddam Hussein's attempt to take over Kuwait, Islamic nations traditionally rally round against aggression by non-Islamic states towards fellow Islamic states. In other words, hot lead ends up in failure and prolongs the tension between the Islamic world and the West. Once again, jaw-jaw would seem cheaper and more effective than war-war, and there are signs (such as the nuclear agreement with Iran), that Huntingdon's advice was being followed. That was until Donald Trump became president of the US.

It is also possible that, in the case of the Yemen, the Western policy of watching from the side-lines is deliberate. In many ways, this is not a civil war but a war between the Sunni and Shia Islamic ideologies. If both parties are weakened by the fight, as seemed likely in 2020, the big winner will be the West, which can discount direct aggression from the protagonists, at least until they rebuild their armouries.

Huntingdon (1996) does not speculate about this splintering in the Islamic world, which may end up being one of the most important political developments in the early 21st century. At the time of writing, it is too early to say whether the Shias or the Sunnis will come out on top. In the past, most observers would probably have put money on Iran and its Shia adherents due to them being more technically sophisticated. At the time of the war in the Yemen, however, there was a major additional factor – namely Israel and its growing relations with Saudi Arabia and the wealthy Gulf states. In this regard, it is notable that, in August 2020, Israel and the UAE recognised each other as sovereign states. Israel has a monopoly on nuclear power in the Middle East, and whichever side it is on has a big advantage. Furthermore, Trump's order to kill the Iranian general Soleimani on 3 January 2020 and the subsequent shooting down by the Iranian authorities of a Ukrainian passenger aircraft leaving Tehran has weakened Iran immeasurably and has strengthened the Sunni camp.

Aside from the strategic considerations related to the Blue Berets, another reason for the decline of the UN is that the Western powers are increasingly inclined to reduce their financial commitments to the UN and its agencies. This is usually in response to disapproval of agency policies or hanky-panky with staffing. In the case of most agencies, the result of cutbacks is a reduction in staff, fewer aid projects and less influence – or at least less influence in the interest of the Western powers. I cannot speak about all the UN agencies, but I am fairly sure from conversations with staff that other agencies had similar problems to those of the FAO.

Around the time I joined the FAO in the mid-1980s, the organisation was in a financial mess. The US was withholding its assessments (national membership dues). The US did not like some of the then DG's policies, and the agency had to borrow from an Italian bank to meet day-to-day costs and salaries for several months. I think collateral for the loan was provided by Saudi Arabia, which, in turn, secured the Cairo-based post of assistant DG for the Middle East. The US did not like the fact that the DG had managed to persuade a majority of the member nations to change the organisation's constitution to extend the term of office of the DG from four to six years. More recently, in 2018, the US and Germany were withholding their assessment payments to the FAO as they did not like some of the policies of the then Brazilian DG. They were unhappy about some of the jobs he had promised to his political friends from Latin America (see *Chapter 2*) and his attempts to secure a third term in office for himself. Politics, as ever, was never far from the scene.

It may be relevant to say that, in the mid-1980s, the USSR was not a member of the FAO, and China was a very small bit player. In other words, the FAO was to all intents and purposes controlled financially by the West, and the DG-related stories are a classic example of the politics of the Cold War, if nothing else. One can hardly blame the emerging powers in Asia and elsewhere for playing similar games now that they can afford to, even if it means Wickstead's (2015) democratic deficit is actually more like a democratic death.

Things are likely to get worse rather than better for the UN, as things stand. Donald Trump is reported (*The Economist*, 2018B) to have talked about withdrawing from the UN altogether, and in May 2020 he pulled the US out of the WHO on the grounds that the agency was taking orders from Beijing. To some extent, the richer developing countries (notably China) picked up the baton, but their price is more influence in how the UN operates and more posts filled by Chinese nationals (CCP members?). President Biden has reversed some of Trump's thinking and actions on the UN and its agencies, as he understands the importance of alliances. However, this moral support also needs the harder support of increased funding if the US is to regain some of its influence over the UN.

The point is that, whatever happens to the Bretton Woods and UN in the future, these institutions will almost certainly have a decreasing role to play in providing traditional development aid. If any firm evidence of this is needed, it is instructive to consider the almost overnight demise of the FAO's Technical Cooperation Department (TCD) in 1990. Up until then, this department had supervised hundreds of technical projects in many developing countries in cooperation with the UNDP, almost all of which was funded by Western aid budgets. After the Berlin Wall fell in 1989 and the Cold War was declared over, the TCD was phased out, and some 400 posts in FAO headquarters were closed.

I do not expect the whole UN to shut up shop. Some UN agencies – such as the WHO, WMO, ICAO, IAEA, UPU, ITU, WIPO and IMO, which cover things of concern to all countries[96]– will survive. That said, the WHO's response to HIV/AIDS was so poor that the UN had to set up a specialist agency, UNAIDS. A little later, it failed to direct and coordinate efforts to contain the Ebola crisis in West Africa in 2014, and it could have handled SARs in 2003 and Covid-19 in 2020 better. Some observers say the agency does not really know what it is for, as its mandate 'to ensure the highest possible level of health for everyone' is too broad and vague. Some medical experts want it abolished, but most call for reform through a focus on advocacy for public health issues, being a forum for research and negotiation, and operating as a director of health interventions. I suspect it will survive and reform slowly.

I see no real reason to keep UNIDO and the United Nations Conference on Trade and Development (UNCTAD) on life support, but they will probably not be axed; instead, they will be allowed to wither slowly on the vine as fewer competent staff are willing to work for them. I also see no real future for UNESCO. China and Russia might decide to keep it on life support if they can see a use for it in promoting their interests. If not, it will almost certainly fade away.

The FAO is also not in good shape. The new DG can count on Chinese support, however, and I expect an increased focus on African agriculture as payback for the votes that saw him elected. As far as the rest of the world is concerned, I expect it will continue its normative global functions such as collating statistics, providing venues for conferences and special meetings, providing programmes on issues of concern (e.g. bird flu, drought, famine and locust control), and playing a role in disease control. It will gradually be reduced in size and, I suspect, will surrender its own in-country offices to take space in UN country offices once again.

There have been numerous attempts at a reform of the UN and, in particular, its role in aid, starting as long ago as 1969 (Jackson, 1969). More recently, in 2006, the United Nations Development Group was set up to maximise synergies and minimise overlaps between agencies. But the agencies are effectively little empires, each of which guards its territory jealously, and there has been little real reform. As far as the UN General Assembly is concerned, a Western country could unilaterally pull out, but the political damage incurred globally would be immense. It would provide non-Western states with perfect ammunition for campaigns to discredit the West, and have things such as reparations for slavery or for the industrial revolution being the instigator of climate change put on the UN agenda.

While I suspect the gradual decline of the UN system will continue in the coming years, there is a faint possibility that the West will wake up in time to the enormous threat of a takeover of the UN by the richer middle-income countries,

---

96. The World Trade Organisation – previously the General Agreement on Trade and Tariffs (GATT) – is not a UN agency, although it has links through the ECOSOC of the UN.

notably China. I say 'enormous' as there is no alternative global talk shop, either at the apex level of the UN General Assembly or for technical matters such as health or telecommunications. If the West loses all influence in the UN, by definition, it is handing that influence on a plate to the newcomers. In theory, the West could withdraw from the current UN systems and allow it to collapse and then start all over again. In practice, this is most unlikely to happen.

The original idea for the UN goes back nearly 100 years to the League of Nations and the end of the First World War. Sadly, in the absence of the US, the League of Nations was a failure. It took the Second World War and US involvement to establish the UN. It is difficult to see how a new UN system could be created without the support of all the major world economies, and if many did withdraw from the existing UN, it is difficult to see how those that did remain would want to support a new initiative. The UN grew out of the fertile ashes of the two world wars of the 20th century and from the unique power of the US after the wars. There is no such situation in 2021.

So, ironically, the only real hope for UN reform has to come from inside. Instead of weakening agencies by withholding funds, the West should increase its financial participation in the UN and also – and perhaps more significantly – ensure a much higher representation of senior Western expertise within the system. This will take time, but it could start by placing very competent young diplomats as ambassadors to the agencies, rather than folk about to go on pension. These guys would follow things carefully and provide early warnings of nonsenses to help nip them in the bud; things such as the constitution changes effected by Saouma and his messing with the WFP. It will take time and cost money, but I see no real alternative, and given we are almost certainly entering a period of global instability not unlike the Cold War, a resurrection of Western support for the UN might pay handsome dividends.

Aid Policy and Change

In addition to being more careful about who gets aid, there is no doubt that a number of donor countries are reviewing their policies on aid more broadly. Penny Mordaunt, the then UK Secretary of State for International Development, advised the Cabinet of the need for major changes to the UK's aid policy. In particular, she challenged the need to spend 0.7% of GNI, equal to some £14 billion annually, on aid. She recommended that much of this money should be used to pay for the services of other UK ministries, notably the armed forces, in a move to align UK aid with national security concerns. She is also on record as calling for a rethink on UK funding of some UN agencies (e.g. UNESCO) and would like the private sector to play a larger role in providing aid.

In March 2019, it was reported that a former Secretary of State for International Development, Priti Patel, was advocating that the UK make the use of its aid funds more relevant and in the national interest. She called for a regearing of support for big international NGOs. This followed scandals associated with staff serving for Oxfam and Save the Children. While these policies are at an early stage of development, there can be no doubt that they reflect a growing awareness that much traditional aid has failed to achieve its objectives. Perhaps the UK is just coming into line with some other rich countries that spend some of their aid funds internally, rather than externally. Italy, for example, spends a considerable amount of money renovating and modernising the headquarters building of the FAO, which is based in Rome.

Given that aid flows are massively dwarfed by remittances and private sector financial flows, and that much traditional aid has not been effective, it could be argued that there is now little need for ODA. To do away with all aid would be very risky, I think. If the rich world were to completely abandon its aid structures and operational procedures, it would have no mechanism to deal with emergencies such as avian influenza, Ebola or Covid-19. The outbreak and containment of Ebola in West Africa in 2016 is a good example of rich countries helping poor countries to overcome a serious problem for both local and international benefit. Luckily, with the exception of a few medical workers who were infected, it was possible to contain the outbreak in Liberia and Sierra Leone.

It seems clear from this that (1) there will still be a need for aid in the coming years in a number of the poorest countries, and (2) just as in its first 70 years, the main motive for rich countries to give aid to poor countries will be politics. The politics will continue to be a mixture of strategic realpolitik and domestic charitable pressures. There is no doubt that many people in rich countries do want to help poorer people elsewhere. However, the goalposts have moved in so far as the focus will no longer be on containing Marxist ideology, but it will be on encouraging the adoption of liberal democracy and governance, containing terrorist threats, responses to emergencies (natural disasters and disease control), climate change, illegal migration, and competing with China.

Epilogue

Most of this book was written before the disease known as Covid-19, caused by the SARS-CoV-2 virus, became the defining influence on all our lives; I have little doubt that the long-term effects of this global pandemic will challenge some, if not all, of my predictions for the future of aid.

One or two things do seem inevitable, however. The most obvious is a reduction in donor funding as a result of the increased debt incurred by almost all countries as a result of the measures taken to control the disease and keep economies going. Furthermore, the priority for the available aid money will be to help poorer countries address the immediate problems associated with the disease (provision of vaccines), rather than more traditional aid projects and programmes. To try to provide a handy summary of what I have written in the earlier chapters, I pose five questions and give my thoughts on each answer.

What Has Aid Achieved Since It Began in Earnest After the Second World War?

The sad answer is not as much as was hoped – certainly as far as economic and social development is concerned. A quick trip around the globe helps to confirm this assessment. It is true that China has been transformed in the last 60 years from one of the poorest countries to a middle-income country. Aid played a role in this transformation, but only a small role, and mainly through a national learning experience and lines of credit. This aid enabled the Chinese to adapt, adopt, develop and follow the paths of economic development worked out in the West. This included things such as education, industrialisation, infrastructure creation, investment, marketing and support for entrepreneurs, especially credit. Significantly, this was achieved by building on an institutional heritage. The Chinese economic miracle had much more to do with the decisions taken by Chinese leaders and the hard work of the Chinese people than aid. It is much the same – although not on such a scale and in different ways – in other successful countries such as Taiwan, Singapore, South Korea and Malaysia.

As is so often the case, India is the odd man out in Asia. It is a liberal democracy with the essential institutions of a modern state, a huge low-cost labour force, and plenty of technical, commercial and financial skills, but its economic growth has massively underperformed compared to China and much of East Asia. Closer examination of the nation suggests that there is a huge difference between its states regarding their economic health and prospects. Many of the southern states and the large cities in central India have done much better than the states of the fertile Indo-Gangetic region. It is difficult not to reflect on whether culture is partly responsible for these economic differences, between India and China. It is not as if India has been starved of aid – during and after the Cold War, India was in receipt of massive amounts of Western aid, although much less than much of Africa on a per capita basis.

It is also notable that a handful of Asian countries have made hardly any progress in terms of poverty reduction, despite large amounts of aid. The most obvious examples are Cambodia, Pakistan, Nepal and the Pacific Island states. I would include Laos, Myanmar and Timor-Leste in this group, although they have received less Western aid. To some greater or lesser extent, these countries have strong traditional cultures but relatively little in the way of the effective national institutions needed for modern economic growth and development.

Between the most and least successful Asian countries is a group of what can be seen as struggling middle-income countries: Bangladesh, Indonesia, the Philippines, Thailand, Sri Lanka and Vietnam. Typically, these countries have weak democracies, poor institutions, a tendency towards massive corruption at all levels of government and, often, a predominant religious faith. They have benefitted from considerable amounts of aid, but this has not helped them address their weaknesses. They have been unable to develop balanced economies and remain heavily dependent on natural resources such as oil or palm oil (Indonesia), niche industries such as tourism (Sri Lanka and Thailand), back-office services (the Philippines), garment-making or remittances.

Moving westwards from Asia to the Middle East, things are pretty dire. Most of the countries with hydrocarbon resources have lots of money, but with few exceptions, it is in the hands of the elites, and most of the people are still very poor. Iran, for example, has the basic resources needed for economic growth, but folk there have not seen their standards of living rise for many years, partly because much national wealth has been and is being spent on ideological wars in the region. People are even poorer in many of the other the countries of the region – such as Yemen, Libya, Iraq and Syria – which have been plagued by war and insurrection. Egypt has avoided insurrection, but its economy has failed to develop, despite massive handouts from Saudi Arabia and a large IMF loan (US$12 billion in 2016). Jordan and Tunisia have also taken IMF loans, but the number of their citizens living below the poverty line has increased, as has unemployment.

Africa – with the exceptions of Mauritius, the Seychelles, São Tomé and Cabo Verde – is a shameful economic disaster. Shameful because it has received masses of aid and most countries have resources to exploit (if only cheap labour), but over three-quarters of the countries of the continent have poorer average per capita incomes at the end of the second decade of the 21st century than they had as colonies. One would have to be very optimistic to believe that traditional aid is suddenly going to help many of the countries in the Middle East and Africa to escape poverty.

Further west across the Atlantic, the Americas is yet another story. With the notable exception of Costa Rica, Central America is little more than a disaster. South America is a mixed bag, but overall, it has not done as well as it should. It has taken some steps towards liberal democracy and has the foundations for the necessary institutions, but growth has generally been halting. By late 2019, it looked as though dictators – albeit civilian rather than military – were making a comeback.

Central Europe and Central Asia have also largely stagnated. It should perhaps be said that North America and much of Western Europe have also had low growth rates (2% per annum) since the turn of the century. However, this is in line with economic expectation in so-called 'mature economies' that do not have untrained, low-cost, young labour forces; infrastructure to create; or new technologies to adopt and exploit.

Why Has It Taken So Long for the Failures of Much Aid To Be Recognised?

The simple explanation is deliberate deception. There has been deception by the aid agencies, by some of the staff of the agencies and, above all, by the politicians committing taxpayers' money to aid agencies. Having convinced their voters that aid money was being used productively, few Western politicians welcomed too much critical appraisal. Andrew Mitchell, a British politician who was once Secretary of State for International Development (2010–12), is on record as saying that aid has achieved much. Conveniently for him, he spoke in generalities and, as far as I recall, has never provided any specific quantified evaluations. I suspect what he really meant is that aid money was well spent in so far as it helped win the Cold War, but he dared not say that for fear of admitting that the whole thing was political and a bit of a fraud. For those companies involved in executing aid projects, it was relatively easy money. In the 1980s, there were more than a dozen UK-based consultancy companies providing agricultural and related engineering expertise in developing countries. By 2020, most had closed or refocused their business models.

Those of us at the coal face might have queried some of the things we were asked to do, but only fools bite the hand that feeds them. The story about Kelly (see 3.8.)

is a good case study, and I am reminded of a chat that occurred one evening in the late 1980s with a fellow traveller at the British Aid Guest House Association[97] in Dhaka, Bangladesh. I was complaining about an investment project that I was involved in preparing, which seemed to me to have very dodgy economics. My fellow traveller, a project economist, explained that it was the easiest thing in the world to juggle the figures and make an investment project come up smelling of roses, however out of line the costs and benefits really were. What he was saying was little more than confirming that the job of the mission economist was to produce a positive outcome.

He also meant that we in development were all involved in a great game of deception one way or another, and that if we did not like it, we should find another job. And this is where the aid industry has created its own problem. A small army of quite well-paid, articulate people is employed in the industry, and understandably, their priority is to retain their jobs and promotion prospects. It is not in their interests to shine too bright a light on some of the nonsenses that they know go on.

Why Did So Much Aid Fail To Generate the Hoped-For Economic Growth?

There are three basic answers to this question. The first is that aid and development were new areas of government practice after the Second World War, and there was little practical experience to build on. True, the Marshall Plan helped to rebuild Europe, but we now know that rebuilding an economy is very different from starting one from scratch. What is more, the views of those few prescient economists who predicted failure early on were not popular with the politicians trying to get out of empire cheaply or others faced with the task of overcoming communism.

The second answer is that it is not entirely fair to blame aid – or more specifically, poorly designed and administered aid – for the poor economic performance of many countries. For sure, some aid was stolen en route between the donor and ultimate recipient, but quite a lot was totally inappropriate (see 3.17.) and was effectively forced on borrowing countries.

Thirdly, the main reason why aid appears to have failed in so many countries is national politics. It is clear from the brief exploratory trip around the globe in this book that economic growth is firmly correlated with the success of the governance of a country, which, in turn, is often linked to a culture that either respects or ignores authority. Discipline and the rule of law are fundamental ingredients in the bake of economic development.

---

97. One of the few places in the country where one could buy a beer in the 1980s.

In China, the rule of law may be a fiction in the eyes of Westerners, but the authority of the CCP is widely respected. Just think about how a country of more than 1 billion people effectively self-isolated during the Covid-19 outbreak in early 2020 when instructed to do so by the powers that be. At the other extreme are countries such as the DRC and much of Central America, where governments have no authority and it is effectively a Wild West, with every man and woman fending for himself or herself. No useful or sustained investment on any scale, even the exploitation of natural resources, is economic in such circumstances.

How Important Is Culture?

The role of culture in development has and probably always will be somewhat contentious, as linking culture with development runs the risk of suggesting some cultures are better than others. In the 1970s, Robert Solow, a Nobel Prize-winning economist, challenged the importance of culture, saying that those who tried to link economic growth to culture ended up in a blaze of amateur sociology. He had no doubt read the works of Margaret Mead (1930) and her fellow anthropologists who had challenged contemporary views of racial superiority.[98] It is also true that, at the time, discounting the importance of culture was helpful as it meant all countries, regardless of culture, were equally eligible for Western aid.

Some 60 years later, this thinking is changing, and it is now acceptable to compare the economic performance of different cultures. In no way do such comparisons have anything to do with race or intelligence. Various academics have demonstrated convincingly that the evidence-based humanistic approach to scientific enquiry during the Enlightenment in Europe led to a shift in behaviour that, in turn, enabled industrialisation and economic growth. According to the book *A Culture of Growth* (Mokyr, 2016, p.8), culture is 'a set of beliefs, values and preferences capable of affecting behaviour that are socially transmitted and are shared by some subset of society' – just think of how the British usually queue calmly and, bizarrely, whatever the circumstance. We are all, in one way or another, subject to the traditions and rituals of our cultures. It is just that the extant culture in many developing countries is usually one that encourages citizens to trust the opinions of traditional leaders or their peers, in preference to the politicians elected by a newly introduced system of voting. It is also the case that it is difficult for people who are used to the seasonal and irregular nature of small-scale agriculture to adapt to the rigours of regular factory work, and this has discouraged investment

---

98. Mead's field studies of primitive cultures, notably in Papua New Guinea, played a major role in successfully challenging the idea, which was prevalent in the first half of the 20th century, that some races are more intelligent than others. Among other things, her work resulted in a conflation of culture and intelligence in the minds of sociologists and others. The result of this conflation was that, for many years, it was taboo for Westerners to criticise other cultures, in case this was seen as suggesting members of these other cultures were less intelligent than aid-giving Westerners.

in manufacturing and the creation of income-earning jobs in many developing countries.

There is also clear evidence that culture or national characteristics, especially those that hold external powers (be they beliefs in the power of the natural world or gods) responsible for day-to-day events, tend to develop more slowly economically than those in which people hold reason, knowledge, themselves and their politicians responsible. The folk in these countries are generally much poorer (Pinker, 2018). An important but often underestimated feature of culture is an endemic resistance to change almost everywhere.

The US diplomat George Kennan (1947) is reported to have said 'Russian communism changed Bolshevism far less than it was changed by Bolshevism.' What he meant was that Lenin's ideas of strong leadership of the masses had to be done by one man.[99] Fast forward 100 years and nothing much has changed in a Russia that continues to need strong, central, almost king-like leadership. We cannot begin to understand the problems of development unless we address culture. For this reason, I devoted much of the previous chapter to a review and analysis of culture and its role in development. As if to confirm that I am not alone in my assessment of the importance of culture, I was intrigued by an article on the subject (*The Economist*, 2020C) that referred to, *inter alia*, 'the revival of cultural explanations for wealth and poverty seems to be a methodological step forward'.

A recent article by Mathew Syed (2021) refers to the importance of 'social trust' as being one of the most important keys to economic development. He provides a number of examples from different countries that show convincingly where the people trust each other, and for that matter the government, people tend to better off. In wealthy Norway more than 70 % of the population think you can trust other people. In contrast, in impoverished Columbia only 4% think people can be trusted. Clearly, social trust is closely related to a nation's culture, and this could provide a useful indicator of where the best results to aid might be achieved.

Given the Relative Failure of Much Aid to Date, Can Yet More Be Justified? If So, What Should the Priorities for Aid Be in the Future?

Some of the problems holding back development in a number of regions across the world, such as pollution in India and population growth in Africa, are so immense that aid will never be able to solve them completely. And if aid policy had not changed in recent years, I would be inclined to think that the honest answer to the first question should be no. But while Western aid alone cannot solve the big

99. Bolshevic was an early leading Russian communist who believed in the violent overthrow of capitalism. He was supported by Lenin.

problems, it can help devise solutions. As for the second question, Western aid policy has changed considerably in the early decades of the 21st century.

If and when the world recovers from Covid-19, I am sure aid will return to being an important feature of global politics for national and international reasons. As far as national reasons are concerned, there is commitment by people in richer countries to help those in poorer countries. Call it charity if you like, but just as the Western world abolished slavery in the 19th century, the reduction in global poverty, disease control and addressing the issues associated with climate change are causes that few in rich countries would vote against. It should be said that some of these interventions are also global public goods, and all mankind stands to benefit from the eradication of any disease or sustainable measures to reduce carbon dioxide emissions. Above all, post Covid-19, there will be an increase in the need for humanitarian aid in the short to medium term, if only to keep millions fed.

Aid is therefore likely to remain in the manifestos of the political parties in most of the richer democracies in the world. However, there is a bitter irony or moral hazard associated with humanitarian aid: the provision of such aid means that national politicians do not have to worry too much about providing basic welfare for the people they represent. In other words, there is a serious risk that humanitarian aid actually prolongs deprivation by allowing governments to ignore the needs of their own people. In future, I suspect some Western humanitarian aid will come with a clear sell-by date. This will be tough in the short run, but is sensible in the medium to long term as it will force governments and warring factions to improve their governance and resolve conflicts. We are already seeing this in the case of the insurrection in Yemen, which has resulted in a massive reduction in aid to the country.

As far as aid-recipient countries are concerned, probably the biggest single change is the phasing out of budget support for poor country treasuries. In early 2020, it became clear from IMF reports that almost all African countries fail to raise enough tax to meet the basic state-provided needs. In other words, for many years, rich-country aid money has essentially allowed poor country governments to get away with having virtually no effective national taxation systems. This moral hazard / magic money tree has now largely been felled, and this will undoubtedly increase hardship for many in the short run, but it will bring about essential changes in how developing governments govern.

A second big change is the redirection of aid money towards the private sector and for job creation rather than to governments, along the lines outlined by the UK with regard to India (see 2.19.). This is because it is now recognised that governments are not good at creating wealth, other than through essential infrastructure investment.

Thirdly, there will be a tendency for rich countries to use aid money to support their own interests and countries where they have geographical and historical ties. And fourthly, Western aid will almost certainly be increasingly focused on fewer countries, and more so on those that have shown they are able to use aid resources effectively; ideally, but not exclusively, countries with active or nascent liberal democratic systems of government.

I am fairly sure that loans for investment in essential infrastructure will also continue to account for much aid, and this is where the competition with China will be the most marked. Greater care by all lenders and borrowers should ensure that these investments generate positive returns to the capital invested. I also foresee increasing efforts to contain disease, especially neglected tropical diseases (NTDs), malaria, TB and HIV/AIDS; in addition, disease emergencies such as outbreaks of Ebola and coronavirus.

There will also almost certainly be an increase in efforts to help countries adapt to and mitigate the effects of climate change, and to improve institutions and aspects of government administration – especially taxation, education and legal systems. I see efforts to develop and transfer adaptation and mitigation measures in response to climate change as being an ever more important component of Western soft power. Few people continue to deny that climate change is a problem, and efforts to address it are a global good – and one that is not tainted by political ideology. If the West can gain the technical and moral high ground by reducing its emissions of greenhouse gases, it will set an example that others can be encouraged to follow with aid support. This is also an arena that the private sector can help with. A Scandinavian consortium of private investors and donor funds has financed and constructed a huge wind power project, covering 162 square kilometres at a cost of over US$ 860 million, in the Turkana region of northern Kenya.

There may also be a small but significant increase in special trade agreements (such as the AGOA of 2000) that allow tariff-free entry of specified goods to the US from Africa. The garment industries in Lesotho and Mauritius have benefitted from AGOA for many years, and in early 2020, Namibia shipped 25 tonnes of beef to Philadelphia under AGOA. There could also be a trickle of CCTs in countries that show signs of establishing effective financial distribution institutions, and there will be aid for emergencies arising from violent weather events and serious disease outbreaks.

An increase in agricultural production will be a key aspect of poverty reduction in much of the developing world, especially in Africa where the population is expected to double by 2050. While this can be achieved to some extent by the adoption of better technology, the biggest single challenge remains land title – or rather the lack of title – in much of sub-Saharan Africa. Until farmers are provided with secure tenure that they can use as collateral for credit, I fear the productivity of African agriculture will remain well below its potential. I believe the aid community must factor land titling into its agendas in future. A start has been made in Rwanda, which needs to be further developed and copied elsewhere.

I would argue that there should be support for more holistic agricultural production. There is a growing body of evidence that suggests highly intensive agriculture – which is based on the heavy use of mineral fertiliser, pesticides, fungicides and herbicides – causes major problems. This is not the place to provide comprehensive details of these problems, but there is no doubt that heavy use of pesticides kills beneficial pollinating insects, overuse of herbicides such as glyphosate leads to tolerance by some weeds, and overuse of mineral fertiliser sanitises the natural soil flora and fauna, which account for much organic fertility. In the West, a number of governments are now encouraging a return to less-intensive farming methods. It is difficult to see that there will be a rapid move away from intensive agriculture in much of the developing world, where food is in short supply, but new food-production technologies will be needed, and aid can play a role in their development and uptake.

However, the economic-development argument has always been only one of the arguments for aid. A more important justification, sadly, is international politics or, more specifically, global security and peace. Of course, there is no counterfactual, but the fact is that the Cold War came to an end without a major conflict between the West and the command economies. Although there is little hard evidence that aid played a major role in this achievement, it is clear that the Western powers provided most of the aid; the USSR never had sufficient financial resources to compete in this arena. It seems more than likely that security concerns will continue to provide the main reason for aid, for much the same reason as before: to secure allegiances.

I do not see that there will be any substantial Western funding of military ventures. Small campaigns, such as those in the Sahel region of West Africa and the DRC, will almost certainly continue, and there will be others, often financed covertly or overtly from the 'aid' budget of donor nations. Although the possibility of large-scale wars always exists in an uncertain world, I do not expect to see any repeats of large-scale military campaigns like those in Afghanistan, Libya, Iraq or Syria.

It is increasingly clear that the Western powers, led by the US, have lost confidence in such large military interventions. Tony Blair's five tests of when to go to war,[100] outlined in a speech he gave in Chicago in 1999, were used by the West to justify humanitarian interventions to stop genocide in places such as Kosovo and Iraq. At the time, there was a belief in Western capitals that the rich world had a moral duty to intervene in such crises. These tests have now been challenged by the interventions in Libya, Iraq and Afghanistan, as they failed to allow for the impossibility of containing Islamists and other extremists.

Some aid funds will continue to go to multilateral programmes such as the UN and the IDA of the World Bank. Although I think and hope that some of the UN agencies will slowly be scaled back, I very much hope the West regains its overall support for international organisations. The West can probably best do this by fine-tuning and using the powers and resources of the World Bank, the UN, and other multilateral and bilateral aid tools built up in earlier years.

The West needs to keep a close eye on China's increasing interest in these institutions. China's move to have greater influence in global institutions is clever as it highlights the current incompetence of the US in the global arena. The undeclared intention is clearly to encourage other countries to knock on China's door, rather than the US's if they want help. This is where the West's soft power should once again be a vital element in its maintenance of world peace.

In addition to concessional loans for essential infrastructure, special loans from the IMF for countries in serious financial difficulty will probably continue to be the most important means of supporting the world economy, maintaining alliances with the West and global peace. The Covid-19 pandemic in 2020/21 (and still ongoing at time of writing) has resulted in loans to developing countries from the World Bank and the IMF of US$6 billion and US$20 billion, respectively, including emergency loans worth US$4 billion to 12 Latin American and Caribbean countries. China too has provided Covid-19 aid to developing countries under the BRI banner, but it is not at all clear that this has achieved much more than glowing media reports.

Apart from such emergency loans, IMF funds prevent financially insecure countries falling into further disarray and/or becoming a security threat to other countries. In 2019, Pakistan – a country often on the brink of financial difficulty – secured another IMF loan of US$6 billion that prevented a total meltdown of its economy, which could have had massive influence in the region. Interestingly, this loan was part of the growing challenge to the Chinese BRI, in that it was dependent on the release of the details of Pakistan's indebtedness to China. This was something China was reluctant to agree to but could not prevent. In contrast, Venezuela, supported

---

100. (1) Are we sure of our case? (2) Have all diplomatic options been tried? (3) Is the intervention militarily sensible and prudent? (4) Are we prepared for a long war? (5) Do we have national interests at stake?

by Russia, was not able to secure any such Western financial support and remained in an economic crisis, and Zimbabwe has been refused IMF aid because Western governments consider its government to be abusing its citizens.

IMF loans are essentially Western loans, as China has limited say in IMF lending decisions.[101] Strictly speaking, IMF funds are loans that have to be repaid, and are not really aid funds. However, special terms and conditions (notably extended repayment periods) can be seen as Keynesian pump-priming initiatives to help governments adjust their financial systems (e.g. the removal of inefficient subsidies and improved taxation), and as such, these are aids for improving economic growth and poverty reduction.

Overall, I think the policy developments outlined previously will result in little or no increase in the total global aid budget. In this context, I do not see too many OECD countries aiming to meet the target of 0.7% GDP/GNI being spent on aid. In real terms, allowing for inflation, this translates into a reduction of aid in the coming years, rather than an expansion. While Covid-19 might delay graduation for some countries, it will not hold back everywhere. This should leave more funding for countries that fail to graduate but that can use aid funds effectively.

Another almost certain change will be fewer job opportunities in aid agencies for Western nationals. In the early days of aid, a large number of Westerners were hired by bilateral and international aid agencies. Since the turn of the century, more and more jobs have been filled by developing-country nationals, and I am sure this trend will continue. So, I would advise against any Westerner planning to make a career out of aid, as many of my generation did.

Finally, the day before I finished the text of this book, as if on cue, the UK government announced that it was going to merge the UK bilateral agency DFID with the Foreign Office. Well, although officially designated a merger, it is in fact more like a takeover, as it means the Foreign Office will get its paws on the DFID budget of £14 billion a year (in 2018/19). While I cannot condone the change, it does tend to confirm what I have been saying in this book, namely that, to a large extent, aid is about politics, not charity, and it has been subject to much review and change over the past 20 years.

---

101. The Chinese yuan or renminbi accounts for just over 10% of IMF funds, giving China a modest influence in IMF lending decisions, which reflect the more than 70% of the funding made up by the US dollar and the euro.

Acronyms/Initialisms

AARS	–	adaptive agricultural research stations
ADB	–	Asian Development Bank
ADG	–	assistant director general
ADP	–	agricultural development project
AFD	–	Agence Française de Développement (French Development Agency)
AfDB	–	African Development Bank
AICS	–	Agenzia Italiana per la Cooperazione allo Sviluppo (Italian Agency for Development Cooperation)
AIDS	–	acquired immune deficiency syndrome
AIIB	–	Asian Infrastructure Investment Bank
ARRI	–	Annual Report on Results and Impact
ASIP	–	Agricultural Sector Investment Programme
BARC	–	Bangladesh Agricultural Research Council
BPH	–	brown plant hopper
BRAC	–	formerly Bangladesh Rehabilitation Assistance Committee
BRI	–	Belt and Road Initiative
BRICS	–	Brazil, Russia, India, China and South Africa
BSB	–	Bangladesh Silk Board
CA	–	Codex Alimentarius
CARE	–	Cooperative for Assistance and Relief Everywhere (previously Cooperative of American Remittances for Europe)
CAS	–	country assistance strategy
CCP	–	Chinese Communist Party (Communist Party of China)
CCT	–	conditional cash transfer
CDB	–	Caribbean Development Bank
CDC Group	–	formerly Commonwealth Development Corporation
CERF	–	Central Emergency Response Fund
CGIAR	–	Consultative Group for International Agricultural Research
CIA	–	Central Intelligence Agency
CP	–	cooperative programme
CPE	–	country programme evaluation
CRIA	–	Central Research Institute for Agriculture (Indonesia)

CRISPR	–	clustered regularly interspaced palindromic repeats
CTA	–	chief technical adviser
DAC	–	Development Assistance Committee (of the OECD)
DFID	–	Department for International Development
DFL	–	disease free layings
DG	–	director general
DRC	–	Democratic Republic of Congo
EAIF	–	Emerging Africa Infrastructure Fund
EBRD	–	European Bank for Reconstruction and Development
EC	–	European Commission
ECOSOC	–	Economic and Social Council
ED	–	executive director
EDF	–	European Development Fund
EU	–	European Union
FAO	–	Food and Agriculture Organization
FAO/CP	–	Food and Agriculture Organization / World Bank Cooperative Programme
FFS	–	farmer field school
GAVI	–	the Vaccine Alliance (originally named the Global Alliance for Vaccines and Immunizations)
GCNA	–	Grenada Co-operative Nutmeg Association
GDP	–	gross domestic product
GIZ	–	Deutsche Gesellschaft für Internationale Zusammenarbeit
Global Fund	–	Global Fund to Fight AIDS, Tuberculosis and Malaria
GM	–	genetically modified
GMO	–	genetically modified organism
GNI	–	gross national income
GOB	–	government of Botswana
HIPC	–	heavily indebted poor country
HIV	–	human immunodeficiency virus
IADB	–	Inter-American Development Bank
IBRD	–	International Bank for Reconstruction and Development
ICAO	–	International Civil Aviation Organization
ICJ	–	International Court of Justice
ICR	–	implementation completion report
IDA	–	International Development Association
IEE	–	Independent External Evaluation

IFAD	–	International Fund for Agricultural Development
IFC	–	International Finance Corporation
IFPRI	–	International Food Policy Research Institute
IGAD	–	Intergovernmental Authority on Development
IITA	–	International Institute for Tropical Agriculture
ILO	–	International Labour Organization
IMF	–	International Monetary Fund
IMO	–	International Maritime Organization
IPM	–	integrated pest management
IRRI	–	International Rice Research Institute
IT	–	information technology
ITU	–	International Telecommunications Union
IUOTPO	–	International Union of Official Tourist Publicity Organisation
JICA	–	Japanese International Cooperation Agency
LEIT	–	low-external-input technology
LIFE	–	Locally Intensified Farm Enterprises
MCC	–	Millennium Challenge Corporation
MDG	–	Millennium Development Goals
MPH	–	Make Poverty History
MPLA	–	Movimento Popular de Libertação de Angola (People's Movement for the Liberation of Angola)
MSF	–	Médecins Sans Frontières (Doctors Without Borders)
NARS	–	National Agricultural Research System
NATO	–	North Atlantic Treaty Organization
NATP I	–	First National Agricultural Technology Project
NATP II	–	Second National Agricultural Technology Project
NGO	–	non-governmental organisation
NOPEST	–	New Options for Pest Management
NordGen	–	Nordic Genetic Resource Center
ODA	–	official development assistance
ODI	–	Overseas Development Institute
ODM	–	Overseas Development Ministry
OECD	–	Organisation of Economic Co-Operation and Development
OED	–	operations evaluation department (World Bank)
OFS	–	Orange Free State
OIC	–	Organisation of Islamic States
OPEC	–	Organization of the Petroleum Exporting Countries

Oxfam	–	Oxford Committee for Famine Relief
P4P	–	Purchase for Progress
pWC	–	Post-Washington Consensus
RCT	–	randomised controlled trial
SAL	–	structural adjustment loan
SDC	–	Swiss Agency for Development Cooperation
SDG	–	Sustainable Development Goal
SDR	–	special drawing rights
SIP	–	sector investment programme
SKAPCO	–	Sudanese Kuwaiti Animal Production Company
SOE	–	state-owned enterprise
SPFS	–	Special Programme for Food Security
SPIN	–	Special Programme in Nepal
SRI	–	System of Rice Intensification
SSC	–	South South Cooperation
T&V	–	Training and Visit
TA	–	technical assistance
TRC	–	technical review committee
UAE	–	United Arab Emirates
UBI	–	universal basic income
UK	–	United Kingdom
ULG	–	Urwick, Lugg & Gould
UN	–	United Nations
UNAIDS	–	Joint United Nations Programme on HIV/AIDS
UNCTAD	–	United Nations Conference on Trade and Development
UNDAF	–	United Nations Development Advisory Framework
UNDP	–	United Nations Development Programme
UNEP	–	United Nations Environment Programme
UNESCO	–	United Nations Education, Scientific and Cultural Organization
UNICEF	–	United Nations International Children's Fund (previously UN International Children's Emergency Fund)
UNIDO	–	United Nations Industrial Development Organization
UNITA	–	National Union for the Total Independence of Angola
UNWTO	–	United Nations World Tourism Organization
UPU	–	Universal Postal Union
US	–	United States of America
USAID	–	United States Agency for International Development

USSR	–	Union of Soviet Socialist Republics
VLW	–	village-level worker
WC	–	Washington Consensus
WFP	–	World Food Programme
WHO	–	World Health Organization
WIPO	–	World Intellectual Property Organization
WMO	–	World Meteorological Organization

References and Further Reading

Achebe, C. 1985. *The trouble with Nigeria*. Enugu: Fourth Dimension Publishers.

Agler, E. 2019. *Under the big tree*. Baltimore, MD: John Hopkins University Press.

Alden, C. 2007. *China in Africa*. London: Zed Books.

Aldrick, P. 2019. Beijing turns to London for advice on world aid. *The Times*, 15 April, 44.

Allen, L. 1971. *Japan: The years of triumph*. London: BPC Unit 75.

Asher, M. 2005. *Khartoum: The ultimate imperial adventure*. London: Viking.

Balogun, K. 1985. *Government in Old Oyo Empire*. Ibadan: Africanus Publishers & Co.

Banerjee, A. and Duflo, E. 2019. *Good economics for hard times*. London: Allen Lane.

Bangladesh Rice Research Knowledge Bank. 2014. *Bangladesh Rice Research Knowledge Bank*. http://knowledgebank-brri.org/

Barrett, T., Pastoret, P.-P. and Taylor, W.P. 2006. *Rinderpest and peste des petits ruminants*. London: Academic Press.

Bauer, P.T. 1971. *Dissent on development*. London: Weidenfeld and Nicolson.

Bauer, T. 1965. Does foreign aid really help? *Daily Telegraph*, 2 August.

Bauer, T. 1971. Economic history as theory. *Economica*, 38(150), 163–179.

Baum, W. and Tolbert, S. 1985. *Investing in Development*. New York, NY: Oxford University Press.

Beatie, A. 2001. IMF puts Africa at heart of work. *Financial Times*, 26 February.

Becker, P. 1966. *Path of blood*. London: Pan.

Berkman, S. 2008. *The World Bank and the gods of lending*. Danvers, MA: Kumarian Press.

Bhagwati, J. 2005. *In defense of globalisation*. Oxford: Oxford University Press.

Birdsall, N. and Fukuyama, F. 2011. The post-Washington consensus. *Foreign Affairs*, 90(2).

Birdsall, N. and Kapur, D. (eds.) 2005. *Rescuing the World Bank*. Washington, DC: The Center for Global Development.

Blackmore, S. 1998. *The meme machine*. Oxford: Oxford University Press.

Blanchard, L.P. and Collins, S.R. 2019. *China's Engagement in Djibouti*. Congressional Research Service. https://crsreports.congress.gov/product/pdf/IF/IF11304/3

Bolton, G. 2008. *Aid and other dirty business*. London: Ebury Press.

Branscheid, V. 1984. *Irrigation water management briefs No 66.* [collected papers] Rome: Food and Agriculture Organisation Investment Centre.

Brautigam, D. 2015. *Will Africa feed China?* Oxford: Oxford University Press.

Bricker, D. and Ibbitson, J. 2018. *Empty planet: The shock of global population.* London: Robinson.

British Broadcasting Corporation. 2018. *Africa Live this week 25–29 June: Anti-terror HQ attacked in Mali.* https://www.bbc.co.uk/news/live/world-africa-44599908

Calderisi, R. 2007. *The trouble with Africa: Why foreign aid isn't working.* London: Yale University Press.

Carr, S. 1989. *Technology for small-scale farmers in sub-Saharan Africa.* [technical paper no. 109]. Washington, DC: World Bank.

Carson, R. 1962. Silent spring. New York, NY: Mariner Books

Cassen, R. & Associates. 1987. *Does aid work?* (2nd edition). 1994. Oxford: Clarendon Press.

Cameron, D. 2018. *Commission on state fragility, growth and development.* Oxford: Blavatnik School of Government and Oxford University.

Caufield, C. 1997. *Masters of illusion.* London: Macmillan/Pan.

China Africa Research Initiative and Boston University Global Development Policy Center. 2018. *Chinese Loans to Africa Database,* Version 2.0. https://chinaafricaloandata.bu.edu/..

Chatzky, A. and McBride, J. 2020. *China's massive Belt and Road Initiative.* Washington, DC: Council on Foreign Relations.

Chen, Y. 2018. *Guest Post – Year of the dogs? A new boom and bust for Chinese construction in Africa. China in Africa,* June 7. http://www.chinaafricarealstory.com/2018/05/year-of-dogs-new-boom-and-bust-for.html

China Focus. 2018. The art of the empty gesture. *The Economist.* 23 June. (Reprinted from Beijing Review).

Chomsky. N. 2006. *Failed States.* London: Hamish Hamilton.

Clapp, J. and Cohen M.J. 2009. *The global food crisis.* Waterloo: Wilfrid Laurier University Press.

Clark, M. 1984. *Modern Italy, 1871–1982.* London: Longman.

Clay, E. and Stokke, O. 2000. *Food aid and human security.* London: Routledge.

Collier, P. 2008A. *The bottom billion.* Oxford: Oxford University Press.

Collier, P. 2008B. The politics of hunger: How illusion and greed fan the food crisis. Foreign Affairs, *87*(6), 67–79.

Commission for Africa. 2005. *Our common interest.* London: Penguin Books.

Commission on State Fragility, Growth and Development. 2018. *Escaping the fragility trap.* London School of Economics, Blavatnik School of Government and International Growth Centre.

Dawkins, R. 1989. *The selfish gene*. Oxford: Oxford University Press.

Dawkins, R. 2007. *The God delusion*. London: Black Swan.

Deaton, A. 2013. *The great escape*. Princeton, NJ: Princeton University Press.

de Soto, H. 2000. *The mystery of capital*. London: Random House.

Devarajan, S., Dollar, D.R. and Holmgren, T. 2001. *Aid and reform in Africa: Lessons from ten case studies*. Washington, DC: World Bank. https://openknowledge.worldbank.org/handle/10986/13894

Diamond, J. 1998. *Guns, germs and steel*. London: Vintage.

Dobermann, A. and Dawe, D. 2008. *Can the System of Rice Intensification Feed Asia?* [occasional paper]. Rome: Food and Agriculture Organization.

Dollar, D. and Kraay A. 2000. *Growth is good for the poor*. World Bank. www.worldbank.org/research/growth/absddolakray.htm

Dowden, R. 2008. *Africa: Altered states, ordinary miracles*. London: Portobello.

Doyle, J. J. and Van Den Berghe, C.H. 1973. *FAO/SIDA Fertilizer Programme LESOTHO Annual Report No 3, May 1973*. Maseru: Food and Agriculture Organization.

Dumont, R. 1966. *False start in Africa*. London: Sphere, in association with Andre Deutsch.

Dunn, J. 2006. *Setting the people free: The story of democracy*. London: Atlantic Books.

Easterly, W. 2002. *The elusive quest for growth*. Cambridge, MA: The MIT Press.

Easterly, W. 2006. *The white man's burden*. New York, NY: Penguin Press.

Easterly, W. 2013. *The tyranny of experts*. New York, NY: Basic Books.

Economy, E.C. 2018. China's new revolution. *Foreign Affairs, 97*(3), 60–74.

Einhorn, J. 2006. Reforming the World Bank. *Foreign Affairs, 85*, 17–22.

Feder, G. Murgai, R. and Quizon, J.B. 2004. Sending farmers back to school: The impact of farmer field schools. *Review of Agricultural Economics, 26*(1), 45–62. DOI:10.1111/j.1467-9353.2003.00161.x

Ferguson, N. 2003. *Empire: How Britain made the modern world*. London: Alan Lane.

Feldman S. and Marks. V. 2009. *Global warming and other bollocks*. London: Metro/John Blake Publishing.

Food and Agriculture Organization. 1985. *FAO: The first 40 years*. Rome: Food and Agriculture Organization.

Food and Agriculture Organization. 2002. *Special Report FAO/WFP crop and food supply assessment mission to Lesotho*. Rome: Food and Agriculture Organization.

Food and Agriculture Organization. 2007A. *The Challenge of Renewal*. Report of the Independent External Evaluation of the Food and Agriculture Organisation conference paper C2007/7A.1 – Rev. 1.

Food and Agriculture Organization. 2007B. *Emerging Issues*. Independent External Evaluation of the Food and Agriculture Organisation paper 07/01/2007.

Food and Agriculture Organization. 2008. GCP/IND/176/NET *Andhra Pradesh Water Management Project: Report of the Evaluation Mission*. http://www.fao.org/fileadmin/user_upload/oed/docs/GCPIND176NET_2008_ER.pdf.

Gaddis, J.L. 2005. *The Cold War*. London: Allen Lane.

Gaitskell, A. 1959. *Gezira: A story of development in the Sudan*. London: Faber and Faber.

Gallagher, J. 2020. *Malaria 'completely stopped' by microbe*. [radio programme] BBC Radio 4, 4 May 2020.

George, S. and Sabelli, F. 1994. *Faith and credit*. London: Penguin Books.

Gill, P. 2010. *Famine and foreigners: Ethiopia since Live Aid*. Oxford: Oxford University Press.

Gill, S. 1993. *A short history of Lesotho*. Morija: Morija Museum and Archives.

Glancy, J. 2018. China Kowtows to Trump over trade. *Sunday Times*, 16 December 2, 27.

Good, K. 2008. *Diamonds, dispossession, and democracy in Botswana*. Oxford: James Currey.

Greening, J. 2015. *UK aid; tackling global challenges in the national interest*. London: HM Treasury Department for International Development.

Guest, R. 2005. *The shackled continent: Africa's past, present and future*. London: Pan.

Gunther, J. 1955. *Inside Africa*. London: Hamish Hamilton Ltd.

Hancock, G. 1991. *Lords of poverty*. London: Mandarin Paperbacks.

Hanhimäki J. 2008. *The United Nations: A very short introduction*. Oxford: Oxford University Press.

Hanlon, J. Barrientos, A. and Hulme, D. 2010. *Just give money to the poor*. Sterling, VA: Kumarian Press.

Hassanali, A., Herren, H., Khan, Z.R., Pickett, J. and Woodcock, C. 2007. Integrated pest management: the push-pull approach for controlling insect pests and weeds of cereals, and its potential for other agricultural systems including animal husbandry. *Philosophical Transactions of the Royal Society B*, *363*, 611–621. http://doi.org/10.1098/rstb.2007.2173

Hausmann, R., Pritchard. L. and Rodrik, D. 2004. *Growth Accelerations*. National Bureau of Economic Research Working Paper No. 10566. https://www.nber.org/papers/w10566

Hawtin, G. (2017) The new CGIAR system takes off. *Agriculture for Development*, *31*, 34–35.

Hayter, T. 1971. *Aid as imperialism*. Harmondsworth: Penguin Books.

Hertz, N. 2004. *I.O.U.: The debt threat and why we must defuse it*. London: Fourth Estate.

Horn, H and Trebesch, C. 2019 *China's overseas lending*. National Bureau of Economic Research Working Paper No. 26050. http://www.nber.org/papers/w26050

Hruska, A. 2021. What the global battle against the fall armyworm reveals about how the US and China see the future of global food production. *Issues in Science & Technology*. Spring.

Hunter, G. 1967. *The best of both worlds?* Oxford: Oxford University Press.

Huntingdon, S. 1996. *The clash of civilizations and the remaking of the world order*. New York, NY: Simon & Schuster.

Hutchinson, J. (ed.) 1969. *Population and food supply*. Cambridge: Cambridge University Press.

Ingram, J. 2006. *Bread and stones: Leadership and the struggle to reform the United Nations World Food Programme*. North Charleston, SC: Booksurge LLC.

International Bank for Reconstruction and Development and International Development Association. 1999. *Summary lending amounts by fiscal year*. Washington, DC: World Bank.

International Bank for Reconstruction and Development and International Development Association. 2019. *Summary lending amounts by fiscal year*. Washington, DC: World Bank.

International Fund for Agricultural Development. 2005. *An independent external evaluation of the International Fund for Agricultural Development*. Independent Office of Evaluation. Rome: International Fund for Agricultural Development.

International Fund for Agricultural Development. 2018. *Annual report on results and impact*. Independent Office of Evaluation. Rome: International Fund for Agricultural Development.

International Monetary Fund. 2021. *Debt relief under the Heavily Indebted Poor Countries (HIPC) Initiative*. https://www.imf.org/en/About/Factsheets/Sheets/2016/08/01/16/11/Debt-Relief-Under-the-Heavily-Indebted-Poor-Countries-Initiative

Jackson, R.G.A. 1969. *A study of the capacity of the United Nations Development System* (two volumes). New York, NY: United Nations. OL14137218M.

Jung, C. and Halliday, J. 2005. *Mao: The unknown story*. London: Johnathan Cape.

Kassm, A. Friedrich,T. and Derpsch, R. 2019. Global spread of conservation agriculture. *International Journal of Environmental Studies, 76*, 29–51.

Kennan, G. 1947. The sources of Soviet conduct. *Foreign Affairs, 25*(4), 566–582.

King, D. 2008. Anti-scientific attitudes towards modern agriculture, especially genetically modified crops, are holding back a green revolution in Africa. *The Times*. 8 September.

Kiruga, M. 2019. Ethiopia's China challenge. *The Africa Report*, 27 March.

Kohler, H.-P., and Thompson, R. 2012. Conditional cash transfers and HIV/AIDS prevention: Unconditionally promising. *The World Bank Economic Review, 26*(2), 165–190.

Kuper, S. 2019. Reasons to be cheerful: For the time being. *FT.COM/Magazine*. April 6/7.

Landes, D. 2000. *The wealth and poverty of nations*. London: Abacus.

Land Matrix. 2021. *Land Matrix*. https://landmatrix.org/

Lankester, T. 2012. *The politics and economics of Britain's foreign aid: The Pergau Dam Affair*. London: Routledge.

Latif, M.A., Islam, M. and Saleque, M.A. 2005. Validation of the System of Rice Intensification (SRI) in Bangladesh. *Field Crops Research, 93*(2–3), 281–292.

Lawson, M. and Morgenstern, E. 2019. *Foreign aid: An introduction to US programs and Policy* (R40213).Washington, DC: Congressional Research Service.

Lewis, B. 2004. *The crisis of Islam: Holy war and unholy terror*. London: Phoenix.

Lugar, R. 2010. *The international financial institutions: A call for change*. [report] Committee on Foreign Relations United States Senate. http://www.gpoaccess.gov/congress/index/html

Lunn, J., Brien, P. and Jozepa, I. 2020. *UK aid: Frequently asked questions*. House of Commons Library Briefing Paper no. 7996. London: House of Commons Library. https://researchbriefings.files.parliament.uk/documents/CBP-7996/CBP-7996.pdf

Maçães, B. 2018. *Belt and road: A Chinese world order*. London: Hurst.

Mackie, J.D. 1991. *A history of Scotland*. London: Penguin.

Magee, B. 1985. *Popper*. London: Fontana Press.

Magnus, G. 2019. *Red flags: Why Xi's China is in jeopardy*. London: Yale.

Mallaby, S. 2004. *The world's banker*. London: Yale University Press.

Manji, A. 2006. *The politics of land reform in Africa*. New York, NY: Zed Books.

Mariotti, S. Pararajasegaram, R. and Resniokofl, S. 2003. Trachoma: Looking forward to Global Elimination of Trachoma by 2020 (GET 2020). *American Journal of Tropical Medicine and Hygiene, 69*(5 Suppl.), 33–35.

Martell, P. 2018. *First raise a flag: How South Sudan won the longest war but lost the peace*. London: Hurst.

Masson-Delmotte, V.P., Zhai, P., Pörtner, H.-O., Roberts, D., Skea, J., Shukla, P.R., Pirani, A., Moufouma-Okia, W., Péan, C., Pidcock, R., Connors, S., Matthews, J.B.R., Chen, Y., Zhou, X., Gomis, M.I., Lonnoy, E., Maycock, T., Tignor, M., and Waterfield, T. (eds.). 2018. Summary for Policymakers. In *Global Warming of 1.5°C. An IPCC Special Report on the impacts of global warming of 1.5°C above pre-industrial levels and related global greenhouse gas emission pathways, in the context of strengthening the global response to the threat of climate change, sustainable development, and efforts to eradicate poverty*. Geneva: World Meteorological Organization. p. 32.

McFaul, M. 2018. *From Cold War to hot peace: An American ambassador in Putin's Russia*. San Diego, CA: Houghton Mifflin Harcourt.

Mead, M. 1930. *Growing up in New Guinea: A comparative study of primitive education*. 2001. New York, NY: Harper Collins.

Mead, W.R. 2007. *God and gold: Britain, America, and the making of the modern world*. New York, NY: Knopf.

Meadows, D.H., Meadows, D.L., Randers, R. and Behrens, W. 1972. *The limits to growth*. New York, NY: Signet.

Meltzer, A.H. 2000. *Report of the International Financial Institution Advisory Commission*. Washington, DC: International Financial Institution Advisory Commission.

'Mercantilism'. 2021. Wikipedia. https://en.wikipedia.org/wiki/Mercantilism

Meredith, M. 2005. *The State of Africa: A history of fifty years of independence*. London: The Free Press.

Miller, C. Tsoka, M. and Reichert, K. 2008. *Impact evaluation of the Mchinji Social Cash Transfer Project*. Washington, DC: USAID, Boston University and Unicef.

Mokyr, J. 2016. *A culture of growth: The origins of the modern economy*. Princeton, NJ: Princeton University Press.

Mordaunt, P. 2019. Replace foreign aid handouts with private donations, says Mordaunt. *The Times*, 30 January, 4.

Mounk, Y. 2018. *The people vs. democracy*. Cambridge, MA: Harvard University Press.

Mounk, Y. and Foa, R.S. 2018. The end of the democratic century. *Foreign Affairs*, 97(3).

Moyo, D. 2009. *Dead aid*. London: Allen Lane.

Myburgh, P. 2019. *Gangster state: Unravelling Ace Magashule's web of capture*. Cape Town: Penguin/Random House.

Neuman, P. 2007. A crisis of identity and the appeal of jihad. *New York International Herald Tribune*. July 6.

Norberg, J. 2016. *Progress*. London: One World.

O'Brien, C.C. 1962. *To Katanga and back: A UN case history*. London: Hutchinson.

Olsen, M. 2000. *Power and prosperity: Outgrowing communist and capitalist dictatorships*. New York, NY: Basic Books.

O'Neill, O. 2002. *A question of trust: The BBC Reith Lectures 2002*. Cambridge: Cambridge University Press.

Organisation of Economic Co-Operation and Development. n.d.A *Official Development Assistance (ODA)*. https://www.oecd.org/dac/financing-sustainable-development/development-finance-standards/official-development-assistance.htm

Organisation of Economic Co-Operation and Development. n.d.B *Statistics on resource flows to developing countries.* https://www.oecd.org/dac/financing-sustainable-development/development-finance-data/statisticsonresourceflowstodevelopingcountries.htm

Ormerod, P. 2005. *Why most things fail: Evolution, extinction and economics.* London: Faber and Faber.

Overseas Development Institute. 2010. *Sector-based approaches in agriculture.* Overseas Development Institute Briefing Paper 58. London: Overseas Development Institute.

Pakenham, T. 1992. *The scramble for Africa.* London: Abacus.

Parks, B., 2019. John Bolton's foreign aid fumble. *The National Interest.* http://nationalinterest.org/feature/john-boltons-foreign-aid-fumble-49177

Phillips, R. 1981. *FAO: Its origins, formation and evolution: 1945–1981.* Rome: Food and Agriculture Organization.

Pinker, S. 2002. *The blank state: The modern denial of human nature.* London: Allen Lane.

Pinker, S. 2018. *Enlightenment now.* London: Allen Lane.

Popper, K. 1945. *The open society and its enemies.* London: Routledge.

Pottinger, B. 2008. *The Mbeki legacy.* Cape Town: Zebra Press.

Reader, J. 1998. *Africa: A biography of the continent.* London: Penguin Books.

Riddell, R. 2007. *Does foreign aid really work?* Oxford: Oxford University Press.

Rodrik, D. Subramanian, A. and Trebbi, F. 2004. 'Institutions Rule'. *Journal of Economic Growth, 9,* 131–165.

Rogoff, K. 2007. *World Business Report.* BBC World Service. 27 May 2007.

Rostow, W.W. 1959. The economic stages for growth. *The Economic History Review New Series, 12*(1), 1–16.

Sachs, J. 2005. *The end of poverty.* London: Penguin.

Sen Amartya. 1999. *Development as freedom.* New York, NY: Anchor Books.

Sen Amartya. 2006. *Identity and violence.* London: Allen Lane.

Simon, D. 2006. *Fifty key thinkers on development.* London: Routledge.

Smillie, I. 2009. *Freedom from want: The remarkable success story of BRAC, the global grassroots organization that's winning the fight against poverty.* Dhaka: The University Press Ltd.

Smith, A. 1776. *The wealth of nations.* 2014. Scotts Valley, CA: CreateSpace Independent Publishing Platform.

Stewart, R. 2014. *The places in between.* London: Picador.

Stirrat, R.L. 2008. Mercenaries, missionaries and misfits: Representations of development personnel. *Critique of Anthropology, 28*(4), 406–425.

Syed. M. 2021. Forget economics and politics – the West's real problem is a moral one. *The Sunday Times*, 20 June, 27.

Tendler, J. 1975. *Inside foreign aid.* Baltimore, MA: John Hopkins University Press.

The Economist. 2002A. Special report: Better than the alternatives. *The Economist.* 18 May.

The Economist. 2002B. Roots of development. *The Economist*, 5 October, 54.

The Economist. 2004. Economic focus | Development piecemeal. *The Economist*, 7 August, 63.

The Economist. 2005. Poor economic growth in Africa. *The Economist.* 24 December.

The Economist. 2008. A scramble in Africa. *The Economist*, 6 September.

The Economist. 2014A. Microfinance: Poor service. *The Economist*, 1 February.

The Economist. 2014B. Aquatic alfalfa: Finding the genome of an extraordinary plant. *The Economist*, 21 June.

The Economist. 2018A. Africa's economies are turning a corner. *The Economist*, 12 May.

The Economist. 2018C. President Joao Lourenco sees himself as an Angolan Deng Xiaoping. *The Economist*, 1 December.

The Economist. 2019A. Malpass v Malpass: The new boss will find that the job is harder to do than it was to get. 13 April 2019, 68–69.

The Economist. 2019B. Seeds of suspicion. *The Economist*, 27 April.

The Economist. 2019B. China courts the world. *The Economist*, 8 June.

The Economist. 2019D. Helicopter money. *The Economist*, 23 November.

The Economist. 2020A. Special Report: China's Belt & Road Initiative. *The Economist*, 8 February, 3–12.

The Economist. 2020B. Africa is changing so rapidly it is becoming hard to ignore. *The Economist*, 28 March.

The Economist 2020. Hard work and black swans. Schools brief. *The Economist*, 5 September.

The Economist. 2021A. Neither predator nor pal. *The Economist*, 3 April.

The Economist. 2021B. The common -sense economist. *The Economist*, 17 April, 86.

The International Financial Institutions: A Call for Change. 2010. *A Report to the Committee on Foreign Relations United States Senate.* 111th Congress 2nd session, 10 March 2010.

Theroux, P. 2003. *Dark star safari: Overland from Cairo to Cape Town*. London: Penguin Books.

Theroux, P. 2005. The failure of aid. *Herald Tribune*, 20 December.

Thompson, H. 2019. Mourning a phantom: The cherished 'rules-based order' never existed. *Prospect*, June, 13.

Thorp, E. 1956. *Ladder of bones*. London: Jonathon Cape.

Tocqueville, A. 1835. *Democracy in America*. 1994. London: Everyman's Library.

Toffler, A. 1971. *Future shock*. London: Pan Books.

Toulmin, C. and Quan, J. 2000. *Evolving land rights, policy and tenure in Africa*. London: IIED.

Tripp, R. 2006. Is low external input technology contributing to sustainable agricultural development? *ODI Natural Resources Perspectives, 102*.

Tyler, G. and Dixie, G. 2013. *Investing in agribusiness*. World Bank: Agriculture & Environmental Services Discussion Paper No. 1. Washington, DC: World Bank.

Union of International Associations. (2020). *Year book of international organisations*. Brussels: Union of International Associations.

United Nations. 2015. *The Millennium Development Goals report*. New York, NY: United Nations.

United States Department of Agriculture Foreign Agricultural Service. 2018. *Bangladesh grain and feed annual*. Global Agricultural Information Network. https://apps.fas.usda.gov/newgainapi/api/report/downloadreportbyfilename?filename=Grain%20and%20Feed%20Annual_Dhaka_Bangladesh_4-3-2018.pdf

Van Den Ban, A.W. and Samanta, R.K. 2006. *Changing roles of agricultural extension in Asian nations*. New Delhi: B.R. Publishing Corporation.

Vertin, Z. 2019. *A rope from the sky*. New York, NY: Pegasus Books.

Wallman, S. 1972. Conditions of non-development: The case of Lesotho. *The Journal of Development Studies, 8(2)*.

Welensky, R. 1964. *4000 days: The life and death of the Federation of Rhodesia and Nyasaland*. London: Collins.

Weiss, T.G. and Daws, S. 2008. *The Oxford handbook on the United Nations*. Oxford: Oxford University Press.

Wickstead, M. 2015. *Aid and development: A brief introduction*. Oxford: Oxford University Press.

World Bank. 2003. *A guide to the World Bank*. Washington, DC: International Bank for Reconstruction and Development.

World Bank Group. 2020. *IFC consolidated financial statement*. Washington, DC: World Bank.

World Health Organisation. 2018. *World malaria report*. Geneva: World Health Organization Publications.

World Health Organisation and Food and Agriculture Organisation of the United Nations. 2019. *Global situation of pesticide management in agriculture and public health*. Report of a 2018 WHO–FAO survey. Geneva: World Health Organisation.

Yergin, D. 1998. *The commanding heights*. New York, NY: Simon & Schuster.

Yunus, M. 2001. *Banker to the poor: Micro-lending and the battle against world poverty*. Dhaka: The University Press Ltd.

Appendices

Appendix A: Development Assistance Committee (DAC) List of Official Development Assistance (ODA) Recipients, 2018–20

Least-Developed Countries	Lower-Middle Income Countries	Upper-Middle Income Countries	Comments
Afghanistan	Armenia	Albania	The UN General Assembly has decided that the following countries are likely to graduate from the least-developed countries: Angola in 2021 and Vanuatu in 2020.
Angola*	Bolivia	Algeria*	
Bangladesh	Cabo Verde*	Antigua and Barbuda	
Benin*	Cameroon*	Argentina	
Bhutan	Congo*	Azerbaijan	
Burkina Faso*	Côte d'Ivoire*	Belarus	
Burundi*	Egypt*	Bosnia and Herzegovina	
Cambodia	El Salvador	Botswana*	
Central African Republic*	Eswatini*	Brazil	
Chad*	Georgia	China (People's Republic of China)	Antigua and Barbuda, and Palau are expected to graduate from the upper-middle-income list by 2020.
Comoros*	Ghana*		
Democratic Republic of Congo*	Guatemala	Colombia	
Djibouti*	Honduras	Cook Islands	
Eritrea*	India	Costa Rica	
Ethiopia*	Indonesia	Cuba	
Gambia*	Jordan	Dominica	
Guinea*	Kenya*	Dominican Republic	The graduation of the Cook Islands is under review.
Guinea-Bissau*	Kosovo	Ecuador	
Haiti	Kyrgyzstan	Equatorial Guinea*	
Kiribati	Micronesia	Fiji	
Laos	Moldova	Gabon*	
Lesotho*	Mongolia	Grenada	
Liberia*	Morocco*	Iran	Tanzania was upgraded to lower-middle income in 2020.
Madagascar*	Nicaragua*	Iraq	
Malawi*	Nigeria*	Jamaica	
Mali*	Pakistan	Kazakhstan	
Mauritania*	Papua New Guinea	Lebanon	
Mozambique*	The Philippines	Libya*	
Myanmar	Sri Lanka	Malaysia	
Nepal	Syria	Maldives	
Niger*	Tajikistan	Marshall Islands	
North Korea	Tokelau	Mauritius*	
Rwanda*	Tunisia*	Mexico	
São Tomé and Príncipe *	Ukraine	Montenegro	
	Uzbekistan	Monserrat	
	Vietnam		
	West Bank and Gaza Strip		

Least-Developed Countries	Lower-Middle Income Countries	Upper-Middle Income Countries	Comments
Senegal*		Namibia*	
Sierra Leone*		Nauru	
Solomon Islands		Palau	
Somalia*		Panama	
South Sudan*		Paraguay	
Sudan*		Peru	
Tanzania		Saint Helena	
Timor-Leste		Saint Lucia	
Togo*		Samoa	
Tuvalu		Serbia	
Uganda*		South Africa*	
Vanuatu		Surinam	
Yemen		Thailand	
Zambia*		Tonga	
Zimbabwe*		Turkey	
		Turkmenistan	
		Venezuela	
		*Wallis and Futuna***	

*African country

** Territory, not a country

Source: List of DAC recipient countries (OECD, n.d.A)

Appendix B: Countries Receiving Heavily Indebted Poor Countries (HIPC) Assistance

Received HIPC Assistance		
Afghanistan	Ethiopia*	Mauritania*
Benin*	The Gambia*	Mozambique*
Bolivia	Ghana*	Nicaragua
Burkina Faso*	Guinea*	Niger*
Burundi*	Guinea-Bissau*	Rwanda*
Cameroon*	Guyana	São Tomé*
Central African Republic*	Haiti	Senegal*
Chad*	Honduras	Sierra Leone*
Comoros*	Liberia*	Tanzania*
Republic of Congo*	Madagascar*	Togo*
Democratic Republic of Congo*	Malawi*	Uganda*
Côte d'Ivoire*	Mali	Zambia*
Potentially Eligible for HIPC Assistance		
Eritrea*	Somalia*	Sudan*

*African country

Source: International Monetary Fund (2021)

Appendix C: The Sustainable Development Goals (SDGs) of the United Nations

1. No poverty
2. Zero hunger
3. Good health and well-being
4. Quality education
5. Gender equality
6. Clean water and sanitation
7. Affordable and clean energy
8. Decent work and economic growth
9. Industry, innovation and infrastructure
10. Reduced inequalities
11. Sustainable cities and communities
12. Responsible production and consumption
13. Climate action
14. Life below water
15. Life on land
16. Peace, justice and strong institutions
17. Partnerships

Appendix D: Major Chinese Investments in Africa and Latin America

Since 2000, Chinese loans to Africa have grown from being under US$1 billion to an estimated peak of US$30 billion in 2016 (the latest year for which data is available is 2018, as shown in the following table). In total, by 2018, China had lent some US$150 billion to the African continent. This lending was for some 1,076 loans. However, little is known about the individual loans.

Since the peak in 2016, lending has fallen, almost certainly as a result of problems associated with servicing loans and China's slower economic growth. The figures shown in Table 6 are for loans, grants and concessional lending. A detailed breakdown by type of financing is not available.

Table 6 Chinese Lending to Africa, 2000–18 (US$ bn)

Year	00	01	02	03	04	05	06	07	08	09
US$ bn	.1	.1	.3	.7	.9	1.6	5	6	4	7

Year	10	11	12	13	14	15	16	17	18
US$ bn	7	10	12	17	12	11	29	14	9

Source: China Africa Research Initiative and Boston University Global Development Policy Center (2018)

The 10 African countries with the biggest debts to China to date are shown in Table 7:

Table 7 The 10 Largest African Borrowers from China (US$ bn)

Country	Angola	Ethiopia	Kenya	Republic of Congo	N. Sudan	Zambia
US$ bn	25	13.5	7.9	7.3	6.4	6.0

Country	Cameroon	Nigeria	Ghana	DRC	Others
US$ bn	5.5	4.8	3.5	3.4	52

Source: China Africa Research Initiative and Boston University Global Development Policy Center (2018)

Limited information is available on what the money has been lent for, but some of the larger loans include the following:

1. Addis Ababa–Djibouti Railway (US $3.13 billion).
2. Metro rail system in Addis Ababa (US$475 million).
3. Railways in Kenya – Mombasa, Nairobi and Kisumu (US$8.2 billion).
4. Loans to Tanzania (US$2 billion).
5. Bagamoyo Port in Tanzania (US$10 billion).
6. Loan for power lines for the Grand Ethiopian Renaissance Dam (US$1.2 billion).
7. Loans to Republic of Congo for infrastructure (US$6 billion) in 2007; only US$1 billion had been spent by 2015.
8. Oil deal with Nigeria (US$2 billion), signed in 2006.
9. Oil deal with Angola (US$3 billion), signed in 2006.
10. Oil and mineral rights deal with Guinea (US$7 billion), was signed in 2008.
11. Zambia copper belt (US$1.2 billion) in 2007.
12. Loan to Zimbabwe (US$2.0 billion) in 2006.
13. Infrastructure (roads, bridges and dams) loan to Ecuador (US$19 billion). The biggest single project is the Coca Codo Sinclair Dam (1,500 MW hydroelectric), which cost US$2.6 billion. It was largely financed and constructed by China in an area near an active volcano. It opened in 2016, but it was running at 50% capacity by 2018 because of serious cracks in the masonry. This is attributed to the use of poor-quality materials during construction. To service this loan and the others, Ecuador provides China with 80% of its oil output annually, and the country has effectively been bankrupted by its debts to China, which were taken out when Correa was president.
14. Loans to Djibouti over the 2000–18 period, including for the port at Doraleh (US$1.5 billion) and to meet the cost of a new free-trade zone (US$3.5 billion) (Blanchard and Collins, 2019). Djibouti has a population of just over 1 million and cannot service its present debt.

A Brief Review of Some Chinese Investments

Work by the World Bank in mid-2020 suggests that China has restructured or relieved debts owed by some 140 poor countries. To date, China has preferred to swap large non-performing loans for a long-term lease of the facility constructed. This may work in some cases but by no means all. Owning a financially failing asset, albeit on a long lease, does not help service the original loan. Indeed, it is not all plain sailing for Beijing as there are already signs of 'creditor imperialism'.[102]

Ethiopia is reported to be having difficulty servicing the loans from China taken out to renovate the railway between Addis Ababa and Djibouti. This project cost US$4.0 billion, of which US$3.3 billion was a loan from the Export-Import Bank of China (Kiruga, 2019). In September 2018, Prime Minister Abiy of Ethiopia announced that China had agreed to restructure the repayment period for its loans to the country from 10 to 30 years. Ethiopia owed China US$12.1 billion in the middle of 2019, and although extending the repayment period will not save any money, it will lower the annual repayments.

Kenya has corruption and overrun problems with the loan taken out to rebuild to the railway from Mombasa to Nairobi. In late 2019, China scaled back its lending to Kenya for the railway extension into the west of the country. No one knows why, but it was clear by then that the loan for the link from Mombasa to Nairobi was not commercially viable, and it hardly makes sense to lend more for what is almost certainly another dud project.

In June 2019, the president of Tanzania suspended the construction of the new port at Bagamoyo, which was being financed by China, as he objected to the Chinese partner's demands for a 99-year lease on the facility.

Prime Minister Mahathir of Malaysia tried to cancel two big Chinese-funded BRI projects in Malaysia on the grounds that he did not want to see a new version of colonialism. In fact, the BRI in Malaysia has been scaled back by one-third as the Chinese would not countenance cancellation.

Sri Lanka had massive problems with the loans taken out to construct the new port at Hambantota in the south of the country, one of the String of Pearls in the Indian Ocean. In late 2017, the Sri Lankan government leased a majority share in the Hambantota port to China Merchant Port Holdings for 99 years in return for US$1.12 billion. In fact, the money was to help the government service the loan taken out to build the port in the first place.

Something very similar seems to be happening in Djibouti, which secured loans of US$1.4 billion from China, much of which was used to pay for the development of a new port. China now owns more than 80% of Djibouti's external debt, and the Chinese ambassador to Djibouti is on record as saying privately that China expects to be repaid in cash or kind. Given Djibouti's limited opportunities to raise cash, the debt almost certainly is falling into the Sri Lankan trap, and the port will very likely also soon be owned by China Merchant Port Holdings.

---

102. 'Creditor imperialism' is a term used to describe a loan from a rich country to a poor country that locks or traps the poor country into long-term commitments that they may not be able to honour, providing the lender with powers to enforce their wishes unilaterally.

A recent article (*The Economist*, 2021A) provides an update on some Chinese lending to emerging nations. Academics at the College of William & Mary in Virginia, US, have looked at 100 Chinese loans to such countries. With the exception of Sierra Leone, which has no international credit rating, all the other countries had poor credit ratings, but this did not seem to bother the Chinese lenders. The interest rates charged – or at least those in the contract documents – were not high at 0.5–4.5 % above the London Inter-Bank Offered Rate (Libor). Again with the exception of Sierra Leone, there were no clauses indicating that the assets would be sequestered if the loans were not serviced. So far so good. However, there were other murky collateral stipulations that might prove onerous. These being clauses that indicate separate bank accounts would have to be opened, which could be seized if repayments were not made; no linkage to other creditors, such as the IMF or regional development banks, meaning that the Chinese loan would not be affected by any other debt rescheduling; and close linkage with other Chinese interests, resulting in a loan recall if the borrower damages the interests of any other Chinese entity. Clearly, China is well aware of the risks of lending to such countries and has taken steps to protect its loans that could actually be counterproductive. Thus, if the protective measures were enforced, this would almost certainly destroy the purpose of the loan, which was to generate goodwill between China and the borrower. China would seem to have more to learn about promoting its soft power.

Appendix E: The Tragedy of the Commons

Around 1990, I was having lunch with a colleague in the FAO who had grown up in South Africa. We were, as usual, talking about development in Africa, and he suggested the real problem was the 'tragedy of the commons'. At the time, I did not ask him to elaborate, thinking he was referring to the common ownership of land that is often a problem in Africa. However, I realised later that he was using it in a much broader sense of the term as a comment on African culture – in particular, village communities.

The tragedy of the commons is a situation in a shared-resource system where individual users, acting independently according to their own self-interest, behave contrary to the common good of all users, depleting or spoiling that resource through their collective action. In simple language, this means that, rather than taking an equal share of a common good (typically land), some take more than their share and reduce the value of the resources for all.

In Lesotho, for example, all land is vested in the Basuto nation or state. Under the 1979 Land Act, holders can secure a long-term lease (10 years) that can be used as security or a sublet. However, the use of the act has been minimal (FAO, 2002), and customary or traditional tenure arrangements predominate. Under these arrangements, land is allocated by traditional community leaders and access is determined by use. Users have exclusive rights to the land for cropping during the cropping season, but the land reverts to communal grazing after the harvest. This hybrid use of exclusivity and usufruct means the land is still really a common asset or shared resource – and so it is vulnerable to the tragedy of the commons. Thus, if a farmer wants to maximise his seasonal-crop production, he needs to use fertiliser (either organic or mineral) as the soils in Lesotho are severely degraded. A farmer who applies fertiliser would also be partly investing on behalf of the whole community, as the residual benefit of the fertiliser would also help improve the quality of the subsequent grazing. In practice, the system tends to discourage the use of fertiliser, as individual farmers are reluctant to invest on behalf of the group, and the group is not willing to contribute to the costs of fertiliser. It may not be a classic example of the tragedy of the commons because the community is not depleting the value of a resource. It is the other side of the coin, however, in so far as it demonstrates how individuals are discouraged from investing on behalf of their community.

In 2005, I spent some time working with a colleague from Malawi. He was well-educated and fairly Western in his attitude to life, and I thought I would ask him about his village experiences. I asked him whether he had to take gifts when he went back to his village. 'Of course,' he said, and he added that he had to take gifts to everyone in the village, even his family's enemies, otherwise the enmity would get worse. He then explained in some detail how the community worked. If a member of the community needed a tool (e.g. an axe or hoe), but did not have one, it would be borrowed from someone who did have one. It all sounded like a very sensible sharing of resources. He then went on to say that if a successful member of the community acquired a bigger and better asset, such as an ox cart or a motorcycle, all members of the whole community would consider they had a right to use it until it broke down or needed maintenance, when it would again become the responsibility of the owner. We went on to talk about starting a business or simple rural enterprise, and my colleague explained how the income would be seen as belonging to the whole community, not the individual entrepreneur. He felt this was a big disincentive to entrepreneurship.

Later that year, I was involved in the evaluation of an investment project in Zambia that was based on providing groups in selected villages with seed money to set up income-generating activities: mainly poultry and livestock rearing. An elected village committee would approve loans to groups that proposed suitable schemes. The groups were to use the loan to buy young stock and feed, and when the fattened animals were sold, the loan would be repaid and the money used to finance another group scheme. There was no difficulty in getting groups to come forward with proposals and to secure loans, but problems arose almost immediately after the loan had been secured. With little or no experience of teamwork or of raising livestock semi-intensively, issues occurred with the group's ability to buy feed and manage the feeding of the pigs and poultry that had been bought, and all such schemes failed. There were fewer problems with goat-rearing subprojects, as the goats were able to forage for themselves and could be surrendered when fattened as repayment for any loans that had been taken out. The only successful proposals were those that involved goats or that were managed by individuals, rather than groups. Of course, the real problem here was the naivety of the funding agency, which had not done its homework.

These few examples cannot be considered a rigorous sociological survey, but I think they do illustrate the strengths and weaknesses of traditional community cultures. On the one hand, they show how poor communities are able to share resources under certain circumstances. However, it is important to recognise that this sharing is actually more of a one-to-one or individual help mechanism than a community benefit.

Some economists (Banerjee and Duflo, 2019) suggest that systems of mutual help are based as much on selfish interest as mutual interest. Therefore, they point out that individuals help others for fear that, if they did not do so, they would not get help when they need it. They also point out that the community spirit breaks down if and when some members have outside opportunities. Furthermore, this community spirit evaporates rapidly when there is a risk that some individuals might benefit more than others. I think they also show how difficult it is to monetarise activities in simple societies that have no tradition of working out how to share the monetary costs of assets or time. In the Zambian case, for group schemes to work, it would have required a rigorous method of attributing the rewards for work done and expenses met to members of the group – an almost totally alien concept to such communities.

Elinor Ostrom, the first female Nobel laureate for economics (and only one of two to date), has challenged the negative aspects of the tragedy of the commons by showing how, in some situations, 'common ownership' of a resource can be more beneficial than private ownership. Essentially, her work looked at risk and whether, if all members of a community followed its rules, the value of the resources (land, forest or water) could be maintained, and if the value were depleted by natural events, the risk was minimised and shared by all equally. But this requires a tradition of mutual trust that rarely exists in simple societies.

Appendix F: The Consultative Group for International Agricultural Research (CGIAR) Centres

1. AfricaRice, Côte d'Ivoire
2. Bioversity International, Rome
3. International Center for Tropical Agriculture (CIAT), Colombia
4. International Maize and Wheat Improvement Center (CIMMYT), Mexico
5. Center for International Forestry Research (CIFOR), Indonesia
6. International Potato Center (CIP), Peru
7. International Center for Agricultural Research in the Dry Areas (ICARDA), Lebanon
8. International Center for Research in Agroforestry (ICRAF), Kenya
9. International Crops Research Institute for the Semi-Arid Tropics (ICRISAT), India
10. International Food Policy Research Institute (IFPRI), US
11. International Institute for Tropical Agriculture (IITA), Nigeria; *International Livestock Center for Africa (ILCA)**
12. International Livestock Research Institute (ILRI), Kenya and Ethiopia; *International Laboratory for Research on Animal Diseases (ILRAD)**
13. International Rice Research Institute (IRRI), Philippines; *International Center for National Agricultural Research (ISNAR), Netherlands***
14. International Water Management Institute (IWMI), Sri Lanka
15. WorldFish, Malaysia

*Subsumed into ILRI in 1994/5

** closed

Appendix G: Long-Serving Leaders by Country

The following lists the long-serving leaders by country. The figures in parentheses show each named individual's number of years in power. Where no figure is shown, the country has not had a long-serving leader.

Algeria: Bouteflika (20)

Angola: Eduardo dos Santos (37)

Benin: Kérékou (29)

Botswana: Seretse Khama (14), Ian Khama (son) (10)

Burkina Faso: Compaoré (27)

Burundi: Nkurunziza (15)

Cameroon: Biya (37)

Cabo Verde: Monteiro (10).

Central African Republic: Bokassa (13), Patassé (10)

Chad: Déby (29 as of 2019)

Comoros: Abdallah (11)

Republic of Congo: Nguesso (35)

DRC: Mobutu Sese Seko (32), Kabila (18)

Djibouti: Aptidon (22), Guelleh (20 as of 2019)

Egypt: Nasser (14), Sadat (11), Mubarak (30)

Ethiopia: Haile Selassie (44), Haile Mariam (14), Meles Zenawi (17)

Eritrea: Afwerki (26 as of 2019)

Equatorial Guinea: Léon M'ba (7)

Gabon: Omar Bongo (42), Ali Bongo (son) (10 as of 2019)

The Gambia: Jawara (29), Jammeh (23)

Ghana: Rawlings (20)

Guinea Bissau: Viera (15)

Guinea: Sékou Touré (26), Conté (24)

Côte d'Ivoire: Houphouët-Boigny (33), Gbagbo (10), Outtara (9 as of 2019)

Kenya: Kenyatta (14), Moi (24), Kibaki (11)

Lesotho: Johnathan (20), Mosisili (16)

Liberia: Doe (10), Sirleaf (12), Tolbert (9)

Libya: Gaddafi (42). Madagascar: Ratsiraka (23), Tsiranana (12)

Malawi: Banda (28), Mutharika, B. (10), Mutharika, A.P. (brother) (5)

Mali: Traoré (22), Konaré (10), Keïta (8)

Mauritania: Daddah (12), Taya (25), Aziz (10)

Mauritius: Jugnauth (23), Ramgoolam (21)

Morocco: King Hassan II (38), Mohammed V (20 as of 2019)

Mozambique: Chissano (18), Machel (11)

Namibia: Nujoma (15), Pohamba (10)

Niger: Diori (13), Kountché (13), Tandja (8), Issoufou (8 as of 2019)

Nigeria: Obasanjo (8), Babangida (7)

South Africa: Mandela (5), Mbeki (9), Zuma (9)

Rwanda: Kagame (30 as of 2020)

São Tomé: Pinto da Costa (21)

Senegal: Senghor (20), Diouf (19), Wade (12)

Seychelles: René (27), Michel (12)

Sierra Leone: Stevens (14), Koroma (10)

Somalia: Siad Barre (22)

Sudan: Bashir (30), Nimiery (14)

South Sudan: Salva Kiir (14)

Eswatini (Swaziland): King Sobhuza II (82), Mswati III (33 as of 2019)

Tanzania: Nyerere, J. (24)

Togo: Gnassingbé, E. (38), Gnassingbé, F. (son) (14 as of 2019)

Tunisia: Bourguiba (33), Ben Ali (22)

Uganda: Museveni (34, as of 2020)

Western Sahara: disputed territory

Zambia: Kaunda (27)

Zimbabwe: Mugabe (37)

Acknowledgements

In the course of my travels associated with my work in development, I met a wide range of interesting and committed people, many of whom became close friends. The list below includes some, but not all, of the many people who shared rides in four-wheel-drive vehicles or in big and little aeroplanes, shared some exotic meals (such as stewed hippo), looked quizzically at me during numerous meetings, and enjoyed gallons of coffee and litres of beer along the way. In their own ways, they all helped me understand a little better what we were all trying to do:

Tullia Aiazzi, Jock Anderson, Bari and Parveen Awan, Mike Barbour, Julia Bevan, Fred Bitanirwe, Nigel Brett, Rowland Burley, Volker Bransheid, Stephen Carr, Don Corbett, Grahame Dixie, Martin Elling, Maurice Fenn, Elon Gilbert, David Giles, Heye Groenewald, Bal Godbole, Lakshman Guatam, Takayuki Hagiwara, Roger Harris, Geoff and Lorna Hawtin, Andrew Hicks, Ian Hill, Jill and Simon Hocombe, Gul Hossein, Wahida Huq, Ian Jones, Masa Kato, Daud Khan, Albert Lieberg, David and Sheelagh Lugg, Andrew MacMillan, Ed Mallorie, John Markie, Chris Mathias, Sudarshan Mathema, John McCartney, Bob McKee, Arun Mitra, David Moffatt, Ashley Morton, Guy Motta, James Muir, Ohene Nyanin, Bob Paterson, David Potter, Michael Rayner, Chris and Karen Redfern, Nuno Santos, Roland Schurmann, Andrew Sergeant, Conrad Smikle, Iqbal Soban, Roderick Stirrat, Tim Stephens, Masami Sugimura, John (Jack) Twyford, Tilo Ulbricht, Jeremy Wall, Ian Walton, Jim Watson, John Weatherhogg, Doug Wolley, Dan Vadnal, and Shami Zingore.

I would also like to thank my wife and family, who patiently tolerated my long absences during trips to developing countries, and listened to many of my stories on return. And also to Alexa Whitten of the Book Refinery Ltd who has helped with typesetting and is also my publisher, and Lindsay Corten for her editing skills.